TOTAL
BASIC SKILLS
Grade 6

GRADE
6

School Specialty
Publishing

Send all inquiries to:
School Specialty Publishing
8720 Orion Place
Columbus, OH 43240-2111

ISBN 0-7696-3716-7

2 3 4 5 6 7 8 9 WAL 09 08 07 06 05

TABLE OF CONTENTS

Reading
Spelling 6–20
Prefixes 21–24
Suffixes 25–32
Dividing Words Into Syllables 33
Synonyms and Antonyms 34–35
Classifying 36–37
Analogies 38–46
Fact or Opinion 47–48
Cause and Effect .49–50
Personification 51
Symbolism 52
Similes and Metaphors 53–55
Generalizations 56–57
Skimming and Scanning 58
Author's Purpose .59–60

Reading Comprehension
Generalization 62–68
Recalling Details and Sequencing 69–74
Using Prior Knowledge 75
Main Idea/Recalling Details 76–90
Using Prior Knowledge/Generalization . . .91–98
Main Idea/Recalling Details 99–102
Venn Diagrams 103
Summarizing 104–113
Review 114

English
Nouns 116
Possessive Nouns 117
Verbs and Verb Tenses 118–122
Irregular Verb Forms 123–124
Nouns and Verbs 125–127
Simple Subjects and Predicates 128–129
Parallel Structure 130
Subject/Verb Agreement 131–132
Pronouns 133–138
Appositives 139
Dangling Modifiers .140
Review 141–143
Adjectives 144–146
Adverbs 147–148
Adjectives and Adverbs 149
Identifying Sentence Parts 150–151
Prepositions 152–154

Direct Objects 155
Indirect Objects 156
Conjunctions 157–158
Frequently Misused Words 159–166

Writing
Capitalization .168–169
Commas 170–171
Semicolons 172
Colons 173
Dashes 174
Quotation Marks 175–176
Apostrophes 177
Contractions 178
Possessives 179–180
Italics 181
Complete Sentences 182
Run-On Sentences 183
Finding Spelling Errors 184–185
Four Types of Sentences 186
Writing Paragraphs 187–189
Writing Description 190–192
Writing Directions 193–194
Stronger Sentences .195
Descriptive Sentences 196
Different Points of View 197–198
Persuasive Writing 199
Characters, Setting, and Plot 200–202
Writing Dialogue 203–204
Paraphrasing 205–206
Summarizing 207
Outlining 208
Friendly Letters 215–216

Math
Place Value/Expanded Notation 218–222
Addition Word Problems 222–223
Subtraction Word Problems 224–225
Multiplication .226–227
Division Word Problems 228–229
Equations 230–231
Rounding and Estimating 232–233
Decimals 234–240
Decimals and Fractions 241–250
Review 251–252
Trial and Error .253–254

Choosing a Method 255–256
Multi-Step Problems .257
Hidden Questions 258
Logic Problems .259–260
Perimeter 261–262
Area 263–265
Volume 266
Geometric Patterns 267–271
Length in Customary/Metric Units 272–273
Weight in Customary/Metric Units 274–275
Capacity in Customary/Metric Units . . .276–277
Temperature in Customary
  and Metric Units 278
Review 279
Ratios 280–282
Percents 283–284
Probability 285–286
Review 287
Data, Tables, and Graphs 288–295
Integers 296–299
Plotting Graphs 300
Ordered Pairs 301
Review 302

Answer Key 303–352

READING

Name _____

Spelling: Words With ā

Directions: Write a sentence for each word. Use a dictionary if you are unsure of the meaning of a word.

1. favorite _____

2. gable _____

3. dangerous _____

_____

4. patient _____

_____

5. lakefront _____

_____

6. statement _____

_____

7. nation _____

_____

8. negotiated _____

9. operate _____

10. decade _____

Directions: Write the answers.

11. Which word means a 10-year period? _____

12. Which word means a triangle-shaped end of a building's roof? _____

13. Which word means arbitrated? _____

Name _____

Spelling: Words With ē

Directions: Write a sentence for each word. Use a dictionary if you are unsure of the meaning of a word.

1. niece _____

2. meaningful _____

3. conceited _____

4. baleen _____

5. field _____

6. disease _____

7. reactivate _____

8. peony _____

9. seafaring _____

10. theme _____

Directions: Write the answers.

11. Which word is a summer-blooming flower?

_____

12. Which word is a type of whale?

_____

13. Which word means an illness?

_____

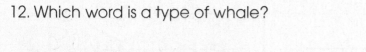

Name _____

Spelling: Words With ī

Directions: Write a sentence for each word. Use a dictionary if you are unsure of the meaning of a word.

1. bisect _____

2. identify _____

3. frightened _____

4. glider _____

5. idol _____

6. library _____

7. pipeline _____

8. hieroglyphic _____

9. rhinoceros _____

10. silent _____

Directions: Write the answers.

11. Which word means to be scared?

_____

12. Which word means to divide into two sections?

_____

13. Which word is an animal?

_____

14. Which word is a type of ancient writing?

_____

Name _____

Spelling: Words With ō

Directions: Write a sentence for each word. Use a dictionary if you are unsure of the meaning of a word.

1. clothing _____

2. slogan _____

3. total _____

4. stethoscope _____

5. voltage _____

6. stereo _____

7. protein _____

8. negotiate _____

9. locust _____

10. locomotive _____

Directions: Write the answers.

11. Which word is an insect?

_____

12. Which word means a train?

_____

13. Which word means a listening device to hear the heart?

_____

14. Which word means to bargain?

_____

Spelling: Words With ū

Directions: Write a sentence for each word. Use a dictionary if you are unsure of the meaning of a word.

1. universe _____

2. cruise _____

3. absolute _____

4. influence _____

5. unanimous _____

6. vacuum _____

7. putrid _____

8. incubate _____

9. peruse _____

10. numerous _____

Directions: Write the answers.

11. Which word means to read carefully?

_____

12. Which word means that everyone is in agreement?

_____

13. Which word means a sea voyage taken for pleasure?

_____

14. Which word means to keep eggs warm until they hatch?

_____

Name _____

Spelling: I Before E, Except After C

Use an **i** before **e**, except after **c** or when **e** and **i** together sound like long **a**.

Examples:
relieve
deceive
neighbor

Exceptions: weird, foreign, height, seize

Directions: Write **C** in the blank if the word in bold is spelled correctly. Draw an **X** in the blank if it is spelled incorrectly. The first one has been done for you.

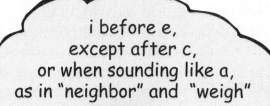

i before e,
except after c,
or when sounding like a,
as in "neighbor" and "weigh"

_C_ 1. They stopped at the crossing for the **freight** train.

____ 2. How much does that **wiegh**?

____ 3. Did you **believe** his story?

____ 4. He **recieved** an A on his paper!

____ 5. She said it was the **nieghborly** thing to do.

____ 6. The guards **seized** the package.

____ 7. That movie was **wierd**!

____ 8. Her **hieght** is five feet, six inches.

____ 9. It's not right to **deceive** others.

____ 10. Your answers should be **breif**.

____ 11. She felt a lot of **grief** when her dog died.

____ 12. He is still **greiving** about his loss.

____ 13. Did the police catch the **thief**?

____ 14. She was their **cheif** source of information.

____ 15. Can you speak a **foreign** language?

Name _____

Spelling: Words With ie and ei

Many people have trouble remembering when to use **ie** and when to use **ei**. The following rules have many exceptions, but they may be helpful to you.

Rule 1: If the two letters are pronounced like ē and are preceded by an s sound, use **ei**, as in receive.

Rule 2: If the two letters are pronounced like ē, but are not preceded by an **s** sound, use **ie** as in believe.

Rule 3: If the two letters are pronounced like ā, use **ei** as in **ei**ght and v**ei**n.

Rule 4: If the two letters are pronounced like ī, use **ei** as in h**ei**ght.

The sound **s** could be produced by the letter **s** as in **single** or the letter **c** as in **cease**.

Directions: Write the words from the box on the lines after the spelling rule that applies.

veil	brief	deceive	belief	niece
reindeer	yield	achieve	height	neighbor
grief	ceiling	weight	vein	seize

Rule 1: _____

Rule 2: _____

Rule 3: _____

Rule 4: _____

Directions: Complete the sentences with words that have the vowel sound shown. Use each word from the box only once.

1. My next-door (ā) _____ wore a long (ā) _____ at her wedding.

2. Will the roof hold the (ā) _____ of Santa's (ā) _____ ?

3. My nephew and (ē) _____ work hard to (ē) _____ their goals.

4. I have a strong (ē) _____ they would never (ē) _____ me.

5. For a (ē) _____ moment, I thought Will would (ē) _____ the game to me.

6. The blood rushed through my (ā) _____ .

7. What is the (ī) _____ of this (ē) _____ ?

Name _____

Spelling: Words With ûr and ôr

The difference between **ûr** and **ôr** is clear in the words **fur** and **for**. The **ûr** sound can be spelled **ur** as in f**ur**, **our** as in j**our**nal, **er** as in h**er** and **ear** as in s**ear**ch.

The **ôr** sound can be spelled **or** as in f**or**, **our** as in f**our**, **oar** as in s**oar** and **ore** as in m**ore**.

Directions: Write the words from the box on the lines to match the sounds.

florist	plural	ignore	courtesy	observe
survey	research	furnish	normal	emergency
tornado	coarse	flourish	source	restore

ûr _____

_____

ôr _____

_____

Directions: Complete the sentences with words that have the sound shown. Use each word only once.

1. We all get along better when we remember to use (**ûr**) _____.

2. My brother likes flowers and wants to be a (**ôr**) _____.

3. What was the (**ôr**) _____ of the (**ûr**) _____ for your report?

4. He waved at her, but she continued to (**ôr**) _____ him.

5. For a plural subject, use a (**ûr**) _____ verb.

6. Beneath the dark clouds a (**ôr**) _____ formed!

7. Firefighters are used to handling an (**ûr**) _____ .

8. When will they be able to (**ôr**) _____ our electricity?

9. How are you going to (**ûr**) _____ your apartment?

Name _____

Spelling: Words Beginning With sh and th

Directions: Write a definition for each word. Use a dictionary if you are unsure of the meaning of a word.

1. shallow: _____

2. thimble: _____

3. shear: _____

4. sheriff: _____

5. thermal: _____

6. throttle: _____

7. shingle: _____

8. shot put: _____

9. thrifty: _____

10. shoreline: _____

11. threaten: _____

12. thyroid: _____

Directions: Use two of the above words in sentences.

13. _____

_____

14. _____

_____

Spelling: Words Beginning With ch

Directions: Write a definition for each word. Use a dictionary if you are unsure of the meaning of a word.

1. chimney: _____

2. china: _____

3. cheetah: _____

4. charity: _____

5. channel: _____

6. chandelier: _____

7. challenge: _____

8. chairman: _____

9. champion: _____

10. cheddar: _____

11. chime: _____

12. chisel: _____

Directions: Write the answers.

13. Which word is a tool for shaping wood?

_____

14. Which word is a type of cheese?

_____

15. Which word is an animal?

_____

Spelling: The Letter Q

In English words, the letter **q** is always followed by the letter **u**.

Examples:
   question
   square
   quick

Directions: Write the correct spelling of each word in the blank. The first one has been done for you.

1. qill   _____*quill*_____

2. eqality   _____

3. qarrel   _____

4. qarter   _____

5. qart   _____

6. qibble   _____

7. qench   _____

8. qeen   _____

9. qip   _____

10. qiz   _____

11. eqipment _____

12. qiet   _____

13. qite   _____

14. eqity   _____

15. eqator   _____

16. eqivalent   _____

17. eqitable   _____

18. eqestrian _____

19. eqation   _____

20. qantity   _____

Name _____

Spelling: Words With kw, ks and gz

The consonant **q** is always followed by **u** in words and is pronounced **kw**. The letter **x** can be pronounced **ks** as in **mix**. When **x** is followed by a vowel, it is usually pronounced **gz** as in **example**.

Directions: Write the words from the box on the lines to match the sounds shown.

expense	exist	aquarium	acquire	request	exact
expand	exit	quality	excellent	quantity	quiz
exhibit	squirm	expression			

kw _____

_____

ks _____

_____

gz _____

Directions: Complete the sentences with words that have the sound shown. Use words from the box only once.

1. We went to the zoo to see the fish (**gz**) _____ .

2. I didn't know its (**gz**) _____ location, so we followed the map.

3. The zoo plans to (**kw**) _____ some sharks for its

   (**kw**) _____ .

4. Taking care of sharks is a big (**ks**) _____ , but a number of people

   have asked the zoo to (**ks**) _____ its display of fish.

5. These people want a better (**kw**) _____ of fish, not a bigger

   (**kw**) _____ of them.

6. I think the zoo already has an (**ks**) _____ display.

7. Some of its rare fish no longer (**gz**) _____ in the ocean.

Reading   17   Total Basic Skills Grade 6

Spelling: Words With Silent Letters

Some letters in words are not pronounced, like the **b** in **crumb**, the **l** in **yolk**, the **n** in **autumn**, the **g** in **design** and the **h** in **hour**.

Directions: Write the words from the box on the lines to match the silent letters. Use a dictionary if you are unsure of the meaning or pronunciation of a word.

condemn	yolk	campaign	assign	salmon
hymn	limb	chalk	tomb	foreign
resign	column	spaghetti	rhythm	solemn

n _____

l _____

g _____

b _____

h _____

Directions: Write words from the box to complete these sentences.

1. What did the teacher (**g**) _____ for homework?

2. She put words in a (**n**) _____ on the board.

3. When she finished writing, her hands were white

   with (**l**) _____ .

4. The church choir clapped in (**h**) _____

   with the (**n**) _____ .

5. While I was cracking an egg, the (**l**) _____ slipped onto the floor.

6. Did the explorers find anything in the ancient (**b**) _____?

7. My favorite dinner of all is (**h**) _____ and meatballs.

8. Do not (**n**) _____ me for making one little mistake.

Spelling: Words With ph or kn

The letters **ph** produce the same sound as the letter **f**. When the letters **kn** are together, the **k** is silent.

Directions: Write a definition for each word. Use a dictionary if you are unsure of the meaning of a word.

1. photographer: _____

2. knowledge: _____

3. knee: _____

4. telephone: _____

5. knock: _____

6. phonics: _____

7. physician: _____

8. knife: _____

9. pharmacy: _____

10. knight: _____

11. knit: _____

12. pheasant: _____

Directions: Write the answers.

13. Which word is a place to buy medicine?

_____

14. Which word is a synonym for doctor?

_____

15. Which word names a bird?

_____

Name _____

Spelling: Words With gh or gn

Directions: Use the clues and the words in the box to complete the crossword puzzle.

recognize	drought	assign
lightning	night	fought
straight	throughout	

Across:

3. My siblings and I _____ occasionally while growing up.
5. The teacher will _____ bus seats for the field trip.
7. _____ the storm, the rescue squads worked without stopping.
8. Do you _____ the woman you are meeting for lunch?

Down:

1. The _____ left farmers without crops.
2. My brother has _____ hair, but mine is curly.
4. Tomorrow _____ we will leave for Florida.
6. _____ struck the old barn on Walnut Hill.

Name _____

Prefixes

A **prefix** is a syllable added to the beginning of a word to change its meaning. The prefix **re** means "back" or "again," as in **re**turn. **Pre** means "before," as in **pre**pare. **Dis** means "do the opposite," as in **dis**appear. **In** and **im** both mean "not," as in **im**possible. (These two prefixes also have other meanings.) **Com** and **con** both mean "with," as in **com**panion and **con**cert. Use **im** and **com** with words that start with **p, b** or **m**. Use **in** and **con** with words that begin with a vowel or other consonants.

Directions: Match each word from the box to its definition.

disbelieve	recite	connotation	impolite	preview
impatient	distrust	configuration	prevision	incomplete
invisible	dislike	confederate	recover	compassion

1. share another's feelings ———————————

2. not finished ———————————

3. another meaning ———————————

4. become normal again ———————————

5. take away confidence ———————————

6. look to the future ———————————

7. arrangement of parts ———————————

8. say from memory ———————————

9. ally ———————————

10. hate ———————————

11. look at ———————————

12. rude ———————————

13. in a hurry ———————————

14. doubt ———————————

15. not seen ———————————

Directions: Add the rest of the word to each prefix in these sentences. Use words from the box only once. Be sure to use the correct form of the word.

16. When he re_____ from his cold, Jeff was im_____ to get back to work.

17. Jonah stared at the ghostly figure with dis_____ and dis_____ .

18. I'd like to re_____ that poem, but my memory of it is in_____.

19. She was very im _____ during the movie pre_____.

Prefixes

A **prefix** is a syllable added to the beginning of a word that changes its meaning. The prefixes **in**, **il**, **ir** and **im** all mean **not**.

Directions: Create new words by adding **in**, **il**, **ir** or **im** to these root words. Use a dictionary to check that the new words are correct. The first one has been done for you.

Prefix		Root Word		New Word
1. _____il_____	+	logical	=	_____illogical_____
2. _____	+	literate	=	_____
3. _____	+	patient	=	_____
4. _____	+	probable	=	_____
5. _____	+	reversible	=	_____
6. _____	+	responsible	=	_____
7. _____	+	active	=	_____
8. _____	+	moral	=	_____
9. _____	+	removable	=	_____
10. _____	+	legible	=	_____
11. _____	+	mature	=	_____
12. _____	+	perfect	=	_____

Name _____

Prefixes

The prefixes **un** and **non** also mean **not**.

Examples:
    Unhappy means not happy.
    Nonproductive means not productive.

Directions: Divide each word into its prefix and root word. The first one has been done for you.

		Prefix	Root Word
1.	unappreciated	un	appreciate
2.	unlikely	_____	_____
3.	unkempt	_____	_____
4.	untimely	_____	_____
5.	nonstop	_____	_____
6.	nonsense	_____	_____
7.	nonprofit	_____	_____
8.	nonresident	_____	_____

Directions: Use the clues in the first sentence to complete the second sentence with one of the words from the box. The first one has been done for you.

9. She didn't reside at school. She was a ___nonresident.___

10. He couldn't stop talking. He talked _____

11. The company did not make a profit. It was a _____ company.

12. She was not talking sense. She was talking _____

13. He visited at a bad time. His visit was _____

14. No one appreciated his efforts. He felt _____

15. He did not "keep up" his hair. His hair was _____

16. She was not likely to come. Her coming was _____

Prefixes

The prefixes **co**, **col**, **com**, **con** and **cor** mean "with" or "together." The prefixes **anti**, **contra** and **ob** mean "against."

Directions: Write each word's prefix and root word in the space provided.

Word	Prefix	Root Word
coexist	co	exist
concurrent		
correlate		
codependent		
antigravity		
contraband		

Directions: Use the words from the chart above to complete the sentences.

1. When airplanes fly very high and then quickly drop down, they cause an

   _____ affect.

2. Materials that are illegal are called _____ .

3. A dog and a cat can _____ in the same house if they get along well.

4. Events that happen at the same time are _____ .

5. When two people rely on each other, they are said to be _____ .

6. The textbook will _____ with the teacher's lectures.

Suffixes

A **suffix** is a syllable added to the end of a root word that changes its meaning.

When a word ends in silent **e**, keep the **e** before adding a suffix beginning with a consonant.

Example: amuse + ment = amusement

Exception: argue + ment = argument

When a word ends in silent **e**, drop the **e** before adding a suffix beginning with a vowel.

Example: amuse = amusing

Exceptions: hoeing, shoeing, canoeing

Directions: Write **C** on the blank if the word in bold is spelled correctly. Draw an **X** in the blank if it is spelled incorrectly. The first one has been done for you.

_C_   1. She was a woman of many **achievements**.

_____   2. He hated to hear their **arguments**.

_____   3. Do you want to go **canoing**?

_____   4. He kept **urgeing** her to eat more dessert.

_____   5. She was not good at **deceiving** others.

_____   6. He **rarely** skipped lunch.

_____   7. Would you repeat that **announcment**?

_____   8. Bicycle **safety** was very important to him.

_____   9. Their constant **argueing** got on my nerves.

_____   10. He found that **shoeing** horses was not easy.

_____   11. The sun felt hot as they were **hoeing**.

_____   12. She was so **relieveed** that she laughed.

Suffixes: Words Ending in Y

If a word ends in a vowel and **y**, keep the **y** when you add a suffix.

Example:
    bray + ed = brayed
    bray + ing = braying

Exception: lay + ed = laid

If a word ends in a consonant and **y**, change the **y** to **i** when you add a suffix unless the suffix begins with **i**.

Example:
    baby + ed = babied
    baby + ing = babying

Directions: Write **C** in the blank if the word in bold is spelled correctly. Draw an **X** if it is spelled incorrectly. The first one has been done for you.

_C_ 1. She was a good student who did well at her **studies**.

_____ 2. Will you please stop **babiing** him?

_____ 3. She **layed** her purse on the couch.

_____ 4. Both the **ferrys** left on schedule.

_____ 5. Could you repeat what he was **saying**?

_____ 6. He was **triing** to do his best.

_____ 7. How many **cherries** are in this pie?

_____ 8. The cat **stayed** away for two weeks.

_____ 9. He is **saveing** all his money.

_____ 10. The lake was **muddier** than I remembered.

_____ 11. It was the **muddyest** lake I've ever seen!

_____ 12. Her mother **babied** her when she was sick.

Name _____

Suffixes: Doubling Final Consonants

If a one-syllable word ends in one vowel and consonant, double the last consonant when you add a suffix that begins with a vowel.

Examples: swim + ing = swimming   big + er = bigger

Directions: Add the suffixes shown to the root words, doubling the final consonants when appropriate. The first one has been done for you.

1. brim + ing = _____brimming_____
2. big + est = _____
3. hop + ing = _____
4. swim + er = _____
5. thin + er = _____
6. spin + ing = _____
7. smack + ing = _____
8. sink + ing = _____
9. win + er = _____
10. thin + est = _____
11. slim + er = _____
12. slim + ing = _____
13. thread + ing = _____
14. thread + er = _____
15. win + ing = _____
16. sing + ing = _____
17. stop + ing = _____
18. thrill + ing = _____
19. drop + ed = _____
20. mop + ing = _____

Name _____

Suffixes

A **suffix** is a syllable added to the end of a word that changes its meaning. Some suffixes change nouns into adjectives.

Examples: fool — **foolish** nation — **national**

Other suffixes change adjectives into adverbs.

Examples: foolish — **foolishly** national — **nationally**

Directions: Match the root words with words from the box.

personal	stylish	obviously	professional
typical	childish	practical	medical
permanently	ticklish	additional	critical
gradually	physical	musical	

1. tickle _____
2. critic _____
3. add _____
4. person _____
5. child _____
6. grade _____
7. practice _____
8. physician _____
9. permanent _____
10. medic _____
11. type _____
12. music _____
13. style _____
14. obvious _____
15. profess _____

Directions: Circle the word or words in each sentence that are a synonym for a word from the box. Write the word from the box on the line. The first one has been done for you.

16. Knowing how to cook is a (useful) skill. ___*practical*___

17. The lake slowly warmed up. _____

18. Clearly, I should have stayed on the path. _____

19. That is a fashionable outfit. _____

20. Wanting your own way all the time is for little kids. _____

21. Getting lost is common for me. _____

22. My grades are a private matter. _____

Name _____

Suffixes: "ion," "tion" and "ation"

The suffixes **ion**, **tion** and **ation** change verbs into nouns.

Examples: imitate + **ion** = imitat**ion**   combine + **ation** = combin**ation**

Directions: Match each word from the box with its definition.

celebration	solution	imitation	exploration	selection
reflection	conversation	population	invitation	suggestion
combination	decoration	appreciation	definition	transportation

1. a copy _____

2. talking _____

3. a request _____

4. the meaning _____

5. a search _____

6. mirror image _____

7. cars, trucks _____

8. ornament _____

9. choice _____

10. a party _____

11. the answer _____

12. people _____

13. a joining _____

14. new idea _____

15. thankfulness _____

Directions: Write the correct forms of the words in the sentences. The first one has been done for you.

16. **transport**   How are we __transporting__ our project to school?

Did anyone arrange __transportation__ ?

17. **decorate**   Today, we are _____ the classroom.

We brought the _____ from home.

18. **solve**   Have you _____ the problem yet?

We need a _____ by the end of the day.

GRADE 6

Name _____

Suffixes: "ment" and "ity"

The suffixes **ment** and **ity** change verbs and some adjectives to nouns.

Examples: treat — **treatment**   able — **ability**

Directions: Circle the word or words in each sentence that are synonyms for words from the box. Write the word from the box on the line. The first one has been done for you.

equipment	responsibility	activity	
accomplishment	adjustment	ability	treatment
assignment	personality	achievement	appointment
popularity	astonishment	advertisement	curiosity

1. The workers are bringing in their (machines.)   __equipment__

2. Whose duty is it to take out the trash?   _____

3. Do you know our homework for tonight?   _____

4. I could see the surprise in his face.   _____

5. Ken is happy with his new position.   _____

6. I was filled with wondering.   _____

7. She lists one achievement in particular.   _____

8. Look at the exercise on page 16.   _____

9. The way you get along with others is part of your character.   _____

10. I heard that commercial a hundred times.   _____

11. Amy has a strong athletic skill.   _____

12. Jason's kindness led to his acceptance by his friends.   _____

13. I need to make a change in my schedule.   _____

14. That is quite an accomplishment!   _____

15. The doctor is trying another way to help my allergies.   _____

Suffixes

The suffix **less** means **lacking** or **without**. The suffix **some** means **full** or **like**.

Examples:

> **Hopeless** means without hope.
> **Awesome** means filled with awe.

Directions: Create new words by adding **some** or **less** to these root words. Use a dictionary to check that the new words are correct. The first one has been done for you.

Root Word		Suffix		New Word
1. heart	+	_____less_____	=	_____heartless_____
2. trouble	+	_____	=	_____
3. home	+	_____	=	_____
4. humor	+	_____	=	_____
5. awe	+	_____	=	_____
6. child	+	_____	=	_____
7. win	+	_____	=	_____

Directions: Use the clues in the first sentence to complete the second sentence with one of the words from the box. The first one has been done for you.

8. Her smile was winning and delightful. She had a _____**winsome**_____ smile .

9. The mean man seemed to have no heart. He was _____

10. She never smiled or laughed. She appeared to be _____

11. The solar system fills me with awe. It is _____

12. The couple had no children. They were _____

13. He had no place to live. He was _____

14. The pet caused the family trouble. It was _____

Name _____

Suffixes: "ship," "ful" and "ist"

Directions: Write the meaning of each word on the line. Use a dictionary if you are unsure of the meaning of a word.

1. biologist: _____

_____

2. citizenship: _____

_____

3. companionship: _____

_____

4. archaeologist: _____

5. typist: _____

6. scholarship: _____

7. doubtful: _____

8. hopeful: _____

9. dictatorship: _____

10. chemist: _____

11. principalship: _____

12. artist: _____

13. spiteful: _____

14. professorship: _____

15. geologist: _____

Name _____

Dividing Words Into Syllables

Directions: Divide these words into syllables by putting a hyphen (-) between each syllable. The first one has done for you.

1. multiplication

   <u>mul-ti-pli-ca-tion</u>

2. discover

   _____

3. ultimate

   _____

4. transfer

   _____

5. continent

   _____

6. follow

   _____

7. British

   _____

8. American

   _____

9. president

   _____

10. discrimination

    _____

11. spectacular

    _____

12. commercial

    _____

13. probability

    _____

14. country

    _____

15. casual

    _____

16. political

    _____

17. wrestle

    _____

18. basketball

    _____

19. particular

    _____

20. cereal

    _____

21. picture

    _____

22. plumber

    _____

23. personal

    _____

24. sentence

    _____

Name _____

Synonyms

A **synonym** is a word that means the same or nearly the same as another word. **Example:** mean and cruel.

Directions: Circle the word or group of words in each sentence that is a synonym for a word in the box. Write the synonym from the box on the line. The first one has been done for you.

florist	courtesy	research	emergency	flourish
plural	observe	furnish	tornado	source
ignored	survey	normally	coarse	restore

1. The children seemed to (thrive) in their new school.   *flourish*

2. Her politeness made me feel welcome. _____

3. The principal came to watch our class. _____

4. Are you going to fix up that old house? _____

5. Six weeks after the disaster, the neighborhood looked as it usually did. _____

6. What was the origin of that rumor? _____

7. The cyclone destroyed two houses. _____

8. She neglected her homework. _____

9. The material had a rough feel to it. _____

10. Did you fill out the questionnaire yet? _____

Directions: Select three words from the box below. Write a sentence for each word that shows you understand the meaning of the word

plural	flourish	source	restore	observe	furnish	research

_____

_____

_____

Name _____

Antonyms

An **antonym** is a word which means the opposite of another word.

Example: hopeful and discouraged

Directions: Circle the word or group of words in each sentence that is an antonym for a word in the box. Write the antonym from the box on the line.

nuisance	considerate
delicate	frivolous
entrance	shiny
divide	parallel
success	valley

1. It seemed as though we'd never make it to the top of the butte. _____

2. Rosa thought the woman was rude to the store clerk. _____

3. The two streets run perpendicular to each other. _____

4. The school carnival was a total failure due to the stormy weather. _____

5. Be sure to wash this sturdy sweater with other heavy items. _____

6. The third grade class worked hard learning to multiply. _____

7. The exit was blocked by a table. _____

8. The purchase of the coat was quite practical. _____

9. The teacher wrote that Colin was a joy to have in class. _____

10. The stone in her ring was dull and cloudy. _____

Name _____

Reading Skills: Classifying

Classifying is placing similar things into categories.

Example: January, May and **October** can be classified as months.

Directions: Write a category name for each group of words.

1. accordion   clarinet   trumpet   _____

2. wasp   bumblebee   mosquito   _____

3. antique   elderly   prehistoric   _____

4. chemist   astronomer   geologist   _____

5. nest   cocoon   burrow   _____

Directions: In each row, draw an **X** through the word that does not belong. Then write a sentence telling why it does not belong.

1. encyclopedia   atlas   novel   dictionary

_____

2. bass   otter   tuna   trout

_____

3. sister   grandmother   niece   uncle

_____

4. bark   beech   dogwood   spruce

_____

5. pebble   gravel   boulder   cement

_____

6. spaniel   Siamese   collie   Doberman

_____

Name _____

Reading Skills: Classifying

Directions: In each row, draw an **X** through the word that does not belong. Then write a word that belongs.

1. monkey   lion   zebra   elephant   dog   _____

2. daisies   roses   violets   ferns   pansies   _____

3. paper   pear   pencil   eraser   stapler   _____

4. sister   cousin   father   aunt   friend   _____

5. hand   mouth   shirt   foot   elbow   _____

6. shy   cry   happy   angry   sad   _____

7. puppy   dog   kitten   cub   lamb   _____

8. red   blue   color   yellow   purple   _____

9. Earth   Jupiter   Saturn   Pluto   Sun   _____

10. sink   bed   desk   dresser   lamp   _____

Directions: Name each category above.

1. _____   6. _____

2. _____   7. _____

3. _____   8. _____

4. _____   9. _____

5. _____   10. _____

Name _____

Writing Analogies

Once you have determined the relationship between the words in the first pair, the next step is to find a similar relationship between another pair of words.

Examples:
   Scissors is to **cut** as **broom** is to **sweep**.
   Black is to **white** as **up** is to **down**.

Scissors cut. Brooms sweep. The first analogy shows the **purpose** of scissors and brooms. In the second example, up and down are **antonyms**, as are black and white.

Directions: Choose the correct word to complete each analogy. The first one has been done for you.

1. **Sky** is to **blue** as **grass** is to
   A. earth   B. green   C. lawn   D. yard   _____green_____

2. **Snow** is to **winter** as **rain** is to
   A. umbrella   B. wet   C. slicker   D. spring   _____

3. **Sun** is to **day** as **moon** is to
   A. dark   B. night   C. stars   D. blackness   _____

4. **5** is to **10** as **15** is to
   A. 50   B. 25   C. 30   D. 40   _____

5. **Collie** is to **dog** as **Siamese** is to
   A. pet   B. kitten   C. baby   D. cat   _____

6. **Letter** is to **word** as **note** is to
   A. tuba   B. music   C. instruments   D. singer   _____

7. **100** is to **10** as **1,000** is to
   A. 10   B. 200   C. 100   D. 10,000   _____

8. **Back** is to **rear** as **pit** is to
   A. peach   B. hole   C. dark   D. punishment   _____

Name _____

Analogies of Purpose

Directions: Choose the correct word to complete each analogy of purpose. The first one has been done for you.

1. **Knife** is to **cut** as **copy machine** is to

   A. duplicate   B. paper   C. copies   D. office   _duplicate_

2. **Bicycle** is to **ride** as **glass** is to

   A. dishes   B. dinner   C. drink   D. break   _____

3. **Hat** is to **cover** as **eraser** is to

   A. chalkboard   B. pencil   C. mistake   D. erase   _____

4. **Mystery** is to **clue** as **door** is to

   A. house   B. key   C. window   D. open   _____

5. **Television** is to **see** as **CD** is to

   A. sound   B. hear   C. play   D. dance   _____

6. **Clock** is to **time** as **ruler** is to

   A. height   B. length   C. measure   D. inches   _____

7. **Fry** is to **pan** as **bake** is to

   A. cookies   B. dinner   C. oven   D. baker   _____

8. **Bowl** is to **fruit** as **wrapper** is to

   A. present   B. candy   C. paper   D. ribbon   _____

Name _____

Antonym Analogies

Directions: Write antonyms for these words.

1. run: _____

2. start: _____

3. laugh: _____

4. dependent: _____

5. young: _____

6. North: _____

7. sink: _____

8. success: _____

9. combine: _____

10. laugh: _____

11. polluted: _____

12. leader: _____

13. fascinate: _____

14. man: _____

15. awake: _____

16. begin: _____

17. increase: _____

18. reverse: _____

19. enlarge: _____

20. East: _____

21. rural: _____

22. amateur: _____

23. patient: _____

24. rich: _____

25. empty: _____

26. fancy: _____

27. introduction: _____

28. modern: _____

Directions: Write two antonym analogies of your own.

29. _____

_____

30. _____

_____

Name _____

Part/Whole Analogies

Directions: Determine whether each analogy is whole to part or part to whole by studying the relationship between the first pair of words. Then choose the correct word to complete each analogy. The first one has been done for you.

1. **Shoestring** is to **shoe** as **brim** is to

    A. cup   B. shade   C. hat   D. scarf   _____hat_____

2. **Egg** is to **yolk** as **suit** is to

    A. clothes   B. shoes   C. business   D. jacket   _____

3. **Stanza** is to **poem** as **verse** is to

    A. rhyme   B. singing   C. song   D. music   _____

4. **Wave** is to **ocean** as **branch** is to

    A. stream   B. lawn   C. office   D. tree   _____

5. **Chicken** is to **farm** as **giraffe** is to

    A. animal   B. zoo   C. tall   D. stripes   _____

6. **Finger** is to **nail** as **leg** is to

    A. arm   B. torso   C. knee   D. walk   _____

7. **Player** is to **team** as **inch** is to

    A. worm   B. measure   C. foot   D. short   _____

8. **Peak** is to **mountain** as **crest** is to

    A. wave   B. ocean   C. beach   D. water   _____

Name _____

Action/Object Analogies

Directions: Determine whether each analogy is action/object or object/action by studying the relationship between the first pair of words. Then choose the correct word to complete each analogy. The first one has been done for you.

1. **Mow** is to **grass** as **shear** is to

   A. cut   B. fleece   C. sheep   D. barber   ___sheep___

2. **Rod** is to **fishing** as **gun** is to

   A. police   B. crime   C. shoot   D. hunting   _____

3. **Ship** is to **captain** as **airplane** is to

   A. fly   B. airport   C. pilot   D. passenger   _____

4. **Car** is to **mechanic** as **body** is to

   A. patient   B. doctor   C. torso   D. hospital   _____

5. **Cheat** is to **exam** as **swindle** is to

   A. criminal   B. business   C. crook   D. crime   _____

6. **Actor** is to **stage** as **surgeon** is to

   A. patient   B. hospital   C. operating room   D. knife   _____

7. **Ball** is to **throw** as **knife** is to

   A. cut   B. spoon   C. dinner   D. silverware   _____

8. **Lawyer** is to **trial** as **surgeon** is to

   A. patient   B. hospital   C. operation   D. operating room   _____

Name _____

Analogies of Association

Directions: Choose the correct word to complete each analogy. The first one has been done for you.

1. **Flowers** are to **spring** as **leaves** are to

   A. rakes   B. trees   C. fall   D. green   ____fall____

2. **Ham** is to **eggs** as **butter** is to

   A. fat   B. toast   C. breakfast   D. spread   _____

3. **Bat** is to **swing** as **ball** is to

   A. throw   B. dance   C. base   D. soft   _____

4. **Chicken** is to **egg** as **cow** is to

   A. barn   B. calf   C. milk   D. beef   _____

5. **Bed** is to **sleep** as **chair** is to

   A. sit   B. couch   C. relax   D. table   _____

6. **Cube** is to **square** as **sphere** is to

   A. circle   B. triangle   C. hemisphere   D. spear   _____

7. **Kindness** is to **friend** as **cruelty** is to

   A. meanness   B. enemy   C. war   D. unkindness   _____

8. **Pumpkin** is to **pie** as **chocolate** is to

   A. cake   B. dark   C. taste   D. dessert   _____

Name _____

Object/Location Analogies

Directions: Write a location word for each object.

1. shirt: _____

2. milk: _____

3. vase: _____

4. screwdriver: _____

5. cow: _____

6. chalkboard: _____

7. shower: _____

8. cucumbers: _____

9. silverware: _____

10. car: _____

11. pages: _____

12. bees: _____

13. money: _____

14. salt water: _____

15. dress: _____

16. ice cream: _____

17. table: _____

18. medicine: _____

19. dog: _____

20. basketball: _____

21. bed: _____

22. roses: _____

23. dishwasher: _____

24. toys: _____

25. cookies: _____

26. bird: _____

27. seashells: _____

28. asteroids: _____

Name _____

Cause/Effect Analogies

Directions: Determine whether the analogy is cause/effect or effect/cause by studying the relationship between the first pair of words. Then choose the correct word to complete each analogy. The first one has been done for you.

You caused this...and now look at the effect!

1. **Ashes** are to **flame** as **darkness** is to

   A. light   B. daylight   C. eclipse   D. sun   _eclipse_

2. **Strong** is to **exercising** as **elected** is to

   A. office   B. senator   C. politician   D. campaigning   _____

3. **Fall** is to **pain** as **disobedience** is to

   A. punishment   B. morals   C. behavior   D. carelessness   _____

4. **Crying** is to **sorrow** as **smiling** is to

   A. teeth   B. mouth   C. joy   D. friends   _____

5. **Germ** is to **disease** as **war** is to

   A. soldiers   B. enemies   C. destruction   D. tanks   _____

6. **Distracting** is to **noise** as **soothing** is to

   A. balm   B. warmth   C. hugs   D. music   _____

7. **Food** is to **nutrition** as **light** is to

   A. vision   B. darkness   C. sunshine   D. bulb   _____

8. **Clouds** are to **rain** as **winds** are to

   A. springtime   B. hurricanes   C. clouds   D. March   _____

Name _____

Synonym Analogies

Directions: Write synonyms for these words.

1. miniature: _____
2. wind: _____
3. picture: _____
4. quiet: _____
5. run: _____
6. cloth: _____
7. mean: _____
8. cup: _____
9. sweet: _____
10. difficult: _____
11. obey: _____
12. plenty: _____
13. scent: _____
14. sudden: _____

15. gigantic: _____
16. rain: _____
17. cabinet: _____
18. loud: _____
19. leap: _____
20. jeans: _____
21. kind: _____
22. dish: _____
23. feline: _____
24. simple: _____
25. beautiful: _____
26. scorch: _____
27. story: _____
28. thaw: _____

Directions: Write two synonym analogies of your own.

29. _____

_____

_____

30. _____

_____

Name _____

Reading Skills: Fact or Opinion?

A **fact** is information that can be proved. An **opinion** is information that tells how someone feels or what he/she thinks about something.

Directions: For each sentence, write **F** for fact or **O** for opinion. The first one has been done for you.

____F____ 1. Each of the countries in South America has its own capital.

_____ 2. All South Americans are good swimmers.

_____ 3. People like the climate in Peru better than in Brazil.

_____ 4. The continent of South America is almost completely surrounded by water.

_____ 5. The only connection with another continent is a narrow strip of land, called the Isthmus of Panama, which links it to North America.

_____ 6. The Andes Mountains run all the way down the western edge of the continent.

_____ 7. The Andes are the longest continuous mountain barrier in the world.

_____ 8. The Andes are the most beautiful mountain range.

_____ 9. The Amazon River is the second longest river in the world—about 4,000 miles long.

_____ 10. Half of the people in South America are Brazilians.

_____ 11. Life in Brazil is better than life in other South American countries.

_____ 12. Brazil is the best place for South Americans to live.

_____ 13. Cape Horn is at the southern tip of South America.

_____ 14. The largest land animal in South America is the tapir, which reaches a length of 6 to 8 feet.

Name _____

Reading Skills: Fact or Opinion?

Directions: Read the paragraphs below. For each numbered sentence, write **F** for fact or **O** for opinion. Write the reason for your answer. The first one has been done for you.

(**1**) The two greatest poems in the history of the world are the *Iliad* and the *Odyssey*. (**2**) The *Iliad* is the story of the Trojan War; the *Odyssey* tells about the wanderings of the Greek hero Ulysses after the war. (**3**) These poems are so long that they each fill an entire book.

(**4**) The author of the poems, according to Greek legend, was a blind poet named Homer. (**5**) Almost nothing is known about Homer. (**6**) This indicates to me that it is possible that Homer never existed. (**7**) Maybe Homer existed but didn't write the *Iliad* and the *Odyssey*.

(**8**) Whether or not there was a Homer does not really matter. We have these wonderful poems, which are still being read more than 2,500 years after they were written.

1. __O__ Reason: <u>This cannot be proven. People have different opinions about which are the greatest poems.</u>

2. _____ Reason: _____

3. _____ Reason: _____

4. _____ Reason: _____

5. _____ Reason: _____

6. _____ Reason: _____

7. _____ Reason: _____

8. _____ Reason: _____

Reading Skills: Cause and Effect

A **cause** is the reason something happens. The **effect** is what happens as the result of the cause.

Directions: Read the paragraphs below. For each numbered sentence, circle the cause or causes and underline the effect or effects. The first one has been done for you.

(1) All living things in the ocean are endangered by humans polluting the water. Pollution occurs in several ways. One way is the dumping of certain waste materials, such as garbage and sewage, into the ocean. (2) The decaying bacteria that feed on the garbage use up much of the oxygen in the surrounding water, so other creatures in the area often don't get enough.

Other substances, such as radioactive waste material, can also cause pollution. These materials are often placed in the water in securely sealed containers. (3) But after years of being exposed to the ocean water, the containers may begin to leak.

Oil is another major source of concern. (4) Oil is spilled into the ocean when tankers run aground and sink or when oil wells in the ocean cannot be capped. (5) The oil covers the gills of fish and causes them to smother. (6) Diving birds get the oil on their wings and are unable to fly. (7) When they clean themselves, they are often poisoned by the oil.

Rivers also can contribute to the pollution of oceans. Many rivers receive the runoff water from farmlands. (8) Fertilizers used on the farms may be carried to the ocean, where they cause a great increase in the amount of certain plants. Too much of some plants can actually be poisonous to fish.

Worse yet are the pesticides carried to the ocean. These chemicals slowly build up in shellfish and other small animals. These animals then pass the pesticides on to the larger animals that feed on them. (9) The buildup of these chemicals in the animals can make them ill or cause their babies to be born dead or deformed.

Reading Skills: Cause and Effect

Directions: Read the following cause and effect statements. If you think the cause and effect are properly related, write **True**. If not, explain why not. The first one has been done for you.

1. The best way to make it rain is to wash your car.

   <u>It does not rain every time you wash your car.</u>

2. Getting a haircut really improved Randy's grades.

   _____

3. Michael got an "A" in geometry because he spent a lot of time studying.

   _____

4. Yesterday I broke a mirror, and today I slammed my thumb in the door.

   _____

5. Helen isn't allowed to go to the dance tonight because she broke her curfew last weekend.

   _____

6. Emily drank a big glass of orange juice and her headache went away.

   _____

7. The Johnsons had their tree cut down because it had Dutch elm disease.

   _____

8. We can't grow vegetables in our backyard because the rabbits keep eating them.

   _____

Reading Skills: Personification

When an author gives an object or animal human characteristics, it is called **personification**.

Example: The dragon quickly <u>thought</u> out its next move in the attack on the village.

Thought is a human process and not associated with mythical creatures, therefore; the dragon is personified in that sentence.

Directions: In the following sentences, underline the personification.

1. The cave's gaping mouth led to internal passageways.

2. The tractor sprang to life with a turn of the key.

3. The lights blinked twice and then died.

4. Crops struggled to survive in the blistering heat, hoping for rainfall.

5. The engine of the car coughed and sputtered as if it wanted to breathe but couldn't.

6. The arrow flew through the air, eyeing its target.

7. Snowmen smile from the safety of their yards.

8. Four-year-old Stephanie's doll sipped tea delicately.

Directions: Write a sentence that personifies the following objects.

1. flower _____

2. stuffed animal _____

3. car _____

Name _____

Reading Skills: Symbolism

Symbolism is the use of something to stand for (symbolize) something else.

Example:

The elderly woman held the pearl necklace in her wrinkled hand and thought back on her life. Many years had gone by since her husband had given her the necklace, as many years as there were pearls. Some of the pearls, she noticed, were darker than others, just as some years in her life had been darker than other years.

The pearl necklace symbolizes the life of the elderly woman. Each pearl stands for a year in her life, and the necklace represents the many years that have passed.

_____

Directions: Write what is being symbolized in the paragraph on the lines below.

The refugees boarded the small ship with high hopes. They had to believe that their destiny was to find the New World and seek shelter there. A few dared to dream of the riches to be found. For them, the boat itself looked like a treasure chest waiting to be discovered.

_____

_____

_____

For 12-year-old Sam, the basketball court was the best place to be. In Sam's neighborhood, crime ran rampant, and it was the one safe place for kids like Sam to play. Sam spent most nights at the court, practicing lay-ups, jump shots and three-point shots. Sam worked hard because for him it wasn't just a sport, it was a golden key.

_____

_____

_____

Name _____

Similes and Metaphors

A **simile** compares two unlike things using the word **like** or **as**.

Example: The fog was **like** a blanket around us. The fog was **as** thick **as** a blanket.

A **metaphor** compares two unlike things without using the word **like** or **as**.

Example: The fog was a blanket around us.

"The fog was thick," is not a simile or a metaphor. **Thick** is an adjective. Similes and metaphors compare two unlike things that are both nouns.

Directions: Underline the two things being compared in each sentence. Then write **S** for simile or **M** for metaphor on the lines.

_____ 1. The florist's shop was a summer garden.

_____ 2. The towels were as rough as sandpaper.

_____ 3. The survey was a fountain of information.

_____ 4. Her courtesy was as welcome as a cool breeze on a hot day.

_____ 5. The room was like a furnace.

Directions: Use similes to complete these sentences.

6. The tornado was as dark as _____

7. His voice was like _____

8. The emergency was as unexpected as _____

9. The kittens were like _____

Directions: Use metaphors to complete these sentences.

10. To me, research was _____

11. The flourishing plants were _____

12. My observation at the hospital was _____

Name _____

Vocabulary Building: Similes

A **simile** is a figure of speech comparing two things using **like** or **as**.

Example: The child was as quiet as a mouse.

Directions: Read the following paragraph. Underline the similes.

The kittens were born on a morning as cold as ice. Although it was late spring, the weather hadn't quite warmed up. There were five kittens in the litter, each quite different from its siblings. The oldest was black as deepest night. There was a calico that looked like Grandma's old quilt. One was as orange as a fall pumpkin, and another was orange and white. The runt was a black and gray tiger. She was as little as a baseball and as quick as lightning to fight for food. The kittens will soon become accepted by the other animals as members of the farm.

Directions: Using the following words, create similes of your own.

Example: piano—The piano keys tinkled like a light rain on a tin roof.

1. fire _____

   _____

2. thunderstorm _____

   _____

3. ocean _____

   _____

4. night _____

   _____

5. rainforest _____

   _____

6. giraffe _____

   _____

Vocabulary Building: Metaphors

A **metaphor** is a figure of speech that directly compares one thing with another.

Example: As it set, the sun was a glowing orange ball of fire.

The sun is being compared to a glowing orange ball of fire.

<u>sun</u>   <u>glowing orange ball of fire</u>

Directions: Underline the metaphor in each sentence.
Then write the two things that are being compared on the lines.

1. The ocean, a swirling mass of anger, released its fury on the shore.

   _____   _____

2. He was a top spinning out of control.

   _____   _____

3. The heat covered the crowd, a blanket smothering them all.

   _____   _____

4. I fed my dog a steak, and it was a banquet for her senses.

   _____   _____

5. The flowers in the garden were a stained glass window.

   _____   _____

Reading Skills: Generalizations

A **generalization** is a statement or rule that applies to many situations or examples.

Example: All children get into trouble at one time or another.

Directions: Read each paragraph, then circle the generalization that best describes the information given.

Although many people think of reptiles as slimy, snakes and other reptiles are covered with scales that are dry to the touch. Scales are outgrowths of the animal's skin. Although in some species they are nearly invisible, in most they form a tile-like covering. The turtle's shell is made up of hardened scales that are fused together. The crocodile has a tough but more flexible covering.

Every reptile has scales.

The scales of all reptiles are alike.

There are many different kinds of scales.

The reptile's scales help to protect it from its enemies and conserve moisture in its body. Some kinds of lizards have fan-shaped scales that they can raise up to scare away other animals. The scales also can be used to court a mate. A reptile called a gecko can hang from a ceiling because of specialized scales on its feet. Some desert lizards have other kinds of scales on their feet that allow them to run over the loose sand.

Scales have many functions.

Scales scare away other animals.

Scales help reptiles adapt to their environments.

A snake will periodically shed its skin, leaving behind a thin impression of its body—scales and all. A lizard sheds its skin too, but it tears off in smaller pieces rather than in one big piece. Before a snake begins this process, which is called molting, its eyes cloud over. The snake will go into hiding until they clear. When it comes out again, it brushes against rough surfaces to pull off the old skin.

Snakes go into hiding before they molt.

Reptiles periodically shed their skin.

A lizard's skin molts in smaller pieces.

Reading Skills: Generalizations

Directions: Identify which statements below are generalizations and which are specific. Write **G** for generalization and **S** for specific.

_____ 1. We want to have lots of good food for the party.

_____ 2. Jenna gave me three pink shirts and two pairs of jeans.

_____ 3. Americans are generous and friendly.

_____ 4. There are ten more female teachers than male teachers at our school.

_____ 5. She wants me to buy watermelon at the grocery store.

_____ 6. She will never believe anything I say.

_____ 7. I got poison ivy because I didn't watch out for the foliage on our hike.

_____ 8. My mom is the best mom in the world.

_____ 9. I get depressed every time the weather turns bad.

_____ 10. The team is so good because they work out and practice every day.

_____ 11. Cats are so bad-tempered.

_____ 12. My dog has a good temperment because he's had lots of training.

_____ 13. Our football team is the best this county has ever seen.

_____ 14. I love the feel of rain on my skin, because it's cool.

_____ 15. That classroom is always out of control.

Name _____

Reading Skills: Skimming and Scanning

Skimming is reading quickly to get a general idea of what a reading selection is about. When skimming, look for headings and key words to give you an overall idea of what you are reading.

Scanning is looking for certain words to find facts or answer questions. When scanning, read or think of questions first.

Directions: Scan the paragraphs below to find the answers to the questions. Then look for specific words that will help you locate the answers. For example, in the second question, scan for the word **smallest**.

There are many different units to measure time. Probably the smallest unit that you use is the second, and the longest unit is the year. While 100 years seems like a very long time to us, in the history of the Earth, it is a smaller amount of time than one second is in a person's entire lifetime.

To describe the history of the Earth, scientists use geologic time. Even a million years is a fairly short period in geologic time. Much of the history of our Earth can only be speculated by scientists before it was written down. Some scientists believe that our planet is about 4,600 million years old. Since a thousand million is a billion, the Earth is believed to be 4.6 billion years old.

1. What kind of time is used to describe the history of the Earth?

    _____

2. For the average person, what is the smallest unit of time used?

    _____

3. In millions of years, how old do some scientists believe the Earth is?

    _____

4. How would you express that in billions of years?

    _____

Name _____

The Author's Purpose

Authors write to entertain, inform or persuade. To entertain means to hold the attention of or to amuse someone. A fiction book about outer space entertains its reader, as does a joke book.

To inform means to give factual information. A cookbook informs the reader of new recipes. A newspaper tells what is happening in the world.

To persuade people means to convince them. Newspaper editorial writers try to persuade readers to accept their opinions. Doctors write health columns to persuade readers to eat nutritious foods.

Directions: Read each of the passages below. Tell whether they entertain, inform or persuade. (They may do more than one.) Give the reasons why.

George Washington was born in a brick house near the Potomac River in Virginia on Feb. 11, 1732. When he was 11 years old, George went to live with his half-brother, Lawrence, at Mount Vernon.

Author's Purpose: _____

Reason: _____

When George Washington was a child, he always measured and counted things. Maybe that is why he became a surveyor when he grew up. Surveyors like to measure and count things, too.

Author's Purpose: _____

Reason: _____

George Washington was the best president America has ever had. He led a new nation to independence. He made all the states feel as if they were part of the United States. All presidents should be as involved with the country as George Washington was.

Author's Purpose: _____

Reason: _____

_____

Name _____

Llamas

Directions: Read each paragraph. Tell whether it informs, entertains or persuades. One paragraph does more than one. Then write your reason on the line below.

A llama (LAH'MAH) is a South American animal that is related to the camel. It is raised for its wool. Also, it can carry heavy loads. Some people who live near mountains in the United States train llamas to go on mountain trips. Llamas are sure-footed because they have two long toes and toenails.

Author's Purpose: _____

Reason: _____

Llamas are the best animals to have if you're planning to backpack in the mountains. They can climb easily and carry your supplies. No one should ever go for a long hiking trip in the mountains without a llama.

Author's Purpose: _____

Reason: _____

Llamas can be stubborn animals. Sometimes they suddenly stop walking for no reason. People have to push them to get them moving again. Stubborn llamas can be frustrating when hiking up a steep mountain.

Author's Purpose: _____

Reason: _____

Greg is an 11-year-old boy who raises llamas to climb mountains. One of his llamas is named Dallas. Although there are special saddles for llamas, Greg likes to ride bareback.

Author's Purpose: _____

Reason: _____

_____

Now use a separate sheet of paper to inform readers about llamas.

READING COMPREHENSION

Name _____

Comprehension: Fun With Photography

The word "photography" means "writing with light." "Photo" is from the Greek word "photos," which means "light." "Graphy" is from the Greek word "graphic," which means "writing." Cameras don't literally write pictures, of course. Instead, they imprint an image onto a piece of film.

Even the most sophisticated camera is basically a box with a piece of light-sensitive film inside. The box has a hole at the opposite end from the film. The light enters the box through the hole—the camera's lens—and shines on the surface of the film to create a picture. The picture that's created on the film is the image the camera's lens is pointed toward.

A lens is a circle of glass that is thinner at the edges and thicker in the center. The outer edges of the lens collect the light rays and draw them together at the center of the lens.

The shutter helps control the amount of light that enters the lens. Too much light will make the picture too light. Too little light will result in a dark picture. Electronic flash—either built into the camera or attached to the top of it—provides light when needed.

Cameras with automatic electronic flashes provide the additional light automatically. Electronic flashes—or simply "flashes," as they are often called—require batteries. If your flash quits working, a dead battery is probably the cause.

Directions: Answer these questions about photography.

1. From what language is the word "photography" derived? _____

2. Where is the camera lens thickest? _____

3. What do the outer edges of the lens do? _____

_____

4. When is a flash needed? _____

_____

5. What does the shutter do? _____

_____

_____

_____

Name _____

Comprehension: Photography Terms

Like other good professionals, photographers make their craft look easy. Their skill—like that of the graceful ice skater—comes from years of practice. Where skaters develop a sense of balance, photographers develop an "eye" for pictures. They can make important technical decisions about photographing, or "shooting," a particular scene in the twinkling of an eye.

It's interesting to know some of the technical language that professional photographers use. "Angle of view" refers to the angle from which a photograph is taken. "Depth of field" is the distance between the nearest point and the farthest point that is in focus in a photo.

"Filling the frame" refers to the amount of space the object being photographed takes up in the picture. A close-up picture of a dog, flower or person would fill the frame. A far-away picture would not.

"ASA" refers to the speed of different types of films. "Speed" means the film's sensitivity to light. The letters **ASA** stand for the American Standards Association. Film manufacturers give their films ratings of 200ASA, 400ASA, and so on to indicate film speed. The higher the number on the film, the higher its sensitivity to light, and the faster its speed. The faster its speed, the better it will be at clearly capturing sports images and other action shots.

Directions: Answer these question about photography terms.

1. Name another term for photographing. _____

2. This is the distance between the nearest point and the farthest point that is in focus in a photo.

_____

3. This refers to the speed of different types of film. _____

4. A close-up picture of someone's face would

☐ provide depth of field.　　☐ create an ASA.　　☐ fill the frame.

5. To photograph a swimming child, which film speed is better?

☐ 200ASA　　　　　☐ 400ASA

th---

Name _____

Comprehension: Photographing Animals

Animals are a favorite subject of many young photographers. Cats, dogs, hamsters and other pets top the list, followed by zoo animals and the occasional lizard.

Because it's hard to get them to sit still and "perform on command," some professional photographers refuse to photograph pets. There are ways around the problem of short attention spans, however.

One way to get an appealing portrait of a cat or dog is to hold a biscuit or treat above the camera. The animal's longing look toward the food will be captured by the camera as a soulful gaze. Because it's above the camera—out of the camera's range—the treat won't appear in the picture. When you show the picture to your friends afterwards, they will be impressed by your pet's loving expression.

If you are using fast film, you can take some good, quick shots of a pet by simply snapping a picture right after calling its name. You'll get a different expression from your pet using this technique. Depending on your pet's disposition, the picture will capture an inquisitive expression or possibly a look of annoyance, especially if you've awakened Rover from a nap!

Taking pictures of zoo animals requires a little more patience. After all, you can't wake up a lion! You may have to wait for a while until the animal does something interesting or moves into a position for you to get a good shot. When photographing zoo animals, don't get too close to the cages, and never tap on the glass or throw things between the bars of a cage! Concentrate on shooting some good pictures, and always respect the animals you are photographing.

Directions: Answer these questions about photographing animals.

1. Why do some professionals dislike photographing animals? _____

_____

2. What speed of film should you use to photograph quick-moving pets? _____

3. To capture a pet's loving expression, hold this out of camera range. _____

4. Compared to taking pictures of pets, what does photographing zoo animals require?

_____

_____

Generalization: Taking Pictures

A **generalization** is a statement that applies to many different situations.

Directions: Read each passage and circle the valid generalization.

1. Most people can quickly be taught to use a simple camera. However, it takes time, talent and a good eye to learn to take professional quality photographs. Patience is another quality that good photographers must possess. Those who photograph nature often will wait hours to get just the right light or shadow in their pictures.

    a. Anyone can learn to use a camera.

    b. Any patient person can become a good photographer.

    c. Good photographers have a good eye for pictures.

2. Photographers such as Diane Arbus, who photograph strange or odd people, also must wait for just the right picture. Many "people photographers" stake out a busy city sidewalk and study faces in the crowd. Then they must leap up quickly and ask to take a picture or sneakily take one without being observed. Either way, it's not an easy task!

    a. Staking out a busy sidewalk is a boring task.

    b. "People photographers" must be patient people and good observers.

    c. Sneak photography is not a nice thing to do to strangers.

3. Whether the subject is nature or humans, many photographers insist that dawn is the best time to take pictures. The light is clear at this early hour, and mist may still be in the air. The mist gives these early morning photos a haunting, "other world" quality that is very appealing.

    a. Morning mist gives an unusual quality to most outdoor photographs.

    b. Photographers all agree that dawn is the best time to take pictures.

    c. Misty light is always important in taking pictures.

Name _____

Generalization: Camera Care

Directions: Read each passage and circle the valid generalization.

1. Professional photographers know it's important to keep their cameras clean and in good working order. Amateur photographers should make sure theirs are, too. However, to take good care of your camera, you must first understand the equipment. Camera shop owners say at least half the "defective" cameras people bring in simply need to have the battery changed!

   a. Cameras are delicate and require constant care so they will work properly.

   b. Many problems amateurs have are caused by lack of familiarity with their equipment.

   c. Amateur photographers don't know how their cameras work.

2. Once a year, some people take their cameras to a shop to be cleaned. Most never have them cleaned at all. Those who know how can clean their cameras themselves. To avoid scratching the lens, they should use the special cloths and tissues professionals rely on. Amateurs are warned never to loosen screws, bolts or nuts inside the camera.

   a. The majority of amateur photographers never bother to have their cameras cleaned.

   b. Cleaning a camera can be tricky and should be left to professionals.

   c. It's hard to find the special cleaning cloths professionals use.

3. Another simple tip from professionals is to make sure your camera works before you take it on vacation. They suggest taking an entire roll of film and having it developed before your trip. That way, if necessary, you'll have time to have the lens cleaned or other repairs made.

   a. Check out your camera before you travel to make sure it's in good working order.

   b. Vacation pictures are often disappointing because the camera needs to be repaired.

   c. Take at least one roll of film along on every vacation.

Name _____

Generalization: Using a Darkroom

The room where photographs are developed is called a "darkroom." Can you guess why? The room must be dark so that light does not get on the film as it is being developed. Specially colored lights allow photographers to see without damaging the film. Because of the darkness and the chemicals used in the developing process, it's important to follow certain darkroom safety procedures.

To avoid shocks while in the darkroom, never touch light switches with wet hands. To avoid touching chemicals, use tongs to transfer prints from one chemical solution to another. When finished with the chemicals, put them back in their bottles. Never leave chemicals out in trays once the developing process is complete.

To avoid skin irritation from chemicals, wipe down all countertops and surfaces when you are finished. Another sensible precaution—make sure you have everything you need before exposing the film to begin the developing process. Any light that enters the darkroom can ruin the pictures being developed.

Directions: Answer these questions about using a darkroom.

1. Which generalization is correct?

    a. Developing pictures is a time-consuming and difficult process.

    b. It's dangerous to develop pictures in a darkroom.

    c. Sensible safety procedures are important for darkroom work.

2. Write directions for working with photography chemicals. _____

_____

_____

_____

3. What is the most important precaution to take to make sure pictures aren't ruined in the darkroom?

_____

_____

_____

Name _____

Comprehension: Colonists Come to America

After Christopher Columbus discovered America in 1492, many people wanted to come live in the new land. During the 17th and 18th centuries, a great many Europeans, especially the English, left their countries and settled along the Atlantic Coast of North America between Florida and Canada. Some came to make a better life for themselves. Others, particularly the Pilgrims, the Puritans and the Quakers, came for religious freedom.

A group of men who wanted gold and other riches from the new land formed the London Company. They asked the king of England for land in America and for permission to found a colony. They founded Jamestown, the first permanent English settlement in America, in 1607. They purchased ships and supplies, and located people who wanted to settle in America.

The voyage to America took about eight weeks and was very dangerous. Often, fierce winds blew the wooden ships off course. Many were wrecked. The ships were crowded and dirty. Frequently, passengers became ill, and some died. Once in America, the early settlers faced even more hardships.

Directions: Answer these questions about the colonists coming to America.

1. How long did it take colonists to travel from England to America? _____

2. Name three groups that came to America to find religious freedom.

1) _____ 2) _____ 3) _____

3. Why was the London Company formed? _____

_____

4. What was Jamestown? _____

_____

5. Why was the voyage to America dangerous? _____

_____

Name _____

Recalling Details: Early Colonial Homes

When the first colonists landed in America, they had to find shelter quickly. Their first homes were crude bark and mud huts, log cabins or dugouts, which were simply caves dug into the hillsides. As soon as possible, the settlers sought to replace these temporary shelters with comfortable houses.

Until the late 17th century, most of the colonial homes were simple in style. Almost all of the New England colonists—those settling in the northern areas of Massachusetts, Connecticut, Rhode Island and New Hampshire—used wood in building their permanent homes. Some of the buildings had thatched roofs. However, they caught fire easily, and so were replaced by wooden shingles. The outside walls also were covered with wooden shingles to make the homes warmer and less drafty.

In the middle colonies—New York, Pennsylvania, New Jersey and Delaware—the Dutch and German colonists often made brick or stone homes that were two-and-a-half or three-and-a-half stories high. Many southern colonists—those living in Virginia, Maryland, North Carolina, South Carolina and Georgia—lived on large farms called plantations. Their homes were usually made of brick.

In the 18th century, some colonists became wealthy enough to replace their simple homes with mansions, often like those being built by the wealthy class in England. They were called Georgian houses because they were popular during the years that Kings George I, George II and George III ruled England. Most were made of brick. They usually featured columns, ornately carved doors and elaborate gardens.

Directions: Answer these questions about early colonial homes.

1. What were the earliest homes of the colonists?

_____

2. What were the advantages of using wooden shingles?

_____

3. What did Dutch and German colonists use to build their homes?

_____

4. What were Georgian homes?

_____

Name _____

Recalling Details: The Colonial Kitchen

The most important room in the home of a colonial family was the kitchen. Sometimes it was the only room in the home. The most important element of the kitchen was the fireplace. Fire was essential to the colonists, and they were careful to keep one burning at all times. Before the man of the house went to bed, he would make sure that the fire was carefully banked so it would burn all night. In the morning, he would blow the glowing embers into flame again with a bellows. If the fire went out, one of the children would be sent to a neighbor's for hot coals. Because there were no matches, it would sometimes take a half hour to light a new fire, using flint, steel and tinder.

The colonial kitchen, quite naturally, was centered around the fireplace. One or two large iron broilers hung over the hot coals for cooking the family meals. Above the fireplace, a large musket and powder horn were kept for protection in the event of an attack and to hunt deer and other game. Also likely to be found near the fireplace was a butter churn, where cream from the family's cow was beaten until yellow flakes of butter appeared.

The furniture in the kitchen—usually benches, a table and chairs—were made by the man or men in the family. It was very heavy and not very comfortable. The colonial family owned few eating utensils—no forks and only a few spoons, also made by members of the family. The dishes included pewter plates, "trenchers"—wooden bowls with handles—and wooden mugs.

Directions: Answer these questions about the colonial kitchen.

1. What was the most important element of the colonial kitchen? _____

2. In colonial days, why was it important to keep a fire burning in the fireplace?

   _____

3. Name two uses of the musket.

   1) _____ 2) _____

4. Who made most of the furniture in the early colonial home?

   _____

Sequencing: Spinning

Most of the colonists could not afford to buy clothes sent over from Europe. Instead, the women and girls, particularly in the New England colonies, spent much time spinning thread and weaving cloth to make their own clothing. They raised sheep for wool and grew flax for linen.

In August, the flax was ready to be harvested and made into linen thread. The plants were pulled up and allowed to dry. Then the men pulled the seed pods from the stalks, bundled the stalks and soaked them in a stream for about five days. The flax next had to be taken out, cleaned and dried. To get the linen fibers from the tough bark and heavy wooden core, the stalks had to be pounded and crushed. Finally, the fibers were pulled through the teeth of a brush called a "hatchel" to comb out the short and broken fibers. The long fibers were spun into linen thread on a spinning wheel.

The spinning wheel was low, so a woman sat down to spin. First, she put flax in the hollow end of a slender stick, called the spindle, at one end of the spinning wheel. It was connected by a belt to a big wheel at the other end. The woman turned the wheel by stepping on a pedal. As it turned, the spindle also turned, twisting the flax into thread. The woman constantly dipped her fingers into water to moisten the flax and keep it from breaking. The linen thread came out through a hole in the side of the spindle. It was bleached and put away to be woven into pieces of cloth.

Directions: Number in order the steps to make linen thread from flax.

_____ The woman sat at the spinning wheel and put flax in the spindle.

_____ Seed pods were pulled from the stalks; stalks were bundled and soaked.

_____ In August, the flax was ready to be harvested and made into thread.

_____ The stalks were pounded and crushed to get the linen fibers.

_____ The thread was bleached and put away to be woven into cloth.

_____ The short fibers were separated out with a "hatchel."

_____ The woman dipped her fingers into water to moisten the flax.

_____ The long fibers were spun into linen thread on a spinning wheel.

_____ The woman turned the wheel by stepping on a pedal, twisting the flax into thread.

_____ The plants were pulled up and allowed to dry.

_____ The linen thread came out through a hole in the side of the spindle.

Name _____

Recalling Details: Clothing in Colonial Times

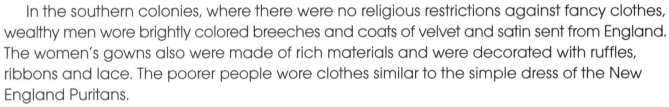

The clothing of the colonists varied from the north to the south, accounting for the differences not only in climate, but also in the religions and ancestries of the settlers. The clothes seen most often in the early New England colonies where the Puritans settled were very plain and simple. The materials—wool and linen—were warm and sturdy.

The Puritans had strict rules about clothing. There were no bright colors, jewelry, ruffles or lace. A Puritan woman wore a long-sleeved gray dress with a big white color, cuffs, apron and cap. A Puritan man wore long woolen stockings and baggy leather "breeches," which were knee-length trousers. Adults and children dressed in the same style of clothing.

In the middle colonies, the clothing ranged from the simple clothing of the Quakers to the colorful, loose-fitting outfits of the Dutch colonists. Dutch women wore more colorful outfits than Puritan women, with many petticoats and fur trim. The men had silver buckles on their shoes and wore big hats decked with curling feathers.

In the southern colonies, where there were no religious restrictions against fancy clothes, wealthy men wore brightly colored breeches and coats of velvet and satin sent from England. The women's gowns also were made of rich materials and were decorated with ruffles, ribbons and lace. The poorer people wore clothes similar to the simple dress of the New England Puritans.

Directions: Answer these questions about clothing in colonial times.

1. Why did the clothing of the colonists vary from the north to the south?

   _____

2. Why did the Puritans wear very plain clothing?

   _____

3. What was the nationality of many settlers in the middle colonies?

   _____

4. From what country did wealthy southern colonists obtain their clothing?

   _____

Name _____

Recalling Details: Venn Diagrams

A **Venn diagram** is used to chart information that shows similarities and differences between two things. The outer part of each circle shows the differences. The intersecting part of the circles shows the similarities.

Example:

Basketball   **Baseball**

Played on a court

Points scored through baskets

Five players on a team

Played with a ball

Two teams

Professional sport

Played on a diamond

Points scored through runs

Nine players on a team

Directions: Complete the Venn diagram below. Think of at least three things to write in the outer part of each circle (differences) and at least three things to write in the intersecting part (similarities).

Colonial Kitchen   **Your Kitchen**

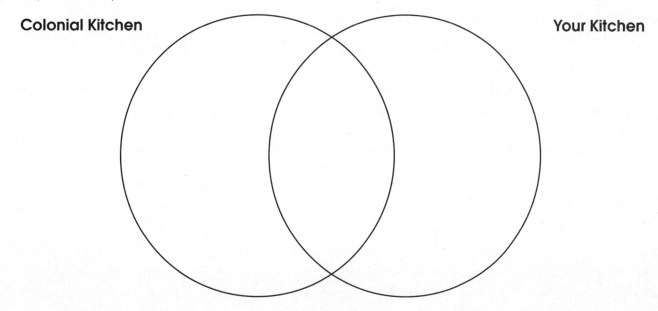

Name _____

Comprehension: Colonial Schools

In early colonial days, there were no schools or teachers. Children learned what they could at home from their parents, but often their parents couldn't read or write either. Later, some women in the New England colonies began teaching in their homes. These first schools were known as "dame schools." Often the books used in these schools were not books at all, but rather "hornbooks"—flat, paddle-shaped wooden boards with the alphabet or Lord's Prayer on the front.

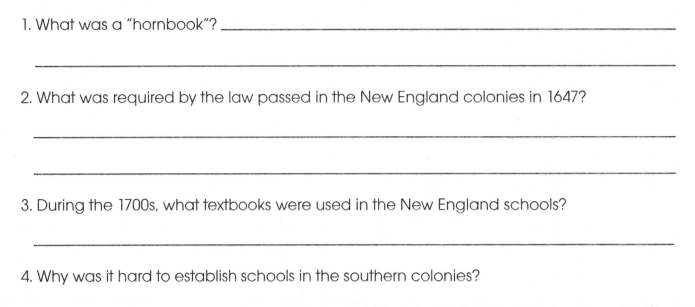

In 1647, a law was passed in the New England colonies requiring every town of 50 or more families to establish an elementary school. By the 1700s, one-room log schoolhouses were common. Children of all ages studied together under one strict schoolmaster. They attended school six days a week, from 7:00 or 8:00 in the morning until 4:00 or 5:00 in the afternoon. Their only textbooks were the Bible and the *New England Primer*, which contained the alphabet, spelling words, poems and questions about the Bible.

Like the New England colonies, the middle colonies also established schools. However, there were few schools in the southern colonies, where most of the people lived on widely separated farms. Wealthy plantation owners hired private teachers from England to teach their children, but the children of poor families received no education.

Directions: Answer these questions about colonial schools.

1. What was a "hornbook"? _____

_____

2. What was required by the law passed in the New England colonies in 1647?

_____

_____

3. During the 1700s, what textbooks were used in the New England schools?

_____

4. Why was it hard to establish schools in the southern colonies?

_____

Name _____

Using Prior Knowledge: Abraham Lincoln and the Civil War

Directions: Before reading about Abraham Lincoln and the Civil War in the following section, answer these questions.

1. The Civil War began because _____

   _____

   _____

2. Abraham Lincoln is famous today because _____

   _____

   _____

   _____

3. What brought about the end of slavery in the United States? _____

   _____

   _____

4. The *Gettysburg Address* begins with the famous line: "Four score and seven years ago. . . . " What does this mean?

   _____

   _____

5. How did Abraham Lincoln die? _____

   _____

   _____

   _____

   _____

Name _____

Main Idea: The *Gettysburg Address*

On November 19, 1863, President Abraham Lincoln gave a short speech to dedicate a cemetery for Civil War soldiers in Gettysburg, Pennsylvania, where a famous battle was fought. He wrote five drafts of the *Gettysburg Address*, one of the most stirring speeches of all time. The war ended in 1865.

Four score and seven years ago, our fathers brought forth on this continent a new nation, conceived in liberty, and dedicated to the proposition that all men are created equal.

Now we are engaged in a great civil war, testing whether that nation, or any nation so conceived and so dedicated, can long endure. We are met on a great battlefield of that war. We have come to dedicate a portion of that field as a final resting place for those who here gave their lives that this nation might live. It is altogether fitting and proper that we should do this.

But, in a larger sense, we cannot dedicate—we cannot consecrate—we cannot hallow—this ground. The brave men, living and dead, who struggled here have consecrated it far above our poor power to add or detract. The world will little note nor long remember what we say here, but it can never forget what they did here. It is for us the living, rather, to be dedicated to the unfinished work which they who fought here have thus far so nobly advanced. It is rather for us to be here dedicated to the great task remaining before us—that from these honored dead we take increased devotion to that cause for which they gave their last full measure of devotion—that we here highly resolve that these dead shall not have died in vain—that this nation, under God, shall have a new birth of freedom—and that government of the people, by the people, for the people shall not perish from this earth.

Directions: Answer the questions about the *Gettysburg Address*.

1. Circle the main idea:

   This speech will be long remembered as a tribute to the dead who died fighting in the Civil War.

   This speech is to honor the dead soldiers who gave their lives so that the nation could have freedom for all citizens.

2. What happened on the ground where the cemetery stood? _____

   _____

   _____

Name _____

Comprehension: The *Gettysburg Address*

Directions: Use context clues or a dictionary to answer these questions about the *Gettysburg Address.*

1. What is the correct definition of **conceived**? _____

_____

2. What is the correct definition of **consecrate**? _____

_____

3. What is the correct definition of **hallow**? _____

_____

4. What is the correct definition of **devotion**? _____

_____

5. What is the correct definition of **resolve**? _____

_____

6. What is the correct definition of **vain**? _____

_____

7. What is the correct definition of **perish**? _____

_____

8. What is the correct definition of **civil**? _____

_____

9. In your own words, what point was President Lincoln trying to make? _____

_____

_____

_____

Name _____

Comprehension:
The *Emancipation Proclamation*

On September 22, 1862, a year before delivering the *Gettysburg Address*, President Lincoln delivered the *Emancipation Proclamation*, which stated that all slaves in Confederate states should be set free. Since the Confederate states had already seceded (withdrawn) from the Union, they ignored the proclamation. However, the proclamation did strengthen the North's war effort. About 200,000 Black men—mostly former slaves—enlisted in the Union Army. Two years later, the 13th Amendment to the Constitution ended slavery in all parts of the United States.

I, Abraham Lincoln, do order and declare that all persons held as slaves within said designated States and parts of States are, and henceforward shall be, free; and that the Executive Government of the United States, including military and naval authorities thereof, shall recognize and maintain the freedom of said persons.

And I hereby enjoin upon the people so declared to be free to abstain from all violence, unless in necessary self-defense; and I recommend to them that, in all cases where allowed, they labor faithfully for reasonable wages.

And I further declare and make known that such persons of suitable condition will be received into the armed forces of the United States to garrison forts, positions, stations, and other places, and to man vessels of all sorts in said service.

(This is not the full text of the *Emancipation Proclamation*.)

Directions: Answer the questions about the *Emancipation Proclamation*.

1. How did the *Emancipation Proclamation* strengthen the North's war effort?

_____

2. Which came first, the *Emancipation Proclamation* or the *Gettysburg Address*?

_____

3. Which amendment to the Constitution grew out of the *Emancipation Proclamation*?

_____

4. **Secede** means to ☐ quit.   ☐ fight.   ☐ withdraw.

Name _____

Comprehension:
The *Emancipation Proclamation*

Directions: Use context clues or a dictionary to answer these questions about the *Emancipation Proclamation.*

1. What is the correct definition of **designated**? _____

_____

2. What is the correct definition of **military**? _____

_____

3. What is the correct definition of **naval**? _____

_____

4. What is the correct definition of **abstain**? _____

_____

5. What is the correct definition of **suitable**? _____

_____

6. What is the correct definition of **garrison**? _____

_____

7. What is the correct definition of **vessels**? _____

_____

8. In your own words, what did the *Emancipation Proclamation* accomplish?

_____

_____

_____

_____

Name _____

Comprehension: Lincoln and the South

Many people think that Abraham Lincoln publicly came out against slavery from the beginning of his term as president. This is not the case. Whatever his private feelings, he did not criticize slavery publicly. Fearful that the southern states would secede, or leave, the Union, he pledged to respect the southern states' rights to own slaves. He also pledged that the government would respect the southern states' runaway slave laws. These laws required all citizens to return runaway slaves to their masters.

Clearly, Lincoln did not want the country torn apart by a civil war. In the following statement, written in 1861 shortly after he became president, he made it clear that the federal government would do its best to avoid conflict with the southern states.

I hold that, in contemplation of the universal law and the Constitution, the Union of these states is perpetual.... No state, upon its own mere motion, can lawfully get out of the Union. ...I shall take care, as the Constitution itself expressly enjoins upon me, that the laws of the Union be faithfully executed in all the states.... The power confided to me will be used to hold, occupy, and possess the property and places belonging to the government, and to collect the duties and imposts....

In your hands, my dissatisfied fellow-countrymen, and not in mine, is the momentous issue of civil war. The government will not assail you. You can have no conflict without yourselves being the aggressors. You have no oath registered in heaven to destroy the government, while I shall have the most solemn one to "preserve, protect and defend" it.

Directions: Use context clues for these definitions.

1. What is the correct definition of **assail**? _____

2. What is the correct definition of **enjoin**? _____

3. What is the correct definition of **contemplation**? _____

_____

Directions: Answer these questions about Lincoln and the southern states.

4. Lincoln is telling the southern states that the government

☐ does want a war.   ☐ doesn't want a war.   ☐ will stop a war.

5. As president, Lincoln pledged to "preserve, protect and defend"

☐ slavery.   ☐ the northern states.   ☐ the Union.

Name _____

Comprehension: Away Down South in Dixie

Although many southerners disapproved of slavery, the pressure to go along with the majority who supported slavery was very strong. Many of those who thought slavery was wrong did not talk about their opinions. It was dangerous to do so!

The main reason the southern states seceded from the Union in 1861 was because they wanted to protect their right to own slaves. They also wanted to increase the number of slaves so they could increase production of cotton and other crops that slaves tended. Many Civil War monuments in the South are dedicated to a war that was described as "just and holy."

"Dixie," a song written in 1859 that is still popular in the South, sums up the attitude of many southerners. As the song lyrics show, southerners' loyalties lay not with the Union representing all the states, but with the South and the southern way of life.

Dixie
I wish I was in Dixie, Hoo-ray! Hoo-ray!
In Dixie land I'll take my stand
To live and die in Dixie.
Away, away, away down south in Dixie!
Away, away, away down south in Dixie!
(This is not the full text of the song.)

Directions: Answer these questions about southerners and "Dixie."

1. Why did southerners who disapproved of slavery keep their opinions to themselves?

_____

_____

2. Why did southerners want more slaves? _____

_____

3. What are the words on some southern Civil War monuments? _____

_____

4. What "stand" is referred to in "Dixie"?

☐ stand for slavery   ☐ stand against slavery   ☐ stand for cotton

Fact and Opinion

Directions: Read each sentence. Then draw an **X** in the box to tell whether it is a fact or opinion.

1. "Dixie" is a beautiful song! ☐ Fact ☐ Opinion

2. It was written in 1859 by a man named Daniel Emmett, who died in 1904. ☐ Fact ☐ Opinion

3. The song became a rallying cry for southerners, because it showed where their loyalties were. ☐ Fact ☐ Opinion

4. I think their loyalty to slavery was absolutely wrong! ☐ Fact ☐ Opinion

5. These four states where people owned slaves did not secede from the Union: Delaware, Maryland, Kentucky and Missouri. ☐ Fact ☐ Opinion

6. The people in these states certainly made the right moral choice. ☐ Fact ☐ Opinion

7. The ownership of one human being by another is absolutely and totally wrong under any circumstances. ☐ Fact ☐ Opinion

8. In the states that did not secede from the Union, some people fought for the Union and others fought for the Confederacy of Southern States. ☐ Fact ☐ Opinion

9. Sometimes brothers fought against brothers on opposite sides of the war. ☐ Fact ☐ Opinion

10. What a horrible situation to be in! ☐ Fact ☐ Opinion

Name _____

Recalling Details: The Island Continent

Australia is the only country that fills an entire continent. It is the smallest continent in the world but the sixth largest country. Australia, called the island continent, is totally surrounded by water—the Indian Ocean on the west and south, the Pacific Ocean on the east and the Arafura Sea, which is formed by these two oceans coming together, to the north.

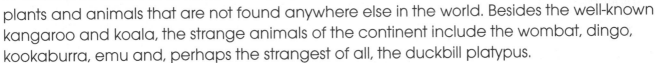

The island continent is, in large part, a very dry, flat land. Yet it supports a magnificent and unusual collection of wildlife. Because of its remoteness, Australia is home to plants and animals that are not found anywhere else in the world. Besides the well-known kangaroo and koala, the strange animals of the continent include the wombat, dingo, kookaburra, emu and, perhaps the strangest of all, the duckbill platypus.

There are many physical features of Australia that also are unique, including the central part of the country known as the "Outback," which consists of three main deserts—the Great Sandy, the Gibson and the Great Victoria. Because much of the country is desert, more than half of all Australians live in large, modern cities along the coast. There are also many people living in the small towns on the edge of the Outback, where there is plenty of grass for raising sheep and cattle. Australia rates first in the world for sheep raising. In fact, there are more than 10 times as many sheep in Australia as there are people!

Directions: Answer these questions about Australia.

1. What are the three large bodies of water that surround Australia?

1) _____ 2) _____ 3) _____

2. Besides the kangaroo and the koala, name three other unusual animals found only in Australia.

1) _____ 2) _____ 3) _____

3. What three deserts make up the "Outback?"

1) _____ 2) _____ 3) _____

Name _____

Comprehension: The Aborigines

The native, or earliest known, people of Australia are the Aborigines (ab-ur-IJ-uh-neez). They arrived on the continent from Asia more than 20,000 years ago. Before the Europeans began settling in Australia during the early 1800s, there were about 300,000 Aborigines. But the new settlers brought diseases that killed many of these native people. Today there are only about 125,000 Aborigines living in Australia, many of whom now live in the cities.

The way of life of the Aborigines, who still live like their ancestors, is closely related to nature. They live as hunters and gatherers and do not produce crops or raise livestock. The Aborigines have no permanent settlements, only small camps near watering places. Because they live off the land, they must frequently move about in search of food. They have few belongings and little or no clothing.

Some tribes of Aborigines, especially those that live in the desert, may move 100 times in a year. They might move more than 1,000 miles on foot during that time. These tribes set up temporary homes, such as tents made of bark and igloo-like structures made of grass.

The Aborigines have no written language, but they have developed a system of hand signals. These are used during hunting when silence is necessary and during their elaborate religious ceremonies when talking is forbidden.

Directions: Circle **True** or **False** for these statements about Aborigines.

1. The Aborigines came from Europe to settle in Australia.   True   False

2. The Aborigines live as hunters and gatherers rather than as farmers.   True   False

3. The tribes move about often to find jobs.   True   False

4. The people move often to help them raise their livestock.   True   False

5. Aborigine tribes always move 200 times a year.   True   False

Name _____

Main Idea/Comprehension: The Boomerang

The Aborigines have developed a few tools and weapons, including spears, flint knives and the boomerang. The boomerang comes in different shapes and has many uses. This curved throwing stick is used for hunting, playing, digging, cutting and even making music.

You may have seen a boomerang that, when thrown, returns to the thrower. This type of boomerang is sometimes used in duck hunting, but it is most often used as a toy and for sporting contests. It is lightweight—about three-fourths of a pound—and has a big curve in it. However, the boomerang used by the Aborigines for hunting is much heavier and is nearly straight. It does not return to its thrower.

Because of its sharp edges, the boomerang makes a good knife for skinning animals. The Aborigines also use boomerangs as digging sticks, to sharpen stone blades, to start fires and as swords and clubs in fighting. Boomerangs sometimes are used to make music—two clapped together provide rhythmic background for dances. Some make musical sounds when they are pulled across one another.

To throw a boomerang, the thrower grasps it at one end and holds it behind his head. He throws it overhanded, adding a sharp flick of the wrist at the last moment. It is thrown into the wind to make it come back. A skillful thrower can do many tricks with his boomerang. He can make it spin in several circles, or make a figure eight in the air. He can even make it bounce on the ground several times before it soars into the air and returns.

Directions: Answer these questions about boomerangs.

1. The main idea is:

   ☐ The Aborigines have developed a few tools and weapons, including spears, flint knives and the boomerang.

   ☐ The boomerang comes in different shapes and has many uses.

2. To make it return, the thrower tosses the boomerang

   ☐ into the wind.   ☐ against the wind.

3. List three uses for the boomerang.

   1) _____

   2) _____

   3) _____

Name _____

Comprehension: The Kangaroo

Many animals found in Australia are not found anywhere else in the world. Because the island continent was separated from the rest of the world for many years, these animals developed in different ways. Many of the animals in Australia are marsupials. Marsupials are animals whose babies are born underdeveloped and are then carried in a pouch on the mother's body until they are able to care for themselves. The kangaroo is perhaps the best known of the marsupials.

There are 45 kinds of kangaroos, and they come in a variety of sizes. The smallest is the musky rat kangaroo, which is about a foot long, including its hairless tail. It weighs only a pound. The largest is the gray kangaroo, which is more than 9 feet long, counting its tail, and can weigh 200 pounds. When moving quickly, a kangaroo can leap 25 feet and move at 30 miles an hour!

A baby kangaroo, called a joey, is totally helpless at birth. It is only three-quarters of an inch long and weighs but a fraction of an ounce. The newly born joey immediately crawls into its mother's pouch and remains there until it is old enough to be independent—which can be as long as eight months.

Kangaroos eat grasses and plants. They can cause problems for farmers and ranchers in Australia because they compete with cattle for pastures. During a drought, kangaroos may invade ranches and even airports looking for food.

Directions: Answer these questions about kangaroos.

1. What are marsupials? _____

_____

2. What is the smallest kangaroo? _____

3. What is a baby kangaroo called? _____

4. Why did Australian animals develop differently from other animals? _____

_____

Comprehension: The Koala

The koala lives in eastern Australia in the eucalyptus (you-ca-LIP-tes) forests. These slow, gentle animals hide by day, usually sleeping in the trees. They come out at night to eat. Koalas eat only certain types of eucalyptus leaves. Their entire way of life centers on this unique diet. The koala's digestive system is specially adapted for eating eucalyptus leaves. In fact, to other animals, these leaves are poisonous!

The wooly, round-eared koala looks like a cuddly teddy bear, but it is not related to any bear. It is a marsupial like the kangaroo. And, like the joey, a baby koala requires a lot of care. It will remain constantly in its mother's pouch until it is six months old. After that, a baby koala will ride piggyback on its mother for another month or two, even though it is nearly as big as she is. Koalas have few babies—only one every other year. While in her pouch, the baby koala lives on its mother's milk. After it is big enough to be on its own, the koala will almost never drink anything again.

Oddly, the mother koala's pouch is backwards—the opening is at the bottom. This leads scientists to believe that the koala once lived on the ground and walked on all fours. But at some point, the koala became a tree dweller. This makes an upside-down pouch very awkward! The babies keep from falling to the ground by holding on tightly with their mouths. The mother koala has developed strong muscles around the rim of her pouch that also help to hold the baby in.

Directions: Answer these questions about koalas.

1. What is the correct definition for **eucalyptus**?

   ☐ enormous   ☐ a type of tree   ☐ rain

2. What is the correct definition for **digestive**?

   ☐ the process in which food is absorbed in the body
   ☐ the process of finding food
   ☐ the process of tasting

3. What is the correct definition for **dweller**?

   ☐ one who climbs   ☐ one who eats   ☐ one who lives in

Name _____

Comprehension: The Wombat

Another animal unique to Australia is the wombat. The wombat has characteristics in common with other animals. Like the koala, the wombat is also a marsupial with a backwards pouch. The pouch is more practical for the wombat, which lives on the ground rather than in trees. The wombat walks on all fours so the baby is in less danger of falling out.

The wombat resembles a beaver without a tail. With its strong claws, it is an expert digger. It makes long tunnels beneath cliffs and boulders in which it sleeps all day. At night, it comes out to look for food. It has strong, beaver-like teeth to chew through the various plant roots it eats. A wombat's teeth have no roots, like a rodent's. Its teeth keep growing from the inside as they are worn down from the outside.

The wombat, which can be up to 4 feet long and weighs 60 pounds when full grown, eats only grass, plants and roots. It is a shy, quiet and gentle animal that would never attack. But when angered, it has a strong bite and very sharp teeth! And, while wombats don't eat or attack other animals, the many deep burrows they dig to sleep in are often dangerous to the other animals living nearby.

Directions: Answer these questions about the wombat.

1. How is the wombat similar to the koala? _____

_____

2. How is the wombat similar to the beaver? _____

_____

3. How is the wombat similar to a rodent? _____

_____

_____

Name _____

Comprehension: The Duckbill Platypus

Australia's duckbill platypus is a most unusual animal. It is very strange-looking and has caused a lot of confusion for people studying it. For many years, even scientists did not know how to classify it. The platypus has webbed feet and a bill like a duck. But it doesn't have wings, has fur instead of feathers and has four legs instead of two. The baby platypus gets milk from its mother, like a mammal, but it is hatched from a tough-skinned egg, like a reptile. A platypus also has a poisonous spur on each of its back legs that is like the tip of a viper's fangs. Scientists have put the platypus—along with another strange animal from Australia called the spiny anteater—in a special class of mammal called "monotremes."

The platypus has an amazing appetite! It has been estimated that a full-grown platypus eats about 1,200 earthworms, 50 crayfish and numerous tadpoles and insects every day. The platypus is an excellent swimmer and diver. It dives under the water of a stream and searches the muddy bottom for food.

A mother platypus lays one or two eggs, which are very small—only about an inch long—and leathery in appearance. During the seven to 14 days it takes for the eggs to hatch, the mother never leaves them, not even to eat. The tiny platypus, which is only a half-inch long, cuts its way out of the shell with a sharp point on its bill. This point is known as an "egg tooth," and it will fall off soon after birth. (Many reptiles and birds have egg teeth, but they are unknown in other mammals.) By the time it is 4 months old, the baby platypus is about a foot long—half its adult size—and is learning how to swim and hunt.

Directions: Answer these questions about the duckbill platypus.

1. In what way is a duckbill platypus like other mammals? _____

_____

2. In what way is it like a reptile? _____

3. What other animal is in the class of mammal called "monotremes"?

_____

4. What makes up the diet of a platypus? _____

5. On what other animals would you see an "egg tooth"? _____

Name _____

Recalling Details: Animals of Australia

Directions: Complete the chart with information from the selection on Australian animals.

	Gray Kangaroo	Koala	Wombat	Platypus
What are the animal's physical characteristics?				
What is the animal's habitat?				
What does the animal eat?				

Name _____

Using Prior Knowledge: Dinosaurs

Everyone is intrigued by dinosaurs. Their size, ferocity and sudden disappearance have fueled scientific investigations for well over a century.

Directions: Before reading about dinosaurs in the following section, answer these questions.

1. Describe what you know about meat-eating dinosaurs. _____

_____

_____

_____

_____

_____

2. Describe what you know about plant-eating dinosaurs. _____

_____

_____

_____

_____

_____

3. Which dinosaur most intrigues you? Why? _____

_____

_____

_____

_____

_____

_____

Name _____

Main Idea: Small Dinosaurs

When most people think of dinosaurs, they visualize enormous creatures. Actually, there were many species of small dinosaurs—some were only the size of chickens.

Like the larger dinosaurs, the Latin names of the smaller ones usually describe the creature. A small but fast species of dinosaur was Saltopus, which means "leaping foot." An adult Saltopus weighed only about 2 pounds and grew to be approximately 2 feet long. Fossils of this dinosaur, which lived about 200 million years ago, have been found only in Scotland.

Another small dinosaur with an interesting name was Compsognathus, which means "pretty jaw." About the same length as the Saltopus, the Compsognathus weighed about three times more. It's unlikely that these two species knew one another, since Compsognathus remains have been found only in France and Germany.

A small dinosaur whose remains have been found in southern Africa is Lesothosaurus, which means "Lesotho lizard." This lizard-like dinosaur was named only partly for its appearance. The first half of its name is based on the place its remains were found—Lesotho, in southern Africa.

Directions: Answer these questions about small dinosaurs.

1. Circle the main idea:

    People who think dinosaurs were big are completely wrong.

    There are several species of small dinosaurs, some weighing only 2 pounds.

2. How much did Saltopus weigh? _____

3. Which dinosaur's name means "pretty jaw"? _____

Name _____

Comprehension: Dinosaur History

Dinosaurs are so popular today that it's hard to imagine this not always being the case. The fact is, no one had any idea that dinosaurs ever existed until about 150 years ago.

In 1841, a British scientist named Richard Owen coined the term **Dinosauria** to describe several sets of recently discovered large fossil bones. **Dinosauria** is Latin for "terrible lizards," and even though some dinosaurs were similar to lizards, modern science now also links dinosaurs to birds. Today's birds are thought to be the closest relatives to the dinosaurs.

Like birds, most dinosaurs had fairly long legs that extended straight down from beneath their bodies. Because of their long legs, many dinosaurs were able to move fast. They were also able to balance themselves well. Long-legged dinosaurs, such as the Iguanodon, needed balance to walk upright.

The Iguanodon walked on its long hind legs and used its stubby front legs as arms. On the end of its arms were five hoof-like fingers, one of which functioned as a thumb. Because it had no front teeth for tearing meat, scientists believe the Iguanodon was a plant eater. Its large, flat back teeth were useful for grinding tender plants before swallowing them.

Directions: Answer these questions about the history of dinosaurs.

1. How were dinosaurs like today's birds? _____

_____

_____

2. This man coined the term **Dinosauria**.

   ☐ Owen Richards   ☐ Richard Owens   ☐ Richard Owen

3. Which of these did the Iguanodon not have?

   ☐ short front legs   ☐ front teeth   ☐ back teeth

4. List other ways you can think of that dinosaurs and birds are alike. _____

_____

_____

_____

_____

Name _____

Recalling Details: Dinosaur Puzzler

Directions: Use the facts you have learned about dinosaurs to complete the puzzle.

Across:

5. This dinosaur had five hoof-like fingers on its short front legs.

6. Dinosaurs with flat back teeth were ____ eaters.

9. Because of where their legs were positioned, dinosaurs had good ____.

Down:

1. Most dinosaurs had ____ legs.

2. The word **Dinosauria** means terrible ____.

3. A bone that has been preserved for many years

4. Dinosaurs were not always as ____ as they are now.

7. Iguanodons walked on their ____ legs.

8. Richard ____ coined the term **Dinosauria**.

9. Dinosaurs are closely related to today's ____.

Name _____

Comprehension: Tyrannosaurus Rex

The largest meat-eating animal ever to roam Earth was Tyrannosaurus Rex. "Rex" is Latin for "king," and because of its size, Tyrannosaurus certainly was at the top of the dinosaur heap. With a length of 46 feet and a weight of 7 tons, there's no doubt this dinosaur commanded respect!

Unlike smaller dinosaurs, Tyrannosaurus wasn't tremendously fast on its huge feet. It could stroll along at a walking speed of 2 to 3 miles an hour. Not bad, considering Tyrannosaurus was pulling along a body that weighed 14,000 pounds! Like other dinosaurs, Tyrannosaurus walked upright, probably balancing its 16-foot-long head by lifting its massive tail.

Compared to the rest of its body, Tyrannosaurus' front claws were tiny. Scientists aren't really sure what the claws were for, although it seems likely that they may have been used for holding food. In that case, Tyrannosaurus would have had to lower its massive head down to its short claws to take anything in its mouth. Maybe it just used the claws to scratch nearby itches!

Because of their low metabolism, dinosaurs did not require a lot of food for survival. Scientists speculate that Tyrannosaurus ate off the same huge piece of meat—usually the carcass of another dinosaur—for several weeks. What do you suppose Tyrannosaurus did the rest of the time?

Directions: Answer these questions about Tyrannosaurus Rex.

1. Why was this dinosaur called "Rex"? _____

_____

2. For what might Tyrannosaurus Rex have used its claws? _____

_____

3. How long was Tyrannosaurus Rex? _____

4. Tyrannosaurus weighed

☐ 10,000 lbs.   ☐ 12,000 lbs.   ☐ 14,000 lbs.

5. Tyrannosaurus ate

☐ plants.   ☐ other dinosaurs.   ☐ birds.

Generalization: Dinosaur Characteristics

Directions: Read each passage and circle the valid generalization.

1. Not surprisingly, Tyrannosaurus had huge teeth in its mammoth head. They were 6 inches long! Because it was a meat eater, Tyrannosaurus' teeth were sharp. They looked like spikes! In comparison, the long-necked, plant-eating Mamenchisaurus had a tiny head and small, flat teeth.

    a. Scientists can't figure out why some dinosaurs had huge teeth.

    b. Tyrannosaurus was probably scarier looking than Mamenchisaurus.

    c. Sharp teeth would have helped Mamenchisaurus chew better.

2. Dinosaurs' names often reflect their size or some other physical trait. For example, Compsognathus means "pretty jaw." Saltopus means "leaping foot." Lesothosaurus means "lizard from Lesotho."

    a. Of the three species, Lesothosaurus was probably the fastest.

    b. Of the three species, Compsognathus was probably the fastest.

    c. Of the three species, Saltopus was probably the fastest.

3. Edmontosaurus, a huge 3-ton dinosaur, had 1,000 teeth! The teeth were cemented into chewing pads in the back of Edmontosaurus' mouth. Unlike the sharp teeth of the meat-eating Tyrannosaurus, this dinosaur's teeth were flat.

    a. Edmontosaurus did not eat meat.

    b. Edmontosaurus did not eat plants.

    c. Edmontosaurus moved very fast.

Name _____

Recalling Details: The Earth's Atmosphere

The most important reason that life can exist on Earth is its atmosphere—the air around us. Without it, plant and animal life could not have developed. There would be no clouds, weather or even sounds, only a deathlike stillness and an endlessly black sky. Without the protection of the atmosphere, the sun's rays would roast the Earth by day. At night, with no blanketing atmosphere, the stored heat would escape into space, dropping the temperature of the planet hundreds of degrees.

Held captive by Earth's gravity, the atmosphere surrounds the planet to a depth of hundreds of miles. However, all but 1 percent of the atmosphere is in a layer about 20 miles deep just above the surface of the Earth. It is made up of a mixture of gases and dusts. About 78 percent of it is a gas called nitrogen, which is very important as food for plants. Most of the remaining gas, 21 percent, is oxygen, which all people and animals depend on for life. The remaining 1 percent is made up of a blend of other gases— including carbon dioxide, argon, ozone and helium—and tiny dust particles. These particles come from ocean salt crystals, bits of rocks and sand, plant pollen, volcanic ash and even meteor dust.

You may not think of air as matter, as something that can be weighed. In fact, the Earth's air weighs billions and billions of tons. Near the surface of the planet, this "air pressure" is greatest. Right now, about 10 tons of air is pressing in on you. Yet, like the fish living near the floor of the ocean, you don't notice this tremendous weight because your body is built to withstand it.

Directions: Answer these questions about the Earth's atmosphere.

1. What is the atmosphere? _____

2. Of what is the atmosphere made? _____

3. What is the most abundant gas in the atmosphere? _____

4. Which of the atmosphere's gases is most important to humans and animals?

   _____

5. What is air pressure? _____

Comprehension: Causes/Effects of Weather

The behavior of the atmosphere, which we experience as weather and climate, affects our lives in many important ways. It is the reason no one lives on the South Pole. It controls when a farmer plants the food we will eat, which crops will be planted and also whether those crops will grow. The weather tells you what clothes to wear and how you will play after school. Weather is the sum of all the conditions of the air that may affect the Earth's surface and its living things. These conditions include the temperature, air pressure, wind and moisture. Climate refers to these conditions but generally applies to larger areas and longer periods of time, such as the annual climate of South America rather than today's weather in Oklahoma City.

Climate is influenced by many factors. It depends first and foremost on latitude. Areas nearest the equator are warm and wet, while the poles are cold and relatively dry. The poles also have extreme seasonal changes, while the areas at the middle latitudes have more moderate climates, neither as cold as the poles nor as hot as the equator. Other circumstances may alter this pattern, however. Land near the oceans, for instance, is generally warmer than inland areas.

Elevation also plays a role in climate. For example, despite the fact that Africa's highest mountain, Kilimanjaro, is just south of the equator, its summit is perpetually covered by snow. In general, high land is cooler and wetter than nearby low land.

Directions: Check the answers to these questions about the causes and effects of weather.

1. What is the correct definition for **atmosphere**?

   ☐ the clouds ☐ the sky ☐ where weather occurs

2. What is the correct definition for **foremost**?

   ☐ most important ☐ highest number ☐ in the front

3. What is the correct definition for **circumstances**?

   ☐ temperatures ☐ seasons ☐ conditions

4. What is the correct definition for **elevation**?

   ☐ height above Earth ☐ nearness to equator ☐ snow covering

5. What is the correct definition for **perpetually**?

   ☐ occasionally ☐ rarely ☐ always

Name _____

Main Idea/Recalling Details: Weather

People have always searched the sky for clues about upcoming weather. Throughout the ages, farmers and sailors have looked to the winds and clouds for signs of approaching storms. But no real understanding of the weather could be achieved without a scientific study of the atmosphere. Such a study depends on being able to measure certain conditions, including pressure, temperature and moisture levels.

A true scientific examination of weather, therefore, was not possible until the development of accurate measuring instruments, beginning in the 17th century. Meteorology—the science of studying the atmosphere—was born in 1643 with the invention of the barometer, which measures atmospheric pressure. The liquid-in-glass thermometer, the hygrometer to measure humidity—the amount of moisture in the air—and the weather map also were invented during the 1600s.

With the measurement of these basic elements, scientists began to work out the relationships between these and other atmospheric conditions, such as wind, clouds and rainfall. Still, their observations failed to show an overall picture of the weather. Such complete weather reporting had to wait two centuries for the rapid transfer of information made possible by the invention of the telegraph during the 1840s.

Today, the forecasts of meteorologists are an international effort. There are thousands of weather stations around the world, both at land and at sea. Upper-level observations are also made by weather balloons and satellites, which continuously send photographs back to earth. All of this information is relayed to national weather bureaus, where meteorologists plot it on graphs and analyze it. The information is then given to the public through newspapers and television and radio stations.

Directions: Answer these questions about studying the weather.

1. The main idea is:

☐ People have always searched the sky for clues about upcoming weather.
☐ A real understanding of weather depends on measuring conditions such as pressure, temperature and moisture levels.

2. List three kinds of instruments used to measure atmospheric conditions, and tell what conditions they measure.

   1) _____   _____

   2) _____   _____

   3) _____   _____

3. During what century were many of these measuring instruments invented? _____

4. Name two things used for upper-level observations.

   1) _____   2) _____

Name _____

Comprehension: Hurricanes

The characteristics of a hurricane are powerful winds, driving rain and raging seas. Although a storm must have winds blowing at least 74 miles an hour to be classified as a hurricane, it is not unusual to have winds above 150 miles per hour. The entire storm system can be 500 miles in diameter, with lines of clouds that spiral toward a center called the "eye." Within the eye itself, which is about 15 miles across, the air is actually calm and cloudless. But this eye is enclosed by a towering wall of thick clouds where the storm's heaviest rains and highest winds are found.

All hurricanes begin in the warm seas and moist winds of the tropics. They form in either of two narrow bands to the north and south of the equator. For weeks, the blistering sun beats down on the ocean water. Slowly, the air above the sea becomes heated and begins to swirl. More hot, moist air is pulled skyward. Gradually, this circle grows larger and spins faster. As the hot, moist air at the top is cooled, great rain clouds are formed. The storm's fury builds until it moves over land or a cold area of the ocean where its supply of heat and moisture is finally cut off.

Hurricanes that strike North America usually form over the Atlantic Ocean. West coast storms are less dangerous because they tend to head out over the Pacific Ocean rather than toward land. The greatest damage usually comes from the hurricanes that begin in the western Pacific, because they often batter heavily populated regions.

Directions: Answer these questions about hurricanes.

1. What is necessary for a storm to be classified as a hurricane? _____

_____

2. What is the "eye" of the hurricane? _____

3. Where do hurricanes come from? _____

4. How does a hurricane finally die down? _____

_____

5. Why do hurricanes formed in the western Pacific cause the most damage?

_____

Comprehension: Tornadoes

Tornadoes, which are also called twisters, occur more frequently than hurricanes, but they are smaller storms. The zigzag path of a tornado averages about 16 miles in length and only about a quarter of a mile wide. But the tornado is, pound for pound, the more severe storm. When one touches the ground, it leaves a trail of total destruction.

The winds in a tornado average about 200 miles per hour. At the center of the funnel-shaped cloud of a tornado is a partial vacuum. In combination with the high winds, this is what makes the storm so destructive. Its force is so great that a tornado can drive a piece of straw into a tree. The extremely low atmospheric pressure that accompanies the storm can cause a building to actually explode.

Unlike hurricanes, tornadoes are formed over land. They are most likely to occur over the central plains of the United States, especially in the spring and early summer months. Conditions for a tornado arise when warm, moist air from the south becomes trapped under colder, heavier air from the north. When the surfaces of the two air masses touch, rain clouds form and a thunderstorm begins. At first, only a rounded bulge hangs from the bottom of the cloud. It gradually gets longer until it forms a column reaching toward the ground. The tornado is white from the moisture when it first forms, but turns black as it sucks up dirt and trash.

Directions: Circle **True** or **False** for these statements about tornadoes.

1. The tornado is a stronger storm than the hurricane.   True   False

2. The path of a tornado usually covers hundreds of miles.   True   False

3. Like the eye of a hurricane, the center of a tornado is calm.   True   False

4. Tornadoes are most likely to occur in the central plains of the
   United States during the spring and early summer months.   True   False

5. High atmospheric pressure usually accompanies a tornado.   True   False

Name _____

Comprehension: Thunderstorms

With warm weather comes the threat of thunderstorms. The rapid growth of the majestic thunderhead cloud and the damp, cool winds that warn of an approaching storm are familiar in most regions of the world. In fact, it has been estimated that at any given time 1,800 such storms are in progress around the globe.

As with hurricanes and tornadoes, thunderstorms are formed when a warm, moist air mass meets with a cold air mass. Before long, bolts of lightning streak across the sky, and thunder booms. It is not entirely understood how lightning is formed. It is known that a positive electrical charge builds near the top of the cloud, and a negative charge forms at the bottom. When enough force builds up, a powerful current of electricity zigzags down an electrically charged pathway between the two, causing the flash of lightning.

The clap of thunder you hear after a lightning flash is created by rapidly heated air that expands as the lightning passes through it. The distant rumbling is caused by the thunder's sound waves bouncing back and forth within clouds or between mountains. When thunderstorms rumble through an area, many people begin to worry about tornadoes. But they need to be just as fearful of thunderstorms. In fact, lightning kills more people than any other severe weather condition. In 1988, lightning killed 68 people in the United States, while tornadoes killed 32.

Directions: Answer these questions about thunderstorms.

1. How many thunderstorms are estimated to be occurring at any given time around the world?

   _____

2. When are thunderstorms formed?

   _____

3. What causes thunder?

   _____

4. On average, which causes more deaths, lightning or tornadoes?

Name _____

Venn Diagram: Storms

Directions: Complete the Venn diagram below. Think of at least three things to write in the outer parts of each circle and at least three things to write in the intersecting parts.

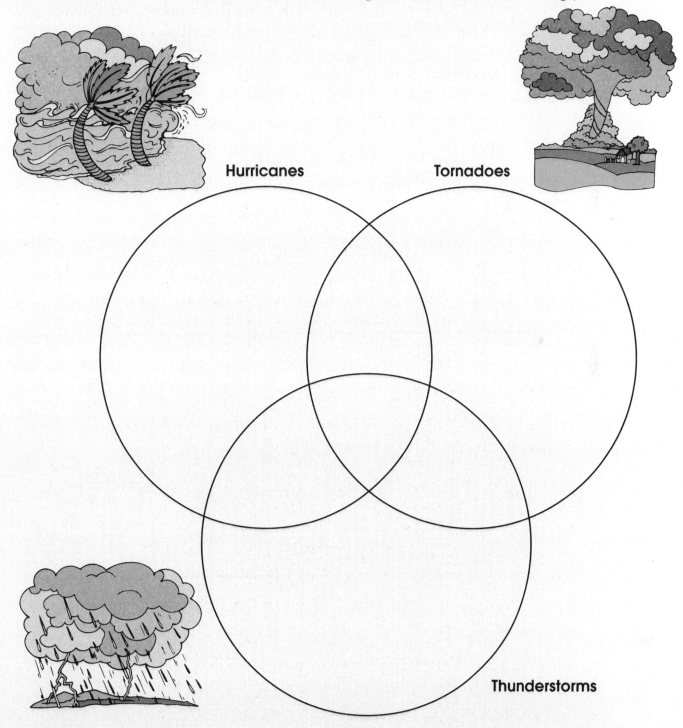

Name _____

Recalling Details: Lightning Safety Rules

Lightning causes more fire damage to forests and property than anything else. More importantly, it kills more people than any other weather event. It is important to know what to do—and what not to do—during a thunderstorm. Here are some important rules to remember:

- **Don't** go outdoors.

- **Don't** go near open doors or windows, fireplaces, radiators, stoves, metal pipes, sinks or plug-in electrical appliances.

- **Don't** use the telephone, as lightning could strike the wires outside.

- **Don't** handle metal objects, such as fishing poles or golf clubs.

- **Don't** go into the water or ride in small boats.

- **Do** stay in an automobile if you are traveling. Cars offer excellent protection.

- **Don't** take laundry off the clothesline.

- **Do** look for shelter if you are outdoors. If there is no shelter, stay away from the highest object in the area. If there are only a few trees nearby, it is best to crouch in the open, away from the trees at a distance greater than the height of the nearest tree. If you are in an area with many trees, avoid the tallest tree. Look for shorter ones.

- **Don't** take shelter near wire fences or clotheslines, exposed sheds or on a hilltop.

- If your hair stands on end or your skin tingles, lightning may be about to strike you. Immediately crouch down, put your feet together and place your hands over your ears.

Directions: Answer these questions about lightning safety rules.

1. Name two things you should avoid if you are looking for shelter outside.

   1) _____

   2) _____

2. What should you do if, during a thunderstorm, your hair stands up or your skin tingles?

   _____

   _____

Name _____

Main Idea/Comprehension: Rainbows

Although there are some violent, frightening aspects of the weather, there is, of course, considerable beauty, too. The rainbow is one simple, lovely example of nature's atmospheric mysteries.

You usually can see a rainbow when the sun comes out after a rain shower or in the fine spray of a waterfall or fountain. Although sunlight appears to be white, it is actually made up of a mixture of colors—all the colors in the rainbow. We see a rainbow because thousands of tiny raindrops act as mirrors and prisms on the sunlight. Prisms are objects that bend light, splitting it into bands of color.

The bands of color form a perfect semicircle. From the top edge to the bottom, the colors are always in the same order—red, orange, yellow, green, blue, indigo and violet. The brightness and width of each band may vary from one minute to the next. You also may notice that the sky framed by the rainbow is lighter than the sky above. This is because the light that forms the blue and violet bands is more bent and spread out than the light that forms the top red band.

You will always see morning rainbows in the west, with the sun behind you. Afternoon rainbows, likewise, are always in the east. To see a rainbow, the sun can be no higher than 42 degrees—nearly halfway up the sky. Sometimes, if the sunlight is strong and the water droplets are very small, you can see a double rainbow. This happens because the light is reflected twice in the water droplets. The color bands are fainter and in reverse order in the second band.

Directions: Answer these questions about rainbows.

1. Check the statement that is the main idea.

   [ ] Although there are violent, frightening aspects of weather, there is considerable beauty, too.

   [ ] The rainbow is one simple, lovely example of nature's atmospheric mysteries.

2. What is the correct definition for **semicircle**?

   [ ] colored circle   [ ] diameter of a circle   [ ] half circle

3. What is a prism? _____

4. In which direction would you look to see an afternoon rainbow? _____

Name _____

Comprehension: Cause and Effect

Directions: Complete the chart by listing the cause and effect of each weather phenomenon.

	Cause	Effect
Thunderstorms		
Hurricanes		
Tornadoes		
Rainbows		
Precipitation		
Drought		

Name _____

Famous Athletes

Athletes are heroes in their fields to both young and old alike. Their stories are sometimes about triumph over amazing odds to become one of the best in their sport. Before beginning the section, answer the following questions as a warm-up.

1. What sport most interests you? Why?

_____

_____

2. What sports figure do you most admire? Why?

_____

_____

3. In your opinion, what makes a person a hero?

_____

_____

4. Try to name a sports legend for each of the sports listed below.

Track and Field _____

Swimming _____

Boxing _____

Baseball _____

Speed Skating _____

Tennis _____

Name _____

Track and Field

Directions: Read the selection. Then answer the questions.

Many people recognize the name "Gail Devers" in the world of track and field. She won a gold medal for the United States at the 1992 Summer Olympics in Barcelona, Spain, in the women's 100-meter dash. However, many people do not know that Gail Devers overcame near insurmountable odds to win that gold medal.

In September, 1990, 24-year-old Gail was diagnosed with Graves' disease, which affects the thyroid gland. She had been fighting this illness for over 2 years before it was finally identified. Graves' disease can cause irregular heartbeat, muscle weakness, nervousness and weight loss. It can also become cancerous. Imagine the difficulties that would create for a person who depends on her muscles in order to compete!

Gail underwent chemotherapy and radiation, which had both good and bad effects on her body. Although the treatments brought her disease under control, the radiation burned her feet so badly that doctors considered amputation.

Amazingly, Gail began her training regimen once again in March, 1991. After competing in several meets and doing well, she went to the United States Olympic Trials and qualified in both the hurdles and the 100-meter dash. Although she came in fifth in the hurdles, the gold medal she claimed in the 100-meter dash represented all her hard work and desire to overcome the odds.

1. Summarize the selection in 3 sentences.

_____

_____

_____

2. Define the following words:

regimen: _____

amputation: _____

thyroid: _____

_____

insurmountable: _____

Name _____

Speed Skating

Directions: Read the selection. Then answer the questions.

Imagine racing around a rink of glassy ice with only a thin blade of metal supporting you. Now, imagine skating so fast that you set a world record! That's exactly what speed skater Bonnie Blair has done all of her life.

Bonnie started skating before she was walking—on the shoulders of her older brothers and sisters. By the time she was 4, Bonnie was competing. At age 7, Bonnie won the 1971 Illinois state championships and dreamed of becoming an Olympian.

That opportunity soon came. Bonnie competed in the 1988, 1992 and 1994 Olympics. She won a gold medal in the 500 meter race and a bronze medal in the 1,000 meter race in 1988, golds in both the 500 and 1,000 meter races in 1992 and repeated the two golds in 1994. No other U.S. woman has ever won five gold medals in the Olympics in any sport. Bonnie Blair is truly a champion!

1. Define the following words:

   opportunity: _____

   meter: _____

2. Bonnie Blair competed over a period of 6 years in the Olympics. What qualities would be necessary to maintain both physical and mental condition to compete for so long?

   _____

   _____

3. Bonnie Blair participated in long-track skating, in which she raced with one other person against a clock for the best time. Do you think this would be easier or more difficult than racing a group to finish first? Why?

   _____

   _____

4. In your opinion, what makes a good athlete?

   _____

   _____

Name _____

Baseball

Directions: Read the selection. Then answer the questions.

Babe Ruth was born George Herman Ruth in 1895. His family lived in Baltimore, Maryland and was quite poor. He overcame poverty to become one of the greatest baseball players of all time.

Babe Ruth's baseball career began with the Baltimore Orioles. He was a pitcher but also a tremendous batter. He later played for the Boston Red Sox and started his home run hitting fame with 29 home runs in 1919.

In 1920, while playing for the New York Yankees, Babe Ruth hit 54 home runs. He had become very popular with baseball fans of all ages. Amazingly, by 1925, he was making more money than the president of the United States! His home-run record of 60 home runs in a single season went unshattered until Roger Maris broke it in 1961 with 61 home runs. Then, in 1998, Mark McGwire hit 70 home runs to become the new "home-run king."

Babe Ruth retired from baseball in 1935 with a career total of 714 home runs. He died in 1948 at age 53.

1. Summarize the selection in 3 sentences.

_____

_____

_____

2. In the early 1900s, life expectancy was shorter than it is today. By today's standards, Babe Ruth died at a relatively young age. What factors have contributed to increased life expectancy?

_____

_____

_____

_____

3. Create a time line of Babe Ruth's life beginning with his birth and ending with his death.

|—————————————————————————————|

Name _____

Swimming

Directions: Read the selection. Then answer the questions.

In 1968, 18-year-old Mark Spitz boasted that he would win six gold medals at the Olympics being held in Mexico. He won two golds in team relay events. Having made this claim and then failing to achieve it made Mark Spitz determined to do better in the 1972 Olympics in Munich.

For the next 4 years, Mark Spitz trained ferociously. Indeed, at the 1972 Olympics, Mark Spitz amazed the world by breaking all records and winning seven gold medals in seven different events. While doing so, he set new world record times in each event. Mark Spitz had accomplished his goal.

1. What feelings do you think Mark Spitz had after the 1968 Olympics?

_____

_____

_____

2. What do you think is the moral to this story?

_____

_____

_____

3. Many Olympians are as young as Mark Spitz was, and some participate at even younger ages. Write one paragraph detailing the advantages of being a young Olympian and one paragraph detailing the disadvantages.

_____

_____

_____

_____

_____

Name _____

Boxing

Directions: Read the selection. Then answer the questions.

Muhammad Ali was born Cassius Clay in Louisville, Kentucky in 1942. He won the amateur Golden Gloves championship in 1959 and 1960 and went on to become the heavyweight champion of the 1960 Olympics. Four years later, he was champion of the world.

However, Ali's athletic fame came with its share of difficulties. He converted to the religion of Islam and thus changed his name from Cassius Clay to Muhammad Ali. It was due to his beliefs in Islam that he refused to comply with the military draft for the Vietnam War. Therefore, he was stripped of his world title and banned from boxing from 1967 to 1970.

Ali regained his title in 1974 and won the world championship again in 1978. This accomplishment made Muhammad Ali the first heavyweight boxer to claim the world championship three times. Most notable about Ali's career is his total 56 wins in the ring with 37 knockouts.

1. Define the following words:

   draft: _____

   banned: _____

   amateur: _____

   notable: _____

   comply: _____

2. Why is it necessary for a country to use the military draft?

   _____

   _____

3. Write a 3-sentence summary of the selection.

   _____

   _____

   _____

Tennis

Directions: Read the selection. Then answer the questions.

Martina Navratilova gained fame as the best women's tennis player of the 1980s. She was born in Czechoslovakia in 1956 and moved to the United States at the age of 19. She became a United States citizen in 1981.

Martina Navratilova excelled in the sport of tennis but she enjoyed the Wimbledon championship the most. She won the singles finals in 1978, 1979, 1982, 1983, 1984, 1985, 1986, 1987 and 1990.

In 1982, she became the first woman professional tennis player to earn over one million dollars in a single season.

1. What physical characteristics are necessary to excel in the sport of tennis?

_____

_____

_____

2. In your opinion, why would an athlete from another country desire to come to the U.S.A. to train and compete?

_____

_____

_____

3. Many athletes find it difficult to adjust to their status as "heroes." What are some possible disadvantages to being an athletic superstar?

_____

_____

_____

_____

_____

_____

Name _____

Review

Directions: Follow the instructions for each section.

1. On the line below, create a time line of the years of birth for the six athletes discussed in this section.

⊢ _____ ⊣

2. What mental and emotional characteristics did all six athletes have in common?

   _____

   _____

   _____

   _____

3. On the line below, create a time line of Muhammad Ali's life.

⊢ _____ ⊣

4. Compare and contrast the sports of tennis and baseball in a two-paragraph essay.

   _____

   _____

   _____

   _____

   _____

   _____

ENGLISH

Metaphor:
Don't be a crab!

Simile:
The wet floor was as slippery as an eel.

Name _____

Nouns

A **noun** names a person, place, thing or idea. There are several types of nouns.

Examples:
  proper nouns: Joe, Jefferson Memorial
  common nouns: dog, town
  concrete nouns: book, stove
  abstract nouns: fear, devotion
  collective nouns: audience, flock

A word can be more than one type of noun.

Example: Dog is both a common and a concrete noun.

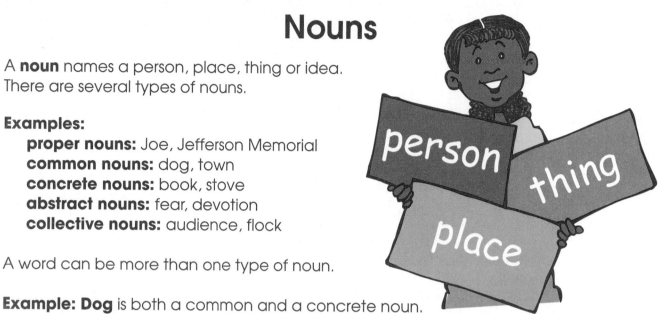

Directions: Write the type or types of each noun on the lines.

1. desk _____
2. ocean _____
3. love _____
4. cat _____
5. herd _____
6. compassion _____
7. reputation _____
8. eyes _____
9. staff _____
10. day _____
11. Roosevelt Building _____
12. Mr. Timken _____
13. life _____
14. porch _____
15. United States _____

Possessive Nouns

A **possessive** noun owns something. To make a singular noun possessive, add an apostrophe and **s. Example:** mayor**'s** campaign.

To make a plural noun possessive when it already ends with **s**, add only an apostrophe. **Example:** dog**s'** tails

To make a plural noun possessive when it doesn't end with **s**, add an apostrophe and **s. Example:** men**'s** shirts

Directions: Write the correct form of the word for each sentence in the group. Words may be singular, plural, singular possessive or plural possessive. The first one has been done for you.

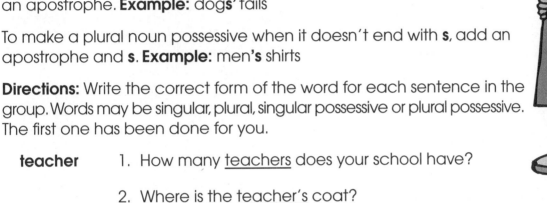

teacher

1. How many <u>teachers</u> does your school have?

2. Where is the <u>teacher's</u> coat?

3. All the <u>teachers'</u> mailboxes are in the school office.

reporter

4. Two _____ were assigned to the story.

5. One _____ car broke down on the way to the scene.

6. The other _____ was riding as a passenger.

7. Both _____ notes ended up missing.

child

8. The _____ are hungry.

9. How much spaghetti can one _____ eat?

10. Put this much on each _____ plate.

11. The _____ spaghetti is ready for them.

mouse

12. Some _____ made a nest under those boards.

13. I can see the _____ hole from here.

14. A baby _____ has wandered away from the nest.

15. The _____ mother is coming to get it.

English

117

Total Basic Skills Grade 6

Verbs

A **verb** is a word that tells what something does or that something exists.

There are two types of verbs: **action** and **state of being**.

Examples:
   Action: run, read
   State of being: feel, sound, taste, stay, look, appear, grow, seem, smell and forms of **be**

Directions: Write **A** if the verb shows action. Write **S** if it shows state of being.

1. _____ He helped his friend.

2. _____ They appear happy and content.

3. _____ Jordi drives to school each day.

4. _____ The snowfall closed schools everywhere.

5. _____ The dog sniffed at its food.

6. _____ The meat tastes funny.

7. _____ Did you taste the ice cream?

8. _____ The young boy smelled the flowers.

9. _____ She looked depressed.

10. _____ The coach announced the dates of the scrimmage.

11. _____ The owner of the store stocks all types of soda.

12. _____ He dribbled the ball down the court.

13. _____ "Everything seems to be in order," said the train conductor.

Verb Tense

Tense is the way a verb is used to express time. To explain what is happening right now, use the **present tense**.

Example: He **is singing** well. He **sings** well.

To explain what has already happened, use the **past tense**.

Example: He **sang** well.

To explain what will happen, use the **future tense**.

Example: He **will sing** well.

Directions: Rewrite each sentence so the verbs are in the same tense. The first one has been done for you.

1. He ran, he jumped, then he is flying.

   <u>He ran, he jumped, then he flew.</u>

2. He was crying, then he will stop.

   _____

3. She feels happy, but she was not sure why.

   _____

4. He is my friend, so was she.

   _____

5. She bit into the cake and says it is good.

   _____

6. He laughs first and then told us the joke.

   _____

Name _____

Spelling Different Forms of Verbs

To show that something is happening in the present, we can use a "plain" verb, or we can use **is** or **are** and add **ing** to the verb.

> is/are + verb + ing
> was/were + verb + ing

Example: We **run**. We **are running**.

To show that something has already happened, we can add **ed** to many verbs, or we can use **was** or **were** and add **ing** to a verb.

Example: The workers **surveyed**. The workers were **surveying**.

If a verb ends in **e**, drop the final **e** before adding an ending that begins with a vowel.

Example: She is **driving**. He **restored** the old car.

If a verb ends in **sh** or **ch**, add **es** instead of **s** to change the form.

Example: He furnish**es**. She watch**es**.

Directions: Complete each sentence with the correct form of the verb given. The first one has been done for you.

1. The florist is (have) a sale this week.   _____having_____

2. Last night's tornado (destroy) a barn.   _____

3. We are (research) the history of our town.   _____

4. My mistake was (use) a plural verb instead of a singular one.   _____

5. She (act) quickly in yesterday's emergency.   _____

6. Our group is (survey) the parents in our community.   _____

7. For our last experiment, we (observe) a plant's growth for 2 weeks.   _____

8. A local company already (furnish) all the materials for this project.   _____

9. Which dairy (furnish) milk to our cafeteria every day?   _____

10. Just (ignore) the mess in here will not help your case.   _____

Name _____

Verb Tense

Directions: Write a sentence using the present tense of each verb.

1. walk _____

_____

2. dream _____

_____

3. achieve _____

_____

Directions: Write a sentence using the past tense of each verb.

4. dance _____

_____

5. study _____

_____

6. hike _____

_____

Directions: Write a sentence using the future tense of each verb.

7. bake _____

_____

8. write _____

_____

9. talk _____

_____

Name _____

Verb Tense

Verbs can be **present**, **past** or **past participle**.

Add **d** or **ed** to form the past tense.

Past-participle verbs also use a helping verb such as **has** or **have**.

Examples:

Present	Past	Past Participle
help	helped	has or have helped
skip	skipped	has or have skipped

Directions: Write the past and past-participle forms of each present tense verb.

Present	Past	Past Participle
1. paint	painted	has (have) painted
2. dream		
3. play		
4. approach		
5. hop		
6. climb		
7. dance		
8. appear		
9. watch		
10. dive		
11. hurry		
12. discover		
13. decorate		
14. close		
15. jump		

English

Name _____

Irregular Verb Forms

The past tense of most verbs is formed by adding **ed**. Verbs that do not follow this format are called **irregular verbs**.

The irregular verb chart shows a few of the many verbs with irregular forms.

Irregular Verb Chart		
Present Tense	**Past Tense**	**Past Participle**
go	went	has, have or had gone
do	did	has, have or had done
fly	flew	has, have or had flown
grow	grew	has, have or had grown
ride	rode	has, have or had ridden
see	saw	has, have or had seen
sing	sang	has, have or had sung
swim	swam	has, have or had swum
throw	threw	has, have or had thrown

The words **had**, **have** and **has** can be separated from the irregular verb by other words in the sentence.

Directions: Choose the correct verb form from the chart to complete the sentences. The first one has been done for you.

1. The pilot had never before ___flown___ that type of plane.

2. She put on her bathing suit and _____ 2 miles.

3. The tall boy had _____ 2 inches over the summer.

4. She insisted she had _____ her homework.

5. He _____ them walking down the street.

6. She _____ the horse around the track.

7. The pitcher has _____ the ball many times.

8. He can _____ safely in the deepest water.

Irregular Verb Forms

Directions: Use the irregular verb chart on the previous page. Write the correct verb form to complete each sentence.

1. Has she ever _____ carrots in her garden?

2. She was so angry she _____ a tantrum.

3. The bird had sometimes _____ from its cage.

4. The cowboy has never _____ that horse before.

5. Will you _____ to the store with me?

6. He said he had often _____ her walking on his street.

7. She insisted she has not _____ taller this year.

8. He _____ briskly across the pool.

9. Have the insects _____ away?

10. Has anyone _____ my sister lately?

11. He hasn't _____ the dishes once this week!

12. Has she been _____ out of the game for cheating?

13. I haven't _____ her yet today.

14. The airplane _____ slowly by the airport.

15. Have you _____ your bike yet this week?

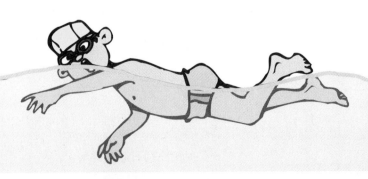

Nouns and Verbs

Some words can be used as both nouns and verbs.

Example:
The **bait** on his hook was a worm.
He couldn't **bait** his hook.

In the first sentence, **bait** is used as a **noun** because it names a thing. In the second sentence, **bait** is used as a **verb** because it shows action.

Directions: Write **noun** or **verb** for the word in bold in each sentence. The first one has been done for you.

verb 1. She **piloted** the small plane across the Pacific Ocean.

_____ 2. Does she **water** her garden every night?

_____ 3. Did you **rebel** against the rules?

_____ 4. Dad will pound the fence **post** into the ground.

_____ 5. That was good **thinking**!

_____ 6. I **object** to your language!

_____ 7. He planned to become a **pilot** after graduation.

_____ 8. The teacher will **post** the new school calendar.

_____ 9. She was **thinking** of a donut.

_____ 10. The **object** of the search was forgotten.

_____ 11. She was a **rebel** in high school.

_____ 12. Would you like fresh **water** for your tea?

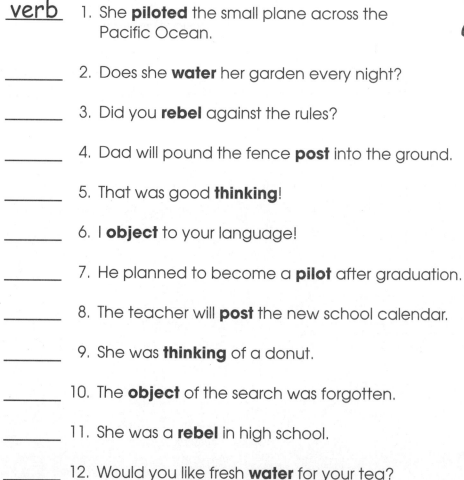

English

125

Total Basic Skills Grade 6

Name _____

Spelling: Plurals

Is **heros** or **heroes** the correct spelling? Many people aren't sure. These rules have exceptions, but they will help you spell the plural forms of most words that end with **o**.
- If a word ends with a consonant and **o**, add **es**: hero**es**.
- If a word ends with a vowel and **o**, add **s**: radio**s**.

Here are some other spelling rules for plurals:
- If a word ends with **s**, **ss**, **x**, **ch** or **sh**, add **es**: bus**es**, kiss**es**, tax**es**, peach**es**, wish**es**.
- If a word ends with **f** or **fe**, drop the **f** or **fe** and add **ves**: lea**f**, lea**ves**; wi**fe**, wi**ves**.
- Some plurals don't end with **s** or **es**: **geese**, **deer**, **children**.

heros or heroes?

Directions: Write the plural forms of the words.

1. Our area doesn't often have (tornado). _____

2. How many (radio) does this store sell every month? _____

3. (Radish) are the same color as apples. _____

4. Does this submarine carry (torpedo)? _____

5. Hawaii has a number of active (volcano). _____

6. Did you pack (knife) in the picnic basket? _____

7. We heard (echo) when we shouted in the canyon. _____

8. Where is the list of (address)? _____

9. What will you do when that plant (reach) the ceiling? _____

10. Sometimes my dad (fix) us milkshakes. _____

11. Every night, my sister (wish) on the first star she sees. _____

12. Who (furnish) the school with pencils and paper? _____

13. The author (research) every detail in her books. _____

Name _____

Spelling: Plurals

Directions: Write the plural form of each word.

1. mother _____
2. ankle _____
3. journey _____
4. ceiling _____
5. governor _____
6. arch _____
7. carnival _____
8. official _____
9. potato _____
10. vacuum _____
11. stereo _____
12. strategy _____
13. column _____
14. architect _____
15. entry _____

16. summary _____
17. issue _____
18. member _____
19. astronomer _____
20. channel _____
21. harmony _____
22. piece _____
23. chicken _____
24. chemical _____
25. journal _____
26. niece _____
27. mayor _____
28. particle _____
29. entrance _____
30. assistant _____

Simple Subjects

The **simple subject** of a sentence tells who or what the sentence is about. It is a noun or a pronoun.

Example: My **mom** is turning forty this year.
   Mom is the simple subject.

Directions: Circle the simple subject in each sentence.

1. The cat ate all its food.

2. They watched the basketball game.

3. Loretta is going to lunch with her friend.

4. José likes strawberry jam on his toast.

5. The reporter interviewed the victim.

6. She turned down the volume.

7. The farm animals waited to be fed.

8. Can you lift weights?

9. The fan did little to cool the hot room.

10. Thomas Jefferson was one of the founding fathers of our country.

11. I have a lot to do tonight.

12. Will you go to the movie with us?

13. We enjoyed the day at the park.

14. Our pet is a dog.

15. She retrieved her homework from the garbage.

Name _____

Simple Predicates

The **simple predicate** of a sentence tells what the subject does, is doing, did or will do. The simple predicate is always a verb.

Example:
My mom **is turning** forty this year.
"Is turning" is the simple predicate.

Directions: Underline the simple predicate in each sentence. Include all helping verbs.

1. I bought school supplies at the mall.

2. The tiger chased its prey.

3. Mark will be arriving shortly.

4. The hamburgers are cooking now.

5. We will attend my sister's wedding.

6. The dental hygienist cleaned my teeth.

7. My socks are hanging on the clothesline.

8. Where are you going?

9. The dog is running toward its owner.

10. Ramos watched the tornado in fear.

11. Please wash the dishes after dinner.

12. My dad cleaned the garage yesterday.

13. We are going hiking at Yellowstone today.

14. The picture shows our entire family at the family picnic.

15. Our coach will give us a pep talk before the game.

Name _____

Parallel Structure

Parts of a sentence are **parallel** when they "match" grammatically and structurally.

Faulty parallelism occurs when the parts of a sentence do not match grammatically and structurally.

For sentences to be parallel, all parts of a sentence—including the verbs, nouns and phrases—must match. This means that, in most cases, verbs should be in the same tense.

Examples:
   Correct: She liked running, jumping and swinging outdoors.
   Incorrect: She liked running, jumping and to swing outdoors.

In the correct sentence, all three of the actions the girl liked to do end in **ing**. In the incorrect sentence, they do not.

Directions: Rewrite the sentences so all elements are parallel. The first one has been done for you.

1. Politicians like making speeches and also to shake hands.

   <u>Politicians like making speeches and shaking hands.</u>

2. He liked singing, acting and to perform in general.

   _____

3. The cake had icing, sprinkles and also has small candy hearts.

   _____

4. The drink was cold, frosty and also is a thirst-quencher.

   _____

5. She was asking when we would arrive, and I told her.

   _____

6. Liz felt like shouting, singing and to jump.

   _____

    130   English

Name _____

Matching Subjects and Verbs

If the subject of a sentence is singular, the verb must be singular. If the subject is plural, the verb must be plural.

Example:
The **dog** with floppy ears **is eating**.
The **dogs** in the yard **are eating**.

Directions: Write the singular or plural form of the subject in each sentence to match the verb.

1. The (yolk) _____ in this egg is bright yellow.

2. The (child) _____ are putting numbers in columns.

3. Both (coach) _____ are resigning at the end of the year.

4. Those three (class) _____ were assigned to the gym.

5. The (lunch) _____ for the children are ready.

6. (Spaghetti) _____ with meatballs is delicious.

7. Where are the (box) _____ of chalk?

8. The (man) _____ in the truck were collecting broken tree limbs.

9. The (rhythm) _____ of that music is exactly right for dancing.

10. Sliced (tomato) _____ on lettuce are good with salmon.

11. The (announcer) _____ on TV was condemning the dictator.

12. Two (woman) _____ are campaigning for mayor of our town.

13. The (group) _____ of travelers was on its way to three foreign countries.

14. The (choir) _____ of thirty children is singing hymns.

15. In spite of the parade, the (hero) _____ were solemn.

Subject/Verb Agreement

Singular subjects require singular verbs. **Plural subjects** require plural verbs. The subject and verb must agree in a sentence.

Example:
   Singular: My dog runs across the field.
   Plural: My dogs run across the field.

Directions: Circle the correct verb in each sentence.

1. Maria (talk/talks) to me each day at lunch.

2. Mom, Dad and I (is/are) going to the park to play catch.

3. Mr. and Mrs. Ramirez (dance/dances) well together.

4. Astronauts (hope/hopes) for a successful shuttle mission.

5. Trees (prevent/prevents) erosion.

6. The student (is/are) late.

7. She (ask/asks) for directions to the senior high gym.

8. The elephants (plod/plods) across the grassland to the watering hole.

9. My friend's name (is/are) Rebecca.

10. Many people (enjoy/enjoys) orchestra concerts.

11. The pencils (is/are) sharpened.

12. My backpack (hold/holds) a lot of things.

13. The wind (blow/blows) to the south.

14. Sam (collect/collects) butterflies.

15. They (love/loves) cotton candy.

Name _____

Personal Pronouns

Personal pronouns take the place of nouns. They refer to people or things. **I**, **me**, **we**, **she**, **he**, **him**, **her**, **you**, **they**, **them**, **us** and **it** are personal pronouns.

Directions: Circle the personal pronouns in each sentence.

1. He is a terrific friend.

2. Would you open the door?

3. Jim and I will arrive at ten o'clock.

4. Can you pick me up at the mall after dinner?

5. What did you do yesterday?

6. They are watching the game on television.

7. Jessie's mom took us to the movies.

8. She writes novels.

9. They gave us the refrigerator.

10. Is this the answer she intended to give?

11. What is it?

12. The dog yelped when it saw the cat.

13. I admire him.

14. We parked the bikes by the tree.

15. The ants kept us from enjoying our picnic.

Name _____

Possessive Pronouns

Possessive pronouns show ownership. **My, mine, your, yours, his, her, hers, their, theirs, our, ours** and **its** are possessive pronouns.

Directions: Circle the possessive pronouns in each sentence.

1. My dogs chase cats continually.

2. Jodi put her sunglasses on the dashboard.

3. His mother and mine are the same age.

4. The cat licked its paw.

5. Their anniversary is February 1.

6. This necklace is yours.

7. We will carry our luggage into the airport.

8. Our parents took us to dinner.

9. My brother broke his leg.

10. Her report card was excellent.

11. Raspberry jam is my favorite.

12. Watch your step!

13. The house on the left is mine.

14. My phone number is unlisted.

15. Our garden is growing out of control.

16. Our pumpkins are ten times larger than theirs.

Name _____

Interrogative Pronouns

An **interrogative pronoun** asks a question. There are three interrogative pronouns: **who**, **what** and **which**.

Use **who** when speaking of persons.
Use **what** when speaking of things.
Use **which** when speaking of persons or things.

Examples:
    Who will go? **What** will you do? **Which** of these is yours?

Who becomes **whom** when it is a direct object or an object of a preposition. The possessive form of **whom** is **whose**.

Examples:
    To **whom** will you write?
    Whose computer is that?

Directions: Write the correct interrogative pronoun.

1. _____ wet raincoat is this?

2. _____ is the president of the United States?

3. _____ is your name?

4. _____ dog made this muddy mess?

5. _____ cat ran away?

6. _____ of you is the culprit?

7. _____ was your grade on the last test?

8. To _____ did you report?

9. _____ do you believe now?

10. _____ is the leader of this English study group?

Personal and Possessive Pronouns

Directions: Write personal or possessive pronouns in the blanks to take the place of the words in bold. The first one has been done for you.

__They   him__   1. **Maisie and Marni** told **Trent** they would see him later.

_____   2. **Spencer** told **Nancee and Sandi** good-bye.

_____   3. **The bike** was parked near **Aaron's** house.

_____   4. **Maria, Matt and Greg** claimed the car was new.

_____   5. The dishes were **the property of Cindy and Jake**.

_____   6. Is this **Carole's**?

_____   7. **Jon** walked near **Jessica and Esau's** house.

_____   8. **The dog** barked all night long!

_____   9. **Dawn** fell and hurt **Dawn's** knee.

_____   10. **Cory and Devan** gave the dog **the dog's** dinner.

_____   11. **Tori and I** gave **Brett and Reggie** a ride home.

_____   12. Do **Josh and Andrea** like cats?

_____   13. **Sasha and Keesha** gave **Josh and me** a ride home.

_____   14. Is this sweater **Marni's**?

_____   15. The cat meowed because **the cat** was hungry.

Name _____

Pronoun/Antecedent Agreement

Often, a **pronoun** is used in place of a noun to avoid repeating the noun again in the same sentence. The noun that a pronoun refers to is called its **antecedent**. The word "antecedent" means "going before."

If the noun is singular, the pronoun that takes its place must also be singular. If the noun is plural, the pronoun that takes its place must also be plural. This is called *agreement* between the pronoun and its antecedent.

Examples:
> **Mary** (singular noun) said **she** (singular pronoun) would dance.
> The **dogs** (plural noun) took **their** (plural pronoun) dishes outside.

When the noun is singular and the gender unknown, it is correct to use either "his" or "his or her."

Directions: Rewrite the sentences so the pronouns and nouns agree. The first one has been done for you.

1. Every student opened their book.

   <u>Every student opened his book.</u>

   Also correct: <u>Every student opened his or her book.</u>

2. Has anyone lost their wallet lately?

   _____

3. Somebody found the wallet under their desk.

   _____

4. Someone will have to file their report.

   _____

5. Every dog has their day!

   _____

6. I felt Ted had mine best interests at heart.

   _____

Name _____

Pronoun/Antecedent Agreement

Directions: Write a pronoun that agrees with the antecedent.

1. Donald said _____ would go to the store.

2. My friend discovered _____ wallet had been stolen.

3. The cat licked _____ paw.

4. Did any woman here lose _____ necklace?

5. Someone will have to give _____ report.

6. Jennifer wished _____ had not come.

7. All the children decided _____ would attend.

8. My grandmother hurt _____ back while gardening.

9. Jerry, Marco and I hope _____ win the game.

10. Sandra looked for _____ missing homework.

11. The family had _____ celebration.

12. My dog jumps out of _____ pen.

13. Somebody needs to remove _____ clothes from this chair.

14. Everything has _____ place in Grandma's house.

15. The team will receive _____ uniforms on Monday.

16. Each artist wants _____ painting to win the prize.

Name _____

Appositives

An **appositive** is a noun or pronoun placed after another noun or pronoun to further identify or rename it. An appositive and the words that go with it are usually set off from the rest of the sentence with commas. Commas are not used if the appositive tells "which one."

Example: Angela's mother, **Ms. Glover**, will visit our school.

Commas are needed because **Ms. Glover** renames Angela's mother.

Example: Angela's neighbor Joan will visit our school.

Commas are not needed because the appositive "Joan" tells **which** neighbor.

Directions: Write the appositive in each sentence in the blank. The first one has been done for you.

Tina   1. My friend Tina wants a horse.

_____ 2. She subscribes to the magazine *Horses*.

_____ 3. Her horse is the gelding "Brownie."

_____ 4. We rode in her new car, a convertible.

_____ 5. Her gift was jewelry, a bracelet.

_____ 6. Have you met Ms. Abbott, the senator?

_____ 7. My cousin Karl is very shy.

_____ 8. Do you eat the cereal Oaties?

_____ 9. Kiki's cat, Samantha, will eat only tuna.

_____ 10. My last name, Jones, is very common.

Name _____

Dangling Modifiers

A **dangling modifier** is a word or group of words that does not modify what it is supposed to modify. To correct dangling modifiers, supply the missing words to which the modifiers refer.

Examples:
Incorrect: While doing the laundry, the dog barked.
Correct: While I was doing the laundry, the dog barked.

In the **incorrect** sentence, it sounds as though the dog is doing the laundry. In the **correct** sentence, it's clear that **I** is the subject of the sentence.

Directions: Rewrite the sentences to make the subject of the sentence clear and eliminate dangling modifiers. The first one has been done for you.

1. While eating our hot dogs, the doctor called.

   <u>While we were eating our hot dogs, the doctor called.</u>

2. Living in Cincinnati, the ball park is nearby.

   _____

3. While watching the movie, the TV screen went blank.

   _____

4. While listening to the concert, the lights went out.

   _____

5. Tossed regularly, anyone can make great salad.

   _____

6. While working, something surprised him.

   _____

   _____

Name _____

Review

Directions: Write **noun** or **verb** to describe the words in bold.

_____ 1. She is one of the fastest **runners** I've seen.

_____ 2. She is **running** very fast!

_____ 3. She **thought** he was handsome.

_____ 4. Please share your **thoughts** with me.

_____ 5. I will **watch** the volleyball game on video.

_____ 6. The sailor fell asleep during his **watch**.

_____ 7. My grandmother believes my purchase was a real **find**.

_____ 8. I hope to **find** my lost books.

Directions: Rewrite the verb in the correct tense.

_____ 9. She **swim** across the lake in 2 hours.

_____ 10. He has **ride** horses for years.

_____ 11. Have you **saw** my sister?

_____ 12. She **fly** on an airplane last week.

_____ 13. My father had **instruct** me in the language.

_____ 14. I **drive** to the store yesterday.

_____ 15. The movie **begin** late.

_____ 16. Where **do** you go yesterday?

Directions: Circle the pronouns.

17. She and I told them to forget it!

18. They all wondered if her dad would drive his new car.

19. We want our parents to believe us.

20. My picture was taken at her home.

English   141   Total Basic Skills Grade 6

Name _____

Review

Directions: Rewrite the sentences to correct the faulty parallels.

1. The cookies were sweet, crunchy and are delicious.

    _____

2. The town was barren, windswept and is empty.

    _____

3. The dog was black, long-haired and is quite friendly.

    _____

4. My favorite dinners are macaroni and cheese, spaghetti and I loved fish.

    _____

Directions: Rewrite the sentences to make the verb tenses consistent.

5. We laughed, cried and were jumping for joy.

    _____

6. She sang, danced and was doing somersaults.

    _____

7. The class researched, studied and were writing their reports.

    _____

8. Bob and Sue talked about their vacation and share their experiences.

    _____

Directions: Circle the pronouns that agree with their antecedents.

9. She left (her/their) purse at the dance.

10. Each dog wagged (its/their) tail.

11. We walked to (our/he) car.

12. The lion watched (his/its) prey.

Name _____

Review

Directions: Rewrite the sentences to correct the dangling modifiers.

1. Living nearby, the office was convenient for her.

   _____

2. While doing my homework, the doorbell rang.

   _____

3. Watching over her shoulder, she hurried away.

   _____

4. Drinking from the large mug, he choked.

   _____

Directions: Circle the correct pronouns.

5. She laughed at my brother and (I/me).

6. At dawn, (he and I/him and me) were still talking.

7. Someone left (his or her/their) coat on the floor.

8. Lauren said (her/she) would not be late.

Directions: Circle the appositive.

9. The school nurse, Ms. Franklin, was worried about him.

10. The car, a Volkswagen, was illegally parked.

11. My hero, Babe Ruth, was an outstanding baseball player.

12. Is that car, the plum-colored one, for sale?

13. Will Mr. Zimmer, Todd's father, buy that car?

Name _____

Adjectives

Adjectives describe nouns.

Examples:
　　tall girl
　　soft voice
　　clean hands

Directions: Circle the adjectives. Underline the nouns they describe. Some sentences may have more than one set of adjectives and nouns.

1.　The lonely man sat in the dilapidated house.

2.　I hope the large crop of grapes will soon ripen.

3.　The white boxes house honeybees.

4.　My rambunctious puppy knocked over the valuable flower vase.

5.　The "unsinkable" *Titanic* sank after striking a gigantic iceberg.

6.　His grades showed his tremendous effort.

7.　There are many purple flowers in the large arrangement.

8.　These sweet peaches are the best I've tasted.

9.　The newsletter describes several educational workshops.

10.　The rodeo featured professional riders and funny clowns.

11.　My evening pottery class is full of very interesting people.

12.　My older brother loves his new pickup truck.

13.　Tami's family bought a big-screen TV.

Name _____

Comparing With Adjectives

When adjectives are used to compare two things, **er** is added at the end of the word for most one-syllable words and some two-syllable words.

Example: It is **colder** today than it was yesterday.

With many two-syllable words and all words with three or more syllables, the word **more** is used with the adjective to show comparison.

Example: Dr. X is **more professional** than Dr. Y.

When adjectives are used to compare three or more things, **est** is added at the end of the word for **most** one-syllable words and some two-syllable words.

Example: Today is the **coldest** day of the year.

With many two-syllable words and all words with three or more syllables, **most** is used with the adjective to show comparison.

Example: Dr. X is the **most professional** doctor in town.

When adding **er** or **est** to one-syllable words, these spelling rules apply.
- Double the last consonant if the word has a short vowel before a final consonant: thinner, fatter.
- If a word ends in **y**, change the **y** to **i** before adding **er** or **est**: earliest, prettiest.
- If a word ends in **e**, drop the final **e** before adding **er** or **est**: simpler, simplest.

Directions: Complete these sentences with the correct form of the adjective.

1. This book is (small) _____ than that one.

2. I want the (small) _____ book in the library.

3. My plan is (practical) _____ than yours.

4. My plan is the (practical) _____ one in the class.

5. I wish the change was (gradual) _____ than it is.

6. My sister is the (childish) _____ girl in her day-care group.

7. There must be a (simple) _____ way to do it than that.

8. This is the (simple) _____ way of the four we thought of.

Name _____

Adjectives: Positive, Comparative and Superlative

There are three degrees of comparison adjectives: **positive**, **comparative** and **superlative**. The **positive degree** is the adjective itself. The **comparative** and **superlative** degrees are formed by adding **er** and **est**, respectively, to most one-syllable adjectives. The form of the word changes when the adjective is irregular, for example, **good**, **better**, **best**.

Most adjectives of two or more syllables require the words "more" or "most" to form the comparative and superlative degrees.

Examples:

Positive:	big	eager	
Comparative:	bigger	more eager	
Superlative:	biggest	most eager	

Directions: Write the positive, comparative or superlative forms of these adjectives.

Positive	Comparative	Superlative
1. hard	_____	_____
2. _____	happier	_____
3. _____	_____	most difficult
4. cold	_____	_____
5. _____	easier	_____
6. _____	_____	largest
7. little	_____	_____
8. _____	shinier	_____
9. round	_____	_____
10. _____	_____	most beautiful

Adverbs

Adverbs tell when, where or how an action occurred.

Examples:
I'll go **tomorrow**. (when)
I sleep **upstairs**. (where)
I screamed **loudly**. (how)

Directions: Circle the adverb and underline the verb it modifies. Write the question (when, where or how) the adverb answers.

1. I ran quickly toward the finish line. _____

2. Today, we will receive our report cards. _____

3. He swam smoothly through the pool. _____

4. Many explorers searched endlessly for
   new lands. _____

5. He looked up into the sky. _____

6. My friend drove away in her new car. _____

7. Later, we will search for your missing wallet. _____

8. Most kings rule their kingdoms regally. _____

9. New plants must be watered daily. _____

10. The stream near our house is heavily polluted. _____

11. My brother likes to dive backward into
    our pool. _____

Name _____

Adverbs: Positive, Comparative and Superlative

There are also three degrees of comparison adverbs: **positive**, **comparative** and **superlative**. They follow the same rules as adjectives.

Example:

Positive:	rapidly	far
Comparative:	more rapidly	farther
Superlative:	most rapidly	farthest

Directions: Write the positive, comparative or superlative forms of these adverbs.

Positive	Comparative	Superlative
1. easily	_____	_____
2. _____	more quickly	_____
3. _____	_____	most hopefully
4. bravely	_____	_____
5. _____	more strongly	_____
6. near	_____	_____
7. _____	_____	most cleverly
8. _____	more gracefully	_____
9. _____	_____	most humbly
10. excitedly	_____	_____
11. _____	more handsomely	_____
12. slowly	_____	_____

Name _____

Adjectives and Adverbs

Directions: Write **adjective** or **adverb** in the blanks to describe the words in bold. The first one has been done for you.

adjective   1. Her **old** boots were caked with mud.

_____   2. The baby was **cranky**.

_____   3. He took the test **yesterday**.

_____   4. I heard the **funniest** story last week!

_____   5. She left her wet shoes **outside**.

_____   6. Isn't that the **fluffiest** cat you've ever seen?

_____   7. He ran **around** the track twice.

_____   8. Our elderly neighbor lady seems **lonely**.

_____   9. His **kind** smile lifted my dragging spirits.

_____   10. **Someday** I'll meet the friend of my dreams!

_____   11. His cat never meows **indoors**.

_____   12. Carlos hung his new shirts **back** in the closet.

_____   13. Put that valuable vase **down** immediately!

_____   14. She is the most **joyful** child!

_____   15. Jonathan's wool sweater is totally **moth-eaten**.

Name _____

Identifying Sentence Parts

The **subject** tells who or what a sentence is about. Sentences can have more than one subject.

Example: Dogs and **cats** make good pets.

The **predicate** tells what the subject does or that it exists. Predicates can be more than one word. A sentence can have more than one predicate.

Examples: She **was walking**. She **walked** and **ran**.

An **adjective** is a word or group of words that describes the subject or another noun.

Example: The **cheerful yellow** bird with **blue** spots flew across the **flower-covered** meadow.

An **adverb** is a word or group of words that tells how, when, where or how often.

Example: He sat **there** waiting **quietly**.

Directions: Write **S** for subject, **P** for predicate, **ADJ** for adjective or **ADV** for adverb above each underlined word or group of words. The first one has been done for you.

```
    ADJ    S      ADJ          P          ADV
```
1. A huge dog with long teeth was barking fiercely.

2. My grandmother usually wore a hat with a veil.

3. My niece and her friend are the same height.

4. The lively reindeer danced and pranced briefly on the rooftop.

Directions: Write sentences containing the sentence parts listed. Mark each part even if the verb part gets separated.

1. Write a question with two subjects, two predicates and two adjectives:

_____

2. Write a statement with one subject, two predicates and two adjectives:

_____

Identifying Sentence Parts

Directions: Write **S** for subject, **P** for predicate, **ADJ** for adjective or **ADV** for adverb above the appropriate words in these sentences.

1. The large cat pounced on the mouse ferociously.

2. Did you remember your homework?

3. My mother is traveling to New York tomorrow.

4. I play basketball on Monday and Friday afternoons.

5. The old, decrepit house sat at the end of the street.

6. Several tiny rabbits nibbled at the grass at the edge of the field.

7. The lovely bride wore a white dress with a long train.

8. We packed the clothes for the donation center in a box.

9. The telephone rang incessantly.

10. The lost child cried helplessly.

11. What will we do with these new puppies?

12. Lauren reads several books each week.

13. The picture hung precariously on the wall.

14. I purchased many new school supplies.

15. Computers have changed the business world.

Name _____

Prepositions

A **preposition** is a word that comes before a noun or pronoun and shows the relationship of that noun or pronoun to some other word in the sentence.

The **object of a preposition** is the noun or pronoun that follows a preposition and adds to its meaning.

A **prepositional phrase** includes the preposition, the object of the preposition and all modifiers.

Example:
She gave him a pat **on his back**.
On is the preposition.
Back is the object of the preposition.
His is a possessive pronoun.

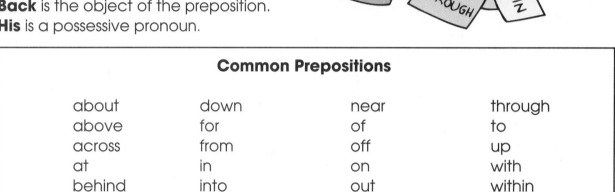

Common Prepositions			
about	down	near	through
above	for	of	to
across	from	off	up
at	in	on	with
behind	into	out	within
by	like	past	without

Directions: Underline the prepositional phrases. Circle the prepositions. Some sentences have more than one prepositional phrase. The first one has been done for you.

1. He claimed he felt (at) home only (on) the West Coast.

2. She went up the street, then down the block.

3. The famous poet was near death.

4. The beautiful birthday card was from her father.

5. He left his wallet at home.

6. Her speech was totally without humor and boring as well.

7. I think he's from New York City.

8. Kari wanted to go with her mother to the mall.

Prepositions

Directions: Complete the sentences by writing objects for the prepositions. The first one has been done for you.

1. He was standing at <u>**the corner of Fifth and Main.**</u>

2. She saw her friend across _____

3. Have you ever looked beyond _____

4. His contact lens fell into _____

5. Have you ever gone outside without _____

6. She was anxious for _____

7. Is that dog from _____

8. She was daydreaming and walked past _____

9. The book was hidden behind _____

10. The young couple had fallen in _____

11. She insisted she was through _____

12. He sat down near _____

13. She forgot her umbrella at _____

14. Have you ever thought of _____

15. Henry found his glasses on _____

Name _____

Object of a Preposition

The **object of a preposition** is the noun or pronoun that follows the preposition and adds to its meaning.

Example:
Correct: Devan smiled **at** (preposition) **Tori** (noun: object of the preposition) and **me** (pronoun: object of the same preposition.)
Correct: Devan smiled at Tori. Devan smiled at me. Devan smiled at Tori and me.
Incorrect: Devan smiled at Tori and I.

Tip: If you are unsure of the correct pronoun to use, pair each pronoun with the verb and say the phrase out loud to find out which pronoun is correct.

Directions: Write the correct pronouns on the blanks. The first one has been done for you.

_____him_____ 1. It sounded like a good idea to Sue and (he/him).

_____ 2. I asked Abby if I could attend with (her/she).

_____ 3. To (we/us), holidays are very important.

_____ 4. Between (we/us), we finished the job quickly.

_____ 5. They gave the award to (he and I/him and me).

_____ 6. The party was for my brother and (I/me).

_____ 7. I studied with (he/him).

_____ 8. Tanya and the others arrived after (we/us).

_____ 9. After the zoo, we stopped at the museum with Bill and (her/she).

_____ 10. The chips for (he/him) are in the bag on top of the refrigerator.

Name _____

Direct Objects

A **direct object** is a noun or pronoun. It answers the question **whom** or **what** after a verb.

Examples:
My mom baked **bread**.
Bread is the direct object. It tells **what** Mom baked.
We saw **Steve**.
Steve is the direct object. It tells **whom** we saw.

Directions: Write a direct object in each sentence.

1. My dog likes _____. WHAT?

2. My favorite drink is _____. WHAT?

3. I saw _____ today. WHOM?

4. The car struck a _____. WHAT?

5. The fan blew _____ through the room. WHAT?

6. I packed a _____ for lunch. WHAT?

7. We watched _____ play basketball. WHOM?

8. I finished my _____. WHAT?

9. The artist sketched the _____. WHAT?

10. He greets _____ at the door. WHOM?

11. The team attended the victory _____. WHAT?

12. The beautician cut my _____. WHAT?

13. Tamika will write _____. WHAT?

Name _____

Indirect Objects

An **indirect object** is a noun or pronoun which tells **to whom or what** or **for whom or what** the action is performed. An indirect object usually is found between a verb and a direct object.

Example:
I gave **Ellen** my address.
Ellen is the indirect object. It tells **to whom** I gave my address.

Directions: Circle the indirect objects. Underline the direct objects.

1. Joann told Mary the secret.

2. Advertisers promise consumers the world.

3. The dogs showed me their tricks.

4. Aunt Martha gave Rhonda a necklace for her birthday.

5. Ramon brought Mom a bouquet of fresh flowers.

6. I sent my niece a package for Christmas.

7. Mr. Dunbar left his wife a note before leaving.

8. Grandma and Grandpa made their friends dinner.

9. The baby handed her mom a toy.

10. Monica told Stephanie the recipe for meatloaf.

11. We sent Grandma a card.

12. The waiter served us dessert.

13. Mom and Dad sold us the farm.

Joining Sentences

Conjunctions are words that join sentences, words or ideas. When two sentences are joined with **and**, they are more or less equal.

Example: Julio is coming, **and** he is bringing cookies.

When two sentences are joined with **but**, the second sentence contradicts the first one.

Example: Julio is coming, **but** he will be late.

When two sentences are joined with **or**, they name a choice.

Example: Julio might bring cookies, **or** he might bring a cake.

When two sentences are joined with **because**, the second one names the reason for the first one.

Example: I'll bring cookies, too, **because** Julio might forget his.

When two sentences are joined with **so**, the second one names a result of the first one.

Example: Julio is bringing cookies, **so** we will have a snack.

Directions: Complete each sentence. The first one has been done for you.

1. We could watch TV, or _we could play Monopoly.®_____

2. I wanted to seize the opportunity, but _____

3. You had better not deceive me, because _____

4. My neighbor was on vacation, so _____

5. Veins take blood back to your heart, and _____

6. You can't always yield to your impulses, because _____

7. I know that is your belief, but _____

8. It could be reindeer on the roof, or _____

9. Brent was determined to achieve his goal, so _____

10. Brittany was proud of her height, because _____

Conjunctions

The conjunctions **and**, **or**, **but** and **nor** can be used to make a compound subject, a compound predicate or a compound sentence.

Examples:
   Compound subject: My friend **and** I will go to the mall.
   Compound predicate: We ran **and** jumped in gym class.
   Compound sentence: I am a talented violinist,
                                   but my father is better.

Directions: Write two sentences of your own in each section.

Compound subject:

1. _____

_____

2. _____

_____

Compound predicate:

1. _____

_____

2. _____

_____

Compound sentence:

1. _____

_____

2. _____

_____

"Affect" and "Effect"

Affect means to act upon or influence.

Example: Studying will **affect** my test grade.

Effect means to bring about a result or to accomplish something.

Example: The **effect** of her smile was immediate!

I HOPE ALL THIS STUDYING AFFECTS MY GRADE!

Directions: Write **affect** or **effect** in the blanks to complete these sentences correctly. The first one has been done for you.

affects   1. Your behavior (affects/effects) how others feel about you.

_____   2. His (affect/effect) on her was amazing.

_____   3. The (affect/effect) of his jacket was striking.

_____   4. What you say won't (affect/effect) me!

_____   5. There's a relationship between cause and (affect/effect).

_____   6. The (affect/effect) of her behavior was positive.

_____   7. The medicine (affected/effected) my stomach.

_____   8. What was the (affect/effect) of the punishment?

_____   9. Did his behavior (affect/effect) her performance?

_____   10. The cold (affected/effected) her breathing.

_____   11. The (affect/effect) was instantaneous!

_____   12. Your attitude will (affect/effect) your posture.

_____   13. The (affect/effect) on her posture was major.

_____   14. The (affect/effect) of the colored lights was calming.

_____   15. She (affected/effected) his behavior.

"Among" and "Between"

Among is a preposition that applies to more than two people or things.

Example: The group divided the cookies **among** themselves.

Between is a preposition that applies to only two people or things.

Example: The cookies were divided **between** Jeremy and Sara.

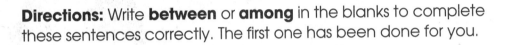

Directions: Write **between** or **among** in the blanks to complete these sentences correctly. The first one has been done for you.

between   1. The secret is (between/among) you and Jon.

_____ 2. (Between/Among) the two of them, whom do you think is nicer?

_____ 3. I must choose (between/among) the cookies, candy and pie.

_____ 4. She threaded her way (between/among) the kids on the playground.

_____ 5. She broke up a fight (between/among) Josh and Sean.

_____ 6. "What's come (between/among) you two?" she asked.

_____ 7. "I'm (between/among) a rock and a hard place," Josh responded.

_____ 8. "He has to choose (between/among) all his friends," Sean added.

_____ 9. "Are you (between/among) his closest friends?" she asked Sean.

_____ 10. "It's (between/among) another boy and me," Sean replied.

_____ 11. "Can't you settle it (between/among) the group?"

_____ 12. "No," said Josh. "This is (between/among) Sean and me."

_____ 13. "I'm not sure he's (between/among) my closest friends."

_____ 14. Sean, Josh and Andy began to argue (between/among) themselves.

_____ 15. I hope Josh won't have to choose (between/among) the two!

Name _____

"All Together" and "Altogether"

All together is a phrase meaning everyone or everything in the same place.

Example: We put the eggs **all together** in the bowl.

Altogether is an adverb that means entirely, completely or in all.

Example: The teacher gave **altogether** too much homework.

THE EGGS ARE ALL TOGETHER

Directions: Write **altogether** or **all together** in the blanks to complete these sentences correctly. The first one has been done for you.

<u>altogether</u>   1. "You ate (altogether/all together) too much food."

_____   2. The girls sat (altogether/all together) on the bus.

_____   3. (Altogether/All together) now: one, two, three!

_____   4. I am (altogether/all together) out of ideas.

_____   5. We are (altogether/all together) on this project.

_____   6. "You have on (altogether/all together) too much makeup!"

_____   7. They were (altogether/all together) on the same team.

_____   8. (Altogether/All together), we can help stop

_____   pollution (altogether/all together).

_____   9. He was not (altogether/all together) happy with his grades.

_____   10. The kids were (altogether/all together) too loud.

_____   11. (Altogether/All together), the babies cried gustily.

_____   12. She was not (altogether/all together) sure what to do.

_____   13. Let's sing the song (altogether/all together).

_____   14. He was (altogether/all together) too pushy for her taste.

_____   15. (Altogether/All together), the boys yelled the school cheer.

Name _____

"Amount" and "Number"

Amount indicates quantity, bulk or mass.

Example: She carried a large **amount** of money in her purse.

Number indicates units.

Example: What **number** of people volunteered to work?

Directions: Write **amount** or **number** in the blanks to complete these sentences correctly. The first one has been done for you.

__number__ 1. She did not (amount/number) him among her closest friends.

_____ 2. What (amount/number) of ice cream should we order?

_____ 3. The (amount/number) of cookies on her plate was three.

_____ 4. His excuses did not (amount/number) to much.

_____ 5. Her contribution (amounted/numbered) to half the money raised.

_____ 6. The (amount/number) of injured players rose every day.

_____ 7. What a huge (amount/number) of cereal!

_____ 8. The (amount/number) of calories in the diet was low.

_____ 9. I can't tell you the (amount/number) of friends she has!

_____ 10. The total (amount/number) of money raised was incredible!

_____ 11. The (amount/number) of gadgets for sale was amazing.

_____ 12. He was startled by the (amount/number) of people present.

_____ 13. He would not do it for any (amount/number) of money.

_____ 14. She offered a great (amount/number) of reasons for her actions.

_____ 15. Can you guess the (amount/number) of beans in the jar?

Name _____

"Irritate" and "Aggravate"

Irritate means to cause impatience, to provoke or annoy.

Example: His behavior **irritated** his father.

Aggravate means to make a condition worse.

Example: Her sunburn was **aggravated** by additional exposure to the sun.

Directions: Write **aggravate** or **irritate** in the blanks to complete these sentences correctly. The first one has been done for you.

aggravated   1. The weeds (aggravated/irritated) his hay fever.

_____   2. Scratching the bite (aggravated/irritated) his condition.

_____   3. Her father was (aggravated/irritated) about her low grade in math.

_____   4. It (aggravated/irritated) him when she switched TV channels.

_____   5. Are you (aggravated/irritated) when the cat screeches?

_____   6. Don't (aggravate/irritate) me like that again!

_____   7. He was in a state of (aggravation/irritation).

_____   8. Picking at the scab (aggravates/irritates) a sore.

_____   9. Whistling (aggravates/irritates) the old grump.

_____   10. She was (aggravated/irritated) when she learned about it.

_____   11. "Please don't (aggravate/irritate) your mother," Dad warned.

_____   12. His asthma was (aggravated/irritated) by too much stress.

_____   13. Sneezing is sure to (aggravate/irritate) his allergies.

_____   14. Did you do that just to (aggravate/irritate) me?

_____   15. Her singing always (aggravated/irritated) her brother.

Name _____

"Principal" and "Principle"

Principal means main, leader or chief, or a sum of money that earns interest.

Examples:
The high school **principal** earned interest on the **principal** in his savings account.
The **principal** reason for his savings account was to save for retirement.

Principle means a truth, law or a moral outlook that governs the way someone behaves.

Example:
Einstein discovered some fundamental **principles** of science.
Stealing is against her **principles**.

Directions: Write **principle** or **principal** in the blanks to complete these sentences correctly. The first one has been done for you.

_____principle_____   1. A (principle/principal) of biology is "the survival of the fittest."

_____   2. She was a person of strong (principles/principals).

_____   3. The (principles/principals) sat together at the district conference.

_____   4. How much of the total in my savings account is (principle/principal)?

_____   5. His hay fever was the (principle/principal) reason for his sneezing.

_____   6. It's not the facts that upset me, it's the (principles/principals) of the case.

_____   7. The jury heard only the (principle/principal) facts.

_____   8. Our school (principle/principal) is strict but fair.

_____   9. Spend the interest, but don't touch the (principle/principal).

_____   10. Helping others is a guiding (principle/principal) of the homeless shelter.

_____   11. In (principle/principal), we agree; on the facts, we do not.

_____   12. The (principle/principal) course at dinner was leg of lamb.

_____   13. Some mathematical (principles/principals) are difficult to understand.

_____   14. The baby was the (principle/principal) reason for his happiness.

"Good" and "Well"

Good is always an adjective. It is used to modify a noun or pronoun.

Examples:
We enjoyed the **good** food.
We had a **good** time yesterday.
It was **good** to see her again.

Well is used to modify verbs, to describe someone's health or to describe how someone is dressed.

Examples:
I feel **well**. He looked **well**.
He was **well**-dressed for the weather.
She sang **well**.

Directions: Write **good** or **well** in the blanks to complete these sentences correctly.

1. She performed _____.

2. You look _____ in that color.

3. These apples are _____.

4. He rides his bike _____.

5. She made a _____ attempt to win the race.

6. The man reported that all was _____ in the coal mine.

7. Jonas said, "I feel _____, thank you."

8. The team played _____.

9. Mom fixed a _____ dinner.

10. The teacher wrote, " _____ work!" on top of my paper.

Name _____

"Like" and "As"

Like means something is similar, resembles something else or describes how things are similar in manner.

Examples:
She could sing **like** an angel.
She looks **like** an angel, too!

As is a conjunction, a joining word, that links two independent clauses in a sentence.

Example: He felt chilly **as** night fell.

Sometimes **as** precedes an independent clause.

Example: As I told you, I will not be at the party.

Directions: Write **like** or **as** in the blanks to complete these sentences correctly. The first one has been done for you.

___as___ 1. He did not behave (like/as) I expected.

_____ 2. She was (like/as) a sister to me.

_____ 3. The puppy acted (like/as) a baby!

_____ 4. (Like/As) I was saying, he will be there at noon.

_____ 5. The storm was 25 miles away, (like/as) he predicted.

_____ 6. He acted exactly (like/as) his father.

_____ 7. The song sounds (like/as) a hit to me!

_____ 8. Grandpa looked (like/as) a much younger man.

_____ 9. (Like/As) I listened to the music, I grew sleepy.

_____ 10. (Like/As) I expected, he showed up late.

_____ 11. She dances (like/as) a ballerina!

_____ 12. (Like/As) she danced, the crowd applauded.

_____ 13. On stage, she looks (like/as) a professional!

_____ 14. (Like/As) I thought, she has taken lessons for years.

WRITING

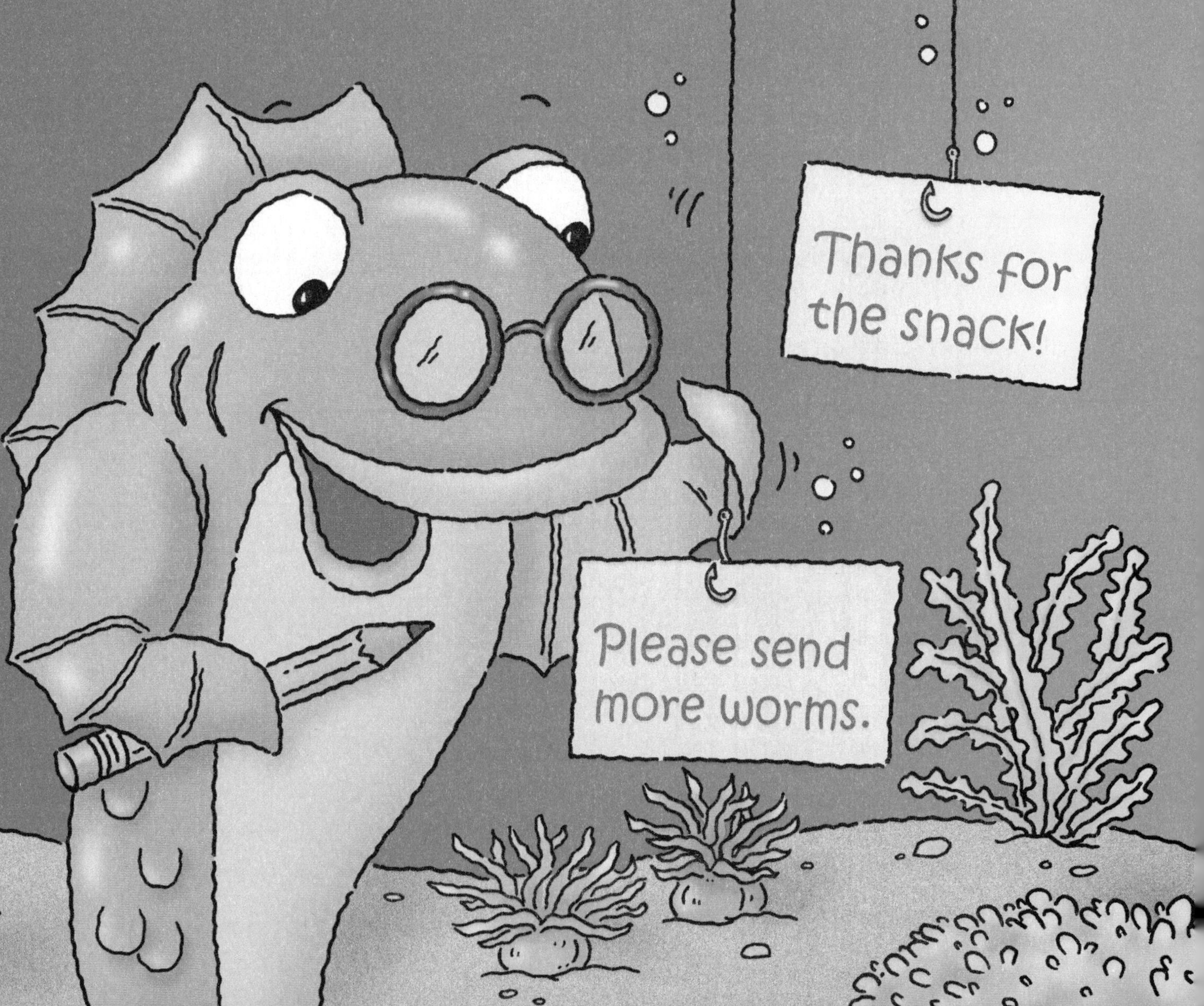

Name _____

Capitalization

Capitalize . . .
>. . . the first word in a sentence
>. . . the first letter of a person's name
>. . . proper nouns, like the names of planets, oceans and mountain ranges
>. . . titles when used with a person's name, even if abbreviated (Dr., Mr., Lt.)
>. . . days of the week and months of the year
>. . . cities, states and countries

Directions: Write **C** in the blank if the word or phrase is capitalized correctly. Rewrite the word or phrase if it is incorrect.

1. _____ President Abraham Lincoln _____
2. _____ Larry D. Walters _____
3. _____ saturn _____
4. _____ benjamin franklin _____
5. _____ August _____
6. _____ professional _____
7. _____ jupiter _____
8. _____ Pacific Ocean _____
9. _____ white house _____
10. _____ pet _____
11. _____ Congress _____
12. _____ Houston _____
13. _____ federal government _____
14. _____ dr. Samuel White _____
15. _____ milwaukee, Wisconsin _____
16. _____ Appalachian mountains _____
17. _____ lake michigan _____
18. _____ Notre Dame College _____
19. _____ department of the Interior _____
20. _____ monday and Tuesday _____

Name _____

Capitalization

Words which name places, people, months and landmarks are always capitalized.

Examples:

Abraham Lincoln	Acme Motor Company
White House	Jefferson Memorial
Fifth Avenue	May, June, July

Directions: Rewrite the sentences using correct capitalization.

1. My family and I visited washington, d.c., in july.

_____

2. We saw the washington monument, the capital building and the white house.

_____

3. I was very impressed by our visit to the smithsonian institution.

_____

4. Our taxi driver, from the american cab company, showed us around town.

_____

5. We drove down pennsylvania avenue.

_____

6. We were unable to see the president of the united states.

_____

7. However, we did see the first lady.

_____

8. My parents and I decided to visit arlington national cemetery.

_____

Commas

Use **commas** . . .
   . . . after introductory phrases
   . . . to set off nouns of direct address
   . . . to set off appositives from the words that go with them
   . . . to set off words that interrupt the flow of the sentence
   . . . to separate words or groups of words in a series

Examples:
   Introductory phrase: Of course, I'd be happy to attend.
   Noun of direct address: Ms. Williams, please sit here.
   To set off appositives: Lee, **the club president**, sat beside me.
   Words interrupting flow: My cousin, **who's 13**, will also be there.
   Words in a series: I ate **popcorn**, **peanuts**, **oats** and **barley**.
        or   I ate **popcorn**, **peanuts**, **oats**, and **barley**.

Note: The final comma is optional when punctuating words in a series.

Directions: Identify how the commas are used in each sentence.
         Write: **I** for introductory phrase
              N for noun of direct address
              A for appositive
              WF for words interrupting flow
              WS for words in a series

_____ 1. Yes, she is my sister.

_____ 2. My teacher, Mr. Hopkins, is very fair.

_____ 3. Her favorite fruits are oranges, plums and grapes.

_____ 4. The city mayor, Carla Ellison, is quite young.

_____ 5. I will buy bread, milk, fruit and ice cream.

_____ 6. Her crying, which was quite loud, soon gave me a headache.

_____ 7. Stephanie, please answer the question.

_____ 8. So, do you know her?

_____ 9. Unfortunately, the item is not returnable.

_____10. My sister, my cousin and my friend will accompany me on vacation.

_____11. My grandparents, Rose and Bill, are both 57 years old.

Name _____

Commas

Directions: Use commas to punctuate these sentences correctly.

Commas are important, and you should know when to use them!

COMMAS

1. I'll visit her however not until I'm ready.

2. She ordered coats gloves and a hat from the catalog.

3. Eun-Jung the new girl looked ill at ease.

4. Certainly I'll show Eun-Jung around school.

5. Yes I'll be glad to help her.

6. I paid nevertheless I was unhappy with the price.

7. I bought stamps envelopes and plenty of postcards.

8. No I told you I was not going.

9. The date November 12 was not convenient.

10. Her earache which kept her up all night stopped at dawn.

11. My nephew who loves bike riding will go with us.

12. He'll bring hiking boots a tent and food.

13. The cat a Himalayan was beautiful.

14. The tennis player a professional in every sense signed autographs.

15. No you can't stay out past 10:00 P.M.

Name _____

Semicolons

A **semicolon** (;) signals a reader to pause longer than tor a comma, but not as long as for a period. Semicolons are used between closely related independent clauses not joined by **and**, **or**, **nor**, **for**, **yet** or **but**.

An **independent clause** contains a complete idea and can stand alone.

Example: Rena was outgoing; her sister was shy.

Directions: Use semicolons to punctuate these sentences correctly. Some sentences require more than one semicolon.

1. Jeff wanted coffee Sally wanted milk.

2. I thought he was kind she thought he was grouchy.

3. "I came I saw I conquered," wrote Julius Caesar.

4. Jessica read books she also read magazines.

5. I wanted a new coat my old one was too small.

6. The airport was fogged-in the planes could not land.

7. Now, he regrets his comments it's too late to retract them.

8. The girls were thrilled their mothers were not.

Directions: Use a semicolon and an independent clause to complete the sentences.

9. She liked him _____

10. I chose a red shirt _____

11. Andrea sang well _____

12. She jumped for joy _____

13. Dancing is good exercise _____

14. The man was kind _____

15. The tire looked flat _____

16. My bike is missing _____

Colons

Use a **colon** . . .

   . . . after the salutation of a business letter
   . . . between the hour and the minute when showing time
   . . . between the volume and page number of a periodical
   . . . between chapters and verses of the Bible
   . . . before a list of three or more items
   . . . to introduce a long statement or quotation

> Dear Mr. Miller:
>
> I would like to place an order for five of your 1 ton scales. Please contact me, concerning price and delivery date.
>
> Sincerely,
> Ms. Jones

Examples:
Salutation: Dear Madame:
Hour and minute: 8:45 P.M.
Periodical volume and page number: *Newsweek* 11:32
Bible chapter and verse: John 3:16
Before a list of three or more items: Buy these: fruit, cereal, cheese
To introduce a long statement or quotation: Author Willa Cather said this about experiencing life: "There are only two or three human stories, and they go on repeating themselves as fiercely as if they had never happened before."

Directions: Use colons to punctuate these sentences correctly. Some sentences require more than one colon.

1. At 12 45 the president said this "Where's my lunch?"

2. Look in Proverbs 1 12 for the answer.

3. Don't forget to order these items boots, socks, shoes and leggings.

4. Ask the librarian for *Weekly Reader* 3 14.

5. Dear Sir Please send me two copies of your report.

6. Avoid these at all costs bad jokes, bad company, bad manners.

7. The statement is in either Genesis 1 6 or Exodus 3 2.

8. At 9 15 P.M., she checked in, and at 6 45 A.M., she checked out.

9. I felt all these things at once joy, anger and sadness.

10. Here's a phrase President Bush liked "A thousand points of light."

Name _____

Dashes

Dashes (—) are used to indicate sudden changes of thought.

Examples:
I want milk—no, make that soda—with my lunch.
Wear your old clothes—new ones would get spoiled.

Directions: If the dash is used correctly in the sentence, write **C** in the blank. If the dash is missing or used incorrectly, draw an **X** in the blank. The first one has been done for you.

__*C*__ 1. No one—not even my dad—knows about the surprise.

_____ 2. Ask—him—no I will to come to the party.

_____ 3. I'll tell you the answer oh, the phone just rang!

_____ 4. Everyone thought—even her brother—that she looked pretty.

_____ 5. Can you please—oh, forget it!

_____ 6. Just stop it I really mean it!

_____ 7. Tell her that I'll—never mind—I'll tell her myself!

_____ 8. Everyone especially Anna is overwhelmed.

_____ 9. I wish everyone could—forgive me—I'm sorry!

_____ 10. The kids—all six of them—piled into the backseat.

Directions: Write two sentences of your own that include dashes.

11. _____

_____

12. _____

_____

Quotation Marks

Quotation marks are used to enclose a speaker's exact words. Use commas to set off a direct quotation from other words in the sentence.

Examples:

Kira smiled and said, "Quotation marks come in handy."
"Yes," Josh said, "I'll take two."

Directions: If quotation marks and commas are used correctly, write **C** in the blank. If they are used incorrectly, write an **X** in the blank. The first one has been done for you.

_**C**_ 1. "I suppose," Elizabeth remarked, "that you'll be there on time."

_____ 2. "Please let me help! insisted Mark.

_____ 3. I'll be ready in 2 minutes!" her father said.

_____ 4. "Just breathe slowly," the nurse said, "and calm down."

_____ 5. "No one understands me" William whined.

_____ 6. "Would you like more milk?" Jasmine asked politely.

_____ 7. "No thanks, her grandpa replied, "I have plenty."

_____ 8. "What a beautiful morning!" Jessica yelled.

_____ 9. "Yes, it certainly is" her mother agreed.

_____ 10. "Whose purse is this?" asked Andrea.

_____ 11. It's mine" said Stephanie. "Thank you."

_____ 12. "Can you play the piano?" asked Heather.

_____ 13. "Music is my hobby." Jonathan replied.

_____ 14. Great!" yelled Harry. Let's play some tunes."

_____ 15. "I practice a lot," said Jayne proudly.

"This is exactly what I'm saying! You can tell by my quotation marks!"

Name _____

Quotation Marks

Directions: Use quotation marks and commas to punctuate these sentences correctly.

"Remember: quotation marks are used to enclose a speaker's exact words."

1. No Ms. Elliot replied you may not go.

2. Watch out! yelled the coach.

3. Please bring my coat called Renee.

4. After thinking for a moment, Paul said I don't believe you.

5. Dad said Remember to be home by 9:00 P.M.

6. Finish your projects said the art instructor.

7. Go back instructed Mom and comb your hair.

8. I won't be needing my winter coat anymore replied Mei-ling.

9. He said How did you do that?

10. I stood and said My name is Rosalita.

11. No said Misha I will not attend.

12. Don't forget to put your name on your paper said the teacher.

13. Pay attention class said our history teacher.

14. As I came into the house, Mom called Dinner is almost ready!

15. Jake, come when I call you said Mother.

16. How was your trip to France Mrs. Shaw? asked Deborah.

Name _____

Apostrophes

Use an **apostrophe** (') in a contraction to show that letters have been left out. A **contraction** is a shortened form of two words, usually a pronoun and a verb.

Add an **apostrophe** and **s** to form the **possessive** of singular nouns. **Plural possessives** are formed two ways. If the noun ends in **s**, simply add an apostrophe at the end of the word. If the noun does not end in **s**, add an apostrophe and **s**.

Examples:
   Contraction: He **can't** button his sleeves.
   Singular possessive: The **boy's** sleeves are too short.
   Plural noun ending in s: The **ladies'** voices were pleasant.
   Plural noun not ending in s: The **children's** song was long.

Directions: Use apostrophes to punctuate the sentences correctly. The first one has been done for you.

1. I can't understand that child's game.

2. The farmers wagons were lined up in a row.

3. She didnt like the chairs covers.

4. Our parents beliefs are often our own.

5. Sandys mothers aunt isnt going to visit.

6. Two ladies from work didnt show up.

7. The citizens group wasnt very happy.

8. The colonists demands werent unreasonable.

9. The mothers babies cried at the same time.

10. Our parents generation enjoys music.

Directions: Write two sentences of your own that include apostrophes.

11. _____

_____

12. _____

_____

Name _____

Contractions

Examples:
 he will = **he'll**
 she is = **she's**
 they are = **they're**
 can not = **can't**

Contraction Chart

Pronoun		Verb		Contraction
I	+	am	=	I'm
we, you, they	+	are	=	we're, you're, they're
he, she, it	+	is	=	he's, she's, it's
I, we, you, they	+	have	=	I've, we've, you've, they've
I, you, we, she, he, they	+	would	=	I'd, you'd, we'd, she'd, he'd, they'd
I, you, we, she, he, they	+	will	=	I'll, you'll, we'll, she'll, he'll, they'll

Directions: Write a sentence using a contraction. The first one has been done for you.

1. I will   _I'll see you tomorrow!_____

2. they are   _____

3. we have   _____

4. she would   _____

5. you are   _____

6. they will   _____

7. she is   _____

8. he would   _____

9. they are   _____

10. I am   _____

Singular Possessives

Directions: Write the singular possessive form of each word. Then, add a noun to show possession. The first one has been done for you.

1. spider _spider's web_____

2. clock _____

3. car _____

4. book _____

5. Mom _____

6. boat _____

7. table _____

8. baby _____

9. woman _____

10. writer _____

11. mouse _____

12. fan _____

13. lamp _____

14. dog _____

15. boy _____

16. house _____

Name _____

Plural Possessives

Directions: Write the plural possessive form of each word. Then add a noun to show possession. The first one has been done for you.

1. kid   _kids' skates_

2. man   _____

3. aunt   _____

4. lion   _____

5. giraffe   _____

6. necklace   _____

7. mouse   _____

8. team   _____

9. clown   _____

10. desk   _____

11. woman   _____

12. worker   _____

Directions: Write three sentences of your own that include plural possessives.

13. _____

_____

14. _____

_____

15. _____

_____

Italics

Use **italics** or **underlining** for titles of books, newspapers, plays, magazines and movies.

Examples:
Book: Have you read *Gone with the Wind*?
Movie: Did you see *The Muppet Movie*?
Newspaper: I like to read *The New York Times*.
Magazine: Some children read *Sports Illustrated*.
Play: *A Doll's House* is a play by Henrik Ibsen.

Since we cannot write in italics, we underline words that should be in italics.

Directions: Underline the words that should be in italics. The first one has been done for you.

1. I read about a play titled <u>Cats</u> in <u>The Cleveland Plain Dealer</u>.

2. You can find The New York Times in most libraries.

3. Audrey Wood wrote Elbert's Bad Word.

4. Parents and Newsweek are both popular magazines.

5. The original Miracle on 34th Street was filmed long ago.

6. Cricket and Ranger Rick are magazines for children.

7. Bon Appetit means "good appetite" and is a cooking magazine.

8. Harper's, The New Yorker and Vanity Fair are magazines.

9. David Copperfield was written by Charles Dickens.

10. Harriet Beecher Stowe wrote Uncle Tom's Cabin.

11. Paul Newman was in a movie called The Sting.

12. Have you read Ramona the Pest by Beverly Cleary?

13. The Louisville Courier Journal is a Kentucky newspaper.

14. Teen and Boy's Life are magazines for young readers.

15. Have you seen Jimmy Stewart in It's a Wonderful Life?

Name _____

Complete Sentences

A **complete sentence** has both a simple subject and a simple predicate. It is a complete thought. Sentences which are not complete are called **fragments**.

Example:
    Complete sentence: The wolf howled at the moon.
    Sentence fragment: Howled at the moon.

Directions: Write **C** on the line if the sentence is complete. Write **F** if it is a fragment.

1. _____ The machine is running.

2. _____ What will we do today?

3. _____ Knowing what I do.

4. _____ That statement is true.

5. _____ My parents drove to town.

6. _____ Watching television all afternoon.

7. _____ The storm devastated the town.

8. _____ Our friends can go with us.

9. _____ The palm trees bent in the wind.

10. _____ Spraying the fire all night.

Directions: Rewrite the sentence fragments from above to make them complete sentences.

_____

_____

_____

_____

_____

Name _____

Run-On Sentences

A **run-on sentence** occurs when two or more sentences are joined together without punctuation or a joining word. Run-on sentences should be divided into two or more separate sentences.

Example:
Run-on sentence: My parents, sister, brother and I went to the park we saw many animals we had fun.
Correct: My parents, sister, brother and I went to the park. We saw many animals and had fun.

Directions: Rewrite the run-on sentences correctly.

1. The dog energetically chased the ball I kept throwing him the ball for a half hour.

_____

_____

_____

2. The restaurant served scrambled eggs and bacon for breakfast I had some and they were delicious.

_____

_____

_____

3. The lightning struck close to our house it scared my little brother and my grandmother called to see if we were safe.

_____

_____

_____

_____

_____

Name _____

Finding Spelling Errors

Directions: One word in each sentence below is misspelled. Write the word correctly on the line.

1. Jeff felt discoraged at the comparison between

   him and his older brother. _____

2. I got inpatient as my curiosity grew. _____

3. She confided that she had not finished the asignment. _____

4. They made the selection after a brief conferrence. _____

5. Obviusly, it's impolite to sneeze on someone. _____

6. This skin cream is practicaly invisible. _____

7. What would prevent you from taking on addtional work? _____

8. I can resite the words to that hymn. _____

9. In a previous columm, the newspaper explained the situation. _____

10. He decieved me so many times that now I distrust him. _____

11. Please have the curtesy to observe the "No Eating" signs. _____

12. The advertisement is so small that it's nearly invisble. _____

13. The best way to communicate is in a face-to-face conservation.

    _____

14. In a cost comparson, salmon is more expensive than tuna. _____

15. Poplarity among friends shouldn't depend on your accomplishments.

    _____

16. Her campaign was quite an acheivement. _____

17. He condemned it as a poor imitation. _____

Finding Spelling Errors

Directions: Circle all misspelled words. Write the words correctly on the lines at the end of each paragraph. If you need help, consult a dictionary.

Sabrina wanted to aquire a saltwater acquarum. She was worried about the expence, though, so first she did some reseach. She wanted to learn the exxact care saltwater fish need, not just to exsist but to florish. One sorce said she needed to put water in the aquarium and wait 6 weeks before she added the fish. "Good greif!" Sabrina thought. She got a kitten from her nieghbor instead.

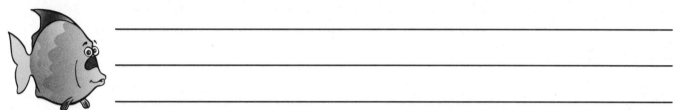

_____

_____

_____

One stormy day, Marcel was babysitting his neice. He happened to obsurve that the sky looked darker than norml. At first he ignorred it, but then he noticed a black cloud exxpand and grow in hieght. Then a tail dropped down from the twisting cloud and siezed a tree! "It's a tornado!" Marcel shouted. "Maybe two tornados! This is an emergensy!" For a breef moment Marcel wished he hadn't shouted, because his niece looked at him with a very frightened expresion. Just then, the cieling began to sag as if it had a heavy wieght on it. "This is an excelent time to visit the basement," he told the little girl as calmy as possible.

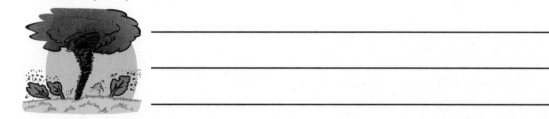

_____

_____

_____

Just before Mother's Day, Bethany went to a flourist to buy some flowers for her mother. "Well, what is your reqest?" the clerk asked. "I don't have much money," Bethany told him. "So make up your mind," he said impatiently. "Do you want qualility or quanity?" Bethany wondered if he was giving her a quizz. She tried not to sqwirm as he stared down at her. Finally she said, "I want cortesy," as she headed for the exxit.

_____

_____

_____

Name _____

Writing: Four Types of Sentences

There are four main types of sentences: A **statement** tells something. It ends in a period. A **question** asks something. It ends in a question mark. A **command** tells someone to do something. It ends in a period or an exclamation mark. An **exclamation** shows strong feeling or excitement. It ends in an exclamation mark.

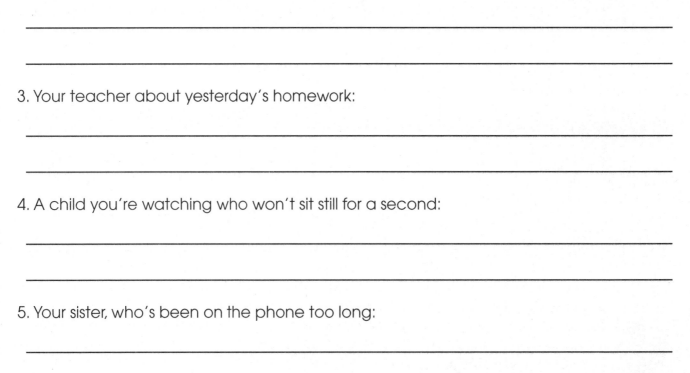

Boy, what a cute cat!

Directions: Write what you would say in each situation. Then tell whether the sentence you wrote was a statement, question, exclamation or command. The first one has been done for you.

Write what you might say to:

1. A friend who has a new cat:
   When did you get the new cat? (question)
   or Boy, what a cute cat! (exclamation)

2. A friend who studied all night for the math test:

   _____

   _____

3. Your teacher about yesterday's homework:

   _____

   _____

4. A child you're watching who won't sit still for a second:

   _____

   _____

5. Your sister, who's been on the phone too long:

   _____

   _____

Name _____

Organizing Paragraphs

A **topic sentence** states the main idea of a paragraph and is usually the first sentence. **Support sentences** follow, providing details about the topic. All sentences in a paragraph should relate to the topic sentence. A paragraph ends with a **conclusion sentence**.

Directions: Rearrange each group of sentences into a paragraph, beginning with the topic sentence. Cross out the sentence in each group that is not related to the topic sentence. Write the new paragraph.

Now, chalk drawings are considered art by themselves. The earliest chalk drawings were found on the walls of caves. Chalk is also used in cement, fertilizer, toothpaste and makeup. Chalk once was used just to make quick sketches. Chalk has been used for drawing for thousands of years. Then the artist would paint pictures from the sketches.

_____

_____

_____

_____

Dams also keep young salmon from swimming downriver to the ocean. Most salmon live in the ocean but return to fresh water to lay their eggs and breed. Dams prevent salmon from swimming upriver to their spawning grounds. Pacific salmon die after they spawn the first time. One kind of fish pass is a series of pools of water that lead the salmon over the dams. Dams are threatening salmon by interfering with their spawning. To help with this problem, some dams have special "fish passes" to allow salmon to swim over the dam.

_____

_____

_____

_____

_____

_____

Building Paragraphs

Directions: Read each group of questions and the topic sentence. On another sheet of paper, write support sentences that answer each question. Number your support sentences in order. Make any necessary changes so the sentences fit together in one paragraph. Then write your paragraph after the topic sentence.

Questions: Why did Jimmy feel sad?
What happened to change how he felt?
How does he feel when he comes to school now?

Jimmy used to look so solemn when he came to school. _____

_____

_____

_____

Questions: Why did Jennifer want to go to another country?
Why couldn't she go?
Does she have any plans to change that?

Jennifer always wanted to visit a foreign country. _____

_____

_____

_____

Questions: What was Paulo's "new way to fix spaghetti"?
Did anyone else like it?
Did Paulo like it himself?

Paulo thought of a new way to fix spaghetti. _____

_____

_____

_____

Name _____

Explaining With Examples

Some paragraphs paint word pictures using adjectives, adverbs, similes and metaphors. Other paragraphs explain by naming examples.

Example:

Babysitting is not an easy way to earn money. For example, the little girl you're watching may be very cranky and cry until her parents come home. Or maybe the family didn't leave any snacks and you have to starve all night. Even worse, the child could fall and get hurt. Then you have to decide whether you can take care of her yourself or if you need to call for help. No, babysitting isn't easy.

Directions: Write examples for each topic sentence on another sheet of paper. Number them in order to put them in paragraph form. Make any necessary changes so the sentences fit together in one paragraph. Then write your paragraphs below after the topic sentences.

1. Sometimes dreams can be scary. _____

_____

_____

_____

_____

_____

_____

2. You can learn a lot by living in a foreign country. _____

_____

_____

_____

_____

_____

_____

_____

Creating Word Pictures

Painters create pictures with colors. Writers create pictures with words. Adding adjectives and adverbs, using specific nouns, verbs, similes and metaphors in sentences help create word pictures.

Notice how much more interesting and informative these two rewritten sentences are.

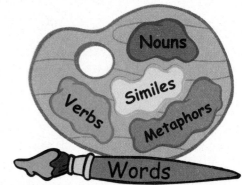

Original Sentence
The animal ate its food.

Rewritten sentences
Like a hungry lion, the starving cocker spaniel wolfed down the entire bowl of food in seconds.

The raccoon delicately washed the berries in the stream before nibbling them slowly, one by one.

Directions: Rewrite each sentence twice, creating two different word pictures.

1. The person built something.

_____

_____

2. The weather was bad.

_____

_____

3. The boy went down the street.

_____

_____

4. The children helped.

_____

_____

Describing People

Often, a writer can show how someone feels by describing how that person looks or what he or she is doing rather than by using emotion words, like angry or happy. This is another way to create word pictures.

Directions: Read the phrases below. Write words to describe how you think that person feels.

1. like a tornado, yelling, raised fists _____

2. slumped, walking slowly, head down _____

3. trembling, breathing quickly, like a cornered animal _____

Directions: Write one or two sentences for each phrase without using emotion words.

4. a runner who has just won a race for his or her school _____

_____

_____

5. a sixth grader on the first day in a new school _____

_____

_____

6. a teenager walking down the street and spotting a house on fire _____

_____

_____

7. a scientist who has just discovered a cure for lung cancer _____

_____

_____

8. a kindergarten child being ignored by his or her best friend _____

_____

_____

Name _____

Describing Events in Order

When we write to explain what happened, we need to describe the events in the same order they occurred. Words and phrases such as **at first, then, after that** and **finally** help us relate the order of events.

Directions: Rewrite the paragraph below, putting the topic sentence first and arranging the events in order.

I got dressed, but I didn't really feel like eating breakfast. By the time I got to school, my head felt hot, so I went to the nurse. This day was terrible from the very beginning. Finally, I ended up where I started—back in my own bed. Then she sent me home again! I just had some toast and left for school. When I first woke up in the morning, my stomach hurt.

_____

_____

_____

_____

_____

_____

Directions: Follow these steps to write a paragraph about what happened the last time you tried to cook something or the last time you tried to fix something that was broken.

1. Write your first draft on another sheet of paper. Start with a topic sentence.
2. Add support sentences to explain what happened. Include phrases to keep things in order: **at first, then, after that, finally, in the middle of it, at last**.
3. Read your paragraph out loud to see if it reads smoothly. Make sure the events are in the correct order.
4. Make any needed changes, then write your paragraph below.

_____

_____

_____

_____

Name _____

Explaining What Happened

Directions: These pictures tell a story, but they're out of order. Follow these steps to write what happened.

1. On another sheet of paper, write a sentence explaining what is happening in each picture.
2. Put your sentences in order and write a topic sentence.
3. Read the whole paragraph to yourself. Add words to show the order in which things happened.
4. Include adjectives and adverbs and maybe even a simile or metaphor to make your story more interesting.
5. Write your paragraph below. Be sure to give it a title.

_____

_____

_____

_____

_____

_____

_____

_____

_____

_____

Name _____

Writing Directions

Directions must be written clearly. They are easiest to follow when they are in numbered steps. Each step should begin with a verb.

How to Peel a Banana:
1. Hold the banana by the stem end.
2. Find a loose edge of peel at the top.
3. Pull the peeling down.
4. Peel the other sections of the banana in the same way.

Directions: Rewrite these directions, number the steps in order and begin with verbs.

How to Feed a Dog
Finally, call the dog to come and eat. Then you carry the filled dish to the place where the dog eats. The can or bag should be opened by you. First, clean the dog's food dish with soap and water. Then get the dog food out of the cupboard. Put the correct amount of food in the dish.

_____

_____

_____

_____

_____

_____

Directions: Follow these steps to write your own directions.

1. On another sheet of paper, draw two symbols, such as a square with a star in one corner or a triangle inside a circle. Don't show your drawing to anyone.
2. On a second sheet of paper, write instructions to make the same drawing. Your directions need to be clear, in order and numbered. Each step needs to begin with a verb.
3. Trade directions (but not pictures) with a partner. See if you can follow each other's directions to make the drawings.
4. Show your partner the drawing you made in step one. Does it look like the one he or she made following your directions? Could you follow your partner's directions? Share what was clear—or not so clear—about each other's instructions.

Writing: Stronger Sentences

Sometimes the noun form of a word is not the best way to express an idea. Compare these two sentences:

They made preparations for the party.
They prepared for the party.

The second sentence, using **prepared** as a verb, is shorter and stronger.

Directions: Write one word to replace a whole phrase. Cross out the words you don't need. The first one has been done for you.

suggested

1. She ~~made a suggestion~~ that we go on Monday.

2. They arranged decorations around the room.

3. Let's make a combination of the two ideas.

4. I have great appreciation for what you did.

5. The buses are acting as transportation for the classes.

6. The group made an exploration of the Arctic Circle.

7. Please make a selection of one quickly.

8. The lake is making a reflection of the trees.

9. The family had a celebration of the holiday.

10. Would you please provide a solution for this problem?

11. Don made an imitation of his cat.

12. Please give a definition of that word.

13. I made an examination of the broken bike.

14. Dexter made an invitation for us to join him.

> Write one word to replace a whole phrase.

Writing: Descriptive Sentences

Descriptive sentences make writing more interesting to the reader. This is done by using adjectives, adverbs, prepositional phrases, similes and metaphors.

Example:
The dog ran down the hill.
The black and white beagle bounded down the steep embankment as though being chased by an invisible dragon.

Directions: Rewrite these sentences so they are more descriptive.

1. Bill likes collecting stamps.

_____

2. Martina drove into town.

_____

3. I enjoy working on the computer.

_____

4. Riverside won the game.

_____

5. Dinner was great.

_____

6. My mom collects antiques.

_____

7. The teacher likes my essay.

_____

8. My brother received a scholarship for college.

_____

Writing: Different Points of View

A **fact** is a statement that can be proved. An **opinion** is what someone thinks or believes.

Directions: Write **F** if the statement is a fact or **O** if it is an opinion.

OPINION

FACT

1. _____ The amusement park near our town just opened last summer.

2. _____ It's the best one in our state.

3. _____ It has a roller coaster that's 300 feet high.

4. _____ You're a chicken if you don't go on it.

Directions: Think about the last movie or TV show you saw. Write one fact and one opinion about it.

Fact: _____

Opinion: _____

In a story, a **point of view** is how one character feels about an event and reacts to it. Different points of view show how characters feel about the same situation.

What if you were at the mall with a friend and saw a CD you really wanted on sale? You didn't bring enough money, so you borrowed five dollars from your friend to buy the CD. Then you lost the money in the store!

Directions: Write a sentence describing what happened from the point of view of each person named below. Explain how each person felt.

Yourself _____

_____

Your friend _____

_____

The store clerk who watched you look for the money _____

_____

The person who found the money _____

_____

Reading Skills: It's Your Opinion

Your opinion is how you feel or think about something. Although other people may have the same opinion, their reasons could not be exactly the same because of their individuality.

When writing an opinion paragraph, it is important to first state your opinion. Then, in at least three sentences, support your opinion. Finally, end your paragraph by restating your opinion in different words.

Example:

   I believe dogs are excellent pets. For thousands of years, dogs have guarded and protected their owners. Dogs are faithful and have been known to save the lives of those they love. Dogs offer unconditional love as well as company for the quiet times in our lives. For these reasons, I feel that dogs make wonderful pets.

Directions: Write an opinion paragraph on whether you would or would not like to have lived in Colonial America. Be sure to support your opinion with at least three reasons.

_____

_____

_____

_____

_____

_____

_____

Writing Checklist

Reread your paragraph carefully.

☐ My paragraph makes sense.   ☐ I have a good opening and ending.

☐ There are no jumps in ideas.   ☐ I used correct spelling.

☐ I used correct punctuation.   ☐ My paragraph is well-organized.

☐ My paragraph is interesting.

Name _____

Persuasive Writing

examples facts reasons

To **persuade** means to convince someone that your opinion is correct. "Because I said so," isn't a very convincing reason. Instead, you need to offer reasons, facts and examples to support your opinion.

Directions: Write two reasons or facts and two examples to persuade someone.

1. Riding a bicycle "no-handed" on a busy street is a bad idea.

Reasons/Facts: _____

_____

Examples: _____

_____

_____

2. Taking medicine prescribed by a doctor for someone else is dangerous.

Reasons/Facts: _____

_____

Examples: _____

_____

_____

3. Learning to read well will help you in every other subject in school.

Reasons/Facts: _____

_____

Examples: _____

_____

_____

Name _____

Describing Characters

When you write a story, your characters must seem like real people. You need to let your reader know not only how they look but how they act, what they look like and how they feel. You could just tell the reader that a character is friendly, scared or angry, but your story will be more interesting if you show these feelings by the characters' actions.

It started like this....

Example:
Character: A frightened child
Adjectives and adverbs: red-haired, freckled, scared, lost, worried
Simile: as frightened as a mouse cornered by a cat
Action: He peeked between his fingers, but his mother was nowhere in sight.

Directions: Write adjectives, adverbs, similes and/or metaphors that tell how each character feels. Then write a sentence that shows how the character feels.

1. an angry woman
   Adjectives and adverbs: _____

   Metaphor or simile: _____

   Sentence: _____

2. a disappointed man
   Adjectives and adverbs: _____

   Metaphor or simile: _____

   Sentence: _____

3. a hungry child
   Adjectives and adverbs: _____

   Metaphor or simile: _____

   Sentence: _____

4. a tired boy
   Adjectives and adverbs: _____

   Metaphor or simile: _____

   Sentence: _____

Name _____

Setting the Scene

Where and when a story takes place is called the **setting**. As with characters, you can tell about a setting—or you can show what the setting is like. Compare these two pairs of sentences:

The sun was shining.
The glaring sun made my eyes burn.

The bus was crowded.
Paige shouldered her way down the aisle, searching for an empty seat on the crowded bus.

If you give your readers a clear picture of your story's setting, they'll feel as if they're standing beside your characters. Include words that describe the sights, sounds, smells, feel and even taste if appropriate.

Directions: Write at least two sentences for each setting, clearly describing it for your readers.

1. an empty kitchen early in the morning _____

_____

_____

2. a locker room after a basketball game _____

_____

_____

3. a dark living room during a scary TV movie _____

_____

_____

4. a classroom on the first day of school _____

_____

_____

5. a quiet place in the woods _____

_____

_____

Name _____

Creating a Plot

When you're writing a story, the **plot** is the problem your characters face and how they solve it. It's helpful to write a plot outline or summary before beginning a story.

In the beginning of a story, introduce the characters, setting and problem.

Example: Scott and Cindy have never met their mother who lives in another state. They decide they would like very much to meet her. They live with their grandmother and father. On the way home from school, they talk about how they can find and contact her.

In the middle, characters try different ways to solve the problem, usually failing at first.

Example: Scott and Cindy hurry home to ask their grandmother if she can help them find their mother. Their grandmother seems nervous and tells Scott and Cindy to discuss the matter with their father when he gets home from work. When Scott and Cindy's father comes home, they tell him about their plan. Their father is very quiet for several minutes. He says he needs some time to think about it and asks if he can let them know tomorrow. Scott and Cindy can hardly sleep that night. Getting through school the next day is tough as well. After school, Scott and Cindy wait by the window for their father's car to pull in the driveway.

In the end, the characters find a way to solve the problem. Not all stories have happy endings. Sometimes, the characters decide they can live with the situation the way it is.

Example: When their father pulls into the driveway, Scott and Cindy rush out to meet him. Their father hands them airplane tickets. Scott and Cindy hug each other. Then they hug their father.

Directions: How do you think this story ends? Write a summary for the ending of this story.

_____

_____

_____

_____

_____

_____

_____

Writing Dialogue

Stories are more interesting when characters talk to each other. Conversations help show the characters' feelings and personalities. Compare these two scenes from a story:

Chad asked Angela to help him with his homework. She said she wouldn't, because she was mad at him for flirting with Nicole.

"Angela, would you be a real friend and help me with this math problem?" Chad asked with a big smile.

"I'm awfully busy, Chad," Angela answered without looking up. "Maybe you should ask Nicole, since you enjoy talking to her so much."

In the second version, we know Angela is angry, even though the writer didn't use that word. You can show how your characters feel by what they say and how they say it.

When you write dialogue, try to make the words sound natural, the way people really talk. Remember to start a new paragraph every time a different person speaks. Put quotation marks around the words the person says. Commas and periods at the ends of sentences go inside the quotation marks.

Directions: Write dialogue for what each character might say to a classmate in this situation. Show how the character feels without using the word for the feeling. Also write the reply from the classmate. Use another sheet of paper for your writing.

The teacher explains a new assignment the class will do in groups. The bell rings and everyone heads for the lunchroom.

1. A discouraged girl who isn't sure she can do the project.

2. A self-confident boy who got an A on the last project.

3. An impatient girl who has an idea and wants to get started.

4. An angry boy who dislikes group projects.

5. A bored girl who doesn't care about the project.

6. A boy who is worried about a different problem in his life.

7. A student who is afraid no one will want him or her for a partner on the project.

Name _____

Writing Dialogue

When it was Megan's turn to present her book report to the class, she dropped all her notecards! Her face turned red, and she wished she was invisible, but all she could do was stand there and say what she could remember without her cards. It was awful!

Directions: Rewrite each paragraph below. Explain the same scenes and feelings using dialogue.

After class, Megan told her friend Sara she had never been so embarrassed in her life. She saw everyone staring at her, and the teacher looked impatient, but there wasn't anything she could do. Sara assured Megan that no one disliked her because of what had happened.

_____

_____

_____

When Megan got home, she told her mother about her book report. By then, she felt like crying. Her mother said not to get discouraged. In a couple of days, she would be able to laugh about dropping the cards.

_____

_____

_____

When Megan's older brother Jed came home, he asked her what was wrong. She briefly told him and said she never was going back to school. He started laughing. Megan got mad because she thought he was laughing at her. Then Jed explained that he had done almost the same thing when he was in sixth grade. He was really embarrassed, too, but not for long.

_____

_____

_____

_____

Name _____

Writing: Paraphrasing

Paraphrasing means to restate something in your own words.

Directions: Write the following sentences in your own words. The first one has been done for you.

1. He sat alone and watched movies throughout the cold, rainy night.

   <u>All through the damp, chilly evening, the boy watched television by himself.</u>

2. Many animals such as elephants, zebras and tigers live in the grasslands.

   _____

   _____

3. In art class, Sarah worked diligently on a clay pitcher, molding and shaping it on the pottery wheel.

   _____

   _____

4. The scientists frantically searched for a cure for the new disease that threatened the entire world population.

   _____

   _____

5. Quietly, the detective crept around the abandoned building, hoping to find the missing man.

   _____

   _____

6. The windmill turned lazily in the afternoon breeze.

   _____

   _____

Name _____

Writing: Paraphrasing

Directions: Using synonyms and different word order, paraphrase the following paragraphs. The first one has been done for you.

Some of the Earth's resources, such as oil and coal, can be used only once. We should always, therefore, be careful how we use them. Some materials that are made from natural resources, including metal, glass and paper, can be reused. This is called recycling.

<u>Many natural resources, including coal and oil, can be used only one time. For this reason, it is necessary to use them wisely. There are other materials made from resources of the Earth that can be recycled, or used again. Materials that can be recycled include metal, glass and paper.</u>

Recycling helps to conserve the limited resources of our land. For example, there are only small amounts of gold and silver ores in the earth. If we can recycle these metals, less of the ores need to be mined. While there is much more aluminum ore in the earth, recycling is still important. It takes less fuel energy to recycle aluminum than it does to make the metal from ore. Therefore, recycling aluminum helps to conserve fuel.

_____

_____

_____

_____

It is impossible to get minerals and fossil fuels from the earth without causing damage to its surface. In the past, people did not think much about making these kinds of changes to the Earth. They did not think about how these actions might affect the future. As a result, much of the land around mines was left useless and ugly. This is not necessary, because such land can be restored to its former beauty.

_____

_____

Writing: Summarizing

A **summary** is a brief retelling of the main ideas of a reading selection. To summarize, write the author's most important points in your own words.

Directions: Write a two-sentence summary for each paragraph.

The boll weevil is a small beetle that is native to Mexico. It feeds inside the seed pods, or bolls, of cotton plants. The boll weevil crossed into Texas in the late 1800s. It has since spread into most of the cotton-growing areas of the United States. The boll weevil causes hundreds of millions of dollars worth of damage to cotton crops each year.

Summary: _____

_____

_____

Each spring, female boll weevils open the buds of young cotton plants with their snouts. They lay eggs inside the buds, and the eggs soon hatch into wormlike grubs. The grubs feed inside the buds, causing the buds to fall from the plant. They eat their way from one bud to another. Several generations of boll weevils may be produced in a single season.

Summary: _____

_____

_____

The coming of the boll weevil to the United States caused tremendous damage to cotton crops. Yet, there were some good results, too. Farmers were forced to plant other crops. In areas where a variety of crops were raised, the land is in better condition than it would have been if only cotton had been grown.

Summary: _____

_____

_____

Name _____

Writing: Outlining

An **outline** is a skeletal description of the main ideas and important details of a reading selection. Making an outline is a good study aid. It is particularly useful when you must write a paper.

Directions: Read the paragraphs, and then complete the outline below.

Weather has a lot to do with where animals live. Cold-blooded animals have body temperatures that change with the temperature of the environment. Cold-blooded animals include snakes, frogs and lizards. They cannot live anywhere the temperatures stay below freezing for long periods of time. The body temperatures of warm-blooded animals do not depend on the environment. Any animal with hair or fur—including dogs, elephants and whales—is warm-blooded. Warm-blooded animals can live anywhere in the world where there is enough food to sustain them.

Some warm-blooded animals live where snow covers the ground all winter. These animals have different ways to survive the cold weather. Certain animals store up food to last throughout the snowy season. For example, the tree squirrel may gather nuts to hide in his home. Other animals hibernate in the winter. The ground squirrel, for example, stays in its burrow all winter long, living off the fat reserves in its body.

Title: _____

Main Topic: I. _____

 Subtopic: A. Cold-blooded animals' temperatures change with environment.

 Detail: 1. _____

 Subtopic: B. _____

 Detail: 1. They can live anywhere there is food.

Main Topic: II. _____

 Subtopic: A. Animals have different ways to survive the cold.

 Details: 1. _____

 2. _____

Name _____

Using the Right Resources

Directions: Decide where you would look to find information on the following topics. After each question, write one or more of the following references:

- **almanac** — contains tables and charts of statistics and information
- **atlas** — collection of maps
- **card/computer catalog** — library resource showing available books by topic, title or author
- **dictionary** — contains alphabetical listing of words with their meanings, pronunciations and origins
- **encyclopedia** — set of books or CD-ROM with general information on many subjects
- *Readers' Guide to Periodical Literature* — an index of articles in magazines and newspapers
- **thesaurus** — contains synonyms and antonyms of words

1. What is the capital of The Netherlands? _____

2. What form of government is practiced there? _____

3. What languages are spoken there? _____

4. What is the meaning of the word **indigenous**? _____

5. Where would you find information on conservation? _____

_____

6. What is a synonym for **catastrophe**? _____

7. Where would you find a review of the play *Cats*? _____

_____

8. Where would you find statistics on the annual rainfall in the Sahara Desert?

_____

9. What is the origin of the word **plentiful**? _____

10. What are antonyms for the word **plentiful**? _____

11. Where would you find statistics for the number of automobiles manufactured in the United States last year? _____

Name _____

Making Inferences: Reference Books

Directions: In the box are four different kinds of reference books. On the line next to each question, write which book you would use to find the information. Some information can be found in more than one reference.

| encyclopedia | almanac | dictionary | thesaurus |

1. A list of words that mean the same as "strong" _____

2. How much rain fell in Iowa in the year 1992 _____

3. What part of speech the word "porch" is _____

4. How many different types of hummingbirds there are _____

5. Weather patterns in Texas for the last 2 years _____

6. A list of words that mean the opposite of "cold" _____

7. Who invented the telescope _____

8. How to pronounce the word "barometer"

_____

9. How many syllables the word "elephant" has

_____

10. What the difference is between African and Asian elephants

_____

11. The population changes in New York between 1935 and 1995

_____

12. How fast a cheetah can run

_____

Name _____

Table of Contents

The **table of contents**, located in the front of books or magazines, tells a lot about what is inside.

A table of contents in books lists the headings and page numbers for each chapter. **Chapters** are the parts into which books are divided. Also listed are chapter numbers and the sections and subsections, if any. Look at the sample table of contents below:

Contents

Chapter 1: Planting a garden 2
        Location 4
        Fences 5
Chapter 2: Seeds 8
        Vegetables
                Potatoes 9
                Beans 10
                Tomatoes 11
        Fruits
                Melons 13
                Pumpkins 14
Chapter 3: Caring for a garden   15
        Weeding 16
        Fertilizing 19

Directions: Using the table of contents above, answer the following questions.

1. How many chapters are in this book?   _____

2. What chapter contains information about things to plant?   _____

3. On what page does information about fences begin?   _____

4. What chapter tells you what you can use to help your garden grow better?   _____

5. What page tells you how to use fertilizer?   _____

6. What page tells you how far apart to plant pumpkin seeds?   _____

7. What is on page 11? _____

8. What is on page 4? _____

Indexes

An **index** is an alphabetical listing ot names, topics and important words and is tound in the back of a book. An index lists every page on which these items appear. For example, in a book about music, dulcimer might be listed this way: Dulcimer 2, 13, 26, 38. Page numbers may also be listed like this: Guitars 18–21. That means that information about guitars begins on page 18 and continues through page 21. **Subject** is the name of the item in an index. **Sub-entry** is a smaller division of the subject. For example, "apples" would be listed under fruit.

Index

N

Neptune 27
NGC 5128 (galaxy) 39
Novas 32

O

Observatories. *See* El Caracol
Orbits of planets 10
Orion rocket 43

P

Planetoids. *See* Asteroids.
Planet rings
  Jupiter 23
  Saturn 9, 25
  Uranus 26
Planets
  discovered by Greeks 7
  outside the solar system 40
  visible with the naked eye 9

See also planet names.
Pleiades 32
Pluto 12, 27
Polaris 35, 36
Pole star. *See* Polaris.
Project Ozma 41

R

Rings. *See* Planet rings.

S

Sagittarius 37
Satellites
  Jupiter 24
  Neptune 27
  Pluto 27
  Saturn 25
  Uranus 26
  See also Galilean satellites
Saturn 25

Directions: Answer the questions about the index from this book about the solar system.

1. On what pages is there information about Pluto? _____

2. On what pages is information about Saturn's first ring found? _____

3. What is on page 41? _____

4. Where is there information about the pole star? _____

5. What is on page 43? _____

6. On what page would you find information about planets that are visible to the eye? _____

7. On what page would you find information about Jupiter's satellites? _____

Name _____

Biographical Research

A **biography** is a written history of a person's life. Often, information for a biography can be obtained from an encyclopedia, especially if a person is famous. Of course, not everyone is listed in a main article in an encyclopedia. Use the encyclopedia's index, which is the last book in the set, to find which volume contains the information you need. Look at this listing taken from an encyclopedia index for Henry Moore, an English artist:

Moore, Henry English sculptor, 1898–1986

    main article Moore 12:106b, illus.
    references in Sculpture 15:290a, illus.

Notice that the listing includes Henry Moore's dates of birth and death and illustrations (illus.). It also includes a short description of his accomplishments: He was an English sculptor. Look below at part of the index from the *Children's Britannica* encyclopedias.

Lincoln, Abraham president of US, 1809–1865
    main article Lincoln 11:49a, illus.
    references in
        Assassination 2:64b
        Caricature, illus. 4:87
        Civil War, American 4:296a fol.
        Confederate States of America 5:113b fol.
        Democracy 6:17a
        Gettysburg, Battle of 8:144a
        Illinois 9:259b
        Thanksgiving Day 17:199a
        United States of America, history of 18:137a fol.
        Westward Movement 19:49a
Lincoln, Benjamin army officer, 1733–1810
    references in American Revolution 1:204b

Lind, Jenny Swedish singer, 1820–87 operatic soprano admired for vocal purity and control; made debut 1838 in Stockholm and sang in Paris and London, becoming known as the "Swedish Nightingale"; toured US with P.T. Barnum 1850; last concert 1883.
    references in Barnum 2:235a
Lindbergh, Anne US author and aviator, b. 1906
    references in Lindbergh 11:53a, illus.
Lindbergh, Charles Augustus US aviator, 1902–1974
    main article Lindbergh 11:53a, illus.
    references in
        Aviation, history of 2:140b, illus.
        Medals and decorations, 11:266b
        Saint Louis, 15:215b
Linde, Karl Von German engineer, 1842–1934
    references in Refrigeration 15:32b

Directions: Answer these questions from the index above.

1. Where is the main article for Abraham Lincoln? _____

2. In addition to the main article, how many other

    places are there references to Abraham Lincoln? _____

3. In which encyclopedia volume is there information about Anne Lindbergh?

_____

CD-ROMs

There are many CD-ROM's which can now assist with biographical research. Often, CD-ROM's not only have written information about an individual's life, but the entry might also include video clips or still-frame pictures. Look for CD-ROM's which are encyclopedias, historical references or famous person indexes.

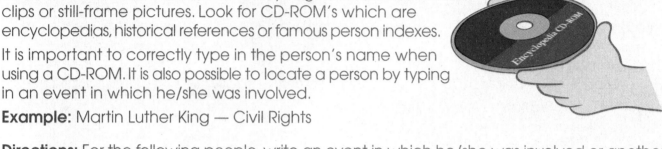

It is important to correctly type in the person's name when using a CD-ROM. It is also possible to locate a person by typing in an event in which he/she was involved.

Example: Martin Luther King — Civil Rights

Directions: For the following people, write an event in which he/she was involved or another category where you might look for additional information.

1. John F. Kennedy _____

2. Rosa Parks _____

3. John Glenn _____

4. Al Gore _____

5. George Burns _____

6. Benjamin Franklin _____

7. Beverly Cleary _____

8. Michael Jordan _____

9. Margaret Thatcher _____

10. Sally Ride _____

11. Thomas Edison _____

12. Marie Curie _____

13. Jonas Salk _____

14. Tiger Woods _____

15. Tara Lipinski _____

16. Alexander Graham Bell _____

Friendly Letters

Directions: Study the format for writing a letter to a friend. Then answer the questions.

your return address	123 Waverly Road Cincinnati, Ohio 45241
date	June 23, 1999
greeting	Dear Josh,
body	How is your summer going? I am enjoying mine so far. I have been swimming twice already this week, and it's only Wednesday! I am glad there is a pool near our house. My parents said that you can stay overnight when your family comes for the 4th of July picnic. Do you want to? We can pitch a tent in the back yard and camp out. It will be a lot of fun! Please write back to let me know if you can stay over on the 4th. I will see you then!
closing **signature**	Your friend, Michael

your return address	Michael Delaney 123 Waverly Road Cincinnati, Ohio 45241
main address	Josh Sommers 2250 West First Ave. Columbus, OH 43212

1. What words are in the greeting? _____

2. What words are in the closing? _____

3. On what street does the writer live? _____

Name _____

Friendly Letters

Directions: Follow the format for writing a letter to a friend. Don't forget to address the envelope!

216

Writing

Name _____

Place Value

Place value is the position of a digit in a number. A digit's place in a number shows its value. Numbers left of the decimal point represent **whole numbers**. Numbers right of the decimal point represent a part, or fraction, of a whole number. These parts are broken down into tenths, hundredths, thousandths, and so on.

Example:

3,443,221.621

millions	hundred thousands	ten thousands	thousands	hundreds	tens	ones	tenths	hundredths	thousandths
3	4	4	3	2	2	1	6	2	1

← —————— **Whole Numbers** —————— → ← —— **Fractions** —— →

Directions: Write the following number words as numbers.

1. Three million, forty-four thousand, six hundred twenty-one _____

2. One million, seventy-seven _____

3. Nine million, six hundred thousand, one hundred two _____

4. Twenty-nine million, one hundred three thousand and nine tenths

   _____

5. One million, one hundred thousand, one hundred seventy-one and

   thirteen hundredths _____

Directions: In each box, write the corresponding number for each place value.

1. 4,822,000.00   ☐   hundreds

2. 55,907,003.00   ☐   thousands

3. 190,641,225.07   ☐   hundred thousands

4. 247,308,211.59   ☐   tenths

5. 7,594,097.33   ☐   millions

6. 201,480,110.01   ☐   hundred thousands

7. 42,367,109,074.25   ☐   hundredths

10.25

Place Value

The chart below shows the place value of each number.

trillions			billions			millions			thousands			ones		
h	t	o	h	t	o	h	t	o	h	t	o	h	t	o
		2	1	4	0	9	0	0	6	8	0	3	5	0

Word form: two trillion, one hundred forty billion, nine hundred million, six hundred eighty thousand, three hundred fifty

Directions: Draw a line to the correct value of each underlined digit. The first one is done for you.

6<u>4</u>3,000 ———————————————————————— 2 hundred million

<u>1</u>3,294,125   9 billion

<u>6</u>78,446 ———————————————————————— 40 thousand

389,<u>2</u>76   2 thousand

1<u>9</u>,000,089,965   2 billion

78,<u>7</u>64   1 hundred thousand

61<u>2</u>,689   9 thousand

<u>2</u>98,154,370   70 thousand

8<u>9</u>,256   10 million

1,<u>3</u>70   30 million

853,6<u>7</u>2,175   7 hundred

<u>2</u>,842,751,360   3 hundred

<u>1</u>63,456   2 hundred

4<u>3</u>8,276,587   6 hundred thousand

8,920,077

Name _____

Expanded Notation

Expanded notation is writing out the value of each digit in a number.

Example:
8,920,077 = 8,000,000 + 900,000 + 20,000 + 70 + 7
Word form: Eight million, nine hundred twenty thousand, seventy-seven

Directions: Write the following numbers using expanded notation.

1. 20,769,033 _____

_____

2. 1,183,541,029 _____

_____

3. 776,003,091 _____

_____

4. 5,920,100,808 _____

_____

5. 14,141,543,760 _____

_____

Directions: Write the following numbers.

1. 700,000 + 900 + 60 + 7 _____

2. 35,000,000 + 600,000 + 400 + 40 + 2 _____

3. 12,000,000 + 700,000 + 60,000 + 4,000 + 10 + 4 _____

4. 80,000,000,000 + 8,000,000,000 + 400,000,000 + 80,000,000 + 10,000 + 400 + 30

_____

5. 4,000,000,000 + 16,000,000 + 30 + 2 _____

Name _____

Addition and Place Value

Directions: Add the problems below in which the digits with the same place value are lined up correctly. Then cross out the problems in which the digits are not lined up correctly.

Find each answer in the diagram and color that section.

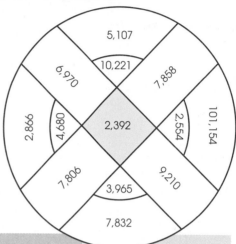

yellow	blue	green	red
638 1,289 + 465 2,392	98 324 + 9,756	4,326 82 + 699	589 95 + 8,526
579 125 + 244	296 2,183 + 75	93,287 36 + 7,831	51 315 + 7,492
83 1,298 + 62	938 3,297 + 445	1,849 964 + 53	198 72 + 68
987 934 + 3,163	46 390 + 9,785	856 642 + 7,462	591 6,352 + 27
57 7,520 + 463	773 3,118 + 74	64 7,430 + 338	919 52 + 6,835

221

Name _____

Addition

Directions: Add the following numbers in your head without writing them out.

1. 17 + 33 = _____

2. 35 + 15 = _____

3. 75 + 25 = _____

4. 41 + 25 = _____

5. 27 + 23 = _____

6. 30 + 20 = _____

7. 12 + 18 = _____

8. 43 + 22 = _____

9. 16 + 34 = _____

10. 9 + 11 + 30 = _____

11. 29 + 21 + 40 = _____

12. 14 + 16 + 20 = _____

13. 37 + 13 + 25 = _____

14. 12 + 22 + 36 = _____

15. 19 + 21 + 57 = _____

16. 21 + 24 + 25 = _____

17. 63 + 14 + 11 = _____

18. 33 + 15 + 42 = _____

19. 25 + 15 + 60 = _____

20. 30 + 20 + 10 = _____

14 + 12 + 7 + 20 + 9 + 18 = ?

Addition Word Problems

Directions: Solve the following addition word problems.

1. 100 students participated in a sports card show in the school gym. Brad brought his entire collection of 2,000 cards to show his friends. He had 700 football cards and 400 basketball cards. If the rest of his cards were baseball cards, how many baseball cards did he bring with him?

   _____

2. Refreshments were set up in one area of the gym. Hot dogs were a dollar, soda was 50 cents, chips were 35 cents and cookies were a quarter. If you purchased two of each item, how much money would you need?

   _____

3. It took each student 30 minutes to set up for the card show and twice as long to put everything away. The show was open for 3 hours. How much time did each student spend on this event?

   _____

4. 450 people attended the card show. 55 were mothers of students, 67 were fathers, 23 were grandparents, 8 were aunts and uncles and the rest were kids. How many kids attended?

   _____

5. Of the 100 students who set up displays, most of them sold or traded some of their cards. Bruce sold 75 cards, traded 15 cards and collected $225. Kevin only sold 15 cards, traded 81 cards and collected $100. Missi traded 200 cards, sold 10 and earned $35. Of those listed, how many cards were sold, how many were traded and how much money was earned?

   sold _____   traded _____   earned $ _____

Name _____

Subtraction

Directions: Subtract the following numbers. When subtracting, begin on the right, especially if you need to regroup and borrow.

$$
\begin{array}{r} 549 \\ -\ 162 \\ \hline \end{array}
\qquad
\begin{array}{r} 823 \\ -\ 417 \\ \hline \end{array}
\qquad
\begin{array}{r} 370 \\ -\ 244 \\ \hline \end{array}
\qquad
\begin{array}{r} 648 \\ -\ 79 \\ \hline \end{array}
$$

$$
\begin{array}{r} 700 \\ -\ 343 \\ \hline \end{array}
\qquad
\begin{array}{r} 475 \\ -\ 299 \\ \hline \end{array}
\qquad
\begin{array}{r} 603 \\ -\ 425 \\ \hline \end{array}
\qquad
\begin{array}{r} 354 \\ -\ 265 \\ \hline \end{array}
$$

$$
\begin{array}{r} 1{,}841 \\ -\ 952 \\ \hline \end{array}
\qquad
\begin{array}{r} 2{,}597 \\ -\ 608 \\ \hline \end{array}
\qquad
\begin{array}{r} 6{,}832 \\ -\ 1{,}774 \\ \hline \end{array}
\qquad
\begin{array}{r} 9{,}005 \\ -\ 3{,}458 \\ \hline \end{array}
$$

$$
\begin{array}{r} 23{,}342 \\ -\ 9{,}093 \\ \hline \end{array}
\qquad
\begin{array}{r} 53{,}790 \\ -\ 40{,}813 \\ \hline \end{array}
\qquad
\begin{array}{r} 29{,}644 \\ -\ 19{,}780 \\ \hline \end{array}
\qquad
\begin{array}{r} 35{,}726 \\ -\ 16{,}959 \\ \hline \end{array}
$$

$$
\begin{array}{r} 109{,}432 \\ -\ 79{,}145 \\ \hline \end{array}
\qquad
\begin{array}{r} 350{,}907 \\ -\ 14{,}185 \\ \hline \end{array}
\qquad
\begin{array}{r} 217{,}523 \\ -\ 44{,}197 \\ \hline \end{array}
\qquad
\begin{array}{r} 537{,}411 \\ -\ 406{,}514 \\ \hline \end{array}
$$

GRADE 6

Name _____

Subtraction Word Problems

Directions: Solve the following subtraction word problems.

1. Last year, 28,945 people lived in Mike's town. This year there are 31,889. How many people have moved in?

   _____

2. Brad earned $227 mowing lawns. He spent $168 on tapes by his favorite rock group. How much money does he have left?

   _____

3. The school year has 180 days. Carrie has gone to 32 school days so far. How many more days does she have left?

   _____

4. Craig wants a skateboard that costs $128. He has saved $47. How much more does he need?

   _____

5. To get to school, Jennifer walks 1,275 steps and Carolyn walks 2,618 steps. How many more steps does Carolyn walk than Jennifer?

   _____

6. Amy has placed 91 of the 389 pieces in a new puzzle she purchased. How many more does she have left to finish?

   _____

7. From New York, it's 2,823 miles to Los Angeles and 1,327 miles to Miami. How much farther away is Los Angeles?

   _____

8. Sheila read that a piece of carrot cake has 236 calories, but a piece of apple pie has 427 calories. How many calories will she save by eating the cake instead of the pie?

   _____

9. Tim's summer camp costs $223, while Sam's costs $149. How much more does Tim's camp cost?

   _____

10. Last year, the nation's budget was $45,000,000,000, but the nation spent $52,569,342,000. How much more than its budget did the nation spend?

    _____

Name _____

Multiplication

Directions: Multiply the following numbers. Be sure to keep the numbers aligned, and place a 0 in the ones place when multiplying by the tens digit.

Example:

Correct	Incorrect
55	55
x 15	x 15
275	275
550	55
825	330

```
1.     12        2.     44        3.     27        4.     92        5.     85
     x  6             x  9             x  7             x  6             x  9
```

```
6.     78        7.     32        8.     19        9.     63        10.    38
     x 24             x 17             x 46             x 12             x 77
```

```
11.   125        12.  641         13.  713         14.  586         15.  294
     x   6             x  25            x   47            x  45            x  79
```

16. 20 x 4 x 7 = _____   17. 9 x 5 x 11 = _____

18. 16 x 2 x 2 = _____   19. 7 x 6 x 3 = _____

20. 33 x 11 x 3 = _____   21. 2 x 8 x 10 = _____

Name _____

Multiplying With Zeros

Directions: Multiply the following numbers. If a number ends with zero, you can eliminate it while calculating the rest of the answer. Then count how many zeros you took off and add them to your answer.

| **Example:** | 550
x 50
27,500 | Take off 2 zeros

Add on 2 zeros | 500
x 5
2,500 | Take off 2 zeros

Add on 2 zeros |

1. 300
    x 6

2. 400
    x 7

3. 620
    x 5

4. 290
    x 7

5. 142
    x 20

6. 505
    x 50

7. 340
    x 70

8. 600
    x 60

9. 550
    x 380

10. 290
     x 150

11. 2,040
     x 360

12. 8,800
     x 200

13. Bruce traveled 600 miles each day of a 10-day trip.
    How far did he go during the entire trip?   _____

14. 30 children each sold 20 items for the school
    fund-raiser. Each child earned $100 for the school.
    How much money did the school collect?   _____

15. 10 x 40 x 2 = _____

16. 30 x 30 x 10 = _____

17. 100 x 60 x 10 = _____

18. 500 x 11 x 2 = _____

19. 9 x 10 x 10 = _____

20. 7,000 x 20 x 10 = _____

Name _____

Division

In a division problem, the **dividend** is the number to be divided, the **divisor** is the number used to divide and the **quotient** is the answer. To check your work, multiply your answer times the divisor and you should get the dividend.

Example: 130 ← **quotient** divisor → 4⟌520 ← **dividend** 4 12 12 00	**Check:** 130 ← **quotient** x 4 ← **divisor** 520 ← **dividend**

Directions: Solve the following division problems.

1. 3⟌546   2. 5⟌720   3. 2⟌458   4. 4⟌796   5. 7⟌896

6. 4⟌128   7. 4⟌376   8. 5⟌225   9. 3⟌684   10. 6⟌924

11. 25⟌475   12. 16⟌768   13. 14⟌840   14. 22⟌418   15. 21⟌693

Directions: Solve these division problems in your head. Challenge yourself for speed and accuracy.

1. 22 ÷ 2 = _____   2. 15 ÷ 3 = _____   3. 72 ÷ 9 = _____

4. 36 ÷ 4 = _____   5. 27 ÷ 9 = _____   6. 56 ÷ 8 = _____

7. 81 ÷ 9 = _____   8. 42 ÷ 6 = _____   9. 63 ÷ 9 = _____

10. 60 ÷ 5 = _____   11. 70 ÷ 10 = _____   12. 98 ÷ 7 = _____

13. 55 ÷ 5 = _____   14. 64 ÷ 8 = _____   15. 84 ÷ 3 = _____

Name _____

Division Word Problems

In the example below, 368 is being divided by 4. 4 won't divide into 3, so move over one position and divide 4 into 36. 4 goes into 36 nine times. Then multiply 4 x 9 to get 36. Subtract 36 from 36. The answer is 0, less than the divisor, so 9 is the right number. Now bring down the 8, divide 4 into it and repeat the process.

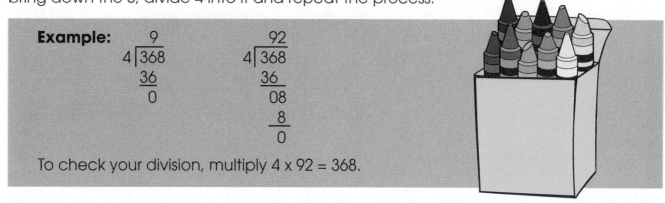

Example:

$$4\overline{)368}$$ with quotient 9, 36, 0

$$4\overline{)368}$$ with quotient 92, 36, 08, 8, 0

To check your division, multiply 4 x 92 = 368.

Directions: Solve the following division problems. (For some problems, you will also need to add or subtract.)

1. Kristy helped the kindergarten teacher put a total of 192 crayons into 8 boxes. How many crayons did they put into each box? _____

2. The scout troop has to finish a 12-mile hike in 3 hours. How many miles an hour will they have to walk? _____

3. At her slumber party, Shelly had 4 friends and 25 pieces of candy. If she kept 5 pieces and divided the rest among her friends, how many pieces did each friend get? _____

4. Kenny's book has 147 pages. He wants to read the same number of pages each day and finish reading the book in 7 days. How many pages should he read each day? _____

5. Brian and 2 friends are going to share 27 marbles. How many will each person get? _____

6. To help the school, 5 parents agreed to sell 485 tickets for a raffle. How many tickets will each person have to sell to do his/her part? _____

7. Tim is going to weed his neighbor's garden for $3 an hour. How many hours does he have to work to make $72? _____

Equations

In an **equation**, the value on the left of the equal sign must equal the value on the right. Remember the order of operations: solve from left to right, multiply or divide numbers before adding or subtracting and do the operation inside parentheses first.

Example:
$$6 + 4 - 2 = 4 \times 2$$
$$10 - 2 = 8$$
$$8 = 8$$

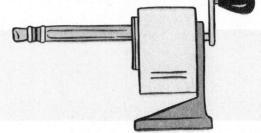

Directions: Write the correct operation signs in the blanks to make accurate equations.

1. (25 _____ 25) _____ 2 = 100 _____ 75

2. (76 _____ 24) _____ 3 = 150 _____ 2

3. 140 _____ 2 _____ 10 = 500 _____ 50 _____ 150

4. 2,100 _____ 2,000 _____ 60 = 80 _____ 2

5. 80 _____ 8 _____ 4 = 160 _____ 160 _____ 160

6. (55 _____ 100) _____ 11 = (1,000 _____ 2) _____ 4

7. 137 _____ 81 _____ 52 = 3 _____ 90

8. 3,000 _____ 10 _____ 10 = (600 _____ 300) _____ 30

9. (720 _____ 20) _____ 4 = 37 _____ 5

10. (457 _____ 43) _____ 500 = (21 _____ 40) x 0

Equations

Directions: Write the correct operation signs in the blanks to make accurate equations.

1. 5 _____ 5 _____ 5 = 3 _____ 5 _____ 0

2. (50 _____ 0) _____ 2 = 25 _____ 2 _____ 2

3. 2 _____ 2 _____ 2 _____ 2 = 2 _____ 2 _____ 4

4. (4 _____ 5) _____ 5 _____ 5 = 2 _____ 3 _____ 5

5. (25 _____ 5) _____ 2 _____ 3 = 3 _____ 6 _____ 2 _____ 5

6. (125 _____ 7) _____ 2 _____ 3 = 100 _____ 2 _____ 4 _____ 70 _____ 10

7. (100 _____ 10) _____ 5 _____ 10 = 10 _____ 5 _____ 100 _____ 10

8. 35 _____ 35 _____ 5 _____ 2 = 5 _____ 3 _____ 2 _____ 5

9. (60 _____ 2) _____ 3 = 3 _____ 3 _____ 3 _____ 0 _____ 15 _____ (5 _____ 15)

10. (120 _____ 4) _____ 7 _____ 3 = (7 _____ 7) _____ (2 _____ 5)

11. (91 _____ 3 _____ 6) _____ 3 = 2 _____ 5 _____ 1 _____ 3 _____ (2 _____ 5)

12. (16 _____ 4) _____ 8 = 5 _____ 5 _____ (3 _____ 3) _____ 6

13. 0 _____ 5 _____ 15 _____ 4 = 3 _____ 3 _____ 3 _____ 8

14. 16 _____ 3 _____ 12 _____ (2 _____ 20) = (2 _____ 2) _____ 6 _____ 10 _____ (2 _____ 7)

15. 21 _____ (3 _____ 3) _____ 3 _____ 1 = 3 _____ 1 _____ 2 _____ 20

Math   231   Total Basic Skills Grade 6

Name _____

Rounding and Estimating

Rounding is expressing a number to the nearest whole number, ten, thousand or other value. **Estimating** is using an approximate number instead of an exact one. When rounding a number, we say a country has 98,000,000 citizens instead of 98,347,425. We can round off numbers to the nearest whole number, the nearest hundred or the nearest million—whatever is appropriate.

Here are the steps: 1) Decide where you want to round off the number. 2) If the digit to the right is less than 5, leave the digit at the rounding place unchanged. 3) If the digit to the right is 5 or more, increase the digit at the rounding place by 1.

Examples: 587 rounded to the nearest hundred is 600.
535 rounded to the nearest hundred is 500.
21,897 rounded to the nearest thousand is 22,000.
21,356 rounded to the nearest thousand is 21,000.

When we estimate numbers, we use rounded, approximate numbers instead of exact ones.

Example: A hamburger that costs $1.49 and a drink that costs $0.79 total about $2.30 ($1.50 plus $0.80).

Directions: Use rounding and estimating to find the answers to these questions. You may have to add, subtract, multiply or divide.

1. Debbi is having a party and wants to fill 11 cups from a 67-ounce bottle of pop. About how many ounces should she pour into each cup? _____

2. Tracy studied 28 minutes every day for 4 days. About how long did she study in all? _____

3. About how much does this lunch cost? $1.19 $0.39 $0.49 _____

4. The numbers below show how long Frank spent studying last week. Estimate how many minutes he studied for the whole week.
Monday: 23 minutes Tuesday: 37 minutes Wednesday: 38 minutes
Thursday: 12 minutes _____

5. One elephant at the zoo weighs 1,417 pounds and another one weighs 1,789 pounds. About how much heavier is the second elephant? _____

6. If Tim studied a total of 122 minutes over 4 days, about how long did he study each day? _____

7. It's 549 miles to Dover and 345 miles to Albany. About how much closer is Albany? _____

Name _____

Rounding

Directions: Round off each number, then estimate the answer. You can use a calculator to find the exact answer.

Round to the nearest ten.	Estimate	Actual Answer
1. $86 \div 9 =$	_____	_____
2. $237 + 488 =$	_____	_____
3. $49 \times 11 =$	_____	_____
4. $309 + 412 =$	_____	_____
5. $625 - 218 =$	_____	_____

Round to the nearest hundred.

6. $790 - 70 =$	_____	_____
7. $690 \div 70 =$	_____	_____
8. $2,177 - 955 =$	_____	_____
9. $4,792 + 3,305 =$	_____	_____
10. $5,210 \times 90 =$	_____	_____

Round to the nearest thousand.

11. $4,078 + 2,093 =$	_____	_____
12. $5,525 - 3,065 =$	_____	_____
13. $6,047 \div 2,991 =$	_____	_____
14. $1,913 \times 4,216 =$	_____	_____
15. $7,227 + 8,449 =$	_____	_____

Name _____

Decimals

A **decimal** is a number that includes a period called a **decimal point**. The digits to the right of the decimal point are a value less than one.

one whole

one tenth

one hundredth

The place value chart below helps explain decimals.

hundreds	tens	ones		tenths	hundredths	thousandths
6	3	2	.	4		
	4	7	.	0	5	
		8	.	0	0	9

A decimal point is read as "and." The first number, 632.4, is read as "six hundred thirty-two and four tenths." The second number, 47.05, is read as "forty-seven and five hundredths." The third number, 8.009, is read as "eight and nine thousandths."

Directions: Write the decimals shown below. Two have been done for you.

1. __**1.4**__   2. _____   3. _____

4. six and five tenths   __**6.5**__

5. twenty-two and nine tenths   _____

6. thirty-six and fourteen hundredths   _____

7. forty-seven hundredths   _____

8. one hundred six and four tenths   _____

9. seven and three hundredths   _____

10. one tenth less than 0.6   _____

11. one hundredth less than 0.34   _____

12. one tenth more than 0.2   _____

Name _____

Adding and Subtracting Decimals

When adding or subtracting decimals, place the decimal points under each other. That way, you add tenths to tenths, for example, not tenths to hundredths. Add or subtract beginning on the right, as usual. Carry or borrow numbers in the same way. Adding 0 to the end of decimals does not change their value, but sometimes makes them easier to add and subtract.

Examples:	39.40	0.064	3.56	6.83
	+ 6.81	+ 0.470	− .09	− 2.14
	46.21	0.534	3.47	4.69

Directions: Solve the following problems.

1. Write each set of numbers in a column and add them.

   a. 2.56 + 0.6 + 76 =   _____

   b. 93.5 + 23.06 + 1.45 =   _____

   c. 3.23 + 91.34 + 0.85 =   _____

2. Write each pair of numbers in a column and subtract them.

   A. 7.89 − 0.56 = _____   B. 34.56 − 6.04 = _____   C. 7.6 − 3.24 = _____

3. In a relay race, Alice ran her part in 23.6 seconds, Cindy did hers in 24.7 seconds and Erin took 20.09 seconds. How many seconds did they take altogether?   _____

4. Although Erin ran her part in 20.09 seconds today, yesterday it took her 21.55 seconds. How much faster was she today?   _____

5. Add this grocery bill:
   potatoes—$3.49; milk—$2.09; bread—$0.99; apples—$2.30   _____

6. A yellow coat cost $47.59, and a blue coat cost $36.79. How much more did the yellow coat cost?   _____

7. A box of Oat Boats cereal has 14.6 ounces. A box of Sugar Circles has 17.85 ounces. How much more cereal is in the Sugar Circles box?   _____

8. The Oat Boats cereal has 4.03 ounces of sugar in it. Sugar Circles cereal has only 3.76 ounces. How much more sugar is in a box of Oats Boats?   _____

Name _____

Mulitplying Decimals by Two-Digit Numbers

To multiply by a 2-digit number, just repeat the same steps. In the example below, first multiply 4 times 9, 4 times 5 and 4 times 3. Then multiply 2 times 9, 2 times 5 and 2 times 3. You may want to place a 0 in the ones place to make sure this answer, 718, is one digit to the left. Now add 1,436 + 7,180 to get the final answer.

Example:	359	359	359	359	359	359
	x 24	x 24	x 24	x 24	x 24	x 24
	6	36	1,436	1,436	1,436	1,436
				80	180	7,180
						8,616

When one or both numbers in a multiplication problem have decimals, check to see how many digits are right of the decimal. Then place the decimal point the same number of places to the left in the answer. Here's how the example above would change if it included decimals:

35.9	3.59
x 0.24	x 24
8.616	86.16

The first example has one digit to the right of the decimal in 35.9 and two more in 0.24, so the decimal point is placed three digits to the left in the answer: 8.616. The second example has two digits to the right of the decimal in 3.59 and none in 24, so the decimal point is placed two digits to the left in the answer: 86.16. (Notice that you do not have to line up the decimals in a multiplication problem.)

Directions: Solve the following problems.

1. Jennie wants to buy 3 T-shirts that cost $15.99 each. How much will they cost altogether? _____

2. Steve is making $3.75 an hour packing groceries. How much will he make in 8 hours? _____

3. Justin made 36 cookies and sold them all at the school carnival for $0.75 each. How much money did he make? _____

4. Last year, the carnival made $467. This year it made 2.3 times as much. How much money did the carnival make this year? _____

5. Troy's car will go 21.8 miles on a gallon of gasoline. His motorcycle will go 1.7 times as far. How far will his motorcycle travel on one gallon of gas? _____

Multiplying Decimals

In some problems, you may need to add zeros in order to place the decimal point correctly.

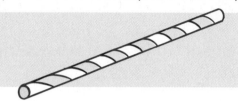

Examples:

$$\begin{array}{r} 0.34 \\ \times\ 0.08 \\ \hline 0.0272 \end{array} \qquad \begin{array}{r} 0.0067 \\ \times\ \ \ \ \ 4 \\ \hline 0.0268 \end{array} \qquad \begin{array}{r} 0.046 \\ \times\ 0.07 \\ \hline 0.00322 \end{array}$$

Directions: Solve the following problems.

1. $\begin{array}{r} 0.15 \\ \times\ 0.02 \\ \hline \end{array}$

2. $\begin{array}{r} 0.67 \\ \times\ 0.08 \\ \hline \end{array}$

3. $\begin{array}{r} 7.3 \\ \times\ 0.06 \\ \hline \end{array}$

4. $\begin{array}{r} 3.59 \\ \times\ 0.08 \\ \hline \end{array}$

5. $\begin{array}{r} 0.061 \\ \times\ 0.014 \\ \hline \end{array}$

6. $\begin{array}{r} 7.10 \\ \times\ 0.042 \\ \hline \end{array}$

7. $\begin{array}{r} 5.05 \\ \times\ 0.08 \\ \hline \end{array}$

8. $\begin{array}{r} 8.75 \\ \times\ 0.067 \\ \hline \end{array}$

9. $\begin{array}{r} 0.0647 \\ \times\ \ \ \ 0.3 \\ \hline \end{array}$

10. $\begin{array}{r} 3.62 \\ \times\ 0.003 \\ \hline \end{array}$

11. $\begin{array}{r} 1.07 \\ \times\ 0.05 \\ \hline \end{array}$

12. $\begin{array}{r} 3.03 \\ \times\ 0.07 \\ \hline \end{array}$

13. $\begin{array}{r} 0.02 \\ \times\ 0.02 \\ \hline \end{array}$

14. $\begin{array}{r} 0.501 \\ \times\ \ 0.03 \\ \hline \end{array}$

15. $\begin{array}{r} 0.321 \\ \times\ \ 0.09 \\ \hline \end{array}$

16. The players and coaches gathered around for refreshments after the soccer game. Of the 30 people there, 0.50 of them had fruit drinks, 0.20 of them had fruit juice and 0.30 of them had soft drinks. How many people had each type of drink?

fruit drink _____

fruit juice _____

soft drink _____

Dividing Decimals by Two-Digit Numbers

Dividing by a 2-digit divisor (34 in the example below) is very similar to dividing by a 1-digit divisor. In this example, 34 will divide into 78 twice. Then multiply 34 x 2 to get 68. Subtract 68 from 78. The answer is 10, which is smaller than the divisor, so 2 was the right number. Now bring down the next 8. 34 goes into 108 three times. Continue dividing as with a 1-digit divisor.

Example:

$$
\begin{array}{r} 2 \\ 34\overline{\smash{)}7{,}888} \\ \underline{68} \\ 10 \end{array}
\qquad
\begin{array}{r} 23 \\ 34\overline{\smash{)}7{,}888} \\ \underline{68} \\ 108 \\ \underline{102} \\ 6 \end{array}
\qquad
\begin{array}{r} 232 \\ 34\overline{\smash{)}7{,}888} \\ \underline{68} \\ 108 \\ \underline{102} \\ 68 \\ \underline{68} \\ 0 \end{array}
$$

To check your division, multiply: 34 x 232 = 7,888.

When the dividend has a decimal, place the decimal point for the answer directly above the decimal point in the dividend.

Examples:

$$
\begin{array}{r} 3.6 \\ 14\overline{\smash{)}50.4} \end{array}
\qquad
\begin{array}{r} 8.92 \\ 34\overline{\smash{)}303.28} \end{array}
$$

Directions: Solve the following problems.

1. $56\overline{\smash{)}7.28}$ 2. $23\overline{\smash{)}18.63}$ 3. $62\overline{\smash{)}255.44}$ 4. $71\overline{\smash{)}82.36}$ 5. $4\overline{\smash{)}8.580}$

6. If socks cost $8.97 for 3 pairs, how much does one pair cost?   _____

7. If candy bars are 6 for $2.58, how much is one candy bar?   _____

8. You buy a bike for $152.25 and agree to make 21 equal payments. How much will each payment be?   _____

9. You and two friends agree to spend several hours loading a truck. The truck driver gives you $36.75 to share. How much will each person get?   _____

10. You buy 14 hamburgers and the bill comes to $32.06. How much did each hamburger cost?   _____

Name _____

Dividing With Zeros

Sometimes you have a remainder in division problems. You can add a decimal point and zeros to the dividend and keep dividing until you have the answer.

Example:

```
        49
25 )1,241
    1 00
      241
      225
       16
```

```
       49.64
25 )1,241.00
    1 00
      241
      225
      160
      150
      100
      100
        0
```

Directions: Solve the following problems.

1. 2)2.5   2. 4)115   3. 12)738   4. 8)586   5. 25)3,415

6. Susie's grandparents sent her a check for $130 to share with her 7 brothers and sisters. How much will each of the 8 children get if the money is divided evenly?   _____

7. A vendor had 396 balloons to sell and 16 workers. How many balloons should each worker sell in order to sell out?   _____

8. Eight of the workers turned in a total of $753. How much did each worker collect if he/she sold the same number of items?   _____

9. A total of 744 tickets were collected from 15 amusement ride operators on the first day of the fair. If each ride required one ticket per person, and they each collected the same number of tickets, how many people rode each ride?   _____

   Do you think that was possible? Why? _____

   _____

10. Five people were hired to clean up the area after the fair closed. They turned in a bill for 26 hours of labor. How many hours did each person work?   _____

Math

239

Total Basic Skills Grade 6

Name _____

Dividing Decimals by Decimals

When a divisor has a decimal, eliminate it before dividing. If there is one digit right of the decimal in the divisor, multiply the divisor and dividend by 10. If there are two digits right of the decimal in the divisor, multiply the divisor and dividend by 100.

Multiply the divisor and dividend by the same number whether or not the dividend has a decimal. The goal is to have a divisor with no decimal.

Examples: $2.3\overline{)89} \times 10 = 23\overline{)890}$ $4.11\overline{)67.7} \times 100 = 411\overline{)6,770}$

$4.9\overline{)35.67} \times 10 = 49\overline{)356.7}$ $0.34\overline{)789} \times 100 = 34\overline{)78,900}$

After removing the decimal from the divisor, work the problem in the usual way.

Directions: Solve the following problems.

1. $3.5\overline{)10.15}$ 2. $6.7\overline{)415.4}$ 3. $0.21\overline{)924}$ 4. $73\overline{)50.37}$

5. The body can burn only 0.00015 of an ounce of alcohol an hour. If an average-sized person has 1 drink, his/her blood alcohol concentration (BAC) is 0.0003. How many hours will it take his/her body to remove that much alcohol from the blood?   _____

6. If the same person has 2 drinks in 1 hour, his/her blood alcohol concentration increases to 0.0006. Burning 0.00015 ounce of alcohol an hour, how many hours will it take that person's body to burn off 2 drinks?   _____

7. If someone has 3 drinks in 1 hour, the blood alcohol concentration rises to 0.0009. At 0.00015 an hour, how many hours will it take to burn off 3 drinks?   _____

8. After a drunk driving conviction, the driver's car insurance can increase by as much as $2,000. Still, this is only 0.57 of the total cost of the conviction. What is the total cost, in round numbers?   _____

9. In Ohio in 1986, about 335 fatal car crashes were alcohol related. That was 0.47 of the total number of fatal car crashes. About how many crashes were there altogether, in round numbers?   _____

Name _____

Decimals and Fractions

A **fraction** is a number that names part of something. The top number in a fraction is called the **numerator**. The bottom number is called the **denominator**. Since a decimal also names part of a whole number, every decimal can also be written as a fraction. For example, 0.1 is read as "one tenth" and can also be written $\frac{1}{10}$. The decimal 0.56 is read as "fifty-six hundredths" and can also be written $\frac{56}{100}$.

Examples:

$$0.7 = \frac{7}{10} \quad 0.34 = \frac{34}{100} \quad 0.761 = \frac{761}{1,000} \quad \frac{5}{10} = 0.5 \quad \frac{58}{100} = 0.58 \quad \frac{729}{1,000} = 0.729$$

Even a fraction that doesn't have 10, 100 or 1,000 as the denominator can be written as a decimal. Sometimes you can multiply both the numerator and denominator by a certain number so the denominator is 10, 100 or 1,000. (You can't just multiply the denominator. That would change the amount of the fraction.)

Examples:

$$\frac{3 \times 2 = 6}{5 \times 2 = 10} = 0.6 \qquad \frac{4 \times 4 = 16}{25 \times 4 = 100} = 0.16$$

Other times, divide the numerator by the denominator.

Examples:

$$\frac{3}{4} = 4\overline{)3.00}^{\,0.75} = 0.75 \qquad \frac{5}{8} = 8\overline{)5.000}^{\,0.625} = 0.625$$

Directions: Follow the instructions below.

1. For each square, write a decimal and a fraction to show the part that is colored. The first one has been done for you.

  a. 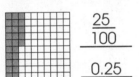 $\frac{25}{100}$ b. 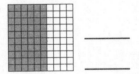   ____   c. 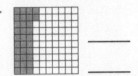   ____

                      0.25   ____   ____

2. Change these decimals to fractions.

  a. 0.6 =   b. 0.54 =   c. 0.751 =   d. 0.73 =   e. 0.592 =   f. 0.2 =

3. Change these fractions to decimals. If necessary, round off the decimals to the nearest hundredth.

  a. $\frac{3}{10} =$ b. $\frac{89}{100} =$ c. $\frac{473}{1,000} =$ d. $\frac{4}{5} =$ e. $\frac{35}{50} =$

  f. $\frac{7}{9} =$ g. $\frac{1}{3} =$ h. $\frac{23}{77} =$ i. $\frac{12}{63} =$ j. $\frac{4}{16} =$

Name _____

Equivalent Fractions and the Lowest Term

Equivalent fractions name the same amount. For example, $\frac{1}{2}$, $\frac{5}{10}$, and $\frac{50}{100}$ are exactly the same amount. They all mean half of something. (And they are all written as the same decimal: 0.5.) To find an equivalent fraction, multiply the numerator and denominator of any fraction by the same number.

Examples: $\dfrac{3 \times 3 = 9 \times 4 = 36}{4 \times 3 = 12 \times 4 = 48}$ Thus, $\dfrac{3}{4}$, $\dfrac{9}{12}$ and $\dfrac{36}{48}$ are all equivalent fractions.

Most of the time, we want fractions in their lowest terms. It's easier to work with $\frac{3}{4}$ than $\frac{36}{48}$. To find a fraction's lowest term, instead of multiplying both parts of a fraction by the same number, divide.

Examples: $\dfrac{36 \div 12 = 3}{48 \div 12 = 4}$ The lowest term for $\dfrac{36}{48}$ is $\dfrac{3}{4}$.

If the numerator and denominator in a fraction can't be divided by any number, the fraction is in its lowest term. The fractions below are in their lowest terms.

Examples: $\dfrac{34}{61}$ $\dfrac{3}{5}$ $\dfrac{7}{9}$ $\dfrac{53}{90}$ $\dfrac{78}{83}$ $\dfrac{3}{8}$

Directions: Follow the instructions below.

1. Write two equivalent fractions for each fraction. Make sure you multiply the numerator and denominator by the same number. The first one is done for you.

a. $\dfrac{1 \times 3 = 3}{2 \times 3 = 6}$ $\dfrac{1 \times 4 = 4}{2 \times 4 = 8}$

b. $\dfrac{2 \times \_\_\_ = \_\_\_}{3 \times \_\_\_ = \_\_\_}$ $\dfrac{2 \times \_\_\_ = \_\_\_}{3 \times \_\_\_ = \_\_\_}$

c. $\dfrac{3 \times \_\_\_ = \_\_\_}{5 \times \_\_\_ = \_\_\_}$ $\dfrac{3 \times \_\_\_ = \_\_\_}{5 \times \_\_\_ = \_\_\_}$

d. $\dfrac{8 \times \_\_\_ = \_\_\_}{9 \times \_\_\_ = \_\_\_}$ $\dfrac{8 \times \_\_\_ = \_\_\_}{9 \times \_\_\_ = \_\_\_}$

2. Find the lowest terms for each fraction. Make sure your answers can't be divided by any other numbers. The first one has been done for you.

a. $\dfrac{2 \div 2 = 1}{36 \div 2 = 18}$

b. $\dfrac{12 \div \_\_\_ = \_\_\_}{25 \div \_\_\_ = \_\_\_}$

c. $\dfrac{12 \div \_\_\_ = \_\_\_}{16 \div \_\_\_ = \_\_\_}$

d. $\dfrac{3 \div \_\_\_ = \_\_\_}{9 \div \_\_\_ = \_\_\_}$

e. $\dfrac{25 \div \_\_\_ = \_\_\_}{45 \div \_\_\_ = \_\_\_}$

f. $\dfrac{11 \div \_\_\_ = \_\_\_}{44 \div \_\_\_ = \_\_\_}$

Name _____

Greatest Common Factor

The **greatest common factor (GCF)** is the largest number that will divide evenly into a set of numbers. In the example, both numbers can be divided evenly by 2 and 4; therefore, 4 is the greatest common factor.

Example: 12 and 20   2, 4 (can be divided evenly into both numbers)
                                  4 (greatest common factor)

Directions: Circle the greatest common factor for each pair of numbers.

1. 56 and 72	6	10	8	2
2. 45 and 81	7	5	9	3
3. 28 and 49	7	11	4	6
4. 10 and 35	3	5	9	7
5. 42 and 30	4	2	5	6
6. 121 and 33	12	9	4	11
7. 96 and 48	48	15	6	3
8. 12 and 132	2	10	12	9
9. 108 and 27	14	9	3	27
10. 44 and 32	4	6	8	10
11. 16 and 88	12	2	8	5
12. 72 and 144	9	11	7	72

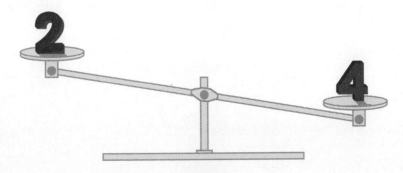

Name _____

Least Common Multiple

The **least common multiple (LCM)** is the lowest possible multiple any pair of numbers have in common.

Examples: 2 and 4
The lowest common multiple is 4, because 4 is a multiple for each number and it is the lowest possible.

6 and 7
Multiples of 6 are 6, 12, 18, 24, 30, 36, 42.
Multiples of 7 are 7, 14, 21, 28, 35, 42.
42 is the lowest multiple that 6 and 7 have in common.

Directions: Find the least common multiple for each pair of numbers.

1. 7 and 8 =

2. 2 and 3 = _____

3. 11 and 4 = _____

4. 5 and 3 = _____

5. 7 and 2 = _____

6. 9 and 4 = _____

7. 2 and 6 = _____

8. 10 and 3 = _____

9. 7 and 5 = _____

10. 9 and 6 = _____

11. 12 and 8 = _____

12. 15 and 3 = _____

Name _____

Comparing Decimals and Fractions

The symbol **>** means greater than. The number on its left is greater than that on its right. The symbol **<** means less than. The number on its left is less than that on its right. An equal sign, **=**, shows the same value on each side.

Directions: Use the sign >, = or < to make each statement true.

1. 0.4 ◯ $\frac{2}{3}$ 2. 1.25 ◯ $\frac{3}{2}$

3. 0.7 ◯ $\frac{4}{5}$ 4. 0.68 ◯ $\frac{5}{7}$

5. 0.1 ◯ $\frac{1}{12}$ 6. 0.45 ◯ $\frac{1}{2}$

7. 0.75 ◯ $\frac{3}{8}$ 8. 0.6 ◯ $\frac{5}{8}$

9. 0.54 ◯ $\frac{2}{5}$ 10. 0.8 ◯ $\frac{4}{6}$

11. 0.25 ◯ $\frac{1}{7}$ 12. 1.8 ◯ $\frac{12}{7}$

13. 0.625 ◯ $\frac{4}{8}$ 14. 0.33 ◯ $\frac{1}{3}$

15. Jenna looked carefully at the labels on two different types of cookies. The chocolate ones had $\frac{3}{4}$ pound in the package. The package of vanilla cookies claimed it had 0.67 pound of cookies inside. Were the chocolate cookies <, > or = to the vanilla cookies? _____

Name _____

Mixed Numbers and Improper Fractions

A **mixed number** is a whole number and a fraction, such as $1\frac{3}{4}$. An **improper fraction** has a numerator that is larger than its denominator, such as $\frac{16}{3}$. To write an improper fraction as a mixed number, divide the numerator by the denominator. The quotient becomes the whole number and the remainder becomes the fraction.

Examples:

$$\frac{16}{3} = 3\overline{)16} = 5\frac{1}{3}$$
$$\quad\;\; 15$$
$$\quad\;\;\; 1$$

$$\frac{28}{5} = 5\overline{)28} = 5\frac{3}{5}$$
$$\quad\;\; 25$$
$$\quad\;\;\; 3$$

To change a mixed number into an improper fraction, multiply the whole number by the denominator and add the numerator.

Examples:

$$4\frac{1}{3} = 4 \times 3 = 12 + 1 = 13 \quad \frac{13}{3}$$

$$8\frac{4}{7} = 8 \times 7 = 56 + 4 = 60 \quad \frac{60}{7}$$

Directions: Follow the instructions below.

1. Change the improper fractions to mixed numbers and reduce to lowest terms. Use another sheet of paper if necessary. The first one has been done for you.

a. $\dfrac{34}{6} = 6\overline{)34} = 5\frac{4}{6} = 5\frac{2}{3}$
   $\quad\quad\;\; 30$
   $\quad\quad\;\;\; 4$

b. $\dfrac{65}{4} =$

c. $\dfrac{23}{8} =$

d. $\dfrac{89}{3} =$

e. $\dfrac{45}{9} =$

f. $\dfrac{32}{5} =$

g. $\dfrac{13}{7} =$

h. $\dfrac{24}{9} =$

i. $\dfrac{31}{2} =$

j. $\dfrac{84}{23} =$

2. Change these mixed numbers into improper fractions. The first one has been done for you.

a. $4\frac{6}{7} = 4 \times 7 = 28 + 6 = \dfrac{34}{7}$

b. $2\frac{1}{9} =$

c. $5\frac{4}{5} =$

d. $12\frac{1}{4} =$

e. $6\frac{7}{8} =$

f. $3\frac{9}{11} =$

g. $8\frac{3}{12} =$

h. $1\frac{6}{14} =$

i. $4\frac{2}{3} =$

j. $9\frac{4}{15} =$

Adding Fractions

When adding fractions, if the denominators are the same, simply add the numerators. When the result is an improper fraction, change it to a mixed number.

Examples: $\frac{3}{5} + \frac{1}{5} = \frac{4}{5}$ $\frac{3}{9} + \frac{7}{9} = \frac{10}{9} = 1\frac{1}{9}$

If the denominators of fractions are different, change them so they are the same. To do this, find equivalent fractions. In the first example below, $\frac{1}{4}$ and $\frac{3}{8}$ have different denominators, so change $\frac{1}{4}$ to the equivalent fraction $\frac{2}{8}$. Then add the numerators. In the second example, $\frac{5}{7}$ and $\frac{2}{3}$ also have different denominators. Find a denominator both 7 and 3 divide into. The lowest number they both divide into is 21. Multiply the numerator and denominator of $\frac{5}{7}$ by 3 to get the equivalent fraction $\frac{15}{21}$. Then multiply the numerator and denominator of $\frac{2}{3}$ by 7 to get the equivalent fraction $\frac{14}{21}$.

Examples:

$$\begin{array}{c} \frac{1 \times 2 = 2}{4 \times 2 = 8} \\ \frac{3}{+8} \end{array} \qquad \begin{array}{c} \frac{2}{8} \\ \frac{3}{+8} \\ \hline \frac{5}{8} \end{array} \qquad \begin{array}{c} \frac{5 \times 3 = 15}{7 \times 3 = 21} \\ \frac{2 \times 7 = 14}{+ 3 \times 7 = 21} \\ \hline \frac{29}{21} = 1\frac{8}{21} \end{array}$$

Directions: Solve the following problems. Find equivalent fractions when necessary.

1. $\frac{3}{5}$ 2. $\frac{7}{8}$ 3. $\frac{1}{9}$ 4. $\frac{2}{6}$ 5. $\frac{2}{15}$
    $\frac{1}{+5}$ $\frac{2}{+16}$ $\frac{2}{+3}$ $\frac{2}{+3}$ $\frac{1}{+5}$

6. Cora is making a cake. She needs $\frac{1}{2}$ cup butter for the cake and $\frac{1}{4}$ cup butter for the frosting. How much butter does she need altogether? _____

7. Henry is painting a wall. Yesterday he painted $\frac{1}{3}$ of it. Today he painted $\frac{1}{4}$ of it. How much has he painted altogether?

8. Nancy ate $\frac{1}{6}$ of a pie. Her father ate $\frac{1}{4}$ of it. How much did they eat altogether? _____

Name _____

Subtracting Fractions

Subtracting fractions is very similar to adding them in that the denominators must be the same. If the denominators are different, use equivalent fractions.

Examples:

$$\begin{array}{r} \frac{3}{4} \\ -\frac{1}{4} \\ \hline \frac{2}{4} = \frac{1}{2} \end{array}$$

$$\begin{array}{r} 2 \times 8 = \frac{16}{40} \\ 5 \times 8 \\ 1 \times 5 = \frac{5}{40} \\ -8 \times 5 \\ \hline \frac{11}{40} \end{array}$$

Adding and subtracting mixed numbers are also similar. Often, though, change the mixed numbers to improper fractions. If the denominators are different, use equivalent fractions.

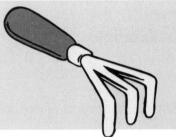

Examples:

$$\begin{array}{r} 2\frac{3}{5} = \frac{13}{5} \\ -1\frac{4}{5} = \frac{9}{5} \\ \hline \frac{4}{5} \end{array}$$

$$\begin{array}{r} 3\frac{3}{14} = \frac{45}{14} \qquad = \frac{45}{14} \\ -2\frac{1}{7} = \frac{15 \times 2}{7 \times 2} = \frac{30}{14} \\ \hline \frac{15}{14} = 1\frac{1}{14} \end{array}$$

Directions: Solve the following problems. Use equivalent fractions and improper fractions where necessary.

1. $\begin{array}{r} \frac{6}{7} \\ \frac{5}{7} \\ - \\ \hline \end{array}$

2. $\begin{array}{r} 1\frac{2}{9} \\ -\frac{4}{9} \\ \hline \end{array}$

3. $\begin{array}{r} 2\frac{3}{6} \\ -\frac{4}{5} \\ \hline \end{array}$

4. $\begin{array}{r} \frac{3}{4} \\ \frac{1}{2} \\ - \\ \hline \end{array}$

5. $\begin{array}{r} 2\frac{1}{3} \\ -\frac{3}{4} \\ \hline \end{array}$

6. Carol promised to weed the flower garden for $1\frac{1}{2}$ hours this morning. So far she has pulled two weeds for $\frac{3}{4}$ of an hour. How much longer does she have to work? _____

7. Dil started out with $1\frac{1}{4}$ gallons of paint. He used $\frac{3}{8}$ gallon of the paint on his boat. How much paint is left? _____

8. A certain movie lasts $2\frac{1}{2}$ hours. Susan has already watched it for $1\frac{2}{3}$ hours. How much longer is the movie? _____

9. Bert didn't finish $\frac{1}{8}$ of the math problems on a test. He made mistakes on $\frac{1}{6}$ of the problems. The rest he answered correctly. What fraction of the problems did he answer correctly? _____

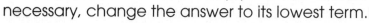

Name _____

Multiplying Fractions

To multiply two fractions, multiply the numerators and then multiply the denominators. If necessary, change the answer to its lowest term.

Examples: $\frac{3}{4} \times \frac{2}{3} = \frac{6}{12} = \frac{1}{2}$ $\frac{1}{8} \times \frac{4}{5} = \frac{4}{40} = \frac{1}{10}$

To multiply a whole number by a fraction, first write the whole number as a fraction (with 1 as the denominator). Then multiply as above. You may need to change an improper fraction to a mixed number.

Examples: $\frac{2}{3} \times \frac{4}{1} = \frac{8}{3} = 2\frac{2}{3}$ $\frac{3}{7} \times \frac{6}{1} = \frac{18}{7} = 2\frac{4}{7}$

Directions: Solve the following problems, writing answers in their lowest terms.

1. $\frac{1}{5} \times \frac{2}{3} =$

2. $\frac{1}{3} \times \frac{4}{7} =$

3. $\frac{2}{8} \times 3 =$

4. $\frac{2}{6} \times \frac{1}{2} =$

5. Tim lost $\frac{1}{8}$ of his marbles. If he had 56 marbles, how many did he lose? _____

6. Jeff is making $\frac{2}{3}$ of a recipe for spaghetti sauce. How much will he need of each ingredient below? _____

   $1\frac{1}{4}$ cups water = _____   2 cups tomato paste = _____

   $\frac{3}{4}$ teaspoon oregano = _____ $4\frac{1}{2}$ teaspoons salt = _____

7. Carrie bought 2 dozen donuts and asked for $\frac{3}{4}$ of them to be chocolate. How many were chocolate? _____

8. Christy let her hair grow 14 inches long and then had $\frac{1}{4}$ of it cut off. How much was cut off? _____

9. Kurt has finished $\frac{7}{8}$ of 40 math problems. How many has he done? _____

10. If Sherryl's cat eats $\frac{2}{3}$ can of cat food every day, how many cans should Sherryl buy for a week? _____

Name _____

Dividing Fractions

Reciprocals are two fractions that, when multiplied together, make 1. To divide a fraction by a fraction, turn one of the fractions upside down and multiply. The upside-down fraction is a reciprocal of its original fraction. If you multiply a fraction by its reciprocal, you always get 1.

Examples of reciprocals: $\frac{2}{3} \times \frac{3}{2} = \frac{6}{6} = 1$ $\frac{9}{11} \times \frac{11}{9} = \frac{99}{99} = 1$

Examples of dividing by fractions: $\frac{1}{2} \div \frac{2}{3} = \frac{1}{2} \times \frac{3}{2} = \frac{3}{4}$ $\frac{2}{5} \div \frac{2}{7} = \frac{2}{5} \times \frac{7}{2} = \frac{14}{10} = \frac{7}{5} = 1\frac{2}{5}$

To divide a whole number by a fraction, first write the whole number as a fraction (with a denominator of 1). (Write a mixed number as an improper fraction.) Then finish the problem as explained above.

Examples: $4 \div \frac{2}{6} = \frac{4}{1} \times \frac{6}{2} = \frac{24}{2} = 12$ $3\frac{1}{2} \div \frac{2}{5} = \frac{7}{2} \times \frac{5}{2} = \frac{35}{4} = 8\frac{3}{4}$

Directions: Solve the following problems, writing answers in their lowest terms. Change any improper fractions to mixed numbers.

1. $\frac{1}{3} \div \frac{2}{5} =$ 2. $\frac{6}{7} \div \frac{1}{3} =$ 3. $3 \div \frac{3}{4} =$ 4. $\frac{1}{4} \div \frac{2}{3} =$

5. Judy has 8 candy bars. She wants to give $\frac{1}{3}$ of a candy bar to everyone in her class. Does she have enough for all 24 students?   _____

6. A big jar of glue holds $3\frac{1}{2}$ cups. How many little containers that hold $\frac{1}{4}$ cup each can you fill?   _____

7. A container holds 27 ounces of ice cream. How many $4\frac{1}{2}$-ounce servings is that?   _____

8. It takes $2\frac{1}{2}$ teaspoons of powdered mix to make 1 cup of hot chocolate. How many cups can you make with 45 teaspoons of mix?   _____

9. Each cup of hot chocolate also takes $\frac{2}{3}$ cup of milk. How many cups of hot chocolate can you make with 12 cups of milk?   _____

Total Basic Skills Grade 6   250   Math

Name _____

Review

Directions: Follow the instructions below.

1. Write each of these decimals as fractions

   a. 0.43 =   b. 0.6 =   c. 0.783 =   d. 0.91 =

2. Write each of these fractions as decimals, rounding them off to the nearest hundredth

   a. $\dfrac{3}{10}$ =   b. $\dfrac{4}{7}$ =   c. $\dfrac{3}{9}$ =   d. $\dfrac{64}{100}$ =

3. Write two equivalent fractions for each of these

   a. $\dfrac{2}{6}$ =   b. $\dfrac{1}{4}$ =   c. $\dfrac{5}{8}$ =

4. Change these fractions into their lowest terms

   a. $\dfrac{4}{16}$ =   b. $\dfrac{6}{18}$ =   c. $\dfrac{5}{90}$ =   d. $\dfrac{9}{24}$ =

5. Change these improper fractions into mixed numbers

   a. $\dfrac{30}{9}$ =   b. $\dfrac{46}{3}$ =   c. $\dfrac{38}{6}$ =   d. $\dfrac{18}{4}$ =

6. Change these mixed numbers into improper fractions

   a. $3\dfrac{1}{6}$ =   b. $7\dfrac{3}{8}$ =   c. $4\dfrac{2}{7}$ =   d. $8\dfrac{1}{9}$ =

7. George has written $1\dfrac{1}{8}$ pages of a report that is supposed to be $3\dfrac{1}{2}$ pages long. How much more does he have to write? _____

8. Jackie ate $\dfrac{3}{8}$ of half a cake. How much of the whole cake did she eat? _____

9. Connie's family is driving to Los Angeles. They drove $\dfrac{1}{6}$ of the way the first day and $\dfrac{1}{5}$ of the way the second day. How much of the trip have they completed so far? _____

10. Kenny gets $6 a week for his allowance. He saved $\dfrac{1}{2}$ of it last week and $\dfrac{1}{3}$ of it this week. How much money did he save in these 2 weeks? _____

11. Of 32 students in one class, $\dfrac{5}{8}$ have a brother or sister. How many students are only children? _____

12. In one class, $\dfrac{1}{5}$ of the students were born in January, $\dfrac{1}{10}$ in February and $\dfrac{1}{10}$ in March. How much of the class was born in these 3 months? _____

Name _____

Review

Directions: Follow the instructions below.

Add.

1. $\frac{4}{16} + \frac{5}{8} =$

2. $\frac{1}{6} + \frac{1}{3} =$

3. $\frac{2}{10} + \frac{4}{5} =$

4. $\frac{3}{5} + \frac{9}{10} =$

Subtract.

1. $\frac{15}{9} - \frac{2}{3} =$

2. $\frac{3}{4} - \frac{3}{8} =$

3. $\frac{4}{7} - \frac{2}{14} =$

4. $\frac{3}{5} - \frac{1}{10} =$

Multiply.

1. $\frac{1}{2} \times \frac{4}{16} =$

2. $\frac{1}{3} \times \frac{4}{9} =$

3. $\frac{5}{12} \times \frac{1}{4} =$

4. $\frac{3}{16} \times \frac{3}{4} =$

Divide.

1. $\frac{3}{5} \div \frac{1}{3} =$

2. $4 \div \frac{1}{2} =$

3. $\frac{1}{4} \div \frac{1}{3} =$

4. $3\frac{3}{4} \div \frac{1}{3} =$

Write >, < or = to make the statements true.

1. 0.5 ◯ $\frac{5}{8}$

2. 0.8 ◯ $\frac{4}{5}$

3. 0.35 ◯ $\frac{2}{5}$

4. 1.3 ◯ $\frac{7}{8}$

Name _____

Trial and Error

Often, the quickest way to solve a problem is to make a logical guess and test it to see if it works. The first guess, or trial, will probably not be the correct answer—but it should help figure out a better, more reasonable guess.

Directions: Use trial and error to find the solutions to these problems.

1. Mr. McFerrson is between 30 and 50 years old. The sum of the digits in his age is 11. His age is an even number. How old is Mr. McFerrson?

   _____

   _____

2. The key for number 5 does not work on Rusty's calculator. How can he use his broken calculator to subtract 108 from 351?

   _____

   _____

3. Tasha likes to swim a certain number of miles each day for 3 days straight. Then, she increases her mileage by 1 for the next 3 days, and so on. Over a nine day period, Tasha swims a total of 27 miles. She swims equal mileage Monday, Tuesday and Wednesday. She swims another amount on Thursday, Friday and Saturday. She swims yet a third amount on Sunday, Monday and Tuesday. How many miles does Tasha swim each day?

   _____ Monday   _____ Tuesday   _____ Wednesday

   _____ Thursday   _____ Friday   _____ Saturday

   _____ Sunday   _____ Monday   _____ Tuesday

Trial and Error

Directions: Use trial and error to complete each diagram so all the equations work.

Example:

$$\underline{\quad 6 \quad},\ \underline{\quad 7 \quad}\ \begin{array}{c} + \rightarrow \underline{\quad 13 \quad} \\ \times \rightarrow \underline{\quad 42 \quad} \end{array}$$

$$\underline{\qquad},\ \underline{\quad 4 \quad}\ \begin{array}{c} + \rightarrow \underline{\qquad} \\ \times \rightarrow \underline{\quad 28 \quad} \end{array} \qquad \underline{\quad 4 \quad},\ \underline{\qquad}\ \begin{array}{c} + \rightarrow \underline{\quad 12 \quad} \\ \times \rightarrow \underline{\qquad} \end{array}$$

$$\underline{\qquad},\ \underline{\qquad}\ \begin{array}{c} + \rightarrow \underline{\quad 8 \quad} \\ \times \rightarrow \underline{\quad 16 \quad} \end{array} \qquad \underline{\quad 7 \quad},\ \underline{\qquad}\ \begin{array}{c} + \rightarrow \underline{\quad 7 \quad} \\ \times \rightarrow \underline{\qquad} \end{array}$$

$$\underline{\qquad},\ \underline{\qquad}\ \begin{array}{c} + \rightarrow \underline{\quad 15 \quad} \\ \times \rightarrow \underline{\quad 56 \quad} \end{array} \qquad \underline{\qquad},\ \underline{\quad 9 \quad}\ \begin{array}{c} + \rightarrow \underline{\quad 17 \quad} \\ \times \rightarrow \underline{\qquad} \end{array}$$

$$\underline{\qquad},\ \underline{\quad 9 \quad}\ \begin{array}{c} + \rightarrow \underline{\qquad} \\ \times \rightarrow \underline{\quad 54 \quad} \end{array} \qquad \underline{\qquad},\ \underline{\quad 16 \quad}\ \begin{array}{c} + \rightarrow \underline{\quad 31 \quad} \\ \times \rightarrow \underline{\qquad} \end{array}$$

$$\underline{\qquad},\ \underline{\qquad}\ \begin{array}{c} + \rightarrow \underline{\quad 11 \quad} \\ \times \rightarrow \underline{\quad 10 \quad} \end{array} \qquad \underline{\qquad},\ \underline{\qquad}\ \begin{array}{c} + \rightarrow \underline{\quad 101 \quad} \\ \times \rightarrow \underline{\quad 100 \quad} \end{array}$$

Choosing a Method

This table explains different methods of computation that can be used to solve a problem.

Method		
Mental Math	– Calculating in your head.	– Use with small numbers, memorized facts and multiples of tens, hundreds, thousands, and so on.
Objects/Diagram	– Drawing or using an object to represent the problem.	– Use to model the situation.
Pencil and Paper	– Calculating the answer on paper.	– Use when a calculator is not available and the problem is too difficult to solve mentally.
Calculator	– Using a calculator or computer to find the solution.	– Use with large numbers or for a quick answer.
Trial and Error	– Making a guess at the answer and trying to see if it works.	– Use when unsure what to do or if none of the methods above work.

Directions: Circle the method of computation that seems best for solving each problem. Then solve the problem.

1. The School Days Fun Fair has 38 booths and 23 games. How many booths and games total are in the fair?

   • Paper and Pencil   Answer: _____

   • Objects/Diagram

2. The lemonade stand was stocked with 230 cups. On the first day, 147 drinks were sold. How many cups were left?

   • Objects/Diagram   Answer: _____

   • Paper and Pencil

3. There are 3 cars in the tram to transport people from the parking lot to the fair. Each car can seat 9 people. How many people can ride the tram at one time?

   • Objects/Diagram   Answer: _____

   • Trial and Error

Choosing a Method

Directions: Write what method you will use for each problem. Then find the answer.

1. Jenna receives an allowance of $3.50 a week. This week, her mother pays her in nickels, dimes and quarters. She received more dimes than quarters. How many of each coin did her mom use to pay her?

   Method: _____

   Answer: _____

2. You are buying your lunch at school. There are 4 people in front of you and 7 people behind you. How many people are standing in line? (Hint: it's not 11 people.)

   Method: _____

   Answer: _____

3. A runner can run 1 mile in 12 minutes. He ran for 30 minutes today. How far did he run?

   Method: _____

   Answer: _____

4. A family of four goes out to dinner. They decide to order a 16-cut pizza. Each person likes something different on his/her pizza, but each will eat equal amounts. Maria likes pepperoni and sausage, Tony likes ham and pineapple, Mom likes cheese only and Dad likes mushrooms. Maria is allergic to mushrooms, so her slices can't be next to Dad's. Mom detests pineapple, so her slices can't be next to Tony's. How will the restaurant arrange their pizza?

   Method: _____

   Answer: _____

5. The Petting Zoo has 72 animals in aquariums, 32 animals in cages and 57 animals fenced in. How many animals does the Petting Zoo have?

   Method: _____

   Answer: _____

Multi-Step Problems

Some problems take more than one step to solve. First, plan each step needed to find the solution. Then solve each part to find the answer.

Example: Tickets for a bargain matinee cost $4 for adults and $3 for children. How much would tickets cost for a family of 2 adults and 3 children?

Step 1: Find the cost of the adults' tickets.

Step 2: Find the cost of the children's tickets.

Step 3: Add to find the sum of the tickets.

2 adults	x	$4 each ticket	=	$8 total
3 children	x	$3 each ticket	=	$9 total
$8 adults	+	$9 children	=	$17 total

The tickets cost $17 total.

Directions: Write the operations you will use to solve each problem. Then find the answer.

1. Arden and her father are riding their bikes 57 miles to Arden's grandma's house. They ride 13 miles, then take a water break. Then they ride 15 miles to a rest area for a picnic lunch. How many miles do Arden and her father have left to ride after lunch?

   Operations: _____

   Answer: _____

2. A triathlete bikes 15 miles at 20 miles per hour, runs 5 miles at 6 miles per hour and swims 1 mile at 4 miles per hour. How long does the triathlon take her to complete?

   Operations: _____

   Answer: _____

3. Ray bought strawberries for $1.99, blueberries for $1.40 and 2 pints of raspberries for $1.25 per pint. How much did Ray spend on berries?

   Operations: _____

   Answer: _____

Name _____

Hidden Questions

When solving a story problem, you may find that some information you want is not stated in the problem. You must ask yourself what information you need and decide how you can use the data in the problem to find this information. The problem contains a hidden question to find before you can solve it.

Example: Chris and his mother are building a birdhouse. He buys 4 pieces of wood for $2.20 each. How much change should he get back from $10?

Step 1: Find the hidden question:
What is the total cost of the wood? $2.20 x 4 = $8.80

Step 2: Use your answer to the hidden
question to solve the problem. $10.00 – $8.80 = $1.20

Directions: Write the hidden questions. Then solve the problems.

1. Chris used 3 nails to attach each board to the frame. After nailing 6 boards, he had 1 nail left. How many nails did Chris have before he started?

   Hidden Question: _____

   Answer: _____

2. Chris sawed a 72-inch post into 3 pieces. Two of the pieces were each 20 inches long. How long was the third piece?

   Hidden Question: _____

   Answer: _____

3. It took Chris and his mom 15 hours to make a birdhouse. They thought it would take 3 days. How many hours early did they complete the job?

   Hidden Question: _____

   Answer: _____

4. It takes Chris 15 hours to make a birdhouse and 9 hours to make a birdfeeder. He worked for 42 hours and made 1 birdhouse and some birdfeeders. How many birdfeeders did Chris make?

   Hidden Question: _____

   Answer: _____

Logic Problems

Directions: Use the clues below to figure out this logic problem.

Three friends all enjoy sports. Each of their favorite sports involves a ball. Two of these sports are played on courts, and one is played on a field.

- Rachel likes to run, and doesn't have to be a good catcher.

- Melinda is a good jumper.

- Betsy is also a good jumper, but she is a good ball handler.

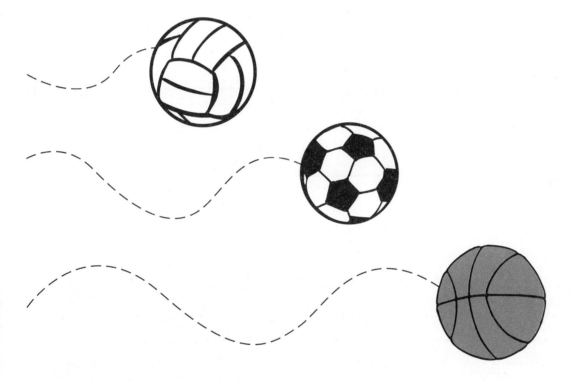

Which sport does each girl play?

Melinda _____

Betsy _____

Rachel _____

A Cool Logic Problem

A family with five children went to the ice-cream shop. The children all ordered different flavors.

Directions: Use the clues and the chart to help you write which child ate which flavor of ice cream. Write a dot in the chart for the correct answer. Cross out all the other boxes in that row and column.

- No person had ice cream with the same first initial as his/her name.

- Neither of the twins, Corey and Cody, like peanut butter. Corey thinks vanilla is boring.

- The children are the twins, Vicki, the brother who got chocolate and the sister who ate peanut butter.

	Rocky Road	Chocolate Chip	Vanilla	Chocolate	Peanut Butter
Corey					
Cody					
Randa					
Vicki					
Paul					

Who ate which flavor?

Corey _____

Cody _____

Randa _____

Vicki _____

Paul _____

Name _____

Perimeter

The **perimeter** is the distance around a shape formed by straight lines, such as a square or triangle. To find the perimeter of a shape, add the lengths of its sides.

Examples:

8 in.

8 in.

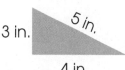

5 in.

4 in.

3 in. 5 in.

4 in.

For the square, add $8 + 8 + 8 + 8 = 32$. Or, write a formula using **P** for **perimeter** and **s** for the **sides**: $P = 4 \times s$
$P = 4 \times 8$
$P = 32$ inches

For the rectangle, add $4 + 5 + 4 + 5 = 18$. Or, use a different formula, using **l** for **length** and **w** for **width**. In formulas with parentheses, first do the adding, multiplying, and so on, in the parentheses:

$P = (2 \times l) + (2 \times w)$
$P = (2 \times 5) + (2 \times 4)$
$P = 10 + 8$
$P = 18$

For the triangle, the sides are all different lengths, so the formula doesn't help. Instead, add the sides: $3 + 4 + 5 = 12$ inches.

Directions: Find the perimeter of each shape below. Use the formula whenever possible.

10 ft.

8 ft.

6 ft.

3 ft.

11 ft.

4 ft.

1. Find the perimeter of the room pictured at left.   P = _____

2. Brandy plans to frame a picture with a sheet of construction paper. Her picture is 8 in. wide and 13 in. long. She wants the frame to extend 1 in. beyond the picture on all sides. How wide and long should the frame be? What is the perimeter of her picture and of the frame?

Length and width of frame: _____

Perimeter of picture: _____

Perimeter of frame: _____

3. A square has a perimeter of 120 feet. How long is each side?   _____

4. A triangle with equal sides has a perimeter of 96 inches.
   How long is each side?   _____

5. A rectangle has two sides that are each 14 feet long and a
   perimeter of 50 feet. How wide is it?   _____

Name _____

Perimeter

Directions: Find the perimeter of each shape below.

1.

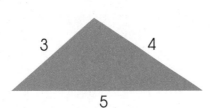

3
4
5

P = _____

2.

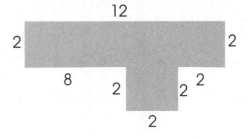

12
2
2
8
2
2
2
2

P = _____

3.

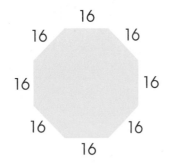

16
16
16
16
16
16
16
16

P = _____

4.

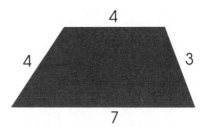

4
4
3
7

P = _____

5.

4
4
4
4

P = _____

6.

3
4
4
3

P = _____

7.

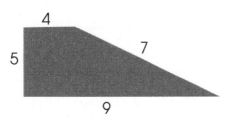

4
5
7
9

P = _____

8.

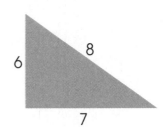

8
6
7

P = _____

Area: Squares and Rectangles

The **area** is the number of square units that covers a certain space. To find the area, multiply the length by the width. The answer is in square units, shown by adding a superscript 2 (^{2}) to the number.

Examples:

 3 in.

 5 in.

8 in.

For the rectangle, use this formula: **A = l x w**
A = 8 x 5
A = 40 in.^{2}

For the square formula, **s** stands for side: **A = s x s** (or s^2)
A = 3 x 3 (or 3^2)
A = 9 in.^{2}

Directions: Find the area of each shape below.

7 ft.

12 ft.

1. Find the area of a room which is 12 feet long and 7 feet wide. A = _____

2. A farmer's field is 32 feet on each side. How many square feet does he have to plow? _____

3. Steve's bedroom is 10 feet by 12 feet. How many square feet of carpeting would cover the floor? _____

4. Two of Steve's walls are 7.5 feet high and 12 feet long. The other two are the same height and 10 feet long. How many square feet of wallpaper would cover all four walls?
   Square feet for 12-foot wall = _____ x 2 = _____
   Square feet for 10-foot wall = _____ x 2 = _____

5. A clothes shop moved from a store that was 35 by 22 feet to a new location that was 53 by 32 feet. How many more square feet does the store have now?

   Square feet for first location = _____

   Square feet for new location = _____ Difference = _____

6. A school wanted to purchase a climber for the playground. The one they selected would need 98 square feet of space. The only space available on the playground was 12 feet long and 8 feet wide. Will there be enough space for the climber? _____

Name _____

Area: Triangles

Finding the area of a triangle requires knowing the size of the base and the height. For the triangle formula, use **b** for **base** and **h** for **height**. Multiply ½ times the size of the base and then multiply by the height. The answer will be in square units.

Example:

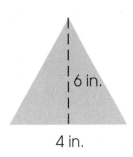

6 in.

4 in.

$$A = \frac{1}{2} \times b \times h$$

$$A = \frac{1}{2} \times 4 \times 6$$

$$A = 12 \text{ in.}^2$$

Directions: Apply the formula to find the area of each triangle below.

1.

3 in.   5 in.

4 in.

A = _____

2.

7 in.

5 in.

A = _____

3.

h = 6 in.

3 in.

A = _____

4.

2 in.

1 in.

A = _____

5. Diane wanted to make a sail for her new boat. The base of the triangular sail would be 7 feet and the height would be 6 feet. Find the area.

A = _____

Area Challenge

When finding the area of an unusual shape, first try to divide it into squares, rectangles or triangles. Find the area of each of those parts, then add your answers together to find the total area of the object.

Directions: Find the area of each shape below.

1.

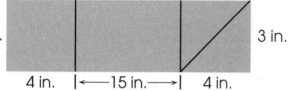

3 in.   4 in. |←——15 in.——→| 4 in.   3 in.

Total area = _____

2.

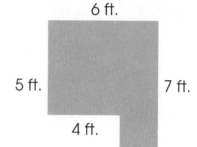

6 ft.

5 ft.   7 ft.

4 ft.

Total area = _____

3.

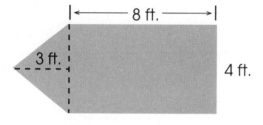

|←——— 8 ft. ———→|

3 ft.   4 ft.

Total area = _____

4.

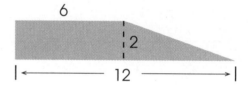

6

2

|←——— 12 ———→|

Total area = _____

5.

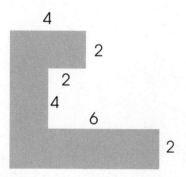

4

2

2

4

6

2

Total area = _____ units²

6.

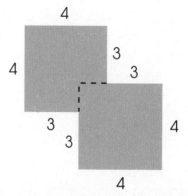

4

3

4   3

3

3   4

3

4

Total area = _____ units²

Name _____

Volume

Volume is the number of cubic units that fills a space. A **cubic unit** has 6 equal sides, like a child's block. To find the volume (**V**) of something, multiply the length (**l**) by the width (**w**) by the height (**h**), or **V = l x w x h**. The answer will be in cubic units (^{3}). Sometimes it's easier to understand volume if you imagine a figure is made of small cubes.

Example: **V = l x w x h**
V = 4 x 6 x 5
V = 120 in.^{3}

Directions: Solve the following problems.

1. What is the volume of a cube that is 7 inches on each side? _____

2. How many cubic inches of cereal are in a box that is 10 inches long, 6 inches wide and 4.5 inches high? _____

3. Jeremy made a tower of five blocks that are each 2.5 inches square. How many cubic inches are in his tower? _____

4. How many cubic feet of gravel are in the back of a full dump truck that measures 7 feet wide by 4 feet tall by 16 feet long? _____

5. Will 1,000 cubic inches of dirt fill a flower box that is 32 inches long, 7 inches wide and 7 inches tall? _____

6. A mouse needs 100 cubic inches of air to live for an hour. Will your pet mouse be okay for an hour in an airtight box that's 4.5 inches wide by 8.25 inches long by 2.5 inches high? _____

7. Find the volume of the figures below. 1 cube = 1 inch^3

A.
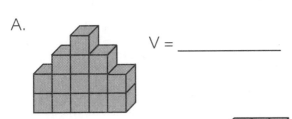
V = _____

C.
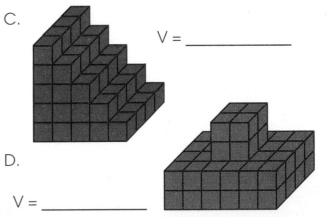
V = _____

B.
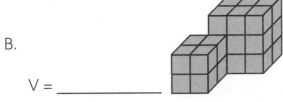
V = _____

D.
V = _____

266

Math

Name _____

Geometric Patterns

Geometric patterns can be described in several ways. **Similar shapes** have the same shape but in differing sizes. **Congruent shapes** have the same geometric pattern but may be facing in different directions. **Symmetrical shapes** are identical when divided in half.

Directions: Use the terms **similar**, **congruent** or **symmetrical** to describe the following patterns.

1.

_____

2.

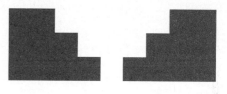

_____

3.

_____

4.

_____

5.

_____

6.

_____

7.

_____

Name _____

Angles

Angles are named according to the number of degrees between the lines. The degrees are measured with a protractor.

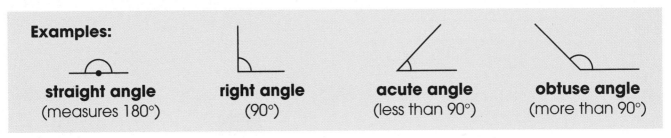

Examples:

straight angle
(measures 180°)

right angle
(90°)

acute angle
(less than 90°)

obtuse angle
(more than 90°)

Directions: Study the examples. Then follow the instructions below.

1. Use a protractor to measure each angle below. Then write whether it is straight, right, acute or obtuse.

A.

Degrees: _____

Kind of angle: _____

C.

Degrees: _____

Kind of angle: _____

B.

_____

Degrees: _____

Kind of angle: _____

D.

Degrees: _____

Kind of angle: _____

2. The angles in this figure are named by letters. Write the number of degrees in each angle and whether it is straight, right, acute or obtuse.

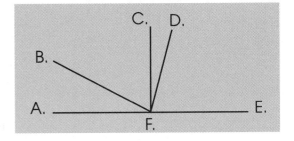

a. Angle AFB   Degrees: _____   Kind of angle: _____

b. Angle AFC   Degrees: _____   Kind of angle: _____

c. Angle AFD   Degrees: _____   Kind of angle: _____

d. Angle AFE   Degrees: _____   Kind of angle: _____

e. Angle BFD   Degrees: _____   Kind of angle: _____

Name _____

Types of Triangles

The sum of angles in all triangles is 180°. However, triangles come in different shapes. They are categorized by the length of their sides and by their types of angles.

Equilateral:

Three equal sides

Acute:

Three acute angles

Isosceles:

Two equal sides

Right:

One right angle

Scalene:

Zero equal sides

Obtuse:

One obtuse angle

One triangle can be a combination of types, such as isosceles and obtuse.

Directions: Study the examples. Then complete the exercises below.

1. Read these directions and color in the correct triangles.

   Color the right scalene triangle blue.
   Color the obtuse scalene triangle red.
   Color the equilateral triangle yellow.
   Color the right isosceles triangle green.
   Color the acute isosceles triangle black.

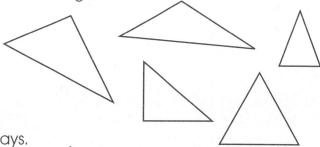

2. Describe each of these triangles in two ways.

   A.

   B.

   _____ _____   _____ _____

3. In the space below, draw the following triangles.

scalene triangle

equilateral triangle

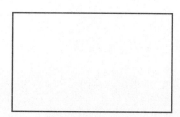
obtuse triangle

Name _____

Finding Angles

All triangles have three angles. The sum of these angles is 180°. Therefore, if we know the number of degrees in two of the angles, we can add them together, then subtract from 180 to find the size of the third angle.

Directions: Follow the instructions below.

1. Circle the number that shows the third angle of triangles A through F. Then describe each triangle two ways. The first one has been done for you.

   A. 60°, 60°   45° 50° (60°)   __equilateral, acute__

   B. 35°, 55°   27° 90° 132°   _____

   C. 30°, 120°   30° 74° 112°   _____

   D. 15°, 78°   65° 87° 98°   _____

   E. 28°, 93°   61° 59° 70°   _____

   F. 12°, 114°   60° 50° 54°   _____

2. Find the number of degrees in the third angle of each triangle below.

A.

40°   40°

_____

B.

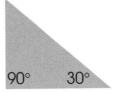

90°   30°

_____

C.

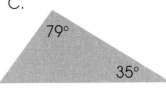

79°

35°

_____

D.

58°   62°

_____

E.

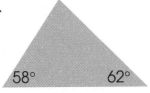

20°   90°

_____

F.

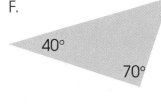

40°

70°

_____

Name _____

Types of Quadrilaterals

A **quadrilateral** is a shape with four sides and four angles. The sum of angles in all quadrilaterals is 360°. Like triangles, quadrilaterals come in different shapes and are categorized by their sides and their angles.

A **square** has four parallel sides of equal length and four 90° angles.

A **rectangle** has four parallel sides, but only its opposite sides are equal length; it has four 90° angles.

A **parallelogram** has four parallel sides, with the opposite sides of equal length.

A **trapezoid** has two opposite sides that are parallel; its sides may or may not be equal length; its angles may include none, one or two that are 90°.

Directions: Study the examples. Then complete the exercises below.

1. Color in the correct quadrilaterals.

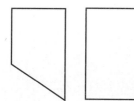  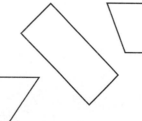 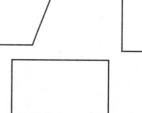

Color two squares blue.   Color two rectangles red.
Color two parallelograms yellow.   Color two trapezoids green.

2. Circle the number that shows the missing angle for each quadrilateral.
   Then name the possible quadrilaterals that could have those angles.

A. 90°, 90°, 90°	45°	90°	180°	_____
B. 65°, 115°, 65°	65°	90°	115°	_____
C. 90°, 110°, 90°	45°	70°	125°	_____
D. 100°, 80°, 80°	40°	80°	100°	_____
E. 90°, 120°, 50°	50°	75°	100°	_____

Name _____

Length in Customary Units

The **customary system** of measurement is the most widely used in the United States. It measures length in inches, feet, yards and miles.

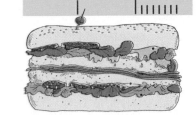

1 ft.   2 ft.   7 in.

Examples:

12 inches (in.) = 1 foot (ft.)
3 ft. (36 in.) = 1 yard (yd.)
5,280 ft. (1,760 yds.) = 1 mile (mi.)

To change to a larger unit, divide. To change to a smaller unit, multiply.

Examples:

To change inches to feet, divide by 12.	24 in. = 2 ft.	27 in. = 2 ft. 3 in.
To change feet to inches, multiply by 12.	3 ft. = 36 in.	4 ft = 48 in.
To change inches to yards, divide by 36.	108 in. = 3 yd.	80 in. = 2 yd. 8 in.
To change feet to yards, divide by 3.	12 ft. = 4 yd.	11 ft. = 3 yd. 2 ft.

Sometimes in subtraction you have to borrow units.

Examples:

```
 3 ft.  4 in.  =  2 ft. 16 in.          3 yd.       =  2 yd.  3 ft.
– 1 ft. 11 in.   – 1 ft. 11 in.       – 1 yd. 2 ft.   – 1 yd.  2 ft.
                   1 ft.  5 in.                          1 yd.  1 ft.
```

Directions: Solve the following problems.

1. 108 in. = ____ ft.

2. 68 in. = ____ ft. ____ in.

3. 8 ft. = ____ yd. ____ ft.

4. 3,520 yd. = ____ mi.

5. What form of measurement (inches, feet, yards or miles) would you use for each item below?

   a. pencil _____

   b. vacation trip _____

   c. playground _____

   d. wall _____

6. One side of a square box is 2 ft. 4 in. What is the perimeter of the box? _____

7. Jason is 59 in. tall. Kent is 5 ft. 1 in. tall. Who is taller and by how much? _____

8. Karen bought a doll 2 ft. 8 in. tall for her little sister. She found a box that is 29 in. long. Will the doll fit in that box? _____

9. Dan's dog likes to go out in the backyard, which is 85 ft. wide. The dog's chain is 17 ft. 6 in. long. If Dan attaches one end of the chain to a pole in the middle of the yard, will his dog be able to leave the yard? _____

Name _____

Length in Metric Units

The **metric system** measures length in meters, centimeters, millimeters, and kilometers.

Examples:
A **meter (m)** is about 40 inches or 3.3 feet.
A **centimeter (cm)** is $\frac{1}{100}$ of a meter or 0.4 inches.
A **millimeter (mm)** is $\frac{1}{1000}$ of a meter or 0.04 inches.
A **kilometer (km)** is 1,000 meters or 0.6 miles.

As before, divide to find a larger unit and multiply to find a smaller unit.

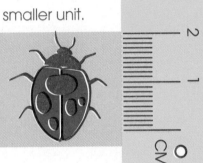

Examples:
To change cm to mm, multiply by 10.
To change cm to meters, divide by 100.
To change mm to meters, divide by 1,000.
To change km to meters, multiply by 1,000.

Directions: Solve the following problems.

1. 600 cm = _____ m   2. 12 cm = _____ mm   3. 47 m = _____ cm   4. 3 km = _____ m

5. In the sentences below, write the missing unit: m, cm, mm or km.

   a. A fingernail is about 1 _____ thick.

   b. An average car is about 5 _____ long.

   c. Someone could walk 1 _____ in 10 minutes.

   d. A finger is about 7 _____ long.

   e. A street could be 3 _____ long.

   f. The Earth is about 40,000 _____ around at the equator.

   g. A pencil is about 17 _____ long.

   h. A noodle is about 4 _____ wide.

   i. A teacher's desk is about 1 _____ wide.

6. A nickel is about 1 mm thick. How many nickels would be in a
   stack 1 cm high?   _____

7. Is something 25 cm long closer to 10 inches or 10 feet?   _____

8. Is something 18 mm wide closer to 0.7 inch or 7 inches?   _____

9. Would you get more exercise running 4 km or 500 m?   _____

10. Which is taller, something 40 m or 350 cm?   _____

Name _____

Weight in Customary Units

Here are the main ways to measure weight in customary units:

16 ounces (oz.) = 1 pound (lb.)
2,000 lb. = 1 ton (tn.)
To change ounces to pounds, divide by 16.
To change pounds to ounces, multiply by 16.

As with measurements of length, you may have to borrow units in subtraction.

BRIDGE
UNSAFE
FOR TRUCKS
OVER
2 TONS

Example:	4 lb. 5 oz.	=	3 lb. 21 oz.
	– 2 lb. 10 oz.		– 2 lb. 10 oz.
			1 lb. 11 oz.

Directions: Solve the following problems.

1. 48 oz. = _____ lb.   2. 39 oz. = _____ lb.   3. 4 lb. = _____ oz.   4. 1.25 tn. = _____ lb.

5. What form of measurement would you use for each of these: ounces, pounds or tons?

   a. pencil _____   b. elephant _____   c. person _____

6. Which is heavier, 0.25 ton or 750 pounds?   _____

7. Twenty-two people, each weighing an average of 150 lb.,
   want to get on an elevator that can carry up to
   1.5 tons. How many of them should wait for the next elevator?   _____

8. A one ton truck is carrying 14 boxes that weigh 125 lb. each. It
   comes to a small bridge with a sign that says, "Bridge unsafe for
   trucks over 2 tons." Is it safe for the truck and the boxes to
   cross the bridge?

   _____

9. A large box of Oat Boats contains 2 lb. 3 oz. of cereal, while
   a box of Honey Hunks contains 1 lb. 14 oz. How many more
   ounces are in the box of Oat Boats?

   _____

10. A can of Peter's Powdered Drink Mix weighs 2 lb. 5 oz.
    A can of Petunia's Powdered Drink Mix weighs 40 oz.
    Which one is heavier?

    _____

11. A can of Peter's Drink Mix is 12 cents an ounce. How much
    does it cost?

    _____

12. How many 5-oz. servings could you get from a fish that weighs
    3 lb. 12 oz.?

    _____

Name _____

Weight in Metric Units

A **gram (g)** is about 0.035 oz.
A **milligram (mg)** is $\frac{1}{1000}$ g or about 0.000035 oz.
A **kilogram (kg)** is 1,000 g or about 2.2 lb.
A **metric ton (t)** is 1,000 kg or about 1.1 tn.

To change g to mg, multiply by 1,000.
To change g to kg, divide by 1,000.
To change kg to g, multiply by 1,000.
To change t to kg, multiply by 1,000.

Directions: Solve the following problems.

1. 3 kg = _____ g

2. 2 g = _____ mg

3. 145 g = _____ kg

4. 3,000 kg = _____ t

5. _____ g = 450 mg

6. 3.5 t = _____ kg

7. Write the missing units below: g, mg, kg or t.

   a. A sunflower seed weighs less than 1 _____.

   b. A serving of cereal contains 14 _____ of sugar.

   c. The same serving of cereal has 250 _____ of salt.

   d. A bowling ball weighs about 7 _____.

   e. A whale weighs about 90 _____.

   f. A math textbook weighs about 1 _____.

   g. A safety pin weighs about 1 _____.

   h. An average car weighs about 1 _____.

8. Is 200 g closer to 7 oz. or 70 oz.? _____

9. Is 3 kg closer to 7 lb. or 70 lb.? _____

10. Does a metric ton weigh more or less than a ton
    measured by the customary system? _____

11. How is a kilogram different from a kilometer? _____

12. Which is heavier, 300 g or 1 kg? _____

Name _____

Capacity in Customary Units

Here are the main ways to measure capacity (how much something will hold) in customary units:

8 fluid ounces (fl. oz.) = 1 cup (c.)
2 c. = 1 pint (pt.)
2 pt. = 1 quart (qt.)
4 qt. = 1 gallon (gal.)

To change ounces to cups, divide by 8.
To change cups to ounces, multiply by 8.
To change cups to pints or quarts, divide by 2.
To change pints to cups or quarts to pints, multiply by 2.

As with measurements of length and weight, you may have to borrow units in subtraction.

Example: 3 gal. 2 qt. =   2 gal. 6 qt.
                  – 1 gal. 3 qt.   – 1 gal. 3 qt.
                  _____   _____
                      1 gal. 3 qt.

Directions: Solve the following problems.

1. 32 fl. oz. = _____ pt.   2. 4 gal. = _____ pt.   3. _____ c. = 24 fl. oz.

4. 5 pt. = _____ qt.   5. 16 pt. = _____ gal.   6. 3 pt. = _____ fl. oz.

7. A large can of soup contains 19 fl. oz. A serving is about 8 oz. How many cans should you buy if you want to serve 7 people?   _____

8. A container of strawberry ice cream holds 36 fl. oz. A container of chocolate ice cream holds 2 pt. Which one has more ice cream? How much more?   _____

9. A day-care worker wants to give 15 children each 6 fl. oz. of milk. How many quarts of milk does she need?   _____

10. This morning, the day-care supervisor bought 3 gal. of milk. The kids drank 2 gal. 3 c. How much milk is left for tomorrow?   _____

11. Harriet bought 3 gal. 2 qt. of paint for her living room. She used 2 gal. 3 qt. How much paint is left over?   _____

12. Jason's favorite punch takes a pint of raspberry sherbet. If he wants to make $1\frac{1}{2}$ times the recipe, how many fl. oz. of sherbet does he need?   _____

Name _____

Capacity in Metric Units

A **liter** (**L**) is a little over 1 quart.
A **milliliter** (**mL**) is $\frac{1}{1000}$ of a liter or about 0.03 oz.
A **kiloliter** (**kL**) is 1,000 liters or about 250 gallons.

Directions: Solve the following problems.

1. 5,000 mL = _____ L

2. 2,000 L = _____ kL

3. 3 L = _____ mL

4. Write the missing unit: L, mL or kL.

    a. A swimming pool holds about 100 _____ of water.

    b. An eyedropper is marked for 1 and 2 _____.

    c. A pitcher could hold 1 or 2 _____ of juice.

    d. A teaspoon holds about 5 _____ of medicine.

    e. A birdbath might hold 5 _____ of water.

    f. A tablespoon holds about 15 _____ of salt.

    g. A bowl holds about 250 _____ of soup.

    h. We drank about 4 _____ of punch at the party.

5. Which is more, 3 L or a gallon?   _____

6. Which is more, 400 mL or 40 oz.?   _____

7. Which is more, 1 kL or 500 L?   _____

8. Is 4 L closer to a quart or a gallon?   _____

9. Is 480 mL closer to 2 cups or 2 pints?   _____

10. Is a mL closer to 4 drops or 4 teaspoonsful?   _____

11. How many glasses of juice containing 250 mL
    each could you pour from a 1-L jug?   _____

12. How much water would you need to water an
    average-sized lawn, 1 kL or 1 L?   _____

Name _____

Temperature in Customary and Metric Units

The customary system measures temperature in Fahrenheit (F°) degrees.

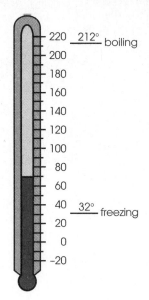

The metric system uses Celsius (C°) degrees.

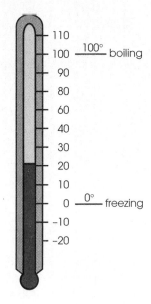

Directions: Study the thermometers and answer these questions.

1. Write in the temperature from both systems:

	Fahrenheit	**Celsius**
a. freezing	_____	_____
b. boiling	_____	_____
c. comfortable room temperature	_____	_____
d. normal body temperature	_____	_____

2. Underline the most appropriate temperature for both systems.

a. a reasonably hot day	34°	54°	84°	10°	20°	35°
b. a cup of hot chocolate	95°	120°	190°	60°	90°	120°
c. comfortable water to swim in	55°	75°	95°	10°	25°	40°

3. If the temperature is 35°C is it summer or winter? _____

4. Would ice cream stay frozen at 35°F? _____

5. Which is colder, –10°C or –10°F? _____

6. Which is warmer, 60°C or 60°F? _____

Name _____

Review

Directions: Complete the following exercises.

1. 372 in. = _____ yd. _____ ft.

2. 4 km = _____ m

3. 1.25 lb. = _____ oz.

4. 2,000 mg = _____ g

5. 1 qt. = _____ oz.

6. 10,000 mL = _____ L

7. Todd has a board that is 6 ft. 3 in. long. He needs to cut it to 4 ft. 9 in. How much should he cut off? _____

8. In a contest, Joyce threw a ball 12 yd. 2 ft. Brenda threw the ball 500 in. Who threw the farthest? _____

9. Would you measure this workbook in mm or cm? _____

10. Which is heavier, a box of books that weighs 4 lb. 6 oz. or a box of dishes that weighs 80 oz.? _____

11. A 1-lb. package has 10 hot dogs. How much of an ounce does each hot dog weigh? _____

12. Would the amount of salt (sodium) in 1 oz. of potato chips be 170 g or 170 mg? _____

13. If someone ate half of a gallon of ice cream, how many fluid ounces would be left? _____

14. You want to serve 6 fl. oz. of ice cream to each of 16 friends at your party. How many quarts of ice cream should you buy? _____

15. Would you measure water in a fish pond with L or kL? _____

16. Would popsicles melt at 5°C? _____

17. Would soup be steaming hot at 100°F? _____

Ratios

A **ratio** is a comparison of two quantities. For example, a wall is 96 in. high; a pencil is 8 in. long. By dividing 8 into 96, you find it would take 12 pencils to equal the height of the wall. The ratio, or comparison, of the wall to the pencil can be written three ways: 1 to 12; 1:12; $\frac{1}{12}$. In this example, the ratio of triangles to circles is 4:6. The ratio of triangles to squares is 4:9. The ratio of circles to squares is 6:9. These ratios will stay the same if we divide both numbers in the ratio by the same number.

Examples: $\frac{4 \div 2 = 2}{6 \div 2 = 3}$ $\frac{6 \div 3 = 2}{9 \div 3 = 3}$ (There is no number that will divide into both 4 and 9.)

By reducing 4:6 and 6:9 to their lowest terms, they are the same—2:3. This means that 2:3, 4:6 and 6:9 are all equal ratios. You can also find equal ratios for all three by multiplying both numbers of the ratio by the same number.

Examples: $\frac{4 \times 3 = 12}{6 \times 3 = 18}$ $\frac{6 \times 5 = 30}{9 \times 5 = 45}$ $\frac{4 \times 4 = 16}{9 \times 4 = 36}$

Directions: Solve the following problems.

1. Write two more equal ratios for each of the following by multiplying or dividing both numbers in the ratio by the same number.

   a. $\frac{1}{2}$ $\frac{2}{4}$ $\frac{3}{6}$ ____ ____

   b. $\frac{1}{4}$ $\frac{2}{8}$ $\frac{4}{16}$ ____ ____

   c. $\frac{8}{24}$ $\frac{1}{3}$ $\frac{3}{9}$ ____ ____

2. Circle the ratios that are equal.

   a. $\frac{1}{6}$ $\frac{3}{6}$

   b. $\frac{15}{25}$ $\frac{3}{5}$

   c. $\frac{2}{7}$ $\frac{10}{35}$

   d. $\frac{2}{3}$ $\frac{6}{10}$

3. Write each ratio three ways.

   a. stars to crosses _____

   b. crosses to trees _____

   c. stars to all other shapes _____

4. Write two equal ratios (multiplying or dividing) for:

   a. stars to crosses _____

   b. crosses to trees _____

   c. stars to all other shapes _____

Name _____

Missing Numbers in Ratios

You can find a missing number (n) in an equal ratio. First, figure out which number has already been multiplied to get the number you know. (In the first example, 3 is multiplied by 3 to get 9; in the second example, 2 is multiplied by 6 to get 12.) Then multiply the other number in the ratio by the same number (3 and 6 in the examples).

Examples: $\frac{3}{4} = \frac{9}{n}$ $\frac{3}{4} \times \frac{3}{3} = \frac{9}{12}$ $n = 12$ $\frac{1}{2} = \frac{n}{12}$ $\frac{1}{2} \times \frac{6}{6} = \frac{6}{12}$ $n = 6$

Directions: Solve the following problems.

1. Find each missing number.

   a. $\frac{1}{2} = \frac{n}{12}$ $n =$ _____   b. $\frac{1}{5} = \frac{n}{15}$ $n =$ _____   c. $\frac{3}{2} = \frac{18}{n}$ $n =$ _____

   d. $\frac{5}{8} = \frac{n}{32}$ $n =$ _____   e. $\frac{8}{3} = \frac{16}{n}$ $n =$ _____   f. $\frac{n}{14} = \frac{5}{7}$ $n =$ _____

2. If a basketball player makes 9 baskets in 12 tries, what is her ratio of baskets to tries, in lowest terms?

    _____

3. At the next game, the player has the same ratio of baskets to tries. If she tries 20 times, how many baskets should she make?

    _____

4. At the third game, she still has the same ratio of baskets to tries. This time she makes 12 baskets. How many times did she probably try?

    _____

5. If a driver travels 40 miles in an hour, what is his ratio of miles to minutes, in lowest terms?   _____

6. At the same speed, how far would the driver travel in 30 minutes?   _____

7. At the same speed, how long would it take him to travel 60 miles?   _____

Name _____

Proportions

A **proportion** is a statement that two ratios are equal. To make sure ratios are equal, called a proportion, we multiply the cross products.

Examples of proportions:	$\frac{1}{5} = \frac{2}{10}$ $\frac{1}{2} \times \frac{10}{5} = \frac{10}{10}$ $\frac{3}{7} = \frac{15}{35}$ $\frac{3}{7} \times \frac{35}{15} = \frac{105}{105}$

These two ratios are not a proportion: $\frac{4}{3} = \frac{5}{6}$ $\frac{4}{3} \times \frac{6}{5} = \frac{24}{15}$

To find a missing number (n) in a proportion, multiply the cross products and divide.

Examples: $\frac{n}{30} = \frac{1}{6}$ $n \times 6 = 1 \times 30$ $n \times 6 = 30$ $n = \frac{30}{6}$ $n = 5$

Directions: Solve the following problems.

1. Write = between the ratios if they are a proportion. Write ≠ if they are not a proportion. The first one has been done for you.

   a. $\frac{1}{2}$ ⬭= $\frac{6}{12}$ b. $\frac{13}{18}$ ◯ $\frac{20}{22}$ c. $\frac{2}{6}$ ◯ $\frac{5}{15}$ d. $\frac{5}{6}$ ◯ $\frac{20}{24}$

2. Find the missing numbers in these proportions.

   a. $\frac{2}{5} = \frac{n}{15}$ $n =$ _____   b. $\frac{3}{8} = \frac{9}{n}$ $n =$ _____   c. $\frac{n}{18} = \frac{4}{12}$ $n =$ _____

3. One issue of a magazine costs $2.99, but if you buy a subscription, 12 issues cost $35.88. Is the price at the same proportion? _____

4. A cookie recipe calls for 3 cups of flour to make 36 cookies. How much flour is needed for 48 cookies? _____

5. The same recipe requires 4 teaspoons of cinnamon for 36 cookies. How many teaspoons is needed to make 48 cookies? (Answer will include a fraction.) _____

6. The recipe also calls for 2 cups of sugar for 36 cookies. How much sugar should you use for 48 cookies? (Answer will include a fraction.) _____

7. If 2 kids can eat 12 cookies, how many can 8 kids eat? _____

Name _____

Percents

Percent means "per 100." A percent is a ratio that compares a number with 100. The same number can be written as a decimal and a percent. To change a decimal to a percent, move the decimal point two places to the right and add the % sign. To change a percent to a decimal, drop the % sign and place a decimal point two places to the left.

Examples:	$0.25 = 25\%$	$0.1 = 10\%$	$1.456 = 145.6\%$
	$32\% = 0.32$	$99\% = 0.99$	$203\% = 2.03$

A percent or decimal can also be written as a ratio or fraction.

Example: $0.25 = 25\% = \dfrac{25}{100} = \dfrac{1}{4} = 1{:}4$

To change a fraction or ratio to a percent, first change it to a decimal. Divide the numerator by the denominator.

Examples: $\dfrac{1}{3} = 3\overline{\smash{)}1.00} = 0.33\tfrac{1}{3} = 33\tfrac{1}{3}\%$ $\dfrac{2}{5} = 5\overline{\smash{)}2.0} = 0.4 = 40\%$

Directions: Solve the following problems.

1. Change the percents to decimals.

   a. 3% = _____   b. 75% = _____   c. 14% = _____   d. 115% = _____

2. Change the decimals and fractions to percents.

   a. 0.56 = _____ %   b. 0.03 = _____ %   c. $\dfrac{3}{4}$ = _____ %   d. $\dfrac{1}{5}$ = _____ %

3. Change the percents to ratios in their lowest terms. The first one has been done for you.

   a. 75% = $\dfrac{75}{100} = \dfrac{3}{4} = \textbf{3:4}$ b. 40% = _____

   c. 35% = _____   d. 70% = _____

4. The class was 45% girls. What percent was boys?   _____

5. Half the shoes in one store were on sale. What percent of the shoes were their ordinary price?   _____

6. Kim read 84 pages of a 100-page book. What percent of the book did she read?   _____

Name _____

Percents

To find the percent of a number, change the percent to a decimal and multiply.

Examples: 45% of $20 = 0.45 x $20 = $9.00
125% of 30 = 1.25 x 30 = 37.50

Directions: Solve the following problems. Round off the answers to the nearest hundredth where necessary.

1. Find the percent of each number.

   a. 26% of 40 = _____   b. 12% of 329 = _____

   c. 73% of 19 = _____   d. 2% of 24 = _____

2. One family spends 35% of its weekly budget of $150 on food. How much do they spend?   _____

3. A shirt in a store usually costs $15.99, but today it's on sale for 25% off. The clerk says you will save $4.50. Is that true?   _____

4. A book that usually costs $12 is on sale for 25% off. How much will it cost?   _____

5. After you answer 60% of 150 math problems, how many do you have left to do?   _____

6. A pet store's shipment of tropical fish was delayed. Nearly 40% of the 1,350 fish died. About how many lived?   _____

7. The shipment had 230 angelfish, which died in the same proportion as the other kinds of fish. About how many angelfish died?   _____

8. A church youth group was collecting cans of food. Their goal was 1,200 cans, but they exceeded their goal by 25%. How many cans did they collect?   _____

Probability

Probability is the ratio of favorable outcomes to possible outcomes in an experiment. You can use probability (P) to figure out how likely something is to happen. For example, six picture cards are turned facedown—3 cards have stars, 2 have triangles and 1 has a circle. What is the probability of picking the circle? Using the formula below, you have a 1 in 6 probability of picking the circle, a 2 in 6 probability of picking a triangle and a 3 in 6 probability of picking a star.

Example: $P = \dfrac{\text{number of favorable outcomes}}{\text{number of trials}}$ $P = \dfrac{1}{6} = 1{:}6$

Directions: Solve the following problems.

1. A class has 14 girls and 15 boys. If all of their names are put on separate slips in a hat, what is the probability of each person's name being chosen? _____

2. In the same class, what is the probability that a girl's name will be chosen? _____

3. In this class, 3 boys are named Mike. What is the probability that a slip with "Mike" written on it will be chosen? _____

4. A spinner on a board game has the numbers 1–8. What is the probability of spinning and getting a 4? _____

5. A paper bag holds these colors of wooden beads: 4 blue, 5 red and 6 yellow. If you select a bead without looking, do you have an equal probability of getting each color? _____

6. Using the same bag of beads, what is the probability of reaching in and drawing out a red bead (in lowest terms)? _____

7. In the same bag, what is the probability of not getting a blue bead? _____

8. In a carnival game, plastic ducks have spots. The probability of picking a duck with a yellow spot is 2:15. There is twice as much probability of picking a duck with a red spot. What is the probability of picking a duck with a red spot? _____

9. In this game, all the other ducks have green spots. What is the probability of picking a duck with a green spot (in lowest terms)? _____

Possible Combinations

Today the cafeteria is offering 4 kinds of sandwiches, 3 kinds of drinks and 2 kinds of cookies. How many possible combinations could you make? To find out, multiply the number of choices together.

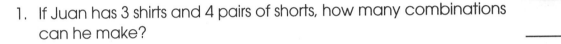

Example: 4 x 3 x 2 = 24 possible combinations

Directions: Solve the following problems.

1. If Juan has 3 shirts and 4 pairs of shorts, how many combinations can he make? _____

2. Janice can borrow 1 book and 1 magazine at a time from her classroom library. The library has 45 books and 16 magazines. How many combinations are possible? _____

3. Kerry's mother is redecorating the living room. She has narrowed her choices to 6 kinds of wallpaper, 3 shades of paint and 4 colors of carpeting that all match. How many possible combinations are there? _____

4. Pam has 6 sweaters that she can combine with pants to make 24 outfits. How many pairs of pants does she have? _____

5. Kenny can get to school by walking, taking a bus, riding his bike or asking his parents for a ride. He can get home the same ways, except his parents aren't available then. How many combinations can he make of ways to get to school and get home? _____

6. Sue's middle school offers 3 different language classes, 3 art classes and 2 music classes. If she takes one class in each area, how many possible combinations are there? _____

7. Bart's school offers 4 language classes, 3 art classes and some music classes. If Bart can make 36 possible combinations, how many music classes are there? _____

8. AAA Airlines schedules 12 flights a day from Chicago to Atlanta. Four of those flights go on to Orlando. From the Orlando airport you can take a bus, ride in a taxi or rent a car to get to Disneyworld. How many different ways are there to get from Chicago to Disneyworld if you make part of your trip on AAA Airlines? _____

Name _____

Review

Directions: Solve the following problems. Round answers to the nearest hundredth where necessary.

1. Write an equal ratio for each of these:

   a. $\dfrac{1}{7} =$ _____

   b. $\dfrac{5}{8} =$ _____

   c. $\dfrac{15}{3} =$ _____

   d. $\dfrac{6}{24} =$ _____

2. State the ratios below in lowest terms.

   a. cats to bugs = _____

   b. cats to dogs = _____

   c. dogs to all other objects = _____

3. If Shawn drives 45 miles an hour, how far could he go in 40 minutes? _____

4. At the same speed, how many minutes would it take Shawn to drive 120 miles?

   _____

5. Mr. Herman is building a doghouse in proportion to his family's house. The family's house is 30 ft. high and the doghouse is 5 ft. high. If the family house is 42 ft. wide, how wide should the doghouse be? _____

6. The family house is 24 ft. from front to back. How big should Mr. Herman make the doghouse? _____

7. Change these numbers to percents:

   a. $0.56 =$ _____

   b. $\dfrac{4}{5} =$ _____

   c. $0.04 =$ _____

   d. $\dfrac{3}{8} =$ _____

8. Which is a better deal, a blue bike for $125 at 25% off or a red bike for $130 at 30% off?

   _____

9. If sales tax is 6%, what would be the total price of the blue bike? _____

10. Richard bought 6 raffle tickets for a free bike. If 462 tickets were sold, what is Richard's probability of winning?

    _____

11. Lori bought 48 tickets in the same raffle. What are her chances of winning?

    _____

Name _____

Comparing Data

Data (**datum**—singular) are gathered information. The **range** is the difference between the highest and lowest number in a group of numbers. The **median** is the number in the middle when numbers are listed in order. The **mean** is the average of the numbers. We can compare numbers or data by finding the range, median and mean.

Example: 16, 43, 34, 78, 8, 91, 26

To compare these numbers, we first need to put them in order: 8 16 26 34 43 78 91. By subtracting the lowest number (8) from the highest one (91), we find the range: 83. By finding the number that falls in the middle, we have the median: 34 (If no number fell exactly in the middle, we would average the two middle numbers.) By adding them and dividing by the number of numbers (7), we get the mean: 42.29 (rounded to the nearest hundredth).

Directions: Solve the following problems. Round answers to the nearest hundredth where necessary.

1. Find the range, median and mean of these numbers: 19, 5, 84, 27, 106, 38, 75.

   Range: _____   Median: _____   Mean: _____

2. Find the range, median and mean finishing times for 6 runners in a race. Here are their times in seconds: 14.2, 12.9, 13.5, 10.3, 14.8, 14.7.

   Range: _____   Median: _____   Mean: _____

3. If the runner who won the race in 10.3 seconds had run even faster and finished in 7 seconds, would the mean time be higher or lower?   _____

4. If that runner had finished in 7 seconds, what would be the median time?   _____

5. Here are the high temperatures in one city for a week: 65, 72, 68, 74, 81, 68, 85. Find the range, median and mean temperatures.

   Range: _____   Median: _____   Mean: _____

6. Find the range, median and mean test scores for this group of students: 41, 32, 45, 36, 48, 38, 37, 42, 39, 36.

   Range: _____   Median: _____   Mean: _____

Name _____

Tables

Organizing data into tables makes it easier to compare numbers. As evident in the example, putting many numbers in a paragraph is confusing. When the same numbers are organized in a table, you can compare numbers in a glance. Tables can be arranged several ways and still be easy to read and understand.

Example: Money spent on groceries:
Family A: week 1 — $68.50; week 2 — $72.25; week 3 — $67.00; week 4 — $74.50.
Family B: week 1 — $42.25; week 2 — $47.50; week 3 — $50.25; week 4 — $53.50.

	Week 1	Week 2	Week 3	Week 4
Family A	$68.50	$72.25	$67.00	$74.50
Family B	$42.25	$47.50	$50.25	$53.50

Directions: Complete the following exercises.

1. Finish the table below, then answer the questions.
   Data: Steve weighs 230 lb. and is 6 ft. 2 in. tall. George weighs 218 lb. and is 6 ft. 3 in. tall. Chuck weighs 225 lb. and is 6 ft. 1 in. tall. Henry weighs 205 lb. and is 6 ft. tall.

	Henry	George	Chuck	Steve
Weight				
Height				

   a. Who is tallest?_____ b. Who weighs the least?_____

2. On another sheet of paper, prepare 2 tables comparing the amount of money made by 3 booths at the school carnival this year and last year. In the first table, write the names of the games in the left-hand column (like **Family A** and **Family B** in the example). In the second table (using the same data), write the years in the left-hand column. Here is the data: fish pond—this year $15.60, last year $13.50; bean-bag toss—this year $13.45, last year $10.25; ring toss—this year $23.80, last year $18.80. After you complete both tables, answer the following questions.

   a. Which booth made the most money this year? _____

   b. Which booth made the biggest improvement from last year to this year? _____

Name _____

Bar Graphs

Another way to organize information is a **bar graph**. The bar graph in the example compares the number of students in 4 elementary schools. Each bar stands for 1 school. You can easily see that School A has the most students and School C has the least. The numbers along the left show how many students attend each school.

Example:

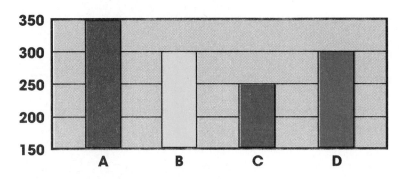

Directions: Complete the following exercises.

1. This bar graph will show how many calories are in 1 serving of 4 kinds of cereal. Draw the bars the correct height and label each with the name of the cereal. After completing the bar graph, answer the questions. Data: Korn Kernals—150 calories; Oat Floats—160 calories; Rite Rice—110 calories; Sugar Shapes—200 calories.

A. Which cereal is the best to eat if you're trying to lose weight? _____

B. Which cereal has nearly the same number of calories as Oat Floats? _____

2. On another sheet of paper, draw your own graph, showing the number of TV commercials in 1 week for each of the 4 cereals in the graph above. After completing the graph, answer the questions. Data: Oat Boats—27 commercials; Rite Rice—15; Sugar Shapes—35; Korn Kernals—28.

A. Which cereal is most heavily advertised? _____

B. What similarities do you notice between the graph of calories and the graph of TV commercials? _____

Name _____

Picture Graphs

Newspapers and textbooks often use pictures in graphs instead of bars. Each picture stands for a certain number of objects. Half a picture means half the number. The picture graph in the example indicates the number of games each team won. The Astros won 7 games, so they have $3\frac{1}{2}$ balls.

Example:

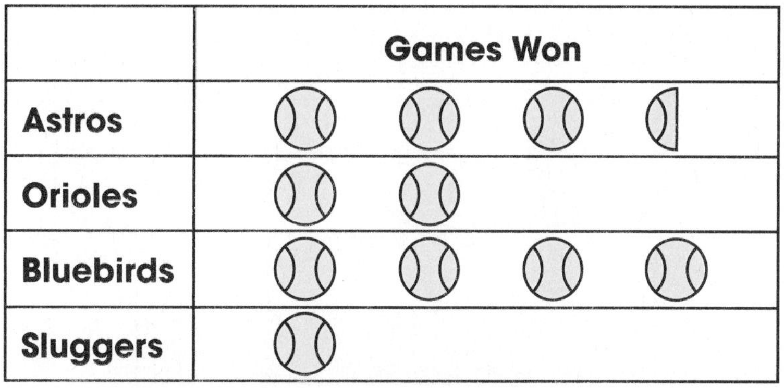

	Games Won			
Astros	⚾	⚾	⚾	◖
Orioles	⚾	⚾		
Bluebirds	⚾	⚾	⚾	⚾
Sluggers	⚾			

(1 ball = 2 games)

Directions: Complete the following exercises.

Finish this picture graph, showing the number of students who have dogs in 4 sixth-grade classes. Draw simple dogs in the graph, letting each drawing stand for 2 dogs.
Data: Class 1—12 dogs; Class 2—16 dogs; Class 3—22 dogs; Class 4—12 dogs.
After completing the graph, answer the questions.

	Dogs Owned by Students
Class 1	
Class 2	
Class 3	
Class 4	

(One dog drawing = 2 students' dogs)

1. Why do you think newspapers use picture graphs?_____
_____

2. Would picture graphs be appropriate to show exact number of dogs living in America? Why or why not?_____
_____

Line Graphs

Still another way to display information is a line graph. The same data can often be shown in both a bar graph and a line graph. Nevertheless, line graphs are especially useful in showing changes over a period of time.

The line graph in the example shows changes in the number of students enrolled in a school over a 5-year period. Enrollment was highest in 1988 and has decreased gradually each year since then. Notice how labeling the years and enrollment numbers make the graph easy to understand.

Example:

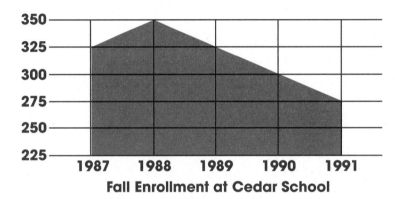

Fall Enrollment at Cedar School

Directions: Complete the following exercises.

1. On another sheet of paper, draw a line graph that displays the growth of a corn plant over a 6-week period. Mark the correct points, using the data below, and connect them with a line. After completing the graph, answer the questions. Data: week 1— 3.5 in.; week 2—4.5 in.; week 3—5 in.; week 4—5.5 in.; week 5—5.75 in.; week 6—6 in.

   a. Between which weeks was the growth fastest? _____

   b. Between which weeks was the growth slowest? _____

2. On another sheet of paper draw a line graph to show how the high temperature varied during one week. Then answer the questions. Data: Sunday—high of 53 degrees; Monday—51; Tuesday—56; Wednesday—60; Thursday—58; Friday—67; Saturday—73. Don't forget to label the numbers.

   a. In general, did the days get warmer or cooler? _____

   b. Do you think this data would have been as clear in a bar graph? _____
      Explain your answer.

   _____

   _____

Name _____

Circle Graphs

Circle graphs are useful in showing how something is divided into parts. The circle graph in the example shows how Carly spent her $10 allowance. Each section is a fraction of her whole allowance. For example, the movie tickets section is $\frac{1}{2}$ of the circle, showing that she spent $\frac{1}{2}$ of her allowance, $5, on movie tickets.

Directions: Complete the following exercises.

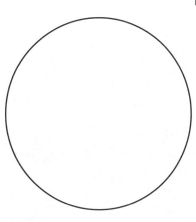

1. When the middle school opened last fall, $\frac{1}{2}$ of the students came from East Elementary, $\frac{1}{4}$ came from West Elementary, $\frac{1}{8}$ came from North Elementary and the remaining students moved into the town from other cities. Make a circle graph showing these proportions. Label each section. Then answer the questions.

   a. What fraction of students at the new school moved into the area from other cities? _____

   b. If the new middle school has 450 students enrolled, how many used to go to East Elementary? _____

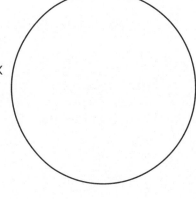

2. This circle graph will show the hair color of 24 students in one class. Divide the circle into 4 sections to show this data: black hair—8 students; brown hair—10 students; blonde hair—4 students; red hair—2 students. (Hint: 8 students are $\frac{8}{24}$ or $\frac{1}{3}$ of the class.) Be sure to label each section by hair color. Then answer the questions.

   a. Looking at your graph, what fraction of the class is the combined group of blonde- and red-haired students? _____

   b. Which two fractions of hair color combine to total half the class? _____

Name _____

Comparing Presentation Methods

Tables and different kinds of graphs have different purposes. Some are more helpful for certain kinds of information. The table and three graphs below all show basically the same information—the amount of money Mike and Margaret made in their lawn-mowing business over a 4-month period.

Combined Income per Month

	Mike	Margaret
June	$34	$36
July	41	35
August	27	28
Sept.	36	40
Totals	$138	$139

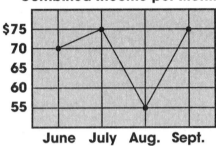

Combined Income per Month

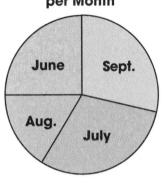

Combined Income per Month

Directions: Study the graphs and table. Then circle the one that answers each question below.

Combined Income per Month

1. Which one shows the fraction of the total income that Mike and Margaret made in August?

        table   line graph   bar graph   circle graph

2. Which one compares Mike's earnings with Margaret's?

        table   line graph   bar graph   circle graph

3. Which one has the most exact numbers?

        table   line graph   bar graph   circle graph

4. Which one has no numbers?

        table   line graph   bar graph   circle graph

5. Which two best show how Mike and Margaret's income changed from month to month?

        table   line graph   bar graph   circle graph

Name _____

Graphing Data

Directions: Complete the following exercises.

1. Use the following information to create a bar graph.

Cities	Population (in 1,000's)
Dover	20
Newton Falls	12
Springdale	25
Hampton	17
Riverside	5

2. Study the data and create a line graph showing the number of baskets Jonah scored during the season.

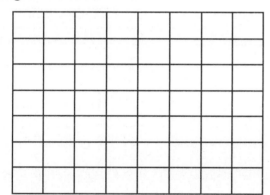

Game 1 — 10
Game 2 — 7
Game 3 — 11
Game 4 — 10
Game 5 — 9
Game 6 — 5
Game 7 — 9

Fill in the blanks.
a. High game: _____
b. Low game: _____
c. Average baskets per game: _____

3. Study the graph, then answer the questions.

a. Which flavor is the most popular? _____

b. Which flavor sold the least? _____

c. What decimal represents the two highest sellers? _____

d. Which flavor had $\frac{1}{10}$ of the sales? _____

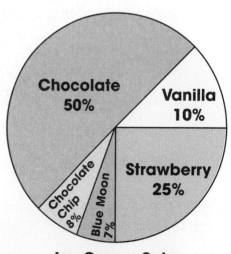

Chocolate 50%
Vanilla 10%
Strawberry 25%
Chocolate Chip 8%
Blue Moon 7%

Ice-Cream Sales

Name _____

Integers

An **integer** is a whole number above or below 0: –2, –1, 0, +1, +2, and so on. **Opposite integers** are two integers the same distance from 0, but in different directions, such as –2 and +2.

Think of the water level in the picture as 0. The part of the iceberg sticking out of the water is positive. The iceberg has +3 feet above water. The part of the iceberg below the water is negative. The iceberg extends – 9 feet under water.

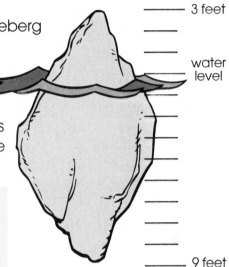

Numbers greater than 0 are **positive** numbers. Numbers less than 0 are **negative** numbers. Pairs of positive and negative numbers are called **opposite integers**.

> **Examples of opposite integers:**
> –5 and +5
> losing 3 pounds and gaining 3 pounds
> earning $12 and spending $12

Directions: Complete the following exercises.

1. Write each of these as an integer. The first one is done for you.

   a. positive 6 = __+6__

   b. losing $5 = _____

   c. 5 degrees below 0 = _____

   d. receiving $12 = _____

2. Write the **opposite** integer of each of these. The first one is done for you.

   a. negative 4 = __+4__

   b. positive 10 = _____

   c. 2 floors below ground level = _____

   d. winning a card game by 6 points = _____

3. Write integers to show each idea.

   a. A train that arrives 2 hours after it was scheduled: _____

   b. A package that has 3 fewer cups than it should: _____

   c. A board that's 3 inches too short: _____

   d. A golf score 5 over par: _____

   e. A paycheck that doesn't cover $35 of a family's expenses: _____

   f. 30 seconds before a missile launch: _____

   g. A team that won 6 games and lost 2: _____

Name _____

Comparing Integers

Comparing two integers can be confusing unless you think of them as being on a number line, as shown below. Remember that the integer farther to the right is greater. Thus, +2 is greater than –3, 0 is greater than –4 and –2 is greater than –5.

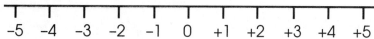

Directions: Study the number line. Then complete the following exercises.

1. Write in integers to complete the number line.

–5 ____ –3 –2 ____ 0 +1 ____ ____ +4 +5

2. Write < for "less than" or > for "greater than" to compare the integers. The first one is done for you.

$-15°$

a. –5 __<__ +5   b. +3 _____ –3   c. +2 _____ –4

d. –4 _____ –3   e. –1 _____ +3   f. –1 _____ –5

3. Write **T** for true or **F** for false. (All degrees are in Fahrenheit.)

a. +7 degrees is colder than –3 degrees.   _____

b. –14 degrees is colder than –7 degrees.   _____

c. +23 degrees is colder than –44 degrees.   _____

d. –5 degrees is colder than +4 degrees.   _____

4. Draw an **X** by the series of integers that are in order from least to greatest.

_____ +2, +3, –4

_____ –3, 0, +1

_____ –7, –4, –1

_____ –3, –4, –5

Adding Integers

The sum of two positive integers is a positive integer.
   Thus, +4 + +1 = +5.
The sum of two negative integers is a negative integer.
   Thus, −5 + −2 = −7.
The sum of a positive and a negative integer has the
sign of the integer that is farther from 0.
   Thus, −6 + +3 = −3.
The sum of opposite integers is 0.
   Thus, +2 + −2 = 0

Directions: Complete the following exercises.

1. Add these integers.

   a. +2 + +7 = _____   b. −4 + −2 = _____   c. +5 + −3 = _____   d. +4 + −4 = _____

   e. −10 + −2 = _____   f. +6 + −1 = _____   g. +45 + −30 = _____   h. −39 + +26 = _____

2. Write the problems as integers. The first one has been done for you.

   a. One cold morning, the temperature was −14 degrees.
      The afternoon high was 20 degrees warmer. What was the
      high temperature that day?

      −14 + +20 = +6

   b. Another day, the high temperature was 26 degrees,
      but the temperature dropped 35 degrees during the
      night. What was the low that night? _____

   c. Sherri's allowance was $7. She paid $4 for a movie ticket.
      How much money did she have left? _____

   d. The temperature in a meat freezer was −10 degrees, but
      the power went off and the temperature rose 6 degrees.
      How cold was the freezer then? _____

   e. The school carnival took in $235, but it had expenses of $185.
      How much money did the carnival make after paying
      its expenses? _____

Name _____

Subtracting Integers

To subtract an integer, change its sign to the opposite and add it. If you are subtracting a negative integer, make it positive and add it: +4 − −6 = +4 + +6 = +10. If you are subtracting a positive integer, make it negative and add it: +8 − +2 = +8 + −2 = +6.

More examples: −5 − −8 = −5 + +8 = +3
                       +3 − +7 = +3 + −7 = −4

Directions: Complete the following exercises.

1. Before subtracting these integers, rewrite each problem. The first one has been done for you.

   −6 − −8 = ____**−6 + +8 = +2**____   +3 − −4 = _____

   +9 − +3 = _____   −1 − −7 = _____

   +7 − −5 = _____   −4 − +3 = _____

2. Write these problems as integers. The first one is done for you.

   a. The high temperature in the Arctic Circle one day was
      −42 degrees. The low was −67 degrees. What
      was the difference between the two?   **−42 − −67 = −42 + +67 = +25**

   b. At the equator one day, the high temperature was
      +106 degrees. The low was +85 degrees. What
      was the difference between the two?   _____

   c. At George's house one morning, the thermometer showed it was
      +7 degrees. The radio announcer said it was −2 degrees. What is the
      difference between the two temperatures? _____

   d. What is the difference between a temperature of +11 degrees
      and a wind-chill factor of −15 degrees?   _____

   e. During a dry spell, the level of a river dropped from 3 feet above
      normal to 13 feet below normal. How many
      feet did it drop?   _____

   f. Here are the average temperatures in a meat freezer for four days:
      −12, −11, −14 and −9 degrees. What is the difference between
      the highest and lowest temperature?   _____

Name _____

Plotting Graphs

A graph with horizontal and vertical number lines can show the location of certain points. The horizontal number line is called the **x axis**, and the vertical number line is called the **y axis**. Two numbers, called the **x coordinate** and the **y coordinate**, show where a point is on the graph.

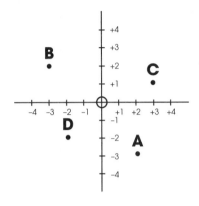

The first coordinate, x, tells how many units to the right or left of 0 the point is located. On the example graph, point A is +2, two units to the right of 0.

The second coordinate, y, tells how many units above or below 0 the point is located. On the example, point A is –3, three units below 0.

Thus, the coordinates of A are +2, –3. The coordinates of B are –3, +2. (Notice the order of the coordinates.) The coordinates of C are +3, +1; and D, –2, –2.

Directions: Study the example. Then answer these questions about the graph below.

1. What towns are at these coordinates?

    +1, +3   _____

    +1, –3   _____

    –4, +1   _____

    –2, –3   _____

    –3, –2   _____

    –3, +3   _____

2. What are the coordinates of these towns?

    Hampton   _____

    Wooster   _____

    Beachwood   _____

    Middletown _____

    Kirby   _____

    Arbor   _____

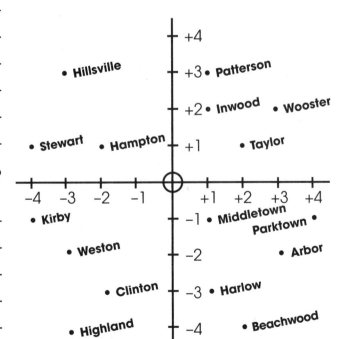

Name _____

Ordered Pairs

Ordered pairs is another term used to describe pairs of integers used to locate points on a graph.

Directions: Complete the following exercises.

1. Place the following points on the graph, using the ordered pairs as data.

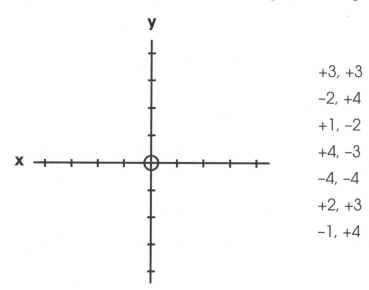

+3, +3

−2, +4

+1, −2

+4, −3

−4, −4

+2, +3

−1, +4

2. Create your own set of ordered pairs. Use your home as the center of your coordinates—zero. Let the x axis serve as East and West. The y axis will be North and South. Now select things to plot on your graph—the school, playground, grocery store, a friend's house, and so on.

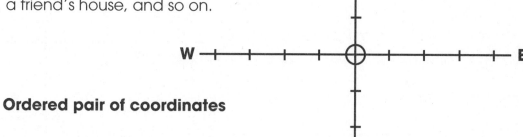

Place	Ordered pair of coordinates
School	_____
Grocery store	_____
Playground	_____
Friend's house	_____

Name _____

Review

Directions: Complete the following exercises.

1. Write the **opposite** integers of the following:

   a. 14 degrees above 0 _____

   b. Spending $21 _____

2. Write integers to show these ideas.

   a. 4 seconds after the launch of the space shuttle _____

   b. A lake 3 feet below its usual level _____

   c. 2 days before your birthday _____

3. Write < for "less than" or > for "greater than" to compare these integers.

   -2 _____ -4   +2 _____ -3   -1 _____ +1

4. Add the integers.

   -14 + -11 = _____   -6 + +5 = _____   -7 + +7 = _____

5. Subtract the integers.

   -4 - -5 = _____   +3 - -6 = _____   +7 - +2 = _____

6. Write **T** for true or **F** for false.

   a. The x coordinate is on the horizontal number line. _____

   b. Add the x and y coordinates to find the location of a point. _____

   c. Always state the x coordinate first. _____

   d. A y coordinate of +2 would be above the horizontal number line. _____

   e. An x coordinate of +2 would be to the right of the vertical number line. _____

CERTIFICATE

Congratulations to

_____
(Your Name)

for finishing this workbook!

_____
(Date)

Page 6

Spelling: Words With ă

Directions: Write a sentence for each word. Use a dictionary if you are unsure of the meaning of a word.

1. favorite
2. gable
3. dangerous
4. patient
5. lakefront
6. statement
7. nation
8. negotiate
9. operate
10. decade

Answers will vary.

Directions: Write the answers.

11. Which word means a 10-year period? __decade__
12. Which word means a triangle-shaped end of a building's roof? __gable__
13. Which word means arbitrated? __negotiated__

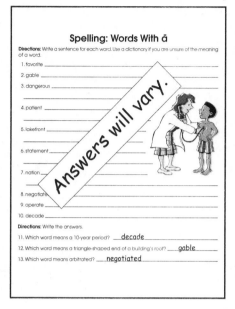

Page 7

Spelling: Words With ē

Directions: Write a sentence for each word. Use a dictionary if you are unsure of the meaning of a word.

1. niece
2. meaningful
3. conceited
4. baleen
5. field
6. disease
7. reactivate
8. peony
9. seafaring
10. theme

Answers will vary.

Directions: Write the answers.

11. Which word is a summer-blooming flower?
    __peony__
12. Which word is a type of whale?
    __baleen__
13. Which word means an illness?
    __disease__

Page 8

Spelling: Words With ī

Directions: Write a sentence for each word. Use a dictionary if you are unsure of the meaning of a word.

1. bisect
2. identify
3. frightened
4. glider
5. idol
6. library
7. pipeline
8. hieroglyphic
9. rhinoceros
10. silent

Answers will vary.

Directions: Write the answers.

11. Which word means to be scared?
    __frightened__
12. Which word means to divide into two sections?
    __bisect__
13. Which word is an animal?
    __rhinoceros__
14. Which word is a type of ancient writing?
    __hieroglyphic__

Page 9

Spelling: Words With ō

Directions: Write a sentence for each word. Use a dictionary if you are unsure of the meaning of a word.

1. clothing
2. slogan
3. total
4. stethoscope
5. voltage
6. stereo
7. protein
8. negotiate
9. locust
10. locomotive

Answers will vary.

Directions: Write the answers.

11. Which word is an insect?
    __locust__
12. Which word means a train?
    __locomotive__
13. Which word means a listening device to hear the heart?
    __stethoscope__
14. Which word means to bargain?
    __negotiate__

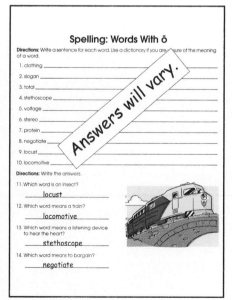

Page 10

Spelling: Words With ū

Directions: Write a sentence for each word. Use a dictionary if you are unsure of the meaning of a word.

1. universe
2. cruise
3. absolute
4. influence
5. unanimous
6. vacuum
7. putrid
8. incubate
9. peruse
10. numerous

Answers will vary.

Directions: Write the answers.

11. Which word means to read carefully?
    __peruse__
12. Which word means that everyone is in agreement?
    __unanimous__
13. Which word means a sea voyage taken for pleasure?
    __cruise__
14. Which word means to keep eggs warm until they hatch?
    __incubate__

Page 11

Spelling: I Before E, Except After C

Use an **i** before **e**, except after **c** or when **e** and **i** together sound like long **a**.

Examples:
relieve
deceive
neighbor

Exceptions: weird, foreign, height, seize

Directions: Write **C** in the blank if the word in bold is spelled correctly. Draw an **X** in the blank if it is spelled incorrectly. The first one has been done for you.

_C_ 1. They stopped at the crossing for the **freight** train.
_X_ 2. How much does that **wiegh**?
_C_ 3. Did you **believe** his story?
_X_ 4. He **recieved** an A on his paper!
_X_ 5. She said it was the **nieghborly** thing to do.
_C_ 6. The guards **seized** the package.
_X_ 7. That movie was **wierd**!
_X_ 8. Her **hieght** is five feet, six inches.
_C_ 9. It's not right to **deceive** others.
_X_ 10. Your answers should be **breif**.
_C_ 11. She felt a lot of **grief** when her dog died.
_X_ 12. He is still **greiving** about his loss.
_C_ 13. Did the police catch the **thief**?
_X_ 14. She was their **cheif** source of information.
_C_ 15. Can you speak a **foreign** language?

i before e,
except after c,
or when sounding like a,
as in "neighbor" and "weigh"

Page 12

Spelling: Words With ie and ei

Many people have trouble remembering when to use **ie** and when to use **ei**. The following rules have many exceptions, but they may be helpful to you.

Rule 1: If the two letters are pronounced like **ē** and are preceded by an **s** sound, use **ei**, as in receive.
Rule 2: If the two letters are pronounced like **ē**, but are not preceded by an **s** sound, use **ie** as in believe.
Rule 3: If the two letters are pronounced like **ā**, use **ei** as in eight and vein.
Rule 4: If the two letters are pronounced like **ī**, use **ei** as in height.

The sound **s** could be produced by the letter **s** as in **single** or the letter **c** as in **cease**.

Directions: Write the words from the box on the lines after the spelling rule that applies.

veil	brief	deceive	belief	niece
reindeer	yield	achieve	height	neighbor
grief	ceiling	weight	vein	seize

Rule 1: __ceiling, deceive, seize__

Rule 2: __grief, brief, yield, achieve, belief, niece__

Rule 3: __veil, reindeer, weight, vein, neighbor__

Rule 4: __height__

Directions: Complete the sentences with words that have the vowel sound shown. Use each word from the box only once.

1. My next-door (ā) __neighbor__ wore a long (ā) __veil__ at her wedding.
2. Will the roof hold the (ā) __weight__ of Santa's (ā) __reindeer__ ?
3. My nephew and (ē) __niece__ work hard to (ē) __achieve__ their goals.
4. I have a strong (ē) __belief__ they would never (ē) __deceive__ me.
5. For a (ē) __brief__ moment, I thought Will would (ē) __yield__ the game to me.
6. The blood rushed through my (ā) __veins__ .
7. What is the (ī) __height__ of this (ē) __ceiling__ ?

Page 13

Spelling: Words With ûr and ôr

The difference between **ûr** and **ôr** is clear in the words **fur** and **for**. The **ûr** sound can be spelled **ur** as in fur, **our** as in journal, **er** as in her and **ear** as in search.

The **ôr** sound can be spelled **or** as in for, **our** as in four, **oar** as in soar and **ore** as in more.

Directions: Write the words from the box on the lines to match the sounds.

florist	plural	ignore	courtesy	observe
survey	research	furnish	normal	emergency
tornado	coarse	flourish	source	restore

ûr __survey, plural, research, furnish, flourish, courtesy,__
   __observe, emergency__

ôr __florist, tornado, coarse, ignore, normal, source, restore__

Directions: Complete the sentences with words that have the sound shown. Use each word only once.

1. We all get along better when we remember to use (ûr) __courtesy__
2. My brother likes flowers and wants to be a (ôr) __florist__
3. What was the (ôr) __source__ of the (ûr) __research__ for your report?
4. He waved at her, but she continued to (ôr) __ignore__ him.
5. For a plural subject, use a (ûr) __plural__ verb.
6. Beneath the dark clouds a (ôr) __tornado__ formed!
7. Firefighters are used to handling an (ur) __emergency__
8. When will they be able to (ôr) __restore__ our electricity?
9. How are you going to (ûr) __furnish__ your apartment?

Page 14

Spelling: Words Beginning With sh and th

Directions: Write a definition for each word. Use a dictionary if you are unsure of the meaning of a word.

th

1. shallow: _____
2. thimble: _____
3. shear: _____
4. sheriff: _____
5. thermal: _____
6. throttle: _____
7. shingle: _____
8. shot put: _____
9. thrifty: _____
10. shoreline: _____
11. threaten: _____
12. thyroid: _____

Answers will vary.

Use two of the above words in sentences.

sh

14. _____

Page 15

Spelling: Words Beginning With ch

Directions: Write a definition for each word. Use a dictionary if you are unsure of the meaning of a word.

1. chimney: _____
2. china: _____
3. cheetah: _____
4. charity: _____
5. channel: _____
6. chandelier: _____
7. challenge _____

Answers will vary.

10. c_____
11. c_____
12. chisel: _____

Directions: Write the answers.

13. Which word is a tool for shaping wood?
__chisel__

14. Which word is a type of cheese?
__cheddar__

15. Which word is an animal?
__cheetah__

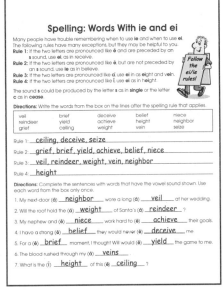

Page 16

Spelling: The Letter Q

In English words, the letter **q** is always followed by the letter **u**.

Examples:
question
square
quick

QUARTERS
QUALITY
QUIET

Directions: Write the correct spelling of each word in the blank. The first one has been done for you.

1. qill — __quill__
2. eqality — __equality__
3. qarrel — __quarrel__
4. qarter — __quarter__
5. qart — __quart__
6. qibble — __quibble__
7. qench — __quench__
8. qeen — __queen__
9. qip — __quip__
10. qiz — __quiz__
11. eqipment — __equipment__
12. qiet — __quiet__
13. qite — __quite__
14. eqity — __equity__
15. eqator — __equator__
16. eqivalent — __equivalent__
17. eqitable — __equitable__
18. eqestrian — __equestrian__
19. eqation — __equation__
20. qantity — __quantity__

EQUAL
ACQUIRE
EQUATOR

Page 17

Spelling: Words With kw, ks and gz

The consonant **q** is always followed by **u** in words and is pronounced **kw**. The letter **x** can be pronounced **ks** as in **mix**. When **x** is followed by a vowel, it is usually pronounced **gz** as in **example**.

Directions: Write the words from the box on the lines to match the sounds shown.

expense	exist	aquarium	acquire	request	exact
expand	exit	quality	excellent	quantity	quiz
exhibit	squirm	expression			

kw __squirm, aquarium, quality, acquire, request, quality, quiz__

ks __expense, expand, expression, excellent__

gz __exhibit, exist, exit, exact__

Directions: Complete the sentences with words that have the sound shown. Use words from the box only once.

1. We went to the zoo to see the fish (gz) __exhibit__
2. I didn't know its (gz) __exact__ location, so we followed the map.
3. The zoo plans to (kw) __acquire__ some sharks for its (kw) __aquarium__
4. Taking care of sharks is a big (ks) __expense__ but a number of people have asked the zoo to (ks) __expand__ its display of fish.
5. These people want a better (kw) __quality__ of fish, not a bigger (kw) __quantity__ of them.
6. I think the zoo already has an (ks) __excellent__ display.
7. Some of its rare fish no longer (gz) __exist__ in the ocean

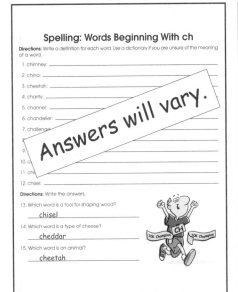

Page 18

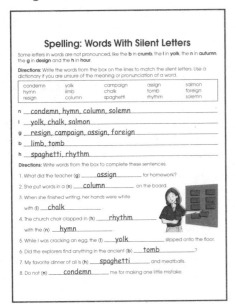

Spelling: Words With Silent Letters

Some letters in words are not pronounced, like the **b** in **crumb**, the **l** in **yolk**, the **n** in **autumn**, the **g** in **design** and the **h** in **hour**.

Directions: Write the words from the box on the lines to match the silent letters. Use a dictionary if you are unsure of the meaning or pronunciation of a word.

condemn	yolk	campaign	assign	salmon
hymn	limb	chalk	tomb	foreign
resign	column	spaghetti	rhythm	solemn

n   condemn, hymn, column, solemn

l   yolk, chalk, salmon

g   resign, campaign, assign, foreign

b   limb, tomb

h   spaghetti, rhythm

Directions: Write words from the box to complete these sentences.

1. What did the teacher (g) **assign** for homework?
2. She put words in a (n) **column** on the board.
3. When she finished writing, her hands were white with (l) **chalk**.
4. The church choir clapped in (h) **rhythm** with the (n) **hymn**.
5. While I was cracking an egg, the (l) **yolk** slipped onto the floor.
6. Did the explorers find anything in the ancient (b) **tomb**?
7. My favorite dinner of all is (h) **spaghetti** and meatballs.
8. Do not (n) **condemn** me for making one little mistake.

Page 19

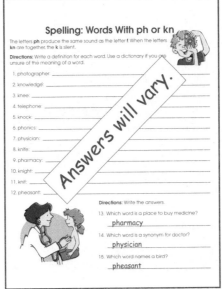

Spelling: Words With ph or kn

The letters **ph** produce the same sound as the letter **f**. When the letters **kn** are together, the **k** is silent.

Directions: Write a definition for each word. Use a dictionary if you are unsure of the meaning of a word.

1. photographer: ____
2. knowledge: ____
3. knee: ____
4. telephone: ____
5. knock: ____
6. phonics: ____
7. physician: ____
8. knife: ____
9. pharmacy: ____
10. knight: ____
11. knit: ____
12. pheasant: ____

Answers will vary.

Directions: Write the answers.

13. Which word is a place to buy medicine?
pharmacy
14. Which word is a synonym for doctor?
physician
15. Which word names a bird?
pheasant

Page 20

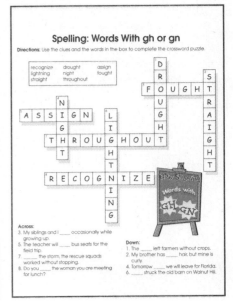

Spelling: Words With gh or gn

Directions: Use the clues and the words in the box to complete the crossword puzzle.

recognize	drought	assign
lightning	night	fought
straight	throughout	

(crossword with answers: DROUGHT, FOUGHT, STRAIGHT, ASSIGN, LIGHTNING, THROUGHOUT, RECOGNIZE, NIGHT)

Across:
3. My siblings and I ____ occasionally while growing up.
5. The teacher will ____ bus seats for the field trip.
7. ____ the storm, the rescue squads worked without stopping.
8. Do you ____ the woman you are meeting for lunch?

Down:
1. The ____ left farmers without crops.
2. My brother has ____ hair, but mine is curly.
4. Tomorrow ____ we will leave for Florida.
6. ____ struck the old barn on Walnut Hill.

Page 21

Prefixes

A **prefix** is a syllable added to the beginning of a word to change its meaning. The prefix **re** means "back" or "again," as in **return**. **Pre** means "before," as in **prepare**. **Dis** means "do the opposite," as in **disappear**. **In** and **im** both mean "not," as in **impossible**. (These two prefixes also have other meanings.) **Com** and **con** both mean "with," as in **companion** and **concert**. Use **im** and **com** with words that start with **p, b** or **m**. Use **in** and **con** with words that begin with a vowel or other consonants.

Directions: Match each word from the box to its definition.

disbelieve	recite	connotation	impolite	preview
impatient	distrust	configuration	prevision	incomplete
invisible	dislike	confederate	recover	compassion

1. share another's feelings **compassion**
2. not finished **incomplete**
3. another meaning **connotation**
4. become normal again **recover**
5. take away confidence **distrust**
6. look to the future **prevision**
7. arrangement of parts **configuration**
8. say from memory **recite**
9. ally **confederate**
10. hate **dislike**
11. look at **preview**
12. rude **impolite**
13. in a hurry **impatient**
14. doubt **disbelieve**
15. not seen **invisible**

Directions: Add the rest of the word to each prefix in these sentences. Use words from the box only once. Be sure to use the correct form of the word.

16. When he re **covered** from his cold, Jeff was im **patient** to get back to work.
17. Jonah stared at the ghostly figure with dis **belief** and dis **trust**.
18. I'd like to re **cite** that poem, but my memory of it is in **complete**.
19. She was very im **polite** during the movie pre **view**.

Page 22

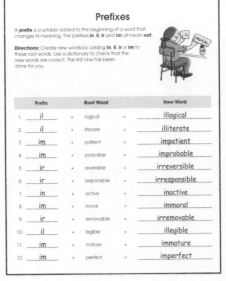

Prefixes

A **prefix** is a syllable added to the beginning of a word that changes its meaning. The prefixes **in, il, ir** and **im** all mean **not**.

Directions: Create new words by adding **in, il, ir** or **im** to these root words. Use a dictionary to check that the new words are correct. The first one has been done for you.

Prefix		Root Word		New Word
1. il	+	logical	=	illogical
2. il	+	literate	=	illiterate
3. im	+	patient	=	impatient
4. im	+	probable	=	improbable
5. ir	+	reversible	=	irreversible
6. ir	+	responsible	=	irresponsible
7. in	+	active	=	inactive
8. im	+	moral	=	immoral
9. ir	+	removable	=	irremovable
10. il	+	legible	=	illegible
11. im	+	mature	=	immature
12. im	+	perfect	=	imperfect

Page 23

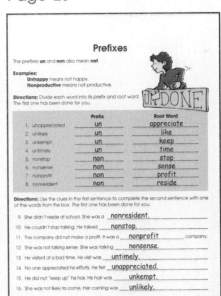

Prefixes

The prefixes **un** and **non** also mean **not**.

Examples:
   Unhappy means not happy.
   Nonproductive means not productive.

Directions: Divide each word into its prefix and root word. The first one has been done for you.

	Prefix	Root Word
1. unappreciated	un	appreciate
2. unlikely	un	like
3. unkempt	un	keep
4. untimely	un	time
5. nonstop	non	stop
6. nonsense	non	sense
7. nonprofit	non	profit
8. nonresident	non	reside

Directions: Use the clues in the first sentence to complete the second sentence with one of the words from the box. The first one has been done for you.

9. She didn't reside at school. She was a **nonresident.**
10. He couldn't stop talking. He talked **nonstop.**
11. The company did not make a profit. It was a **nonprofit** company.
12. She was not talking sense. She was talking **nonsense.**
13. He visited at a bad time. His visit was **untimely.**
14. No one appreciated his efforts. He felt **unappreciated.**
15. He did not "keep up" his hair. His hair was **unkempt.**
16. She was not likely to come. Her coming was **unlikely.**

Answer Key   **305**   Total Basic Skills Grade 6

Page 24

Prefixes

The prefixes **co, col, com, con** and **cor** mean "with" or "together." The prefixes **anti, contra** and **ob** mean "against."

Directions: Write each word's prefix and root word in the space provided.

Word	Prefix	Root Word
coexist	co	exist
concurrent	con	current
correlate	cor	relate
codependent	co	depend
antigravity	anti	gravity
contraband	contra	band

Directions: Use the words from the chart above to complete the sentences.

1. When airplanes fly very high and then quickly drop down, they cause an __antigravity__ affect.

2. Materials that are illegal are called __contraband__.

3. A dog and a cat can __coexist__ in the same house if they get along well.

4. Events that happen at the same time are __concurrent__.

5. When two people rely on each other, they are said to be __codependent__.

6. The textbook will __correlate__ with the teacher's lectures.

Page 25

Suffixes

A **suffix** is a syllable added to the end of a root word that changes its meaning.

When a word ends in silent **e**, keep the **e** before adding a suffix beginning with a consonant.

Example: amuse + ment = amusement

Exception: argue + ment = argument

When a word ends in silent **e**, drop the **e** before adding a suffix beginning with a vowel.

Example: amuse + ing = amusing

Exceptions: hoeing, shoeing, canoeing

Directions: Write **C** on the blank if the word in bold is spelled correctly. Draw an **X** in the blank if it is spelled incorrectly. The first one has been done for you.

C 1. She was a woman of many **achievements**.
C 2. He hated to hear their **arguments**.
X 3. Do you want to go **canoing**?
X 4. He kept **urgeing** her to eat more dessert.
C 5. She was not good at **deceiving** others.
C 6. He **rarely** skipped lunch.
X 7. Would you repeat that **announcment**?
C 8. Bicycle **safety** was very important to him.
X 9. Their constant **argueing** got on my nerves.
C 10. He found that **shoeing** horses was not easy.
C 11. The sun felt hot as they were **hoeing**.
X 12. She was so **relieveed** that she laughed.

Page 26

Suffixes: Words Ending in Y

If a word ends in a vowel and **y**, keep the **y** when you add a suffix.

Example:
bray + ed = brayed
bray + ing = braying

Exception: lay + ed = laid

If a word ends in a consonant and **y**, change the **y** to **i** when you add a suffix unless the suffix begins with **i**.

Example:
baby + ed = babied
baby + ing = babying

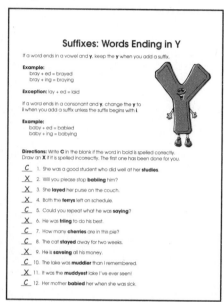

Directions: Write **C** in the blank if the word in bold is spelled correctly. Draw an **X** if it is spelled incorrectly. The first one has been done for you.

C 1. She was a good student who did well at her **studies**.
X 2. Will you please stop **babling** him?
X 3. She **layed** her purse on the couch.
X 4. Both the **ferrys** left on schedule.
C 5. Could you repeat what he was **saying**?
X 6. He was **trling** to do his best.
C 7. How many **cherries** are in this pie?
C 8. The cat **stayed** away for two weeks.
X 9. He is **savoing** all his money.
C 10. The lake was **muddier** than I remembered.
X 11. It was the **muddyest** lake I've ever seen!
C 12. Her mother **babied** her when she was sick.

Page 27

Suffixes: Doubling Final Consonants

If a one-syllable word ends in one vowel and consonant, double the last consonant when you add a suffix that begins with a vowel.

Examples: swim + ing = swimming   big + er = bigger

Directions: Add the suffixes shown to the root words, doubling the final consonants when appropriate. The first one has been done for you.

1. brim + ing = brimming
2. big + est = biggest
3. hop + ing = hopping
4. swim + er = swimmer
5. thin + er = thinner
6. spin + ing = spinning
7. smack + ing = smacking
8. sink + ing = sinking
9. win + er = winner
10. thin + est = thinnest
11. slim + er = slimmer
12. slim + ing = slimming
13. thread + ing = threading
14. thread + er = threader
15. win + ing = winning
16. sing + ing = singing
17. stop + ing = stopping
18. thrill + ing = thrilling
19. drop + ed = dropped
20. mop + ing = mopping

Page 28

Suffixes

A **suffix** is a syllable added to the end of a word that changes its meaning. Some suffixes change nouns into adjectives.

Examples: fool — **foolish**   nation — **national**

Other suffixes change adjectives into adverbs.

Examples: foolish — **foolishly**   national — **nationally**

Directions: Match the root words with words from the box.

personal	stylish	obviously	professional
typical	childish	practical	medical
permanently	ticklish	additional	
gradually	physical	musical	

1. tickle __ticklish__
2. critic __critical__
3. add __additional__
4. person __personal__
5. child __childish__
6. grade __gradually__
7. practice __practical__
8. physician __physical__
9. permanent __permanently__
10. medic __medical__
11. type __typical__
12. music __musical__
13. style __stylish__
14. obvious __obviously__
15. profess __professional__

Directions: Circle the word or words in each sentence that are a synonym for a word from the box. Write the word from the box on the line. The first one has been done for you.

16. Knowing how to cook is a (useful) skill. __practical__
17. The lake (slowly) warmed up. __gradually__
18. (Clearly) I should have stayed on the path. __Obviously__
19. That is a (fashionable) outfit. __stylish__
20. Wanting your own way all the time is (for little kids). __childish__
21. Getting lost is (common) for me. __typical__
22. My grades are (a private matter). __personal__

Page 29

Suffixes: "ion," "tion" and "ation"

The suffixes **ion, tion** and **ation** change verbs into nouns.

Examples: imitate + **ion** = imitation   combine + **ation** = combination

Directions: Match each word from the box with its definition.

celebration	solution	imitation	exploration	selection
reflection	conversation	population	invitation	suggestion
combination	decoration	appreciation	definition	transportation

1. a copy __imitation__
2. talking __conversation__
3. a request __invitation__
4. the meaning __definition__
5. a search __exploration__
6. mirror image __reflection__
7. cars, trucks __transportation__
8. ornament __decoration__
9. choice __selection__
10. a party __celebration__
11. the answer __solution__
12. people __population__
13. a joining __combination__
14. new idea __suggestion__
15. thankfulness __appreciation__

Directions: Write the correct forms of the words in the sentences. The first one has been done for you.

16. transport   How are we __transporting__ our project to school?
Did anyone arrange __transportation__?

17. decorate   Today, we are __decorating__ the classroom.
We brought the __decorations__ from home.

18. solve   Have you __solved__ the problem yet?
We need a __solution__ by the end of the day.

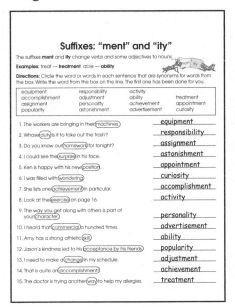

Page 30

Suffixes: "ment" and "ity"

The suffixes **ment** and **ity** change verbs and some adjectives to nouns.

Examples: treat — **treatment**   able — **ability**

Directions: Circle the word or words in each sentence that are synonyms for words from the box. Write the word from the box on the line. The first one has been done for you.

equipment	responsibility	activity	
accomplishment	adjustment	ability	treatment
assignment	personality	achievement	appointment
popularity	astonishment	advertisement	curiosity

1. The workers are bringing in their (machines). — **equipment**
2. Whose (duty) is it to take out the trash? — **responsibility**
3. Do you know our (homework) for tonight? — **assignment**
4. I could see the (surprise) in his face. — **astonishment**
5. Ken is happy with his new (position). — **appointment**
6. I was filled with (wondering). — **curiosity**
7. She lists one (achievement) in particular. — **accomplishment**
8. Look at the (exercise) on page 16. — **activity**
9. The way you get along with others is part of your (character). — **personality**
10. I heard that (commercial) a hundred times. — **advertisement**
11. Amy has a strong athletic (skill). — **ability**
12. Jason's kindness led to his (acceptance by his friends). — **popularity**
13. I need to make a (change) in my schedule. — **adjustment**
14. That is quite an (accomplishment). — **achievement**
15. The doctor is trying another (way) to help my allergies. — **treatment**

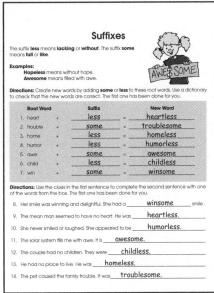

Page 31

Suffixes

The suffix **less** means **lacking** or **without**. The suffix **some** means **full** or **like**.

Examples:
Hopeless means without hope.
Awesome means filled with awe.

Directions: Create new words by adding **some** or **less** to these root words. Use a dictionary to check that the new words are correct. The first one has been done for you.

	Root Word		Suffix		New Word
1.	heart	+	less	=	heartless
2.	trouble	+	some	=	troublesome
3.	home	+	less	=	homeless
4.	humor	+	less	=	humorless
5.	awe	+	some	=	awesome
6.	child	+	less	=	childless
7.	win	+	some	=	winsome

Directions: Use the clues in the first sentence to complete the second sentence with one of the words from the box. The first one has been done for you.

8. Her smile was winning and delightful. She had a **winsome** smile.
9. The mean man seemed to have no heart. He was **heartless.**
10. She never smiled or laughed. She appeared to be **humorless.**
11. The solar system fills me with awe. It is **awesome.**
12. The couple had no children. They were **childless.**
13. He had no place to live. He was **homeless.**
14. The pet caused the family trouble. It was **troublesome.**

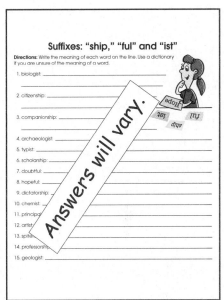

Page 32

Suffixes: "ship," "ful" and "ist"

Directions: Write the meaning of each word on the line. Use a dictionary if you are unsure of the meaning of a word.

1. biologist: _____
2. citizenship: _____
3. companionship: _____
4. archaeologist: _____
5. typist: _____
6. scholarship: _____
7. doubtful: _____
8. hopeful: _____
9. dictatorship: _____
10. chemist: _____
11. principal: _____
12. artist: _____
13. spite: _____
14. professorship: _____
15. geologist: _____

Answers will vary.

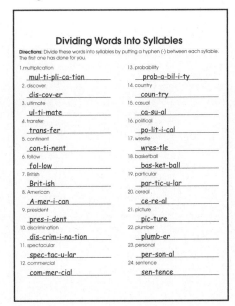

Page 33

Dividing Words Into Syllables

Directions: Divide these words into syllables by putting a hyphen (-) between each syllable. The first one has done for you.

1. multiplication — **mul-ti-pli-ca-tion**
2. discover — **dis-cov-er**
3. ultimate — **ul-ti-mate**
4. transfer — **trans-fer**
5. continent — **con-ti-nent**
6. follow — **fol-low**
7. British — **Brit-ish**
8. American — **A-mer-i-can**
9. president — **pres-i-dent**
10. discrimination — **dis-crim-i-na-tion**
11. spectacular — **spec-tac-u-lar**
12. commercial — **com-mer-cial**
13. probability — **prob-a-bil-i-ty**
14. country — **coun-try**
15. casual — **ca-su-al**
16. political — **po-lit-i-cal**
17. wrestle — **wres-tle**
18. basketball — **bas-ket-ball**
19. particular — **par-tic-u-lar**
20. cereal — **ce-re-al**
21. picture — **pic-ture**
22. plumber — **plumb-er**
23. personal — **per-son-al**
24. sentence — **sen-tence**

Page 34

Synonyms

A **synonym** is a word that means the same or nearly the same as another word. **Example:** mean and cruel.

Directions: Circle the word or group of words in each sentence that is a synonym for a word in the box. Write the synonym from the box on the line. The first one has been done for you.

florist	courtesy	research	emergency	flourish
plural	observe	furnish	tornado	source
ignored	survey	normally	coarse	restore

1. The children seemed to (thrive) in their new school. — **flourish**
2. Her (politeness) made me feel welcome. — **courtesy**
3. The principal came to (watch) our class. — **observe**
4. Are you going to (fix up) that old house? — **restore**
5. Six weeks after the (disaster) the neighborhood looked as it usually did. — **emergency**
6. What was the (origin) of that rumor? — **source**
7. The (cyclone) destroyed two houses. — **tornado**
8. She (neglected) her homework. — **ignored**
9. The material had a (rough) feel to it. — **coarse**
10. Did you fill out the (questionnaire) yet? — **survey**

Directions: Select three words from the box below. Write a sentence for each word that shows you understand the meaning of the word

plural	flourish	source	restore	observe	furnish	research

Answers will vary.

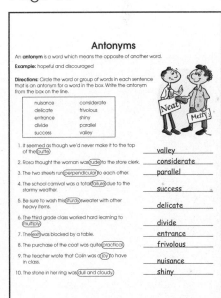

Page 35

Antonyms

An **antonym** is a word which means the opposite of another word.

Example: hopeful and discouraged

Directions: Circle the word or group of words in each sentence that is an antonym for a word in the box. Write the antonym from the box on the line.

nuisance	considerate
delicate	frivolous
entrance	shiny
divide	parallel
success	valley

1. It seemed as though we'd never make it to the top of the (butte). — **valley**
2. Rosa thought the woman was (rude) to the store clerk. — **considerate**
3. The two streets run (perpendicular) to each other. — **parallel**
4. The school carnival was a total (failure) due to the stormy weather. — **success**
5. Be sure to wash this (sturdy) sweater with other heavy items. — **delicate**
6. The third grade class worked hard learning to (multiply). — **divide**
7. The (exit) was blocked by a table. — **entrance**
8. The purchase of the coat was quite (practical). — **frivolous**
9. The teacher wrote that Colin was a (joy) to have in class. — **nuisance**
10. The stone in her ring was (dull and cloudy). — **shiny**

Page 36

Reading Skills: Classifying

Classifying is placing similar things into categories.

Example: January, May and **October** can be classified as months.

Directions: Write a category name for each group of words.

1. accordion	clarinet	trumpet	musical instruments
2. wasp	bumblebee	mosquito	insects
3. antique	elderly	prehistoric	words for "old"
4. chemist	astronomer	geologist	scientists
5. nest	cocoon	burrow	animal homes

Directions: In each row, draw an **X** through the word that does not belong. Then write a sentence telling why it does not belong.

1. encyclopedia   atlas   no**X**el   dictionary
A novel is not a reference book.

2. bass   ot**X**er   tuna   trout
An otter is not a fish.

3. sister   grandmother   niece   un**X**le
An uncle is not a female relative.

4. b**X**rk   beech   dogwood   spruce
Bark is not a type of tree.

5. pebble   gravel   boulder   ce**X**ent
Cement is not a form of rock.

6. spaniel   Sia**X**ese   collie   Doberman
A Siamese is not a type of dog.

Page 37

Reading Skills: Classifying

Directions: In each row, draw an **X** through the word that does not belong. Then write a word that belongs.

Sample answers:

1. monkey		**X**phant	d**X**g			giraffe
2. daisies	roses	violets	fe**X**ts	pansies		tulips
3. paper	pe**X**r	pencil	eraser	stapler		pen
4. sister	cousin	father	aunt	fri**X**nd		mother
5. hand	mouth	sh**X**rt	foot	elbow		leg
6. shy	c**X**t	happy	angry	sad		grumpy
7. puppy	d**X**g	kitten	cub	lamb		chick
8. red	blue	c**X**lor	yellow	purple		green
9. Earth	Jupiter	Saturn	Pluto	S**X**n		Mars
10. s**X**k	bed	desk	dresser	lamp		chair

Directions: Name each category above.

1. African animals
2. flowers
3. school supplies
4. relatives
5. body parts
6. feelings
7. baby animals
8. colors
9. planets
10. bedroom furniture

Page 38

Writing Analogies

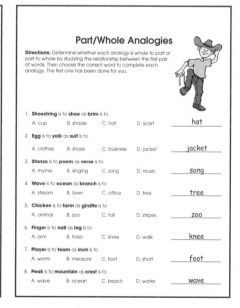

Once you have determined the relationship between the words in the first pair, the next step is to find a similar relationship between another pair of words.

Examples:
Scissors is to **cut** as **broom** is to **sweep**.
Black is to **white** as **up** is to **down**.

Scissors cut. Brooms sweep. The first analogy shows the **purpose** of scissors and brooms. In the second example, up and down are **antonyms**, as are black and white.

Directions: Choose the correct word to complete each analogy. The first one has been done for you.

1. **Sky** is to **blue** as **grass** is to
A. earth   B. green   C. lawn   D. yard   — green

2. **Snow** is to **winter** as **rain** is to
A. umbrella   B. wet   C. slicker   D. spring   — spring

3. **Sun** is to **day** as **moon** is to
A. dark   B. night   C. stars   D. blackness   — night

4. **5** is to **10** as **15** is to
A. 50   B. 25   C. 30   D. 40   — 30

5. **Collie** is to **dog** as **Siamese** is to
A. pet   B. kitten   C. baby   D. cat   — cat

6. **Letter** is to **word** as **note** is to
A. tuba   B. music   C. instruments   D. singer   — music

7. **100** is to **10** as **1,000** is to
A. 10   B. 200   C. 100   D. 10,000   — 100

8. **Back** is to **rear** as **pit** is to
A. peach   B. hole   C. dark   D. punishment   — hole

Page 39

Analogies of Purpose

Directions: Choose the correct word to complete each analogy of purpose. The first one has been done for you.

1. **Knife** is to **cut** as **copy machine** is to
A. duplicate   B. paper   C. copies   D. office   — duplicate

2. **Bicycle** is to **ride** as **glass** is to
A. dishes   B. dinner   C. drink   D. break   — drink

3. **Hat** is to **cover** as **eraser** is to
A. chalkboard   B. pencil   C. mistake   D. erase   — erase

4. **Mystery** is to **clue** as **door** is to
A. house   B. key   C. window   D. open   — key

5. **Television** is to **see** as **CD** is to
A. sound   B. hear   C. play   D. dance   — hear

6. **Clock** is to **time** as **ruler** is to
A. height   B. length   C. measure   D. inches   — measure

7. **Fry** is to **pan** as **bake** is to
A. cookies   B. dinner   C. oven   D. baker   — oven

8. **Bowl** is to **fruit** as **wrapper** is to
A. present   B. candy   C. paper   D. ribbon   — candy

Page 40

Antonym Analogies

Directions: Write antonyms for these words.

Answers will vary but may include:

1. run:	walk	15. awake:	asleep
2. start:	stop	16. begin:	end
3. laugh:	cry	17. increase:	decrease
4. dependent:	independent	18. reverse:	forward
5. young:	old	19. enlarge:	shrink
6. North:	South	20. East:	West
7. sink:	float	21. rural:	urban
8. success:	failure	22. amateur:	professional
9. combine:	separate	23. patient:	impatient
10. laugh:	cry	24. rich:	poor
11. polluted:	clean	25. empty:	full
12. leader:	follower	26. fancy:	plain
13. fascinate:	bore	27. introduction:	conclusion
14. man:	woman	28. modern:	old-fashion

Directions: Write two antonym analogies of your own.

29.

30.   Answers will vary.

Page 41

Part/Whole Analogies

Directions: Determine whether each analogy is whole to part or part to whole by studying the relationship between the first pair of words. Then choose the correct word to complete each analogy. The first one has been done for you.

1. **Shoestring** is to **shoe** as **brim** is to
A. cup   B. shade   C. hat   D. scarf   — hat

2. **Egg** is to **yolk** as **suit** is to
A. clothes   B. shoes   C. business   D. jacket   — jacket

3. **Stanza** is to **poem** as **verse** is to
A. rhyme   B. singing   C. song   D. music   — song

4. **Wave** is to **ocean** as **branch** is to
A. stream   B. lawn   C. office   D. tree   — tree

5. **Chicken** is to **farm** as **giraffe** is to
A. animal   B. zoo   C. tall   D. stripes   — zoo

6. **Finger** is to **nail** as **leg** is to
A. arm   B. torso   C. knee   D. walk   — knee

7. **Player** is to **team** as **inch** is to
A. worm   B. measure   C. foot   D. short   — foot

8. **Peak** is to **mountain** as **crest** is to
A. wave   B. ocean   C. beach   D. water   — wave

GRADE 6

Page 42

Action/Object Analogies

Directions: Determine whether each analogy is action/object or object/action by studying the relationship between the first pair of words. Then choose the correct word to complete each analogy. The first one has been done for you.

1. **Mow** is to **grass** as **shear** is to — <u>sheep</u>
   A. cut   B. fleece   C. sheep   D. barber

2. **Rod** is to **fishing** as **gun** is to — <u>hunting</u>
   A. police   B. crime   C. shoot   D. hunting

3. **Ship** is to **captain** as **airplane** is to — <u>pilot</u>
   A. fly   B. airport   C. pilot   D. passenger

4. **Car** is to **mechanic** as **body** is to — <u>doctor</u>
   A. patient   B. doctor   C. torso   D. hospital

5. **Cheat** is to **exam** as **swindle** is to — <u>business</u>
   A. criminal   B. business   C. crook   D. crime

6. **Actor** is to **stage** as **surgeon** is to — <u>operating room</u>
   A. patient   B. hospital   C. operating room   D. knife

7. **Ball** is to **throw** as **knife** is to — <u>cut</u>
   A. cut   B. spoon   C. dinner   D. silverware

8. **Lawyer** is to **trial** as **surgeon** is to — <u>operation</u>
   A. patient   B. hospital   C. operation   D. operating room

Page 43

Analogies of Association

Directions: Choose the correct word to complete each analogy. The first one has been done for you.

1. **Flowers** are to **spring** as **leaves** are to — <u>fall</u>
   A. rakes   B. trees   C. fall   D. green

2. **Ham** is to **eggs** as **butter** is to — <u>toast</u>
   A. fat   B. toast   C. breakfast   D. spread

3. **Bat** is to **swing** as **ball** is to — <u>throw</u>
   A. throw   B. dance   C. base   D. soft

4. **Chicken** is to **egg** as **cow** is to — <u>milk</u>
   A. barn   B. calf   C. milk   D. beef

5. **Bed** is to **sleep** as **chair** is to — <u>sit</u>
   A. sit   B. couch   C. relax   D. table

6. **Cube** is to **square** as **sphere** is to — <u>circle</u>
   A. circle   B. triangle   C. hemisphere   D. spear

7. **Kindness** is to **friend** as **cruelty** is to — <u>enemy</u>
   A. meanness   B. enemy   C. war   D. unkindness

8. **Pumpkin** is to **pie** as **chocolate** is to — <u>cake</u>
   A. cake   B. dark   C. taste   D. dessert

Page 44

Object/Location Analogies

Directions: Write a location word for each object. Answers will vary but may include:

1. shirt:	closet		15. dress:		dress shop
2. milk:	carton		16. ice cream:		freezer
3. vase:	table		17. table:		dining room
4. screwdriver:	toolbox		18. medicine:		pharmacy
5. cow:	barn		19. dog:		doghouse
6. chalkboard:	classroom		20. basketball:		hoop
7. shower:	bathroom		21. bed:		bedroom
8. cucumbers:	garden		22. roses:		vase
9. silverware:	drawer		23. dishwasher:		kitchen
10. car:	garage		24. toys:		toy box
11. pages:	book		25. cookies:		cookie jar
12. bees:	beehive		26. bird:		birdhouse
13. money:	bank		27. seashells:		beach
14. salt water:	sea		28. asteroids:		sky

Page 45

Cause/Effect Analogies

Directions: Determine whether the analogy is cause/effect or effect/cause by studying the relationship between the first pair of words. Then choose the correct word to complete each analogy. The first one has been done for you.

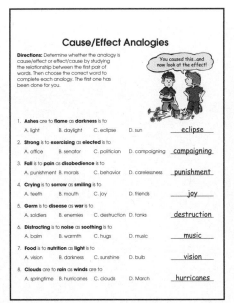

You caused this...and now look at the effect!

1. **Ashes** are to **flame** as **darkness** is to — <u>eclipse</u>
   A. light   B. daylight   C. eclipse   D. sun

2. **Strong** is to **exercising** as **elected** is to — <u>campaigning</u>
   A. office   B. senator   C. politician   D. campaigning

3. **Fall** is to **pain** as **disobedience** is to — <u>punishment</u>
   A. punishment   B. morals   C. behavior   D. carelessness

4. **Crying** is to **sorrow** as **smiling** is to — <u>joy</u>
   A. teeth   B. mouth   C. joy   D. friends

5. **Germ** is to **disease** as **war** is to — <u>destruction</u>
   A. soldiers   B. enemies   C. destruction   D. tanks

6. **Distracting** is to **noise** as **soothing** is to — <u>music</u>
   A. balm   B. warmth   C. hugs   D. music

7. **Food** is to **nutrition** as **light** is to — <u>vision</u>
   A. vision   B. darkness   C. sunshine   D. bulb

8. **Clouds** are to **rain** as **winds** are to — <u>hurricanes</u>
   A. springtime   B. hurricanes   C. clouds   D. March

Page 46

Synonym Analogies

Directions: Write synonyms for these words. Answers will vary but may include:

1. miniature:	tiny		15. gigantic:		huge
2. wind:	gale		16. rain:		shower
3. picture:	photo		17. cabinet:		cupboard
4. quiet:	silent		18. loud:		noisy
5. run:	jog		19. leap:		jump
6. cloth:	material		20. jeans:		pants
7. mean:	nasty		21. kind:		nice
8. cup:	mug		22. dish:		plate
9. sweet:	tasty		23. feline:		cat
10. difficult:	hard		24. simple:		easy
11. obey:	do		25. beautiful:		pretty
12. plenty:	lots		26. scorch:		burn
13. scent:	smell		27. story:		tale
14. sudden:	quick		28. thaw:		unfreeze

Directions: Write two synonym analogies of your own.

29. _____

30. *Answers will vary.*

Page 47

Reading Skills: Fact or Opinion?

A **fact** is information that can be proved. An **opinion** is information that tells how someone feels or what he/she thinks about something.

Directions: For each sentence, write **F** for fact or **O** for opinion. The first one has been done for you.

F 1. Each of the countries in South America has its own capital.

O 2. All South Americans are good swimmers.

O 3. People like the climate in Peru better than in Brazil.

F 4. The continent of South America is almost completely surrounded by water.

F 5. The only connection with another continent is a narrow strip of land, called the Isthmus of Panama, which links it to North America.

F 6. The Andes Mountains run all the way down the western edge of the continent.

F 7. The Andes are the longest continuous mountain barrier in the world.

O 8. The Andes are the most beautiful mountain range.

F 9. The Amazon River is the second longest river in the world—about 4,000 miles long.

F 10. Half of the people in South America are Brazilians.

O 11. Life in Brazil is better than life in other South American countries.

O 12. Brazil is the best place for South Americans to live.

F 13. Cape Horn is at the southern tip of South America.

F 14. The largest land animal in South America is the tapir, which reaches a length of 6 to 8 feet.

Page 48

Reading Skills: Fact or Opinion?

Directions: Read the paragraphs below. For each numbered sentence, write **F** for fact or **O** for opinion. Write the reason for your answer. The first one has been done for you.

(1) The two greatest poems in the history of the world are the *Iliad* and the *Odyssey*. (2) The *Iliad* is the story of the Trojan War; the *Odyssey* tells about the wanderings of the Greek hero Ulysses after the war. (3) These poems are so long that they each fill an entire book.

(4) The author of the poems, according to Greek legend, was a blind poet named Homer. (5) Almost nothing is known about Homer. (6) This indicates to me that it is possible that Homer never existed. (7) Maybe Homer existed but didn't write the *Iliad* and the *Odyssey*.

(8) Whether or not there was a Homer does not really matter. We have these wonderful poems, written more than 2,500 years after they were written.

Sample answers:

1. **O** Reason: This cannot be proven. People have different opinions about which are the greatest poems.
2. **F** Reason: explains what the poems are about
3. **F** Reason: tells how long the poems are
4. **F** Reason: tells a fact about a Greek legend
5. **F** Reason: tells that not much is known about Homer
6. **O** Reason: not everyone thinks Homer did not exist
7. **O** Reason: some people may believe this and some may not
8. **O** Reason: some people may not agree with this

Page 49

Reading Skills: Cause and Effect

A **cause** is the reason something happens. The **effect** is what happens as the result of the cause.

Directions: Read the paragraphs below. For each numbered sentence, circle the cause or causes and underline the effect or effects. The first one has been done for you.

(1) All living things in the ocean are endangered by (humans polluting the water.) Pollution occurs in several ways. One way is the dumping of certain waste materials, such as garbage and sewage, into the ocean. (2) (The decaying bacteria that feed on the garbage use up much of the oxygen in the surrounding water) so other creatures in the area often don't get enough.

Other substances, such as radioactive waste material, can also cause pollution. These materials are often placed in water in securely sealed containers. (3) But (after years of being exposed to the ocean water) the containers may begin to leak.

Oil is another major source of concern. (4) Oil is spilled into the ocean when (tankers run aground and sink or when oil wells in the ocean cannot be capped.) (5) The (oil covers the gills of fish) and causes them to smother. (6) (Diving birds get the oil on their wings) and are unable to fly. (7) (When they clean themselves,) they are often poisoned by the oil.

Rivers also can contribute to the pollution of oceans. Many rivers receive the runoff water from farmlands. (8) (Fertilizers used on the farms may be carried to the ocean,) where they cause a great increase in the amount of certain plants. Too much of some plants can actually be poisonous to fish.

Worse yet are the pesticides carried to the ocean. These chemicals slowly build up in shellfish and other small animals. These animals then pass the pesticides on to the larger animals that feed on them. (9) (The buildup of these chemicals in the animals) can make them ill or cause their babies to be born dead or deformed.

Page 50

Reading Skills: Cause and Effect

Directions: Read the following cause-and-effect statements. If you think the cause and effect are properly related, write **True**. If not, explain why not. The first one has been done for you.

1. The best way to make it rain is to wash your car.
   It does not rain every time you wash your car.

2. Getting a haircut really improved Randy's grades.
   Getting your hair cut doesn't improve your grades.

3. Michael got an "A" in geometry because he spent a lot of time studying.
   True

4. Yesterday I broke a mirror, and today I slammed my thumb in the door.
   You don't slam your thumb in a door because you break a mirror.

5. Helen isn't allowed to go to the dance tonight because she broke her curfew last weekend.
   True

6. Emily drank a big glass of orange juice and her headache went away.
   Drinking orange juice doesn't cure a headache.

7. The Johnsons had their tree cut down because it had Dutch elm disease.
   True

8. We can't grow vegetables in our backyard because the rabbits keep eating them.
   True

Page 51

Reading Skills: Personification

When an author gives an object or animal human characteristics, it is called **personification**.

Example: The dragon quickly thought out its next move in the attack on the village.

Thought is a human process and not associated with mythical creatures, therefore; the dragon is personified in that sentence.

Directions: In the following sentences, underline the personification.

1. The cave's gaping mouth led to internal passageways.
2. The tractor sprang to life with a turn of the key.
3. The lights blinked twice and then died.
4. Crops struggled to survive in the blistering heat, hoping for rainfall.
5. The engine of the car coughed and sputtered as if it wanted to breathe but couldn't.
6. The arrow flew through the air, eyeing its target.
7. Snowmen smile from the safety of their yards.
8. Four-year-old Stephanie's doll sipped tea delicately.

Directions: Write a sentence that personifies the following objects.

1. flower
2. stuffed animal   Answers will vary.
3. car

Page 52

Reading Skills: Symbolism

Symbolism is the use of something to stand for (symbolize) something else.
Example:
The elderly woman held the pearl necklace in her wrinkled hand and thought back on her life. Many years had gone by since her husband had given her the necklace, as many years as there were pearls. Some of the pearls, she noticed, were darker than others, just as some years in her life had been darker than other years.

The pearl necklace symbolizes the life of the elderly woman. Each pearl stands for a year in her life, and the necklace represents the many years that have passed.

Directions: Writ **Sample answers:** ed in the paragraph on the lines below.

The refugees boarded the small ship with high hopes. They had to believe that their destiny was to find the New World and seek shelter there. A few dared to dream of the riches to be found. For them, the boat itself looked like a treasure chest waiting to be discovered.

The boat symbolizes a treasure chest as something that holds riches and excitement for a great future.

For 12-year-old Sam, the basketball court was the best place to be. In Sam's neighborhood, crime ran rampant, and it was the one safe place for kids like Sam to play. Sam spent most nights at the court, practicing lay-ups, jump shots and three-point shots. Sam worked hard because for him it wasn't just a sport, it was a golden key.

Basketball symbolizes a golden key, because if Sam becomes good enough at it, it could be the "key" to getting him into a good school and giving him a good future.

Page 53

Similes and Metaphors

A **simile** compares two unlike things using the word **like** or **as**.

Example: The fog was **like** a blanket around us. The fog was **as** thick **as** a blanket.

A **metaphor** compares two unlike things without using the word **like** or **as**.

Example: The fog was a blanket around us.

"The fog was thick." is not a simile or a metaphor. **Thick** is an adjective. Similes and metaphors compare two unlike things that are both nouns.

Directions: Underline the two things being compared in each sentence. Then write **S** for simile or **M** for metaphor on the lines.

M 1. The florist's shop was a summer garden.
S 2. The towels were as rough as sandpaper.
M 3. The survey was a fountain of information.
S 4. Her courtesy was as welcome as a cool breeze on a hot day.
S 5. The room was like a furnace.

Directions: Use similes to complete these sentences.

6. The tornado was as dark as
7. His voice was like
8. The emergency was as unexpected as
9. The kittens were like

Directions: Use metaphors to complete the

10. To me, research was
11. The flourishing plants were
12. My observation at the hospital was

Answers will vary.

Page 54

Vocabulary Building: Similes

A **simile** is a figure of speech comparing two things using **like** or **as**.

Example: The child was as quiet as a mouse.

Directions: Read the following paragraph. Underline the similes.

The kittens were born on a morning as cold as ice. Although it was late spring, the weather hadn't quite warmed up. There were five kittens in the litter, each quite different from its siblings. The oldest was black as deepest night. There was a calico that looked like Grandma's old quilt. One was as orange as a fall pumpkin, and another was orange and white. The runt was a black and gray tiger. She was as little as a baseball and as quick as lightning to fight for food. The kittens will soon become accepted by the other animals as members of the farm.

Directions: Using the following words, create similes of your own.

Example: piano—The piano keys tinkled like a light rain on a tin roof.

1. fire The fire was as hot as a furnace.
2. thunderstorm The thunderstorm was like an angry old man.
3. ocean The ocean was as blue as the sky.
4. night The night was as black as pitch.
5. rainforest The rainforest was like a breath of fresh air.
6. giraffe The giraffe is as tall as our house!

Sample answers:

Page 55

Vocabulary Building: Metaphors

A **metaphor** is a figure of speech that directly compares one thing with another.

Example: As it set, the sun was a glowing orange ball of fire.

The sun is being compared to a glowing orange ball of fire.

<u>sun</u>   <u>glowing orange ball of fire</u>

Directions: Underline the metaphor in each sentence. Then write the two things that are being compared on the lines.

1. The ocean, a swirling mass of anger, released its fury on the shore.

   <u>ocean</u>   <u>swirling mass of anger</u>

2. He was a top spinning out of control.

   <u>He</u>   <u>top spinning out of control</u>

3. The heat covered the crowd, a blanket smothering them all.

   <u>heat</u>   <u>blanket smothering them all</u>

4. I fed my dog a steak, and it was a banquet for her senses.

   <u>steak</u>   <u>banquet for her senses</u>

5. The flowers in the garden were a stained glass window.

   <u>flowers</u>   <u>stained glass window</u>

Page 56

Reading Skills: Generalizations

A **generalization** is a statement or rule that applies to many situations or examples.

Example: All children get into trouble at one time or another.

Directions: Read each paragraph, then circle the generalization that best describes the information given.

Although many people think of reptiles as slimy, snakes and other reptiles are covered with scales that are dry to the touch. Scales are outgrowths of the animal's skin. Although in some species they are nearly invisible, in most they form a tile-like covering. The turtle's shell is made up of hardened scales that are fused together. The crocodile has a tough but more flexible covering.

(Every reptile has scales.)

The scales of all reptiles are alike.

There are many different kinds of scales.

The reptile's scales help to protect it from its enemies and conserve moisture in its body. Some kinds of lizards have fan-shaped scales that they can raise up to scare away other animals. The scales also can be used to court a mate. A reptile called a gecko can hang from a ceiling because of specialized scales on its feet. Some desert lizards have other kinds of scales on their feet that allow them to run over the loose sand.

(Scales have many functions.)

Scales scare away other animals.

Scales help reptiles adapt to their environments.

A snake will periodically shed its skin, leaving behind a thin impression of its body—scales and all. A lizard sheds its skin too, but it tears off in smaller pieces rather than in one big piece. Before a snake begins this process, which is called molting, its eyes cloud over. The snake will go into hiding until they clear. When it comes out again, it brushes against rough surfaces to pull off the old skin.

Snakes go into hiding before they molt.

(Reptiles periodically shed their skin.)

A lizard's skin molts in smaller pieces.

Page 57

Reading Skills: Generalizations

Directions: Identify which statements below are generalizations and which are specific. Write G for generalization and S for specific.

- G 1. We want to have lots of good food for the party.
- S 2. Jenna gave me three pink shirts and two pairs of jeans.
- G 3. Americans are generous and friendly.
- S 4. There are ten more female teachers than male teachers at our school.
- S 5. She wants me to buy watermelon at the grocery store.
- G 6. She will never believe anything I say.
- S 7. I got poison ivy because I didn't watch out for the foliage on our hike.
- G 8. My mom is the best mom in the world.
- S 9. I get depressed every time the weather turns bad.
- S 10. The team is so good because they work out and practice every day.
- G 11. Cats are so bad-tempered.
- S 12. My dog has a good temperment because he's had lots of training.
- G 13. Our football team is the best this county has ever seen.
- S 14. I love the feel of rain on my skin, because it's cool.
- G 15. That classroom is always out of control.

Page 58

Reading Skills: Skimming and Scanning

Skimming is reading quickly to get a general idea of what a reading selection is about. When skimming, look for headings and key words to give you an overall idea of what you are reading.

Scanning is looking for certain words to find facts or answer questions. When scanning, r or think of questions first.

Directions: Scan the paragraphs below to find the answers to the questions. Then look for specific words that will help you locate the answers. For example, in the second question, scan for the word **smallest**.

There are many different units to measure time. Probably the smallest unit that you use is the second, and the longest is the year. While 100 years seems like a very long time to us, in the history of the Earth, it is a smaller amount of time than one second is in a person's entire lifetime. To describe the history of the Earth, scientists use geologic time. Even a million years is a fairly short period in geologic time. Much of the history of our Earth can only be speculated by scientists before it was written down. Some scientists believe that our planet is about 4,600 million years old. Since a thousand million is a billion, the Earth is believed to be 4.6 billion years old.

1. What kind of time is used to describe the history of the Earth?

   geologic time

2. For the average person, what is the smallest unit of time used?

   the second

3. In millions of years, how old do some scientists believe the Earth is?

   4,600 million years

4. How would you express that in billions of years?

   4.6 billion years

Page 59

The Author's Purpose

Authors write to entertain, inform or persuade. To entertain means to hold the attention of or to amuse someone. A fiction book about outer space entertains its reader, as does a joke book.

To inform means to give factual information. A cookbook informs the reader of new recipes. A newspaper tells what is happening in the world.

To persuade people means to convince them. Newspaper editorial writers try to persuade readers to accept their opinions. Doctors write health columns to persuade readers to eat nutritious foods.

Directions: Read each of the passages below. Tell whether they entertain, inform or persuade. (They may do more than one.) Give the reasons why.

George Washington was born... a brick house on the Potomac River in Virginia on Feb. 11, 1732. When he was 11... his half-brother, Lawrence, at Mount Vernon.   *Answers may include:*

Author's Purpose: Inform

Reason: The passage contains only facts about George Washington.

When George Washington was a child, he always measured and counted things. Maybe that is why he became a surveyor when he grew up. Surveyors like to measure and count things, too.

Author's Purpose: Persuade and inform

Reason: The passage gives the author's opinion, as well as some facts.

George Washington was the best president America has ever had. He led a new nation to independence. He made all the states feel as if they were part of the United States. All presidents should be as involved with the country as George Washington was.

Author's Purpose: Persuade

Reason: Most of the information in this passage is opinion. The author tries to persuade the reader to agree with his point of view.

Page 60

Llamas

Directions: Read each paragraph. Tell whether it informs, entertains or persuades. One paragraph does more than one. Then write your reason on the line below.

A llama (LAH'MAH) is a South American animal that is related to the camel. It is raised for its wool. Also, it can carry heavy loads. Some people who live near mountains in the United States train llamas to go on mount~~ains~~. [Answers may include:] ~~because~~ they have two long toe~~s~~.

Author's Purpose: inform

Reason: All information is factual.

Llamas are the best animals to have if you're planning to backpack in the mountains. They can climb easily and carry your supplies. No one should ever go for a long hiking trip in the mountains without a llama.

Author's Purpose: persuade/inform

Reason: The paragraph contains some opinion and some fact.

Llamas can be stubborn animals. Sometimes they suddenly stop walking for no reason. People have to push them to get them moving again. Stubborn llamas can be frustrating when hiking up a steep mountain.

Author's Purpose: inform

Reason: All information is factual.

Greg is an 11-year-old boy who raises llamas to climb mountains. One of his llamas is named Dallas. Although there are special saddles for llamas, Greg likes to ride bareback.

Author's Purpose: entertain

Reason: This information is presented to interest the reader. It tells a story.

Now use a separate sheet of paper to inform readers about llamas.

Page 62

Comprehension: Fun With Photography

The word "photography" means "writing with light." "Photo" is from the Greek word "photos," which means "light." "Graphy" is from the Greek word "graphic," which means "writing." Cameras don't literally write pictures, of course. Instead, they imprint an image onto a piece of film.

Even the most sophisticated camera is basically a box with a piece of light-sensitive film inside. The box has a hole at the opposite end from the film. The light enters the box through the hole—the camera's lens—and shines on the surface of the film to create a picture. The picture that's created on the film is the image the camera's lens is pointed toward.

A lens is a circle of glass that is thinner at the edges and thicker in the center. The outer edges of the lens collect the light rays and draw them together at the center of the lens.

The shutter helps control the amount of light that enters the lens. Too much light will make the picture too light. Too little light will result in a dark picture. Electronic flash—either built into the camera or attached to the top of it—provides light when needed.

Cameras with automatic electronic flashes provide the additional light automatically. Electronic flashes—or simply "flashes," as they are often called—require batteries. If your flash quits working, a dead battery is probably the cause.

Directions: Answer these questions about photography.

1. From what language is the word "photography" derived? __Greek__
2. Where is the camera lens thickest? __in the center__
3. What do the outer edges of the lens do? __collect the light rays and draw them together to the center of the lens__
4. When is a flash needed? __when there isn't enough light__
5. What does the shutter do? __It helps control the amount of light that enters the lens.__

Page 63

Comprehension: Photography Terms

Like other good professionals, photographers make their craft look easy. Their skill—like that of the graceful ice skater—comes from years of practice. Where skaters develop a sense of balance, photographers develop an "eye" for pictures. They can make important technical decisions about photographing, or "shooting," a particular scene in the twinkling of an eye.

It's interesting to know some of the technical language that professional photographers use. "Angle of view" refers to the angle from which a photograph is taken. "Depth of field" is the distance between the nearest point and the farthest point that is in focus in a photo.

"Filling the frame" refers to the amount of space the object being photographed takes up in the picture. A close-up picture of a dog, flower or person would fill the frame. A far-away picture would not.

"ASA" refers to the speed of different types of film. "Speed" means the film's sensitivity to light. The letters **ASA** stand for the American Standards Association. Film manufacturers give their films ratings of 200ASA, 400ASA, and so on to indicate film speed. The higher the number on the film, the higher its sensitivity to light, and the faster its speed. The faster its speed, the better it will be at clearly capturing sports images and other action shots.

Directions: Answer these question about photography terms.

1. Name another term for photographing. __"shooting"__
2. This is the distance between the nearest point and the farthest point that is in focus in a photo. __depth of field__
3. This refers to the speed of different types of film. __ASA__
4. A close-up picture of someone's face would
   ☐ provide depth of field.　☐ create an ASA.　☒ fill the frame.
5. To photograph a swimming child, which film speed is better?
   ☐ 200ASA　☒ 400ASA

Page 64

Comprehension: Photographing Animals

Animals are a favorite subject of many young photographers. Cats, dogs, hamsters and other pets top the list, followed by zoo animals and the occasional lizard.

Because it's hard to get them to sit still and "perform on command," some professional photographers refuse to photograph pets. There are ways around the problem of short attention spans, however.

One way to get an appealing portrait of a cat or dog is to hold a biscuit or treat above the camera. The animal's longing look toward the food will be captured by the camera as a soulful gaze. Because it's above the camera—out of the camera's range—the treat won't appear in the picture. When you show the picture to your friends afterwards, they will be impressed by your pet's loving expression.

If you are using fast film, you can take some good, quick shots of a pet by simply snapping a picture right after calling its name. You'll get a different expression from your pet using this technique. Depending on your pet's disposition, the picture will capture an inquisitive expression or possibly a look of annoyance, especially if you've awakened Rover from a nap!

Taking pictures of zoo animals requires a little more patience. After all, you can't wake up a lion! You may have to wait for a while until the animal does something interesting or moves into a position for you to get a good shot. When photographing zoo animals, don't get too close to the cages, and never tap on the glass or throw things between the bars of a cage! Concentrate on shooting some good pictures, and always respect the animals you are photographing.

Directions: Answer these questions about photographing animals.

1. Why do some professionals dislike photographing animals? __because it's difficult to get them to sit still__
2. What speed of film should you use to photograph quick-moving pets? __fast__
3. To capture a pet's loving expression, hold this out of camera range. __a treat__
4. Compared to taking pictures of pets, what does photographing zoo animals require? __more patience__

Page 65

Generalization: Taking Pictures

A **generalization** is a statement that applies to many different situations.

Directions: Read each passage and circle the valid generalization.

1. Most people can quickly be taught to use a simple camera. However, it takes time, talent and a good eye to learn to take professional quality photographs. Patience is another quality that good photographers must possess. Those who photograph nature often will wait hours to get just the right light or shadow in their pictures.
   a. (Anyone can learn to use a camera.)
   b. Any patient person can become a good photographer.
   c. Good photographers have a good eye for pictures.

2. Photographers such as Diane Arbus, who photograph strange or odd people, also must wait for just the right picture. Many "people photographers" stake out a busy city sidewalk and study faces in the crowd. Then they must leap up quickly and ask to take a picture or sneakily take one without being observed. Either way, it's not an easy task!
   a. Staking out a busy sidewalk is a boring task.
   b. ("People photographers" must be patient people and good observers.)
   c. Sneak photography is not a nice thing to do to strangers.

3. Whether the subject is nature or humans, many photographers insist that dawn is the best time to take pictures. The light is clear at this early hour, and mist may still be in the air. The mist gives these early morning photos a haunting, "other world" quality that is very appealing.
   a. (Morning mist gives an unusual quality to most outdoor photographs.)
   b. Photographers all agree that dawn is the best time to take pictures.
   c. Misty light is always important in taking pictures.

Page 66

Generalization: Camera Care

Directions: Read each passage and circle the valid generalization.

1. Professional photographers know it's important to keep their cameras clean and in good working order. Amateur photographers should make sure theirs are, too. However, to take good care of your camera, you must first understand the equipment. Camera shop owners say at least half the "defective" cameras people bring in simply need to have the battery changed!

   a. Cameras are delicate and require constant care so they will work properly.

   b. (Many problems amateurs have are caused by lack of familiarity with their equipment.)

   c. Amateur photographers don't know how their cameras work.

2. Once a year, some people take their cameras to a shop to be cleaned. Most never have them cleaned at all. Those who know how can clean their cameras themselves. To avoid scratching the lens, they should use the special cloths and tissues professionals rely on. Amateurs are warned never to loosen screws, bolts or nuts inside the camera.

   a. (The majority of amateur photographers never bother to have their cameras cleaned.)

   b. Cleaning a camera can be tricky and should be left to professionals.

   c. It's hard to find the special cleaning cloths professionals use.

3. Another simple tip from professionals is to make sure your camera works before you take it on vacation. They suggest taking an entire roll of film and having it developed before your trip. That way, if necessary, you'll have time to have the lens cleaned or other repairs made.

   a. (Check out your camera before you travel to make sure it's in good working order.)

   b. Vacation pictures are often disappointing because the camera needs to be repaired.

   c. Take at least one roll of film along on every vacation.

Page 67

Generalization: Using a Darkroom

The room where photographs are developed is called a "darkroom." Can you guess why? The room must be dark so that light does not get on the film as it is being developed. Specially colored lights allow photographers to see without damaging the film. Because of the darkness and the chemicals used in the developing process, it's important to follow certain darkroom safety procedures.

To avoid shocks while in the darkroom, never touch light switches with wet hands. To avoid touching chemicals, use tongs to transfer prints from one chemical solution to another. When finished with the chemicals, put them back in their bottles. Never leave chemicals out in trays once the developing process is complete.

To avoid skin irritation from chemicals, wipe down all countertops and surfaces when you are finished. Another sensible precaution—make sure you have everything you need before exposing the film to begin the developing process. Any light that enters the darkroom can ruin the pictures being developed.

Directions: Answer these questions about using a darkroom.

1. Which generalization is correct?

   a. Developing pictures is a time-consuming and difficult process.

   b. It's dangerous to develop pictures in a darkroom.

   c. (Sensible safety procedures are important for darkroom work.)

2. Write directions for working with photography chemicals. Use tongs to transfer prints from one chemical solution to another. Put chemicals away when finished. Clean surfaces when you finish.

3. What is the most important precaution to take to make sure pictures aren't ruined in the darkroom? The room must be kept dark while developing photographs.

Page 68

Comprehension: Colonists Come to America

After Christopher Columbus discovered America in 1492, many people wanted to come live in the new land. During the 17th and 18th centuries, a great many Europeans, especially the English, left their countries and settled along the Atlantic Coast of North America between Florida and Canada. Some came to make a better life for themselves. Others, particularly the Pilgrims, the Puritans and the Quakers, came for religious freedom.

A group of men who wanted gold and other riches from the new land formed the London Company. They asked the king of England for land in America and for permission to found a colony. They founded Jamestown, the first permanent English settlement in America, in 1607. They purchased ships and supplies, and located people who wanted to settle in America.

The voyage to America took about eight weeks and was very dangerous. Often, fierce winds blew the wooden ships off course. Many were wrecked. The ships were crowded and dirty. Frequently, passengers became ill, and some died. Once in America, the early settlers faced even more hardships.

Directions: Answer these questions about the colonists coming to America.

1. How long did it take colonists to travel from England to America? 8 weeks

2. Name three groups that came to America to find religious freedom.

   1) Pilgrims   2) Puritans   3) Quakers

3. Why was the London Company formed? to ask the king of England if they could found a colony in America

4. What was Jamestown? the first permanent English settlement in America

5. Why was the voyage to America dangerous? Many ships wrecked. They were crowded and dirty, and passengers became ill.

Page 69

Recalling Details: Early Colonial Homes

When the first colonists landed in America, they had to find shelter quickly. Their first homes were crude bark and mud huts, log cabins or dugouts, which were simply caves dug into the hillsides. As soon as possible, the settlers sought to replace these temporary shelters with comfortable houses.

Until the late 17th century, most of the colonial homes were simple in style. Almost all of the New England colonists—those settling in the northern areas of Massachusetts, Connecticut, Rhode Island and New Hampshire—used wood in building their permanent homes. Some of the buildings had thatched roofs. However, they caught fire easily, and so were replaced by wooden shingles. The outside walls also were covered with wooden shingles to make the houses warmer and less drafty.

In the middle colonies—New York, Pennsylvania, New Jersey and Delaware—the Dutch and German colonists often made brick or stone homes that were two-and-a-half or three-and-a-half stories high. Many southern colonists—those living in Virginia, Maryland, North Carolina, South Carolina and Georgia—lived on large farms called plantations. Their homes were usually made of brick.

In the 18th century, some colonists became wealthy enough to replace their simple homes with mansions, often like those being built by the wealthy class in England. They were called Georgian houses because they were popular during the years that Kings George I, George II and George III ruled England. Most were made of brick. They usually featured columns, ornately carved doors and elaborate gardens.

Directions: Answer these questions about early colonial homes.

1. What were the earliest homes of the colonists? bark and mud huts, log cabins, dugouts

2. What were the advantages of using wooden shingles? They didn't catch fire as easily as thatched roofs.

3. What did Dutch and German colonists use to build their homes? brick and stone

4. What were Georgian homes? mansions with columns, ornate doors and elaborate gardens

Page 70

Recalling Details: The Colonial Kitchen

The most important room in the home of a colonial family was the kitchen. Sometimes it was the only room in the home. The most important element of the kitchen was the fireplace. Fire was essential to the colonists, and they were careful to keep one burning at all times. Before the man of the house went to bed, he would make sure that the fire was carefully banked so it would burn all night. In the morning, he would blow the glowing embers into flame again with a bellows. If the fire went out, one of the children would be sent to a neighbor's for hot coals. Because there were no matches, it would sometimes take a half hour to light a new fire, using flint, steel and tinder.

The colonial kitchen, quite naturally, was centered around the fireplace. One or two large iron broilers hung over the hot coals for cooking the family meals. Above the fireplace, a large musket and powder horn were kept for protection in the event of an attack and to hunt deer and other game. Also likely to be found near the fireplace was a butter churn, where cream from the family's cow was beaten until yellow flakes of butter appeared.

The furniture in the kitchen—usually benches, a table and chairs—was made by the man or men in the family. It was very heavy and not very comfortable. The colonial family owned few eating utensils—no forks and only a few spoons, also made by members of the family. The dishes included pewter plates, "trenchers"—wooden bowls with handles—and wooden mugs.

Directions: Answer these questions about the colonial kitchen.

1. What was the most important element of the colonial kitchen? fireplace

2. In colonial days, why was it important to keep a fire burning in the fireplace? There were no matches, and fires were hard to start.

3. Name two uses of the musket.

   1) hunting   2) protection

4. Who made most of the furniture in the early colonial home? men in the family

Page 71

Sequencing: Spinning

Most of the colonists could not afford to buy clothes sent over from Europe. Instead, the women and girls, particularly in the New England colonies, spent much time spinning thread and weaving cloth to make their own clothing. They raised sheep for wool and grew flax for linen.

In August, the flax was ready to be harvested and made into linen thread. The plants were pulled up and allowed to dry. Then the men pulled the seed pods from the stalks, bundled the stalks and soaked them in a stream for about five days. The flax next had to be taken out, cleaned and dried. To get the linen fibers from the tough bark and heavy wooden core, the stalks had to be pounded and crushed. Finally, the fibers were pulled through the teeth of a brush called a "hatchel" to comb out the short and broken fibers. The long fibers were spun into linen thread on a spinning wheel.

The spinning wheel was low, so a woman sat down to spin. First, she put flax in the hollow end of a slender stick, called the spindle, at one end of the spinning wheel. It was connected by a belt to a big wheel at the other end. The woman turned the wheel by stepping on a pedal. As it turned, the spindle also turned, twisting the flax into thread. The woman constantly dipped her fingers into water to moisten the flax and keep it from breaking. The linen thread came out through a hole in the side of the spindle. It was bleached and put away to be woven into pieces of cloth.

Directions: Number in order the steps to make linen thread from flax.

7 The woman sat at the spinning wheel and put flax in the spindle.

3 Seed pods were pulled from the stalks; stalks were bundled and soaked.

1 In August, the flax was ready to be harvested and made into thread.

4 The stalks were pounded and crushed to get the linen fibers.

11 The thread was bleached and put away to be woven into cloth.

5 The short fibers were separated out with a "hatchel."

9 The woman dipped her fingers into water to moisten the flax.

6 The long fibers were spun into linen thread on a spinning wheel.

8 The woman turned the wheel by stepping on a pedal, twisting the flax into thread.

2 The plants were pulled up and allowed to dry.

10 The linen thread came out through a hole in the side of the spindle.

Page 72

Recalling Details: Clothing in Colonial Times

The clothing of the colonists varied from the north to the south, accounting for the differences not only in climate, but also in the religions and ancestries of the settlers. The clothes seen most often in the early New England colonies where the Puritans settled were very plain and simple. The materials—wool and linen—were warm and sturdy.

The Puritans had strict rules about clothing. There were no bright colors, jewelry, ruffles or lace. A Puritan woman wore a long-sleeved gray dress with a big white color, cuffs, apron and cap. A Puritan man wore long woolen stockings and baggy leather "breeches," which were knee-length trousers. Adults and children dressed in the same style of clothing.

In the middle colonies, the clothing ranged from the simple clothing of the Quakers to the colorful, loose-fitting outfits of the Dutch colonists. Dutch women wore more colorful outfits than Puritan women, with many petticoats and fur trim. The men also wore big hats decked with curling feathers.

In the southern colonies, where there were no religious restrictions against fancy clothes, wealthy men wore brightly colored breeches and coats of velvet and satin sent from England. The women's gowns also were made of rich materials and were decorated with ruffles, ribbons and lace. The poorer people wore clothes similar to the simple dress of the New England Puritans.

Directions: Answer these questions about clothing in colonial times.

1. Why did the clothing of the colonists vary from the north to the south?
differences in climate, religions and ancestries

2. Why did the Puritans wear very plain clothing?
They had very strict rules and religious restrictions.

3. What was the nationality of many settlers in the middle colonies?
Dutch

4. From what country did wealthy southern colonists obtain their clothing?
England

Page 73

Recalling Details: Venn Diagrams

A **Venn diagram** is used to chart information that shows similarities and differences between two things. The outer part of each circle shows the differences. The intersecting part of the circles shows the similarities.

Example:

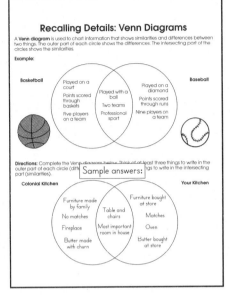

Basketball — Baseball

Played on a court / Points scored through baskets / Five players on a team

Played with a ball / Two teams / Professional sport

Played on a diamond / Points scored through runs / Nine players on a team

Directions: Complete the Venn diagram below. Think of at least three things to write in the outer part of each circle (differences) and at least three things to write in the intersecting part (similarities).

Sample answers:

Colonial Kitchen — Your Kitchen

Furniture made by family / No matches / Fireplace / Butter made with churn

Table and chairs / Most important room in house

Furniture bought at store / Matches / Oven / Butter bought at store

Page 74

Comprehension: Colonial Schools

In early colonial days, there were no schools or teachers. Children learned what they could at home from their parents, but often their parents couldn't read or write either. Later, some women in the New England colonies began teaching in their homes. These first schools were known as "dame schools." Often the books used in these schools were not books at all, but rather "hornbooks"—flat, paddle-shaped wooden boards with the alphabet or Lord's Prayer on the front.

In 1647, a law was passed in the New England colonies requiring every town of 50 or more families to establish an elementary school. By the 1700s, one-room log schoolhouses were common. Children of all ages studied together under one strict schoolmaster. They attended school six days a week, from 7:00 or 8:00 in the morning until 4:00 or 5:00 in the afternoon. Their only textbooks were the Bible and the *New England Primer*, which contained the alphabet, spelling words, poems and questions about the Bible.

Like the New England colonies, the middle colonies also established schools. However, there were few schools in the southern colonies, where most of the people lived on widely separated farms. Wealthy plantation owners hired private teachers from England to teach their children, but the children of poor families received no education.

Directions: Answer these questions about colonial schools.

1. What was a "hornbook"? **flat wooden boards with the alphabet or Lord's Prayer on the front**

2. What was required by the law passed in the New England colonies in 1647? **Every town with 50 or more families had to establish an elementary school.**

3. During the 1700s, what textbooks were used in the New England schools? **the Bible and the *New England Primer***

4. Why was it hard to establish schools in the southern colonies? **Most people lived on widely seperated farms.**

Page 75

Using Prior Knowledge: Abraham Lincoln and the Civil War

Directions: Before reading about Abraham Lincoln and the Civil War in the following section, answer these questions.

1. The Civil War began because _____

2. Abraham Lincoln is famous today because _____

3. What brought about the end of slavery? _____

Answers will vary.

4. The *Gettysburg Address* begins with this line: "Four score and seven years ago. . . ." "What does _____

5. How did Abraham Lincoln die? _____

Page 76

Main Idea: The *Gettysburg Address*

On November 19, 1863, President Abraham Lincoln gave a short speech to dedicate a cemetery for Civil War soldiers in Gettysburg, Pennsylvania, where a famous battle was fought. He wrote five drafts of the *Gettysburg Address*, one of the most stirring speeches of all time. The war ended in 1865.

Four score and seven years ago, our fathers brought forth on this continent a new nation, conceived in liberty, and dedicated to the proposition that all men are created equal.

Now we are engaged in a great civil war, testing whether that nation, or any nation so conceived and so dedicated, can long endure. We are met on a great battlefield of that war. We have come to dedicate a portion of that field as a final resting place for those who here gave their lives that this nation might live. It is altogether fitting and proper that we should do this.

But, in a larger sense, we cannot dedicate—we cannot consecrate—we cannot hallow—this ground. The brave men, living and dead, who struggled here have consecrated it far above our poor power to add or detract. The world will little note nor long remember what we say here, but it can never forget what they did here. It is for us the living, rather, to be dedicated to the unfinished work which they who fought here have thus far so nobly advanced. It is rather for us to be here dedicated to the great task remaining before us—that from these honored dead we take increased devotion to that cause for which they gave their last full measure of devotion—that we here highly resolve that these dead shall not have died in vain—that this nation, under God, shall have a new birth of freedom—and that government of the people, by the people, for the people shall not perish from this earth.

Directions: Answer the questions about the *Gettysburg Address*.

1. Circle the main idea:

This speech will be long remembered as a tribute to the dead who died fighting in the Civil War.

(This speech is to honor the dead soldiers who gave their lives so that the nation could have freedom for all citizens.)

2. What happened on the ground where the cemetery stood? **A great battle was fought and many lives were lost.**

Page 77

Comprehension: The *Gettysburg Address*

Directions: Use context clues or a dictionary to answer these questions about the *Gettysburg Address.*

1. What is the correct definition of **conceived**? **to form an idea**

2. What is the correct definition of **consecrate**? **bless**

3. What is the correct definition of **hallow**? **to revere as holy**

4. What is the correct definition of **devotion**? **dedication to**

5. What is the correct definition of **resolve**? **end, finish, to find a solution**

6. What is the correct definition of **vain**? **without cause or reason**

7. What is the correct definition of **perish**? **to die**

8. What is the correct definition of **civil**? **pertaining to a community, country or civilians**

9. In your own words, what point was President Lincoln trying to make? **Answers will vary.**

Page 78

Comprehension:
The *Emancipation Proclamation*

On September 22, 1862, a year before delivering the *Gettysburg Address*, President Lincoln delivered the *Emancipation Proclamation*, which stated that all slaves in Confederate states should be set free. Since the Confederate states had already seceded (withdrawn) from the Union, they ignored the proclamation. However, the proclamation did strengthen the North's war effort. About 200,000 Black men—mostly former slaves—enlisted in the Union Army. Two years later, the 13th Amendment to the Constitution ended slavery in all parts of the United States.

I, Abraham Lincoln, do order and declare that all persons held as slaves within said designated States and parts of States are, and henceforward shall be, free; and that the Executive Government of the United States, including military and naval authorities thereof, shall recognize and maintain the freedom of said persons.

And I hereby enjoin upon the people so declared to be free to abstain from all violence, unless in necessary self-defense; and I recommend to them that, in all cases where allowed, they labor faithfully for reasonable wages.

And I further declare and make known that such persons of suitable condition will be received into the armed forces of the United States to garrison forts, positions, stations, and other places, and to man vessels of all sorts in said service.

(This is not the full text of the *Emancipation Proclamation*.)

Directions: Answer the questions about the *Emancipation Proclamation*.

1. How did the *Emancipation Proclamation* strengthen the North's war effort?
   About 200,000 Black men enlisted in the Union army.

2. Which came first, the *Emancipation Proclamation* or the *Gettysburg Address*?
   The *Emancipation Proclamation*

3. Which amendment to the Constitution grew out of the *Emancipation Proclamation*?
   13th

4. **Secede** means to ☐ quit. ☐ fight. ☒ withdraw.

Page 79

Comprehension:
The *Emancipation Proclamation*

Directions: Use context clues or a dictionary to answer these questions about the *Emancipation Proclamation*.

1. What is the correct definition of **designated**? appointed

2. What is the correct definition of **military**? an army

3. What is the correct definition of **naval**? related to warships

4. What is the correct definition of **abstain**? keep away from, refrain from

5. What is the correct definition of **suitable**? appropriate

6. What is the correct definition of **garrison**? a fort

7. What is the correct definition of **vessels**? ships

8. In your own words, what did the *Emancipation Proclamation* accomplish?
   Answers will vary.

Page 80

Comprehension: Lincoln and the South

Many people think that Abraham Lincoln publicly came out against slavery from the beginning of his term as president. This is not the case. Whatever his private feelings, he did not criticize slavery publicly. Fearful that the southern states would secede, or leave, the Union, he pledged to respect the southern states' rights to own slaves. He also pledged that the government would respect the southern states' runaway slave laws. These laws required all citizens to return runaway slaves to their masters.

Clearly, Lincoln did not want the country torn apart by a civil war. In the following statement, written in 1861 shortly after he became president, he made it clear that the federal government would do its best to avoid conflict with the southern states.

I hold that, in contemplation of the universal law and the Constitution, the Union of these states is perpetual.... No state, upon its own mere motion, can lawfully get out of the Union. ...I shall take care, as the Constitution itself expressly enjoins upon me, that the laws of the Union be faithfully executed in all the states....The power confided to me will be used to hold, occupy, and possess the property and places belonging to the government, and to collect the duties and imposts....

In your hands, my dissatisfied fellow-countrymen, and not in mine, is the momentous issue of civil war. The government will not assail you. You can have no conflict without yourselves being the aggressors. You have no oath registered in heaven to destroy the government, while I shall have the most solemn one to "preserve, protect and defend" it.

Directions: Use context clues for these definitions.

1. What is the correct definition of **assail**? to attack, to confront

2. What is the correct definition of **enjoin**? to impose a rule or law

3. What is the correct definition of **contemplation**? meditation, considering before making a decision

Directions: Answer these questions about Lincoln and the southern states.

4. Lincoln is telling the southern states that the government
   ☐ does want a war. ☒ doesn't want a war. ☐ will stop a war.

5. As president, Lincoln pledged to "preserve, protect and defend"
   ☐ slavery. ☐ the northern states. ☒ the Union.

Page 81

Comprehension: Away Down South in Dixie

Although many southerners disapproved of slavery, the pressure to go along with the majority who supported slavery was very strong. Many of those who thought slavery was wrong did not talk about their opinions. It was dangerous to do so!

The main reason the southern states seceded from the Union in 1861 was because they wanted to protect their right to own slaves. They also wanted to increase the number of slaves so they could increase production of cotton and other crops that slaves tended. Many Civil War monuments in the South are dedicated to a war that was described as "just and holy."

"Dixie," a song written in 1859 that is still popular in the South, sums up the attitude of many southerners. As the song lyrics show, southerners' loyalties lay not with the Union representing all the states, but with the South and the southern way of life.

Dixie
I wish I was in Dixie, Hoo-ray! Hoo-ray!
In Dixie land I'll take my stand
To live and die in Dixie.
Away, away, away down south in Dixie!
Away, away, away down south in Dixie!
(This is not the full text of the song.)

Directions: Answer these questions about southerners and "Dixie."

1. Why did southerners who disapproved of slavery keep their opinions to themselves?
   It was dangerous to express their opinions.

2. Why did southerners want more slaves? to increase production of cotton and other crops

3. What are the words on some southern Civil War monuments? "just and holy"

4. What "stand" is referred to in "Dixie"?
   ☒ stand for slavery ☐ stand against slavery ☐ stand for cotton

Page 82

Fact and Opinion

Directions: Read each sentence. Then draw an **X** in the box to tell whether it is a fact or opinion.

1. "Dixie" is a beautiful song! ☐ Fact ☒ Opinion

2. It was written in 1859 by a man named Daniel Emmett, who died in 1904. ☒ Fact ☐ Opinion

3. The song became a rallying cry for southerners, because it showed where their loyalties were. ☒ Fact ☐ Opinion

4. I think their loyalty to slavery was absolutely wrong! ☐ Fact ☒ Opinion

5. These four states where people owned slaves did not secede from the Union: Delaware, Maryland, Kentucky and Missouri. ☒ Fact ☐ Opinion

6. The people in these states certainly made the right moral choice. ☐ Fact ☒ Opinion

7. The ownership of one human being by another is absolutely and totally wrong under any circumstances. ☐ Fact ☒ Opinion

8. In the states that did not secede from the Union, some people fought for the Union and others fought for the Confederacy of Southern States. ☒ Fact ☐ Opinion

9. Sometimes brothers fought against brothers on opposite sides of the war. ☒ Fact ☐ Opinion

10. What a horrible situation to be in! ☐ Fact ☒ Opinion

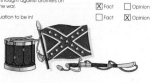

Page 83

Recalling Details: The Island Continent

Australia is the only country that fills an entire continent. It is the smallest continent in the world but the sixth largest country. Australia, called the island continent, is totally surrounded by water—the Indian Ocean on the west and south, the Pacific Ocean on the east and the Arafura Sea, which is formed by these two oceans coming together, to the north.

The island continent is, in large part, a very dry, flat land. Yet it supports a magnificent and unusual collection of wildlife. Because of its remoteness, Australia is home to plants and animals that are not found anywhere else in the world. Besides the well-known kangaroo and koala, the strange animals of the continent include the wombat, dingo, kookaburra, emu and, perhaps the strangest of all, the duckbill platypus.

There are other physical features of Australia that also are unique, including the central part of the country known as the "Outback," which consists of three main deserts—the Great Sandy, the Gibson and the Great Victoria. Because much of the country is desert, more than half of all Australians live in large, modern cities along the coast. There are also many people living in the small towns on the edge of the Outback, where there is plenty of grass for raising sheep and cattle. Australia rates first in the world for sheep raising. In fact, there are more than 10 times as many sheep in Australia as there are people!

Directions: Answer these questions about Australia.

1. What are the three large bodies of water that surround Australia?
   1) Indian Ocean 2) Pacific Ocean 3) Arafura Sea

2. Besides the kangaroo and the koala, name three other unusual animals found only in Australia. Answers also include: kookaburra and duckbill platypus
   1) Wombat 2) Emu 3) Dingo

3. What three deserts make up the "Outback"?
   1) Great Sandy 2) Gibson 3) Great Victoria

Page 84

Comprehension: The Aborigines

The native, or earliest known, people of Australia are the Aborigines (ab-ur-LI-uh-neez). They arrived on the continent from Asia more than 20,000 years ago. Before the Europeans began settling in Australia during the early 1800s, there were about 300,000 Aborigines. But the new settlers brought diseases that killed many of these native people. Today there are only about 125,000 Aborigines living in Australia, many of whom now live in the cities.

The way of life of the Aborigines, who still live like their ancestors, is closely related to nature. They live as hunters and gatherers and do not produce crops or raise livestock. The Aborigines have no permanent settlements, only small camps near watering places. Because they live off the land, they must frequently move about in search of food. They have few belongings and little or no clothing.

Some tribes of Aborigines, especially those that live in the desert, may move 100 times in a year. They might move more than 1,000 miles on foot during that time. These tribes set up temporary homes, such as tents made of bark and igloo-like structures made of grass.

The Aborigines have no written language, but they have developed a system of hand signals. These are used during hunting when silence is necessary and during their elaborate religious ceremonies when talking is forbidden.

Directions: Circle **True** or **False** for these statements about Aborigines.

1. The Aborigines came from Europe to settle in Australia. True (False)
2. The Aborigines live as hunters and gatherers rather than as farmers. (True) False
3. The tribes move about often to find jobs. True (False)
4. The people move often to help them raise their livestock. True (False)
5. Aborigine tribes always move 200 times a year. True (False)

Page 85

Main Idea/Comprehension: The Boomerang

The Aborigines have developed a few tools and weapons, including spears, flint knives and the boomerang. The boomerang comes in different shapes and has many uses. This curved throwing stick is used for hunting, playing, digging, cutting and even making music.

You may have seen a boomerang that, when thrown, returns to the thrower. This type of boomerang is sometimes used in duck hunting, but it is most often used as a toy and for sporting contests. It is lightweight—about three-fourths of a pound—and has a big curve in it. However, the boomerang used by the Aborigines for hunting is much heavier and is nearly straight. It does not return to its thrower.

Because of its sharp edges, the boomerang makes a good knife for skinning animals. The Aborigines also use boomerangs as digging sticks, to sharpen stone blades, to start fires and as swords and clubs in fighting. Boomerangs sometimes are used to make music—two clapped together provide rhythmic background for dances. Some make musical sounds when they are pulled across one another.

To throw a boomerang, the thrower grasps it at one end and holds it behind his head. He throws it overhanded, adding a sharp flick of the wrist at the last moment. It is thrown into the wind to make it come back. A skillful thrower can do many tricks with his boomerang. He can make it spin in several circles, or make a figure eight in the air. He can even make it bounce on the ground several times before it soars into the air and returns.

Directions: Answer these questions about boomerangs.

1. The main idea is:
   ☐ The Aborigines have developed a few tools and weapons, including spears, flint knives and the boomerang.
   ☒ The boomerang comes in different shapes and has many uses.

2. To make it return, the thrower tosses the boomerang
   ☒ into the wind. ☐ against the wind.

3. List three uses for the boomerang.   Sample answers:
   1) hunting
   2) playing
   3) digging

Page 86

Comprehension: The Kangaroo

Many animals found in Australia are not found anywhere else in the world. Because the island continent was separated from the rest of the world for many years, these animals developed in different ways. Many of the animals in Australia are marsupials. Marsupials are animals whose babies are born underdeveloped and are then carried in a pouch on the mother's body until they are able to care for themselves. The kangaroo is perhaps the best known of the marsupials.

There are 45 kinds of kangaroos, and they come in a variety of sizes. The smallest is the musky rat kangaroo, which is about a foot long, including its hairless tail. It weighs only a pound. The largest is the gray kangaroo, which is more than 9 feet long, counting its tail, and can weigh 200 pounds. When moving quickly, a kangaroo can leap 25 feet and move at 30 miles an hour!

A baby kangaroo, called a joey, is totally helpless at birth. It is only three-quarters of an inch long and weighs but a fraction of an ounce. The newly born joey immediately crawls into its mother's pouch and remains there until it is old enough to be independent—which can be as long as eight months.

Kangaroos eat grasses and plants. They can cause problems for farmers and ranchers in Australia because they compete with cattle for pastures. During a drought, kangaroos may invade ranches and even airports looking for food.

Directions: Answer these questions about kangaroos.

1. What are marsupials? animals whose babies are born underdeveloped and are carried in a pouch on the mother until they can care for themselves

2. What is the smallest kangaroo? musky rat kangaroo

3. What is a baby kangaroo called? joey

4. Why did Australian animals develop differently from other animals? The island continent was separated from the rest of the world for many years.

Page 87

Comprehension: The Koala

The koala lives in eastern Australia in the eucalyptus (you-ca-LIP-tes) forests. These slow, gentle animals hide by day, usually sleeping in the trees. They come out at night to eat. Koalas eat only certain types of eucalyptus leaves. Their entire way of life centers on this unique diet. The koala's digestive system is specially adapted for eating eucalyptus leaves. In fact, to other animals, these leaves are poisonous!

The wooly, round-eared koala looks like a cuddly teddy bear, but it is not related to any bear. It is a marsupial like the kangaroo. And, like the joey, a baby koala requires a lot of care. It will remain constantly in its mother's pouch until it is six months old. After that, a baby koala will ride piggyback on its mother for another month or two, even though it is nearly as big as she is. Koalas have few babies—only one every other year. While in her pouch, the baby koala lives on its mother's milk. After it is big enough to be on its own, the koala will almost never drink anything again.

Oddly, the mother koala's pouch is backwards—the opening is at the bottom. This leads scientists to believe that the koala once lived on the ground and walked on all fours. But at some point, the koala became a tree dweller. This makes an upside-down pouch very awkward! The babies keep from falling to the ground by holding on tightly with their mouths. The mother koala has developed strong muscles around the rim of her pouch that also help to hold the baby in.

Directions: Answer these questions about koalas.

1. What is the correct definition for **eucalyptus**?
   ☐ enormous ☒ a type of tree ☐ rain

2. What is the correct definition for **digestive**?
   ☒ the process in which food is absorbed in the body
   ☐ the process of finding food
   ☐ the process of tasting

3. What is the correct definition for **dweller**?
   ☐ one who climbs ☐ one who eats ☒ one who lives in

Page 88

Comprehension: The Wombat

Another animal unique to Australia is the wombat. The wombat has characteristics in common with other animals. Like the koala, the wombat is also a marsupial with a backwards pouch. The pouch is more practical for the wombat, which lives on the ground rather than in trees. The wombat walks on all fours, so the baby is in less danger of falling out.

The wombat resembles a beaver without a tail. With its strong claws, it is an expert digger. It makes long tunnels beneath cliffs and boulders in which it sleeps all day. At night, it comes out to look for food. It has strong, beaver-like teeth to chew through the various plant roots it eats. A wombat's teeth have no roots, like a rodent's. Its teeth keep growing from the inside as they are worn down from the outside.

The wombat, which can be up to 4 feet long and weighs 60 pounds when full grown, eats only grass, plants and roots. It is a shy, quiet and gentle animal that would never attack. But when angered, it has a strong bite and very sharp teeth! And, while wombats don't eat or attack other animals, the many deep burrows they dig to sleep in are often dangerous to the other animals living nearby.

Directions: Answer these questions about the wombat.

1. How is the wombat similar to the koala? It is a marsupial with a backwards pouch.

2. How is the wombat similar to the beaver? It has strong claws to dig and strong teeth to chew through plants.

3. How is the wombat similar to a rodent? Its teeth have no roots but keep growing from the inside as they are worn down from the outside.

Page 89

Comprehension: The Duckbill Platypus

Australia's duckbill platypus is a most unusual animal. It is very strange-looking and has caused a lot of confusion for people studying it. For many years, even scientists did not know how to classify it. The platypus has webbed feet and a bill like a duck. But it doesn't have wings, has fur instead of feathers and has four legs instead of two. The baby platypus gets milk from its mother, like a mammal, but it is hatched from a tough-skinned egg, like a reptile. A platypus also has a poisonous spur on each of its back legs that is like the tip of a viper's fangs. Scientists have put the platypus—along with another strange animal from Australia called the spiny anteater—in a special class of mammal called "monotremes."

The platypus has an amazing appetite! It has been estimated that a full-grown platypus eats about 1,200 earthworms, 50 crayfish and numerous tadpoles and insects every day. The platypus is an excellent swimmer and diver. It dives under the water of a stream and searches the muddy bottom for food.

A mother platypus lays one or two eggs, which are very small—only about an inch long—and leathery in appearance. During the seven to 14 days it takes for the eggs to hatch, the mother never leaves them, not even to eat. The tiny platypus, which is only a half-inch long, cuts its way out of the shell with a sharp point on its bill. This point is known as an "egg tooth," and it will fall off soon after birth. (Many reptiles and birds have egg teeth, but they are unknown in other mammals.) By the time it is 4 months old, the baby platypus is about a foot long—half its adult size—and is learning how to swim and hunt.

Directions: Answer these questions about the duckbill platypus.

1. In what way is a duckbill platypus like other mammals? It gets milk from its mother.

2. In what way is it like a reptile? It hatches from a tough-skinned egg.

3. What other animal is in the class of mammal called "monotremes"? the spiny anteater

4. What makes up the diet of a platypus? earthworms, crayfish, tadpoles and insects

5. On what other animals would you see an "egg tooth"? many reptiles and birds

Page 90

Recalling Details: Animals of Australia

Directions: Complete the chart with information from the selection on Australian animals.

	Gray Kangaroo	Koala	Wombat	Platypus
What are the animal's physical characteristics?	9 feet long 200 pounds marsupial good leaper fast mover	wooly round-eared marsupial good climber	marsupial walks on all fours strong claws and teeth up to 4 feet long 60 pounds	webbed feet duck-like bill fur, four legs hatches from egg poisonous spur 2 feet long good swimmer
What is the animal's habitat?	farmland of Australia	eucalyptus forests of eastern Australia	tunnels beneath cliffs and boulders	streams with muddy bottoms
What does the animal eat?	grasses, plants	eucalyptus leaves	grass, plants, roots	earthworms, crayfish, tadpoles, insects

Page 91

Using Prior Knowledge: Dinosaurs

Everyone is intrigued by dinosaurs. Their size, ferocity and sudden disappearance have fueled scientific investigations for well over a century.

Directions: Before reading about dinosaurs in the following section, answer these questions.

1. Describe what you know about meat-eating dinosaurs. _____

2. Describe what you know about plant-eatin_____

3. Which dinosaur _____ why? _____

Answers will vary.

Page 92

Main Idea: Small Dinosaurs

When most people think of dinosaurs, they visualize enormous creatures. Actually, there were many species of small dinosaurs—some were only the size of chickens.

Like the larger dinosaurs, the Latin names of the smaller ones usually describe the creature. A small but fast species of dinosaur was Saltopus, which means "leaping foot." An adult Saltopus weighed only about 2 pounds and grew to be approximately 2 feet long. Fossils of this dinosaur, which lived about 200 million years ago, have been found only in Scotland.

Another small dinosaur with an interesting name was Compsognathus, which means "pretty jaw." About the same length as the Saltopus, the Compsognathus weighed about three times more. It's unlikely that these two species knew one another, since Compsognathus remains have been found only in France and Germany.

A small dinosaur whose remains have been found in southern Africa is Lesothosaurus, which means "Lesotho lizard." This lizard-like dinosaur was named only partly for its appearance. The first half of its name is based on the place its remains were found—Lesotho, in southern Africa.

Directions: Answer these questions about small dinosaurs.

1. Circle the main idea:

People who think dinosaurs were big are completely wrong.

(There are several species of small dinosaurs, some weighing only 2 pounds.)

2. How much did Saltopus weigh? __about 2 pounds__

3. Which dinosaur's name means "pretty jaw"? __Compsognathus__

Page 93

Comprehension: Dinosaur History

Dinosaurs are so popular today that it's hard to imagine this not always being the case. The fact is, no one had any idea that dinosaurs ever existed until about 150 years ago.

In 1841, a British scientist named Richard Owen coined the term **Dinosauria** to describe several sets of recently discovered large fossil bones. **Dinosauria** is Latin for "terrible lizards," and even though some dinosaurs were similar to lizards, modern science now also links dinosaurs to birds. Today's birds are thought to be the closest relatives to the dinosaurs.

Like birds, most dinosaurs had fairly long legs that extended straight down from beneath their bodies. Because of their long legs, many dinosaurs were able to move fast. They were also able to balance themselves well. Long-legged dinosaurs, such as the Iguanodon, needed balance to walk upright.

The Iguanodon walked on its long hind legs and used its stubby front legs as arms. On the end of its arms were five hoof-like fingers, one of which functioned as a thumb. Because it had no front teeth for tearing meat, scientists believe the Iguanodon was a plant eater. Its large, flat back teeth were useful for grinding tender plants before swallowing them.

Directions: Answer these questions about the history of dinosaurs.

1. How were dinosaurs like today's birds? __most had fairly long, straight legs that extended straight down beneath their bodies__

2. This man coined the term **Dinosauria**.
☐ Owen Richards ☐ Richard Owens ☒ Richard Owen

3. Which of these did the Iguanodon not have?
☐ short front legs ☒ front teeth ☐ back teeth

4. List other ways you can think of that dinosaurs and birds are alike. __Answers will vary.__

Page 94

Recalling Details: Dinosaur Puzzler

Directions: Use the facts you have learned about dinosaurs to complete the puzzle.

Across:
5. This dinosaur had five hoof-like fingers on its short front legs.
6. Dinosaurs with flat back teeth were ____ eaters.
9. Because of where their legs were positioned, dinosaurs had good ____.

Down:
1. Most dinosaurs had ____ legs.
2. The word **Dinosauria** means terrible ____.
3. A bone that has been preserved for many years
4. Dinosaurs were not always as ____ as they are now.
7. Iguanodons walked on their ____ legs.
8. Richard ____ coined the term **Dinosauria**.
9. Dinosaurs are closely related to today's ____.

Crossword answers:
- IGUANODON
- PLANT
- BALANCE
- POPULAR
- LIZARDS
- FOSSIL
- LONG
- HIND
- OWEN
- BIRDS

Page 95

Comprehension: Tyrannosaurus Rex

The largest meat-eating animal ever to roam Earth was Tyrannosaurus Rex. "Rex" is Latin for "king," and because of its size, Tyrannosaurus certainly was at the top of the dinosaur heap. With a length of 46 feet and a weight of 7 tons, there's no doubt this dinosaur commanded respect!

Unlike smaller dinosaurs, Tyrannosaurus wasn't tremendously fast on its huge feet. It could stroll along at a walking speed of 2 to 3 miles an hour. Not bad, considering Tyrannosaurus was pulling along a body that weighed 14,000 pounds! Like other dinosaurs, Tyrannosaurus walked upright, probably balancing its 16-foot-long head by lifting its massive tail.

Compared to the rest of its body, Tyrannosaurus' front claws were tiny. Scientists aren't really sure what the claws were for, although it seems likely that they may have been used for holding food. In that case, Tyrannosaurus would have had to lower its massive head down to its short claws to take anything in its mouth. Maybe it just used the claws to scratch nearby itches!

Because of their low metabolism, dinosaurs did not require a lot of food for survival. Scientists speculate that Tyrannosaurus ate off the same huge piece of meat—usually the carcass of another dinosaur—for several weeks. What do you suppose Tyrannosaurus did the rest of the time?

Directions: Answer these questions about Tyrannosaurus Rex.

1. Why was this dinosaur called "Rex"? __It means king.__

2. For what might Tyrannosaurus Rex have used its claws? __to hold food__

3. How long was Tyrannosaurus Rex? __about 46 feet__

4. Tyrannosaurus weighed
☐ 10,000 lbs. ☐ 12,000 lbs. ☒ 14,000 lbs.

5. Tyrannosaurus ate
☐ plants. ☒ other dinosaurs. ☐ birds.

Page 96

Generalization: Dinosaur Characteristics

Directions: Read each passage and circle the valid generalization.

1. Not surprisingly, Tyrannosaurus had huge teeth in its mammoth head. They were 6 inches long! Because it was a meat eater, Tyrannosaurus' teeth were sharp. They looked like spikes! In comparison, the long-necked, plant-eating Mamenchisaurus had a tiny head and small, flat teeth.

   a. Scientists can't figure out why some dinosaurs had huge teeth.

   b. Tyrannosaurus was probably scarier looking than Mamenchisaurus.

   c. (Sharp teeth would have helped Mamenchisaurus chew better.)

2. Dinosaurs' names often reflect their size or some other physical trait. For example, Compsognathus means "pretty jaw." Saltopus means "leaping foot." Lesothosaurus means "lizard from Lesotho."

   a. Of the three species, Lesothosaurus was probably the fastest.

   b. Of the three species, Compsognathus was probably the fastest.

   c. (Of the three species, Saltopus was probably the fastest.)

3. Edmontosaurus, a huge 3-ton dinosaur, had 1,000 teeth! The teeth were cemented into chewing pads in the back of Edmontosaurus' mouth. Unlike the sharp teeth of the meat-eating Tyrannosaurus, this dinosaur's teeth were flat.

   a. (Edmontosaurus did not eat meat.)

   b. Edmontosaurus did not eat plants.

   c. Edmontosaurus moved very fast.

Page 97

Recalling Details: The Earth's Atmosphere

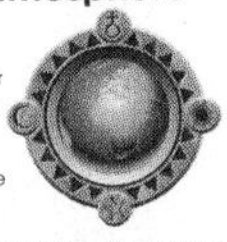

The most important reason that life can exist on Earth is its atmosphere—the air around us. Without it, plant and animal life could not have developed. There would be no clouds, weather or even sounds, only a deathlike stillness and an endlessly black sky. Without the protection of the atmosphere, the sun's rays would roast the Earth by day. At night, with no blanketing atmosphere, the stored heat would escape into space, dropping the temperature of the planet hundreds of degrees.

Held captive by Earth's gravity, the atmosphere surrounds the planet to a depth of hundreds of miles. However, all but 1 percent of the atmosphere is in a layer about 20 miles deep just above the surface of the Earth. It is made up of a mixture of gases and dusts. About 78 percent of it is a gas called nitrogen, which is very important as food for plants. Most of the remaining gas, 21 percent, is oxygen, which all people and animals depend on for life. The remaining 1 percent is made up of a blend of other gases—including carbon dioxide, argon, ozone and helium—and tiny dust particles. These particles come from ocean salt crystals, bits of rocks and sand, plant pollen, volcanic ash and even meteor dust.

You may not think of air as matter, as something that can be weighed. In fact, the Earth's air weighs billions and billions of tons. Near the surface of the planet, this "air pressure" is greatest. Right now, about 10 tons of air is pressing in on you. Yet, like the fish living near the floor of the ocean, you don't notice this tremendous weight because your body is built to withstand it.

Directions: Answer these questions about the Earth's atmosphere.

1. What is the atmosphere? the air around us
2. Of what is the atmosphere made? a mixture of gases and dusts
3. What is the most abundant gas in the atmosphere? nitrogen
4. Which of the atmosphere's gases is most important to humans and animals? oxygen
5. What is air pressure? the weight of the air on Earth

Page 98

Comprehension: Causes/Effects of Weather

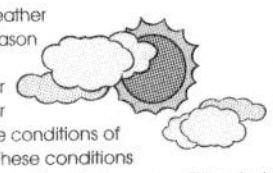

The behavior of the atmosphere, which we experience as weather and climate, affects our lives in many important ways. It is the reason no one lives on the South Pole. It controls when a farmer plants the food we will eat, which crops will be planted and also whether those crops will grow. The weather tells you what clothes to wear and how you will play after school. Weather is the sum of all the conditions of the air that may affect the Earth's surface and its living things. These conditions include the temperature, air pressure, wind and moisture. Climate refers to these conditions but generally applies to larger areas and longer periods of time, such as the annual climate of South America rather than today's weather in Oklahoma City.

Climate is influenced by many factors. It depends first and foremost on latitude. Areas nearest the equator are warm and wet, while the poles are cold and relatively dry. The poles also have extreme seasonal changes, while the areas at the middle latitudes have more moderate climates, neither as cold as the poles nor as hot as the equator. Other circumstances may alter this pattern, however. Land near the oceans, for instance, is generally warmer than inland areas.

Elevation also plays a role in climate. For example, despite the fact that Africa's highest mountain, Kilimanjaro, is just south of the equator, its summit is perpetually covered by snow. In general, high land is cooler and wetter than nearby low land.

Directions: Check the answers to these questions about the causes and effects of weather.

1. What is the correct definition for **atmosphere**?
   - ☐ the clouds ☐ the sky ☒ where weather occurs
2. What is the correct definition for **foremost**?
   - ☒ most important ☐ highest number ☐ in the front
3. What is the correct definition for **circumstances**?
   - ☐ temperatures ☐ seasons ☒ conditions
4. What is the correct definition for **elevation**?
   - ☒ height above Earth ☐ nearness to equator ☐ snow covering
5. What is the correct definition for **perpetually**?
   - ☐ occasionally ☐ rarely ☒ always

Page 99

Main Idea/Recalling Details: Weather

People have always searched the sky for clues about upcoming weather. Throughout the ages, farmers and sailors have looked to the winds and clouds for signs of approaching storms. But no real understanding of the weather could be achieved without a scientific study of the atmosphere. Such a study depends on being able to measure certain conditions, including pressure, temperature and moisture levels.

A true scientific examination of weather, therefore, was not possible until the development of accurate measuring instruments, beginning in the 17th century. Meteorology—the science of studying the atmosphere—was born in 1643 with the invention of the barometer, which measures atmospheric pressure. The liquid-in-glass thermometer, the hygrometer to measure humidity—the as amount of moisture in the air—and the weather map also were invented during the 1600s.

With the measurement of these basic elements, scientists began to work out the relationships between these and other atmospheric conditions, such as wind, clouds and rainfall. Still, their observations failed to show an overall picture of the weather. Such complete weather reporting had to wait two centuries for the rapid transfer of information made possible by the invention of the telegraph during the 1840s.

Today, the forecasts of meteorologists are an international effort. There are thousands of weather stations around the world, both at land and at sea. Upper-level observations are also made by weather balloons and satellites, which continuously send photographs back to earth. All of this information is relayed to national weather bureaus, where meteorologists plot it on graphs and analyze it. The information is then given to the public through newspapers and television and radio stations.

Directions: Answer these questions about studying the weather.

1. The main idea is:
   - ☐ People have always searched the sky for clues about upcoming weather.
   - ☒ A real understanding of weather depends on measuring conditions such as pressure, temperature and moisture levels.
2. List three kinds of instruments used to measure atmospheric conditions, and tell what conditions they measure.
   1) barometer — atmospheric pressure
   2) hygrometer — humidity
   3) liquid-in-glass thermometer — temperature
3. During what century were many of these measuring instruments invented? 17th
4. Name two things used for upper-level observations.
   1) weather balloon 2) satellite

Page 100

Comprehension: Hurricanes

The characteristics of a hurricane are powerful winds, driving rain and raging seas. Although a storm must have winds blowing at least 74 miles an hour to be classified as a hurricane, it is not unusual to have winds above 150 miles per hour. The entire storm system can be 500 miles in diameter, with lines of clouds that spiral toward a center called the "eye." Within the eye itself, which is about 15 miles across, the air is actually calm and cloudless. But this eye is enclosed by a towering wall of thick clouds where the storm's heaviest rains and highest winds are found.

All hurricanes begin in the warm seas and moist winds of the tropics. They form in either of two narrow bands to the north and south of the equator. For weeks, the blistering sun beats down on the ocean water. Slowly, the air above the sea becomes heated and begins to swirl. More hot, moist air is pulled skyward. Gradually, this circle grows larger and spins faster. As the hot, moist air at the top is cooled, great rain clouds are formed. The storm's fury builds until it moves over land or a cold area of the ocean where its supply of heat and moisture is finally cut off.

Hurricanes that strike North America usually form over the Atlantic Ocean. West coast storms are less dangerous because they tend to head out over the Pacific Ocean rather than toward land. The greatest damage usually comes from the hurricanes that begin in the western Pacific, because they often batter heavily populated regions.

Directions: Answer these questions about hurricanes.

1. What is necessary for a storm to be classified as a hurricane? winds blowing at least 74 miles an hour
2. What is the "eye" of the hurricane? lines of clouds that spiral toward the center
3. Where do hurricanes come from? warm seas and moist winds of the tropics
4. How does a hurricane finally die down? It moves over land or a cold area of the ocean where its supply of heat and moisture is cut off.
5. Why do hurricanes formed in the western Pacific cause the most damage? They often batter heavily populated areas.

Page 101

Comprehension: Tornadoes

Tornadoes, which are also called twisters, occur more frequently than hurricanes, but they are smaller storms. The zigzag path of a tornado averages about 16 miles in length and only about a quarter of a mile wide. But the tornado is, pound for pound, the more severe storm. When one touches the ground, it leaves a trail of total destruction.

The winds in a tornado average about 200 miles per hour. At the center of the funnel-shaped cloud of a tornado is a partial vacuum. In combination with the high winds, this is what makes the storm so destructive. Its force is so great that a tornado can drive a piece of straw into a tree. The extremely low atmospheric pressure that accompanies the storm can cause a building to actually explode.

Unlike hurricanes, tornadoes are formed over land. They are most likely to occur over the central plains of the United States, especially in the spring and early summer months. Conditions for a tornado arise when warm, moist air from the south becomes trapped under colder, heavier air from the north. When the surfaces of the two air masses touch, rain clouds form and a thunderstorm begins. At first, only a rounded bulge hangs from the bottom of the cloud. It gradually gets longer until it forms a column reaching toward the ground. The tornado is white from the moisture when it first forms, but turns black as it sucks up dirt and trash.

Directions: Circle **True** or **False** for these statements about tornadoes.

1. The tornado is a stronger storm than the hurricane. (True) False
2. The path of a tornado usually covers hundreds of miles. True (False)
3. Like the eye of a hurricane, the center of a tornado is calm. True (False)
4. Tornadoes are most likely to occur in the central plains of the United States during the spring and early summer months. (True) False
5. High atmospheric pressure usually accompanies a tornado. True (False)

Page 102

Comprehension: Thunderstorms

With warm weather comes the threat of thunderstorms. The rapid growth of the majestic thunderhead cloud and the damp, cool winds that warn of an approaching storm are familiar in most regions of the world. In fact, it has been estimated that at any given time 1,800 such storms are in progress around the globe.

As with hurricanes and tornadoes, thunderstorms are formed when a warm, moist air mass meets with a cold air mass. Before long, bolts of lightning streak across the sky, and thunder booms. It is not entirely understood how lightning is formed. It is known that a positive electrical charge builds near the top of the cloud, and a negative charge forms at the bottom. When enough force builds up, a powerful current of electricity zigzags down an electrically charged pathway between the two, causing the flash of lightning.

The clap of thunder you hear after a lightning flash is created by rapidly heated air that expands as the lightning passes through it. The distant rumbling is caused by the thunder's sound waves bouncing back and forth within clouds or between mountains. When thunderstorms rumble through an area, many people begin to worry about tornadoes. But they need to be just as fearful of thunderstorms. In fact, lightning kills more people than any other severe weather condition. In 1988, lightning killed 68 people in the United States, while tornadoes killed 32.

Directions: Answer these questions about thunderstorms.

1. How many thunderstorms are estimated to be occurring at any given time around the world?

   1,800

2. When are thunderstorms formed?

   when a warm, moist air mass meets a cold air mass

3. What causes thunder?

   rapidly heated air that expands as lightning passes through it

4. On average, which causes more deaths, lightning or tornadoes?

   lightning

Page 103

Venn Diagram: Storms

Directions: Complete the Venn diagram below. Think of at least three things to write in the outer parts of each circle and at least three things to write in the intersecting parts.

Sample answers:

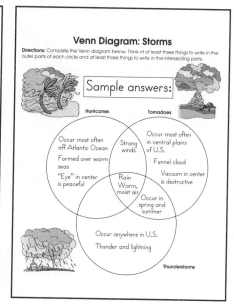

Hurricanes
- Occur most often off Atlantic Ocean
- Formed over warm seas
- "Eye" in center is peaceful

Tornadoes
- Occur most often in central plains of U.S.
- Funnel cloud
- Vacuum in center is destructive

(Hurricanes ∩ Tornadoes) Strong winds

(center) Rain Warm, moist air

(Tornadoes) Occur in spring and summer

Thunderstorms
- Occur anywhere in U.S.
- Thunder and lightning

Page 104

Recalling Details: Lightning Safety Rules

Lightning causes more fire damage to forests and property than anything else. More importantly, it kills more people than any other weather event. It is important to know what to do—and what not to do—during a thunderstorm. Here are some important rules to remember:

- **Don't** go outdoors.
- **Don't** go near open doors or windows, fireplaces, radiators, stoves, metal pipes, sinks or plug-in electrical appliances.
- **Don't** use the telephone, as lightning could strike the wires outside.
- **Don't** handle metal objects, such as fishing poles or golf clubs.
- **Don't** go into the water or ride in small boats.
- **Do** stay in an automobile if you are traveling. Cars offer excellent protection.
- **Don't** take laundry off the clothesline.
- **Do** look for shelter if you are outdoors. If there is no shelter, stay away from the highest object in the area. If there are only a few trees nearby, it is best to crouch in the open, away from the trees at a distance greater than the height of the nearest tree. If you are in an area with many trees, avoid the tallest tree. Look for shorter ones.
- **Don't** take shelter near wire fences or clotheslines, exposed sheds or on a hilltop.
- If your hair stands on end or your skin tingles, lightning may be about to strike you. Immediately crouch down, put your feet together and place your hands over your ears.

Directions: Answer these questions about lightning safety rules.

1. Name two things you should avoid if you are looking for shelter outside.

   1) the highest object in the area
   2) the tallest tree

2. What should you do if, during a thunderstorm, your hair stands up or your skin tingles?

   Immediately crouch down, put your feet together and place your hands over your ears.

Page 105

Main Idea/Comprehension: Rainbows

Although there are some violent, frightening aspects of the weather, there is, of course, considerable beauty, too. The rainbow is one simple, lovely example of nature's atmospheric mysteries.

You usually can see a rainbow when the sun comes out after a rain shower or in the fine spray of a waterfall or fountain. Although sunlight appears to be white, it is actually made up of a mixture of colors—all the colors in the rainbow. We see a rainbow because thousands of tiny raindrops act as mirrors and prisms on the sunlight. Prisms are objects that bend light, splitting it into bands of color.

The bands of color form a perfect semicircle. From the top edge to the bottom, the colors are always in the same order—red, orange, yellow, green, blue, indigo and violet. The brightness and width of each band may vary from one minute to the next. You also may notice that the sky framed by the rainbow is lighter than the sky above. This is because the light that forms the blue and violet bands is more bent and spread out than the light that forms the top red band.

You will always see morning rainbows in the west, with the sun behind you. Afternoon rainbows, likewise, are always in the east. To see a rainbow, the sun can be no higher than 42 degrees—nearly halfway up the sky. Sometimes, if the sunlight is strong and the water droplets are very small, you can see a double rainbow. This happens because the light is reflected twice in the water droplets. The color bands are fainter and in reverse order in the second band.

Directions: Answer these questions about rainbows.

1. Check the statement that is the main idea.

   ☐ Although there are violent, frightening aspects of weather, there is considerable beauty, too.

   ☒ The rainbow is one simple, lovely example of nature's atmospheric mysteries.

2. What is the correct definition for **semicircle**?

   ☐ colored circle   ☐ diameter of a circle   ☒ half circle

3. What is a prism? an object that bends light and splits it into bands of color

4. In which direction would you look to see an afternoon rainbow? east

Page 106

Comprehension: Cause and Effect

Directions: Complete the chart by listing the cause and effect of each weather phenomenon.

	Cause	Effect
Thunderstorms	warm, moist air mass collides with cold air mass	lightning, thunder, rain
Hurricanes	air above the sea heats and swirls; hot, moist air is pulled up and spins faster	rain clouds form; spiraling wind
Tornadoes	warm, moist air gets trapped under cold, heavy air	rain clouds form; thunderstorms occur; tornado develops
Rainbows	sun comes out after rain	raindrops reflect sun's light like mirrors and act like prisms, bending light into bands of color
Precipitation	warm, moist air; low pressure system	rain
Drought	lack of rain and dew	dry earth, loss of livestock, dust bowl conditions

Page 107

Famous Athletes

Athletes are heroes in their fields to both young and old alike. Their stories are sometimes about triumph over amazing odds to become one of the best in their sport. Before beginning the section, answer the following questions as a warm-up.

1. What sport most interests you? Why?

2. What sports figure do you most admire? Why?

Answers will vary.

3. In your opinion, what makes a person a hero?

4. Try to name a sports legend for each of the sports Answers may include:

Track and Field Carl Lewis, Gail Devers
Swimming Esther Williams, Mark Spitz
Boxing Muhammad Ali, George Forman
Baseball Babe Ruth, Sammy Sosa
Speed Skating Dan Jansen, Bonnie Blair
Tennis John McEnroe, Martina Navratilova, Chris Everett

Page 108

Track and Field

Directions: Read the selection. Then answer the questions.

Many people recognize the name "Gail Devers" in the world of track and field. She won a gold medal for the United States at the 1992 Summer Olympics in Barcelona, Spain, in the women's 100-meter dash. However, many people do not know that Gail Devers overcame near insurmountable odds to win that gold medal.

In September, 1990, 24-year-old Gail was diagnosed with Graves' disease, which affects the thyroid gland. She had been fighting this illness for over 2 years before it was finally identified. Graves' disease can cause irregular heartbeat, muscle weakness, nervousness and weight loss. It can also become cancerous. Imagine the difficulties that would create for a person who depends on her muscles in order to compete!

Gail underwent chemotherapy and radiation, which had both good and bad effects on her body. Although the treatments brought her disease under control, the radiation burned her feet so badly that doctors considered amputation.

Amazingly, Gail began her training regimen once again in March, 1991. After competing in several meets and doing well, she went to the United States Olympic Trials and qualified in both the hurdles and the 100-meter dash. Although she came in fifth in the hurdles, the gold medal she claimed in the 100-meter dash represented all her hard work and desire to overcome the odds.

1. Summarize the selection in 3 sentences.

Answers will vary.

2. Define the following words:

Answers may include:

regimen: a regulated course of treatment or behavior

amputation: cutting off

thyroid: a large gland at the base of the neck which affects growth, development and metabolism.

insurmountable: incapable of being overcome

Page 109

Speed Skating

Directions: Read the selection. Then answer the questions.

Imagine racing around a rink of glassy ice with only a thin blade of metal supporting you. Now, imagine skating so fast that you set a world record! That's exactly what speed skater Bonnie Blair has done all of her life.

Bonnie started skating before she was walking—on the shoulders of her older brothers and sisters. By the time she was 4, Bonnie was competing. At age 7, Bonnie won the 1971 Illinois state championships and dreamed of becoming an Olympian.

That opportunity soon came. Bonnie competed in the 1988, 1992 and 1994 Olympics. She won a gold medal in the 500 meter race and a bronze medal in the 1,000 meter race in 1988, golds in both the 500 and 1,000 meter races in 1992 and repeated the two golds in 1994. No other U.S. woman has ever won five gold medals in the Olympics in any sport. Bonnie Blair is truly a champion!

Answers may include:

1. Define the following words:

opportunity: a favorable combination of circumstances, time and place.

meter: the basic metric unit of length (equals 39.37 inches)

2. Bonnie Blair competed over a period of 6 years in the Olympics. What qualities would be necessary to maintain both physical and mental condition to compete for so long?

3. Bonnie Blair participated in long-track skating ... with one other person against a clock for the best time. Do yo ... ier or more difficult than racing a group to finish first? Why?

4. In your opinio ... d athlete?

Answers may vary.

Page 110

Baseball

Directions: Read the selection. Then answer the questions.

Babe Ruth was born George Herman Ruth in 1895. His family lived in Baltimore, Maryland and was quite poor. He overcame poverty to become one of the greatest baseball players of all time.

Babe Ruth's baseball career began with the Baltimore Orioles. He was a pitcher but also a tremendous batter. He later played for the Boston Red Sox and started his home run hitting fame with 29 home runs in 1919.

In 1920, while playing for the New York Yankees, Babe Ruth hit 54 home runs. He had become very popular with baseball fans of all ages. Amazingly, by 1925, he was making more money than the president of the United States! His home-run record of 60 home runs in a single season went unshattered until Roger Maris broke it in 1961 with 61 home runs. Then, in 1998, Mark McGwire hit 70 home runs to become the new "home-run king."

Babe Ruth retired from baseball in 1935 with a career total of 714 home runs. He died in 1948 at age 53.

1. Summarize the selection in 3 sentences.

Answers will vary.

2. In the early 1900s, life ex ... today's standards, Babe Ruth died at a relatively ... uted to increased life expectancy?

Better medical care: people are more educated about self-care: the invention of new medicines: better medical facilities.

Babe Ruth born	B.R. hit 29 home runs with Boston Red Sox	B.R. hit 54 home runs with N.Y. Yankees	B.R. retired from baseball 714 home runs	Babe Ruth died
1895	1919	1920	1935	1948

Page 111

Swimming

Directions: Read the selection. Then answer the questions.

In 1968, 18-year-old Mark Spitz boasted that he would win six gold medals at the Olympics being held in Mexico. He won two golds in team relay events. Having made this claim and then failing to achieve it made Mark Spitz determined to do better in the 1972 Olympics in Munich.

For the next 4 years, Mark Spitz trained ferociously. Indeed, at the 1972 Olympics, Mark Spitz amazed the world by breaking all records and winning seven gold medals in seven different events. While doing so, he set new world record times in each event. Mark Spitz had accomplished his goal.

1. What feelings do you think Mark Spitz had after the 1968 Olympics?

2. What do you think is the moral to this story?

Answers may vary.

3. Many Olym ... ark Spitz was, and some participate at even younger age ... Write one paragraph detailing the advantages of being a young Olympian and one paragraph detailing the disadvantages.

Page 112

Boxing

Directions: Read the selection. Then answer the questions.

Muhammad Ali was born Cassius Clay in Louisville, Kentucky in 1942. He won the amateur Golden Gloves championship in 1959 and 1960 and went on to become the heavyweight champion of the 1960 Olympics. Four years later, he was champion of the world.

However, Ali's athletic fame came with its share of difficulties. He converted to the religion of Islam and thus changed his name from Cassius Clay to Muhammad Ali. It was due to his beliefs in Islam that he refused to comply with the military draft for the Vietnam War. Therefore, he was stripped of his world title and banned from boxing from 1967 to 1970.

Ali regained his title in 1974 and won the world championship again in 1978. This accomplishment made Muhammad Ali the first heavyweight boxer to claim the world championship three times. Most notable about Ali's career is his total 56 wins in the ring.

Answers may include:

1. Define the following words:

draft: to select, usually forcing someone to do something

banned: forbidden

amateur: a non-professional who engages in his/her pursuit for pleasure

notable: worthy of notice

comply: to go along with

2. Why is it necessary for a country to use the military draft?

3. Write a 3-sen...

Answers will vary.

Page 113

Tennis

Directions: Read the selection. Then answer the questions.

Martina Navratilova gained fame as the best women's tennis player of the 1980s. She was born in Czechoslovakia in 1956 and moved to the United States at the age of 19. She became a United States citizen in 1981.

Martina Navratilova excelled in the sport of tennis but she enjoyed the Wimbledon championship the most. She won the singles finals in 1978, 1979, 1982, 1983, 1984, 1985, 1986, 1987 and 1990.

In 1982, she became the first woman professional tennis player to earn over one million dollars in a single season.

1. What physical characteristics are necessary to excel in the sport of tennis?

2. In your opinion, why would an ath ... ome to the U.S.A. to train ...

Answers will vary.

3. Many athletes find it difficult to adjust to their status as "heroes." What are some possible disadvantages to being an athletic superstar?

Page 114

Review

Directions: Follow the instructions for each section.

1. On the line below, create a time line of the years of birth for the six athletes discussed in this section.

```
                    1950              1964
                 Mark Spitz        Bonnie Blair
1895          1942          1956          1966
Babe Ruth   Cassius Clay  Martina Navratilova  Gail Devers
```

2. What mental and emotional characteristics did all six athletes have in common?

_____
Answers will vary.
_____

3. On the line below, create a time line of Muhammad Ali's life.

```
    M.A. won Golden      Heavyweight champion
    Gloves Championship  1960  of the world      1967  1970
1942 1959          M.A. won                    M.A. banned from boxing
          Olympics      1964              and stripped of world title
```

4. Compare and contrast the sports of tennis and baseball in a two-paragraph essay.

_____
Answers will vary.
_____

Page 116

Nouns

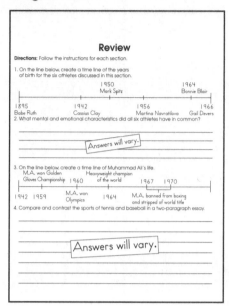

A **noun** names a person, place, thing or idea. There are several types of nouns.

Examples:
  proper nouns: Joe, Jefferson Memorial
  common nouns: dog, town
  concrete nouns: book, stove
  abstract nouns: fear, devotion
  collective nouns: audience, flock

A word can be more than one type of noun.

Example: Dog is both a common and a concrete noun.

Directions: Write the type or types of each noun on the lines.

1. desk — common, concrete
2. ocean — common, concrete
3. love — common, abstract
4. cat — common, concrete
5. herd — common, concrete, collective
6. compassion — common, abstract
7. reputation — common, abstract
8. eyes — common, concrete
9. staff — common, concrete, collective
10. day — common, concrete
11. Roosevelt Building — proper, concrete
12. Mr. Timken — proper, concrete
13. life — common, abstract
14. porch — common, concrete
15. United States — proper, concrete or abstract

Page 117

Possessive Nouns

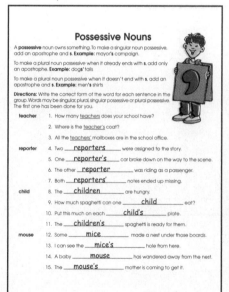

A **possessive** noun owns something. To make a singular noun possessive, add an apostrophe and **s. Example:** mayor**'s** campaign.

To make a plural noun possessive when it already ends with **s**, add only an apostrophe. **Example:** dogs**'** tails

To make a plural noun possessive when it doesn't end with **s**, add an apostrophe and **s. Example:** men**'s** shirts

Directions: Write the correct form of the word for each sentence in the group. Words may be singular, plural, singular possessive or plural possessive. The first one has been done for you.

teacher
1. How many <u>teachers</u> does your school have?
2. Where is the <u>teacher's</u> coat?
3. All the <u>teachers'</u> mailboxes are in the school office.

reporter
4. Two <u>reporters</u> were assigned to the story.
5. One <u>reporter's</u> car broke down on the way to the scene.
6. The other <u>reporter</u> was riding as a passenger.
7. Both <u>reporters'</u> notes ended up missing.

child
8. The <u>children</u> are hungry.
9. How much spaghetti can one <u>child</u> eat?
10. Put this much on each <u>child's</u> plate.
11. The <u>children's</u> spaghetti is ready for them.

mouse
12. Some <u>mice</u> made a nest under those boards.
13. I can see the <u>mice's</u> hole from here.
14. A baby <u>mouse</u> has wandered away from the nest.
15. The <u>mouse's</u> mother is coming to get it.

Page 118

Verbs

A **verb** is a word that tells what something does or that something exists.

There are two types of verbs: **action** and **state of being**.

Examples:
  Action: run, read
  State of being: feel, sound, taste, stay, look, appear, grow, seem, smell and forms of **be**

Directions: Write **A** if the verb shows action. Write **S** if it shows state of being.

1. **A** He helped his friend.
2. **S** They appear happy and content.
3. **A** Jordi drives to school each day.
4. **A** The snowfall closed schools everywhere.
5. **A** The dog sniffed at its food.
6. **S** The meat tastes funny.
7. **A** Did you taste the ice cream?
8. **A** The young boy smelled the flowers.
9. **S** She looked depressed.
10. **A** The coach announced the dates of the scrimmage.
11. **A** The owner of the store stocks all types of soda.
12. **A** He dribbled the ball down the court.
13. **S** "Everything seems to be in order," said the train conductor.

Page 119

Verb Tense

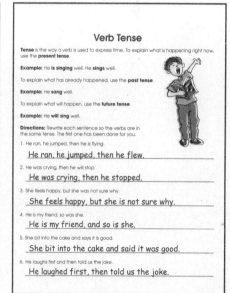

Tense is the way a verb is used to express time. To explain what is happening right now, use the **present tense.**

Example: He is singing well. He **sings** well.

To explain what has already happened, use the **past tense.**

Example: He sang well.

To explain what will happen, use the **future tense.**

Example: He will sing well.

Directions: Rewrite each sentence so the verbs are in the same tense. The first one has been done for you.

1. He ran, he jumped, then he is flying.
   He ran, he jumped, then he flew.

2. He was crying, then he will stop.
   He was crying, then he stopped.

3. She feels happy, but she was not sure why.
   She feels happy, but she is not sure why.

4. He is my friend, so was she.
   He is my friend, and so is she.

5. She bit into the cake and says it is good.
   She bit into the cake and said it was good.

6. He laughs first and then told us the joke.
   He laughed first, then told us the joke.

GRADE 6

Page 120

Spelling Different Forms of Verbs

To show that something is happening in the present, we can use a "plain" verb, or we can use **is** or **are** and add **ing** to the verb.

is/are + verb + ing
was/were + verb + ing

Example: We run. We **are running**.

To show that something has already happened, we can add **ed** to many verbs, or we can use **was** or **were** and add **ing** to a verb.

Example: The workers **surveyed**. The workers were **surveying**.

If a verb ends in **e**, drop the final **e** before adding an ending that begins with a vowel.

Example: She is **driving**. He **restored** the old car.

If a verb ends in **sh** or **ch**, add **es** instead of **s** to change the form.

Example: He furnish**es**. She watch**es**.

Directions: Complete each sentence with the correct form of the verb given. The first one has been done for you.

1. The florist is (have) a sale this week. _**having**_
2. Last night's tornado (destroy) a barn. _**destroyed**_
3. We are (research) the history of our town. _**researching**_
4. My mistake was (use) a plural verb instead of a singular one. _**using**_
5. She (act) quickly in yesterday's emergency. _**acted**_
6. Our group is (survey) the parents in our community. _**surveying**_
7. For our last experiment, we (observe) a plant's growth for 2 weeks. _**observed**_
8. A local company already (furnish) all the materials for this project. _**furnished**_
9. Which dairy (furnish) milk to our cafeteria every day? _**furnishes**_
10. Just (ignore) the mess in here will not help your case. _**ignoring**_

Page 121

Verb Tense

Directions: Write a sentence using the present tense of each verb.

1. walk
2. dream
3. achieve

Directions: ...

4. danc...
5. study
6. hike

Directions: Write a sentence using the future tense of each verb.

7. bake
8. write
9. talk

Answers will vary.

Page 122

Verb Tense

Verbs can be **present**, **past** or **past participle**.

Add **d** or **ed** to form the past tense.

Past-participle verbs also use a helping verb such as **has** or **have**.

Examples:

Present	Past	Past Participle
help	helped	has or have helped
skip	skipped	has or have skipped

Directions: Write the past and past-participle forms of each present tense verb.

	Present	Past	Past Participle
1.	paint	painted	has (have) painted
2.	dream	dreamed	has (have) dreamed
3.	play	played	has (have) played
4.	approach	approached	has (have) approached
5.	hop	hopped	has (have) hopped
6.	climb	climbed	has (have) climbed
7.	dance	danced	has (have) danced
8.	appear	appeared	has (have) appeared
9.	watch	watched	has (have) watched
10.	dive	dove, dived	has (have) dived
11.	hurry	hurried	has (have) hurried
12.	discover	discovered	has (have) discovered
13.	decorate	decorated	has (have) decorated
14.	close	closed	has (have) closed
15.	jump	jumped	has (have) jumped

Page 123

Irregular Verb Forms

The past tense of most verbs is formed by adding **ed**. Verbs that do not follow this format are called **irregular verbs**.

The irregular verb chart shows a few of the many verbs with irregular forms.

Irregular Verb Chart

Present Tense	Past Tense	Past Participle
go	went	has, have or had gone
do	did	has, have or had done
fly	flew	has, have or had flown
grow	grew	has, have or had grown
ride	rode	has, have or had ridden
see	saw	has, have or had seen
sing	sang	has, have or had sung
swim	swam	has, have or had swum
throw	threw	has, have or had thrown

The words **had**, **have** and **has** can be separated from the irregular verb by other words in the sentence.

Directions: Choose the correct verb form from the chart to complete the sentences. The first one has been done for you.

1. The pilot had never before _**flown**_ that type of plane.
2. She put on her bathing suit and _**swam**_ 2 miles.
3. The tall boy had _**grown**_ 2 inches over the summer.
4. She insisted she had _**done**_ her homework.
5. He _**saw**_ them walking down the street.
6. She _**rode**_ the horse around the track.
7. The pitcher has _**thrown**_ the ball many times.
8. He can _**swim**_ safely in the deepest water.

Page 124

Irregular Verb Forms

Directions: Use the irregular verb chart on the previous page. Write the correct verb form to complete each sentence.

1. Has she ever _**grown**_ carrots in her garden?
2. She was so angry she _**threw**_ a tantrum.
3. The bird had sometimes _**flown**_ from its cage.
4. The cowboy has never _**ridden**_ that horse before.
5. Will you _**go**_ to the store with me?
6. He said he had often _**seen**_ her walking on his street.
7. She insisted she has not _**grown**_ taller this year.
8. He _**swam**_ briskly across the pool.
9. Have the insects _**flown**_ away?
10. Has anyone _**seen**_ my sister lately?
11. He hasn't _**done**_ the dishes once this week!
12. Has she been _**thrown**_ out of the game for cheating?
13. I haven't _**seen**_ her yet today.
14. The airplane _**flew**_ slowly by the airport.
15. Have you _**ridden**_ your bike yet this week?

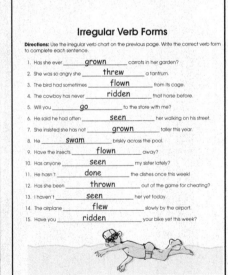

Page 125

Nouns and Verbs

Some words can be used as both nouns and verbs.

Example:
The **bait** on his hook was a worm.
He couldn't **bait** his hook.

In the first sentence, **bait** is used as a **noun** because it names a thing. In the second sentence, **bait** is used as a **verb** because it shows action.

Directions: Write **noun** or **verb** for the word in bold in each sentence. The first one has been done for you.

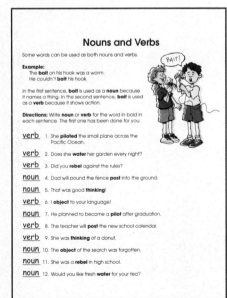

verb 1. She **piloted** the small plane across the Pacific Ocean.
verb 2. Does she **water** her garden every night?
verb 3. Did you **rebel** against the rules?
noun 4. Dad will pound the fence **post** into the ground.
noun 5. That was good **thinking**.
verb 6. I **object** to your language!
noun 7. He planned to become a **pilot** after graduation.
verb 8. The teacher will **post** the new school calendar.
verb 9. She was **thinking** of a donut.
noun 10. The **object** of the search was forgotten.
noun 11. She was a **rebel** in high school.
noun 12. Would you like fresh **water** for your tea?

Total Basic Skills Grade 6   322   Answer Key

Page 126

Spelling: Plurals

Is **heros** or **heroes** the correct spelling? Many people aren't sure. These rules have exceptions, but they will help you spell the plural forms of most words that end with **o**.
- If a word ends with a consonant and **o**, add **es**: heroes.
- If a word ends with a vowel and **o**, add **s**: radios.

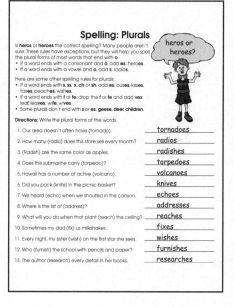

Here are some other spelling rules for plurals:
- If a word ends with **s**, **ss**, **x**, **ch** or **sh**, add **es**: buses, kisses, taxes, peaches, wishes.
- If a word ends with **f** or **fe**, drop the **f** or **fe** and add **ves**: leaf, leaves; wife, wives.
- Some plurals don't end with **s** or **es**: geese, deer, children.

Directions: Write the plural forms of the words.

1. Our area doesn't often have (tornado). **tornadoes**
2. How many (radio) does this store sell every month? **radios**
3. (Radish) are the same color as apples. **radishes**
4. Does this submarine carry (torpedo)? **torpedoes**
5. Hawaii has a number of active (volcano). **volcanoes**
6. Did you pack (knife) in the picnic basket? **knives**
7. We heard (echo) when we shouted in the canyon. **echoes**
8. Where is the list of (address)? **addresses**
9. What will you do when that plant (reach) the ceiling? **reaches**
10. Sometimes my dad (fix) us milkshakes. **fixes**
11. Every night, my sister (wish) on the first star she sees. **wishes**
12. Who (furnish) the school with pencils and paper? **furnishes**
13. The author (research) every detail in her books. **researches**

Page 127

Spelling: Plurals

Directions: Write the plural form of each word.

1. mother — **mothers**
2. ankle — **ankles**
3. journey — **journeys**
4. ceiling — **ceilings**
5. governor — **governors**
6. arch — **arches**
7. carnival — **carnivals**
8. official — **officials**
9. potato — **potatoes**
10. vacuum — **vacuums**
11. stereo — **stereos**
12. strategy — **strategies**
13. column — **columns**
14. architect — **architects**
15. entry — **entries**
16. summary — **summaries**
17. issue — **issues**
18. member — **members**
19. astronomer — **astronomers**
20. channel — **channels**
21. harmony — **harmonies**
22. piece — **pieces**
23. chicken — **chickens**
24. chemical — **chemicals**
25. journal — **journals**
26. niece — **nieces**
27. mayor — **mayors**
28. particle — **particles**
29. entrance — **entrances**
30. assistant — **assistants**

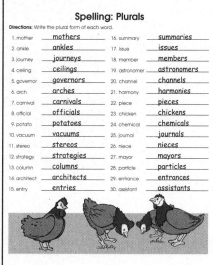

Page 128

Simple Subjects

The **simple subject** of a sentence tells who or what the sentence is about. It is a noun or a pronoun.

Example: My mom is turning forty this year.
Mom is the simple subject.

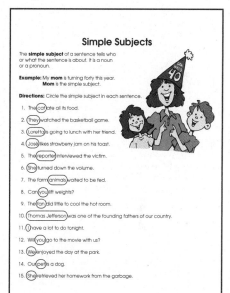

Directions: Circle the simple subject in each sentence.

1. The (cat) ate all its food.
2. (They) watched the basketball game.
3. (Loretta) is going to lunch with her friend.
4. (Jose) likes strawberry jam on his toast.
5. The (reporter) interviewed the victim.
6. (She) turned down the volume.
7. The farm (animals) waited to be fed.
8. Can (you) lift weights?
9. The (fan) did little to cool the hot room.
10. (Thomas Jefferson) was one of the founding fathers of our country.
11. (I) have a lot to do tonight.
12. Will (you) go to the movie with us?
13. (We) enjoyed the day at the park.
14. Our (pet) is a dog.
15. (She) retrieved her homework from the garbage.

Page 129

Simple Predicates

The **simple predicate** of a sentence tells what the subject does, is doing, did or will do. The simple predicate is always a verb.

Example:
My mom is turning forty this year.
"Is turning" is the simple predicate.

Directions: Underline the simple predicate in each sentence. Include all helping verbs.

1. I <u>bought</u> school supplies at the mall.
2. The tiger <u>chased</u> its prey.
3. Mark <u>will be arriving</u> shortly.
4. The hamburgers <u>are cooking</u> now.
5. We <u>will attend</u> my sister's wedding.
6. The dental hygienist <u>cleaned</u> my teeth.
7. My socks <u>are hanging</u> on the clothesline.
8. Where <u>are</u> you going?
9. The dog <u>is running</u> toward its owner.
10. Ramos <u>watched</u> the tornado in fear.
11. Please <u>wash</u> the dishes after dinner.
12. My dad <u>cleaned</u> the garage yesterday.
13. We <u>are going</u> hiking at Yellowstone today.
14. The picture <u>shows</u> our entire family at the family picnic.
15. Our coach <u>will give</u> us a pep talk before the game.

Page 130

Parallel Structure

Parts of a sentence are **parallel** when they "match" grammatically and structurally.

Faulty parallelism occurs when the parts of a sentence do not match grammatically and structurally.

For sentences to be parallel, all parts of a sentence—including the verbs, nouns and phrases—must match. This means that, in most cases, verbs should be in the same tense.

Examples:
Correct: She liked running, jumping and swinging outdoors.
Incorrect: She liked running, jumping and to swing outdoors.

In the correct sentence, all three of the actions the girl liked to do end in **ing**. In the incorrect sentence, they do not.

Directions: Rewrite the sentences so all elements are parallel. The first one has been done for you.

1. Politicians like making speeches and also to shake hands.
   Politicians like making speeches and shaking hands.
2. He liked singing, acting and to perform in general.
   He liked singing, acting and performing in general.
3. The cake had icing, sprinkles and also has small candy hearts.
   The cake had icing, sprinkles and small candy hearts.
4. The drink was cold, frosty and also is a thirst-quencher.
   The drink was cold, frosty and a thirst-quencher.
5. She was asking when we would arrive, and I told her.
   She asked when we would arrive, and I told her.
6. Liz felt like shouting, singing and to jump.
   Liz felt like shouting, singing and jumping.

Page 131

Matching Subjects and Verbs

If the subject of a sentence is singular, the verb must be singular. If the subject is plural, the verb must be plural.

Example:
The **dog** with floppy ears **is eating**.
The **dogs** in the yard **are eating**.

Directions: Write the singular or plural form of the subject in each sentence to match the verb.

1. The (yolk) **yolk** in this egg is bright yellow.
2. The (child) **children** are putting numbers in columns.
3. Both (coach) **coaches** are resigning at the end of the year.
4. Those three (class) **classes** were assigned to the gym.
5. The (lunch) **lunches** for the children are ready.
6. (Spaghetti) **Spaghetti** with meatballs is delicious.
7. Where are the (box) **boxes** of chalk?
8. The (man) **men** in the truck were collecting broken tree limbs.
9. The (rhythm) **rhythm** of that music is exactly right for dancing.
10. Sliced (tomato) **tomatoes** on lettuce are good with salmon.
11. The (announcer) **announcer** on TV was condemning the dictator.
12. Two (woman) **women** are campaigning for mayor of our town.
13. The (group) **group** of travelers was on its way to three foreign countries.
14. The (choir) **choir** of thirty children is singing hymns.
15. In spite of the parade, the (hero) **heroes** were solemn.

Page 132

Subject/Verb Agreement

Singular subjects require singular verbs. **Plural subjects** require plural verbs. The subject and verb must agree in a sentence.

Example:
Singular: My dog runs across the field.
Plural: My dogs run across the field.

Directions: Circle the correct verb in each sentence.

1. Maria (talk/**talks**) to me each day at lunch.
2. Mom, Dad and I (is/**are**) going to the park to play catch.
3. Mr. and Mrs. Ramirez (**dance**/dances) well together.
4. Astronauts (**hope**/hopes) for a successful shuttle mission.
5. Trees (**prevent**/prevents) erosion.
6. The student (**is**/are) late.
7. She (ask/**asks**) for directions to the senior high gym.
8. The elephants (**plod**/plods) across the grassland to the watering hole.
9. My friend's name (**is**/are) Rebecca.
10. Many people (**enjoy**/enjoys) orchestra concerts.
11. The pencils (is/**are**) sharpened.
12. My backpack (hold/**holds**) a lot of things.
13. The wind (blow/**blows**) to the south.
14. Sam (collect/**collects**) butterflies.
15. They (**love**/loves) cotton-candy.

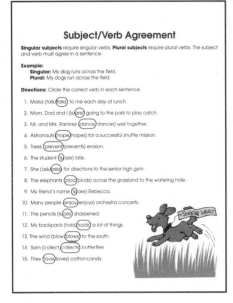

Page 133

Personal Pronouns

Personal pronouns take the place of nouns. They refer to people or things. **I, me, we, she, he, him, her, you, they, them, us** and **it** are personal pronouns.

Directions: Circle the personal pronouns in each sentence.

1. **He** is a terrific friend.
2. Would **you** open the door?
3. Jim and **I** will arrive at ten o'clock.
4. Can **you** pick **me** up at the mall after dinner?
5. What did **you** do yesterday?
6. **They** are watching the game on television.
7. Jessie's mom took **us** to the movies.
8. **She** writes novels.
9. **They** gave **us** the refrigerator.
10. Is this the answer **she** intended to give?
11. What is **it**?
12. The dog yelped when **it** saw the cat.
13. **I** admire **him**.
14. **We** parked the bikes by the tree.
15. The ants kept **us** from enjoying **our** picnic.

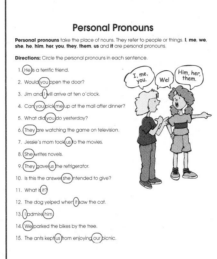

Page 134

Possessive Pronouns

Possessive pronouns show ownership. **My, mine, your, yours, his, her, hers, their, theirs, our, ours** and **its** are possessive pronouns.

Directions: Circle the possessive pronouns in each sentence.

1. **My** dogs chase cats continually.
2. Jodi put **her** sunglasses on the dashboard.
3. **His** mother and **mine** are the same age.
4. The cat licked **its** paw.
5. **Their** anniversary is February 1.
6. This necklace is **yours**.
7. We will carry **our** luggage into the airport.
8. **Our** parents took us to dinner.
9. **My** brother broke **his** leg.
10. **Her** report card was excellent.
11. Raspberry jam is **my** favorite.
12. Watch **your** step!
13. The house on the left is **mine**.
14. **My** phone number is unlisted.
15. **Our** garden is growing out of control.
16. **Our** pumpkins are ten times larger than **theirs**.

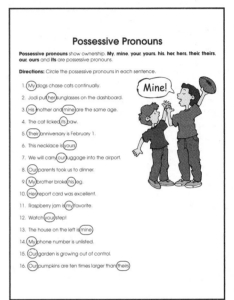

Page 135

Interrogative Pronouns

An **interrogative pronoun** asks a question. There are three interrogative pronouns: **who, what** and **which**.

Use **who** when speaking of persons.
Use **what** when speaking of things.
Use **which** when speaking of persons or things.

Examples:
Who will go? **What** will you do? **Which** of these is yours?

Who becomes **whom** when it is a direct object or an object of a preposition. The possessive form of **whom** is **whose**.

Examples:
To **whom** will you write?
Whose computer is that?

Directions: Write the correct interrogative pronoun.

1. **Whose** wet raincoat is this?
2. **Who** is the president of the United States?
3. **What** is your name?
4. **Whose** dog made this muddy mess?
5. **Whose** cat ran away?
6. **Which** of you is the culprit?
7. **What** was your grade on the last test?
8. To **whom** did you report?
9. **Whom** do you believe now?
10. **Who** is the leader of this English study group?

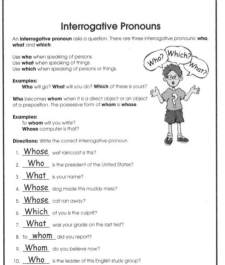

Page 136

Personal and Possessive Pronouns

Directions: Write personal or possessive pronouns in the blanks to take the place of the words in bold. The first one has been done for you.

They him 1. **Maisie and Marni** told **Trent** they would see him later.
He them 2. **Spencer** told **Nancee and Sandi** good-bye.
It his 3. **The bike** was parked near **Aaron's** house.
They 4. **Maria, Matt and Greg** claimed the car was new.
theirs 5. The dishes were **the property of Cindy and Jake**.
hers 6. Is this **Carole's**?
He their 7. **Jon** walked near **Jessica and Esau's** house.
It 8. **The dog** barked all night long!
She her 9. **Dawn** fell and hurt **Dawn's** knee.
They its 10. **Cory and Devan** gave the dog **the dog's** dinner.
We them 11. **Tori and I** gave **Brett and Reggie** a ride home.
they 12. Do **Josh and Andrea** like cats?
They us 13. **Sasha and Keesha** gave **Josh and me** a ride home.
hers 14. Is this sweater **Marni's**?
it 15. The cat meowed because **the cat** was hungry.

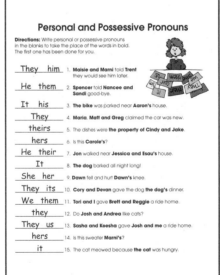

Page 137

Pronoun/Antecedent Agreement

Often, a **pronoun** is used in place of a noun to avoid repeating the noun again in the same sentence. The noun that a pronoun refers to is called its **antecedent**. The word "antecedent" means "going before."

If the noun is singular, the pronoun that takes its place must also be singular. If the noun is plural, the pronoun that takes its place must also be plural. This is called *agreement* between the pronoun and its antecedent.

Examples:
Mary (singular noun) said **she** (singular pronoun) would dance.
The **dogs** (plural noun) took **their** (plural pronoun) dishes outside.

When the noun is singular and the gender unknown, it is correct to use either "his" or "his or her."

Directions: Rewrite the sentences so the pronouns and nouns agree. The first one has been done for you.

1. Every student opened their book.
   Every student opened his book.
   Also correct: Every student opened his or her book.
2. Has anyone lost their wallet lately?
   Has anyone lost his or her wallet lately?
3. Somebody found the wallet under their desk.
   Somebody found the wallet under his desk.
4. Someone will have to file their report.
   Someone will have to file his or her report.
5. Every dog has their day!
   Every dog has its day!
6. I felt Ted had mine best interests at heart.
   I felt Ted had my best interests at heart.

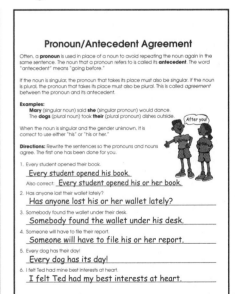

Page 138

Pronoun/Antecedent Agreement

Directions: Write a pronoun that agrees with the antecedent.

1. Donald said ___he___ would go to the store.
2. My friend discovered ___his (or her)___ wallet had been stolen.
3. The cat licked ___its___ paw.
4. Did any woman here lose ___her___ necklace?
5. Someone will have to give ___his (or her)___ report.
6. Jennifer wished ___she___ had not come.
7. All the children decided ___they___ would attend.
8. My grandmother hurt ___her___ back while gardening.
9. Jerry, Marco and I hope ___we___ win the game.
10. Sandra looked for ___her___ missing homework.
11. The family had ___its___ celebration.
12. My dog jumps out of ___its___ pen.
13. Somebody needs to remove ___his (or her)___ clothes from this chair.
14. Everything has ___its___ place in Grandma's house.
15. The team will receive ___their___ uniforms on Monday.
16. Each artist wants ___his (or her)___ painting to win the prize.

Page 139

Appositives

An **appositive** is a noun or pronoun placed after another noun or pronoun to further identify or rename it. An appositive and the words that go with it are usually set off from the rest of the sentence with commas. Commas are not used if the appositive tells "which one."

Example: Angela's mother, **Ms. Glover**, will visit our school.

Commas are needed because **Ms. Glover** renames Angela's mother.

Example: Angela's neighbor Joan will visit our school.

Commas are not needed because the appositive "Joan" tells **which** neighbor.

Directions: Write the appositive in each sentence in the blank. The first one has been done for you.

___Tina___	1. My friend Tina wants a horse.
___Horses___	2. She subscribes to the magazine *Horses*.
___"Brownie"___	3. Her horse is the gelding "Brownie."
___convertible___	4. We rode in her new car, a convertible.
___bracelet___	5. Her gift was jewelry, a bracelet.
___senator___	6. Have you met Ms. Abbott, the senator?
___Karl___	7. My cousin Karl is very shy.
___Oaties___	8. Do you eat the cereal Oaties?
___Samantha___	9. Kiki's cat, Samantha, will eat only tuna.
___Jones___	10. My last name, Jones, is very common.

Page 140

Dangling Modifiers

A **dangling modifier** is a word or group of words that does not modify what it is supposed to modify. To correct dangling modifiers, supply the missing words to which the modifiers refer.

Examples:
Incorrect: While doing the laundry, the dog barked.
Correct: While I was doing the laundry, the dog barked.

In the **incorrect** sentence, it sounds as though the dog is doing the laundry. In the **correct** sentence, it's clear that **I** is the subject of the sentence.

Directions: Rewrite the sentences to make the subject of the sentence clear and eliminate dangling modifiers. The first one has been done for you.

1. While eating our hot dogs, the doctor called.
   While we were eating our hot dogs, the doctor called.
2. Living in Cincinnati, the ball park is nearby.
   I live in Cincinnati, and the ball park is nearby.
3. While watching the movie, the TV screen went blank.
   While we were watching the movie, the TV screen went blank.
4. While listening to the concert, the lights went out.
   While we were listening to the concert, the lights went out.
5. Tossed regularly, anyone can make great salad.
   Anyone can make a great salad if it's tossed regularly.
6. While working, something surprised him.
   While he was working, something surprised him.

Page 141

Review

Directions: Write **noun** or **verb** to describe the words in bold.

noun	1. She is one of the fastest **runners** I've seen.
verb	2. She is **running** very fast!
verb	3. She **thought** he was handsome.
noun	4. Please share your **thoughts** with me.
verb	5. I will **watch** the volleyball game on video.
noun	6. The sailor fell asleep during his **watch**.
noun	7. My grandmother believes my purchase was a real **find**.
verb	8. I hope to **find** my lost books.

Directions: Rewrite the verb in the correct tense.

swam	9. She **swim** across the lake in 2 hours.
ridden	10. He has **ride** horses for years.
seen	11. Have you **saw** my sister?
flew	12. She **fly** on an airplane last week.
instructed	13. My father had **instruct** me in the language.
drove	14. I **drive** to the store yesterday.
began	15. The movie **begin** late.
did	16. Where **do** you go yesterday?

Directions: Circle the pronouns.

17. (She) and (I) told (them) to forget (it).
18. (They) all wondered if (her) dad would drive (his) new car.
19. (We) want (our) parents to believe (us).
20. (My) picture was taken at (her) home.

Page 142

Review

Directions: Rewrite the sentences to correct the faulty parallels.

1. The cookies were sweet, crunchy and are delicious.
   The cookies were sweet, crunchy and delicious.
2. The town was barren, windswept and is empty.
   The town was barren, windswept and empty.
3. The dog was black, long-haired and is quite friendly.
   The dog was black, long-haired and quite friendly.
4. My favorite dinners are macaroni and cheese, spaghetti and I loved fish.
   My favorite dinners are macaroni and cheese, spaghetti and fish.

Directions: Rewrite the sentences to make the verb tenses consistent.

5. We laughed, cried and were jumping for joy.
   We laughed, cried and jumped for joy.
6. She sang, danced and was doing somersaults.
   She sang, danced and did somersaults.
7. The class researched, studied and were writing their reports.
   The class researched, studied and wrote their reports.
8. Bob and Sue talked about their vacation and share their experiences.
   Bob and Sue talked about their vacation and shared their experiences.

Directions: Circle the pronouns that agree with their antecedents.

9. She left (her/their) purse at the dance.
10. Each dog wagged (its/their) tail.
11. We walked to (our/he) car.
12. The lion watched (his/its) prey.

Page 143

Review Answers may vary.

Directions: Rewrite the sentences to correct the dangling modifiers.

1. Living nearby, the office was convenient for her.
   She lived nearby and the office was convenient for her.
2. While doing my homework, the doorbell rang.
   While I was doing my homework, the doorbell rang.
3. Watching over her shoulder, she hurried away.
   She watched over her shoulder and hurried away.
4. Drinking from the large mug, he choked.
   While he was drinking from the large mug, he choked.

Directions: Circle the correct pronouns.

5. She laughed at my brother and (I/me).
6. At dawn, (he and I/him and me) were still talking.
7. Someone left (his or her/their) coat on the floor.
8. Lauren said (her/she) would not be late.

Directions: Circle the appositive.

9. The school nurse, (Ms. Franklin) was worried about him.
10. The car (a Volkswagen) was illegally parked.
11. My hero, (Babe Ruth) was an outstanding baseball player.
12. Is that car (the plum-colored one) for sale?
13. Will Mr. Zimmer, (Todd's father) buy that car?

REVIEW
NOUNS VERBS
SIMPLE SUBJECTS
PERSONAL PRONOUNS
POSSESSIVE PRONOUNS
INTERROGATIVE PRONOUNS
ANTECEDENTS
APPOSITIVES
SIMPLE PREDICATES

Answer Key   325   Total Basic Skills Grade 6

Page 144

Adjectives

Adjectives describe nouns.

Examples:
tall girl
soft voice
clean hands

Directions: Circle the adjectives. Underline the nouns they describe. Some sentences may have more than one set of adjectives and nouns.

1. The lonely man sat in the dilapidated house.
2. I hope the large crop of grapes will soon ripen.
3. The white boxes house honeybees.
4. My rambunctious puppy knocked over the valuable flower vase.
5. The unsinkable Titanic sank after striking a gigantic iceberg.
6. His grades showed his tremendous effort.
7. There are many purple flowers in the large arrangement.
8. These sweet peaches are the best I've tasted.
9. The newsletter describes several educational workshops.
10. The rodeo featured professional riders and funny clowns.
11. My evening pottery class is full of very interesting people.
12. My older brother loves his new pickup truck.
13. Tami's family bought a big-screen TV.

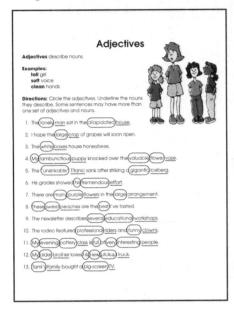

Page 145

Comparing With Adjectives

When adjectives are used to compare two things, **er** is added at the end of the word for most one-syllable words and some two-syllable words.

Example: It is **colder** today than it was yesterday.

With many two-syllable words and all words with three or more syllables, the word **more** is used with the adjective to show comparison.

Example: Dr. X is **more professional** than Dr. Y.

When adjectives are used to compare three or more things, **est** is added at the end of the word for **most** one-syllable words and some two-syllable words.

Example: Today is the **coldest** day of the year.

With many two-syllable words and all words with three or more syllables, **most** is used with the adjective to show comparison.

Example: Dr. X is the **most professional** doctor in town.

When adding **er** or **est** to one-syllable words, these spelling rules apply.
• Double the last consonant if the word has a short vowel before a final consonant: thinner, fatter.
• If a word ends in **y**, change the y to **i** before adding **er** or **est**: earliest, prettiest.
• If a word ends in **e**, drop the final **e** before adding **er** or **est**: simpler, simplest.

Directions: Complete these sentences with the correct form of the adjective.

1. This book is (small) __smaller__ than that one.
2. I want the (small) __smallest__ book in the library.
3. My plan is (practical) __more practical__ than yours.
4. My plan is (practical) __most practical__ one in the class.
5. I wish the change was (gradual) __more gradual__ than it is.
6. My sister is the (childish) __most childish__ girl in her day-care group.
7. There must be a (simple) __simpler__ way to do it than that.
8. This is the (simple) __simplest__ way of the four we thought of.

Page 146

Adjectives: Positive, Comparative and Superlative

There are three degrees of comparison adjectives: **positive**, **comparative** and **superlative**. The **positive degree** is the adjective itself. The **comparative** and **superlative** degrees are formed by adding **er** and **est**, respectively, to most one-syllable adjectives. The form of the word changes when the adjective is irregular; for example, **good**, **better**, **best**.

Most adjectives of two or more syllables require the words "more" or "most" to form the comparative and superlative degrees.

Examples:
Positive: big / eager
Comparative: bigger / more eager
Superlative: biggest / most eager

Directions: Write the positive, comparative or superlative forms of these adjectives.

Positive	Comparative	Superlative
1. hard	harder	hardest
2. happy	happier	happiest
3. difficult	more difficult	most difficult
4. cold	colder	coldest
5. easy	easier	easiest
6. large	larger	largest
7. little	less	least
8. shiny	shinier	shiniest
9. round	rounder	roundest
10. beautiful	more beautiful	most beautiful

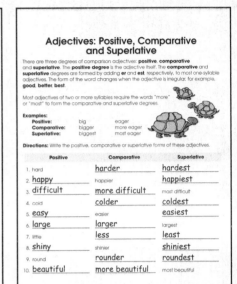

Page 147

Adverbs

Adverbs tell when, where or how an action occurred.

Examples:
I'll go **tomorrow**. (when)
I sleep **upstairs**. (where)
I screamed **loudly**. (how)

Directions: Circle the adverb and underline the verb it modifies. Write the question (when, where or how) the adverb answers.

1. I ran quickly toward the finish line. — how
2. Today we will receive our report cards. — when
3. He swam smoothly through the pool. — how
4. Many explorers searched endlessly for new lands. — how
5. He looked up into the sky. — where
6. My friend drove away in her new car. — where
7. Later we will search for your missing wallet. — when
8. Most kings rule their kingdoms regally. — how
9. New plants must be watered daily. — when
10. The stream near our house is heavily polluted. — how
11. My brother likes to dive backward into our pool. — how

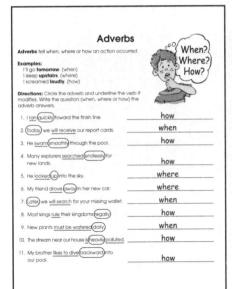

Page 148

Adverbs: Positive, Comparative and Superlative

There are also three degrees of comparison adverbs: **positive**, **comparative** and **superlative**. They follow the same rules as adjectives.

Example:
Positive: rapidly / far
Comparative: more rapidly / farther
Superlative: most rapidly / farthest

Directions: Write the positive, comparative or superlative forms of these adverbs.

Positive	Comparative	Superlative
1. easily	more easily	most easily
2. quickly	more quickly	most quickly
3. hopefully	more hopefully	most hopefully
4. bravely	more bravely	most bravely
5. strongly	more strongly	most strongly
6. near	nearer	nearest
7. cleverly	more cleverly	most cleverly
8. gracefully	more gracefully	most gracefully
9. humbly	more humbly	most humbly
10. excitedly	more excitedly	most excitedly
11. handsomely	more handsomely	most handsomely
12. slowly	more slowly	most slowly

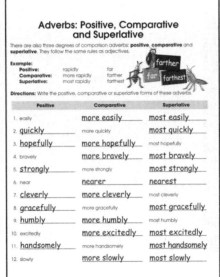

Page 149

Adjectives and Adverbs

Directions: Write **adjective** or **adverb** in the blanks to describe the words in bold. The first one has been done for you.

1. adjective — Her **old** boots were caked with mud.
2. adjective — The baby was **cranky**.
3. adverb — He took the test **yesterday**.
4. adjective — I heard the **funniest** story last week!
5. adverb — She left her wet shoes **outside**.
6. adjective — Isn't that the **fluffiest** cat you've ever seen?
7. adverb — He ran **around** the track twice.
8. adjective — Our elderly neighbor lady seems **lonely**.
9. adjective — His **kind** smile lifted my dragging spirits.
10. adverb — **Someday** I'll meet the friend of my dreams!
11. adverb — His cat never meows **indoors**.
12. adverb — Carlos hung his new shirts **back** in the closet.
13. adverb — Put that valuable vase **down** immediately!
14. adjective — She is the most **joyful** child!
15. adjective — Jonathan's wool sweater is totally **moth-eaten**.

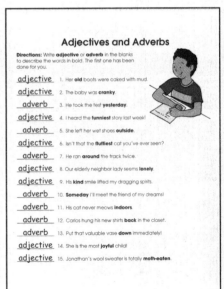

Page 150

Identifying Sentence Parts

The **subject** tells who or what a sentence is about. Sentences can have more than one subject.

Example: Dogs and **cats** make good pets.

The **predicate** tells what the subject does or that it exists. Predicates can be more than one word. A sentence can have more than one predicate.

Examples: She **was walking**. She **walked** and **ran**.

An **adjective** is a word or group of words that describes the subject or another noun.

Example: The **cheerful yellow** bird with **blue** spots flew across the **flower-covered** meadow.

An **adverb** is a word or group of words that tells how, when, where or how often.

Example: He sat **there** waiting **quietly**.

Directions: Write **S** for subject, **P** for predicate, **ADJ** for adjective or **ADV** for adverb above each underlined word or group of words. The first one has been done for you.

ADJ S ADJ P ADV
1. A huge dog with long teeth was barking fiercely.

S ADV P
2. My grandmother usually wore a hat with a veil.

S S P ADJ
3. My niece and her friend are the same height.

ADJ S P P ADV
4. The lively reindeer danced and pranced briefly on the rooftop.

Directions: Write sentences containing the sentence parts listed. Mark each part even if the verb part gets separated.

1. Write a question with two subjects, two predicates and two adjectives:

2. Write a statement with ___ *Answers will vary.* ___ dicates and two adjectives:

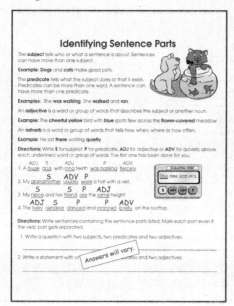

Page 151

Identifying Sentence Parts

Directions: Write **S** for subject, **P** for predicate, **ADJ** for adjective or **ADV** for adverb above the appropriate words in these sentences.

ADJ S P ADV
1. The large cat pounced on the mouse ferociously.

P S P
2. Did you remember your homework?

S P ADV
3. My mother is traveling to New York tomorrow.

S P ADJ ADJ
4. I play basketball on Monday and Friday afternoons.

ADJ S P
5. The old decrepit house sat at the end of the street.

ADJ S P
6. Several tiny rabbits nibbled at the grass at the edge of the field.

ADJ S P ADJ ADJ
7. The lovely bride wore a white dress with a long train.

S P ADJ
8. We packed the clothes for the donation center in a box.

S P ADV
9. The telephone rang incessantly.

ADJ S P ADV
10. The lost child cried helplessly.

P S P ADJ ADJ
11. What will we do with these new puppies?

S P ADV
12. Lauren reads several books each week.

S P ADV
13. The picture hung precariously on the wall.

S P ADJ
14. I purchased many new school supplies.

S P ADJ
15. Computers have changed the business world.

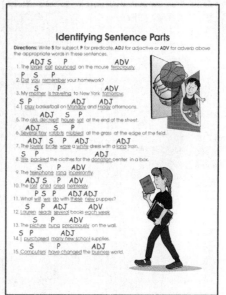

Page 152

Prepositions

A **preposition** is a word that comes before a noun or pronoun and shows the relationship of that noun or pronoun to some other word in the sentence.

The **object of a preposition** is the noun or pronoun that follows a preposition and adds to its meaning.

A **prepositional phrase** includes the preposition, the object of the preposition and all modifiers.

Example:
She gave him a pat **on his back**.
On is the preposition.
Back is the object of the preposition.
His is a possessive pronoun.

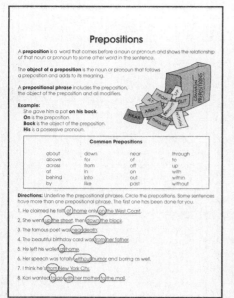

Common Prepositions

about	down	near	through
above	for	of	to
across	from	off	up
at	in	on	with
behind	into	out	within
by	like	past	without

Directions: Underline the prepositional phrases. Circle the prepositions. Some sentences have more than one prepositional phrase. The first one has been done for you.

1. He claimed he felt at home only on the West Coast.
2. She went up the street, then down the block.
3. The famous poet was near death.
4. The beautiful birthday card was from her father.
5. He left his wallet at home.
6. Her speech was totally without humor and boring as well.
7. I think he's from New York City.
8. Kari wanted to go with her mother to the mall.

Page 153

Prepositions

Directions: Complete the sentences by writing objects for the prepositions. The first one has been done for you.

1. He was standing in **the corner of Fifth and Main.**

2. She saw her friend across _____

3. Have you ever looked beyond _____

4. His contact lens fell into _____

5. Have you ___

6. She w___ *Answers will vary.*

7. Is that___

8. She was daydreaming and walked past _____

9. The book was hidden behind _____

10. The young couple had fallen in _____

11. She insisted she was through _____

12. He sat down near _____

13. She forgot her umbrella at _____

14. Have you ever thought of _____

15. Henry found his glasses on _____

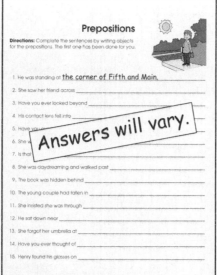

Page 154

Object of a Preposition

The **object of a preposition** is the noun or pronoun that follows the preposition and adds to its meaning.

Example:
Correct: Devan smiled **at** (preposition) **Tori** (noun: object of the preposition) and **me** (pronoun: object of the same preposition.)
Correct: Devan smiled at Tori. Devan smiled at me. Devan smiled at Tori and me.
Incorrect: Devan smiled at Tori and I.

Tip: If you are unsure of the correct pronoun to use, pair each pronoun with the verb and say the phrase out loud to find out which pronoun is correct.

Directions: Write the correct pronouns on the blanks. The first one has been done for you.

him	1. It sounded like a good idea to Sue and (he/him).
her	2. I asked Abby if I could attend with (her/she).
us	3. To (we/us), holidays are very important.
us	4. Between (we/us), we finished the job quickly.
him and me	5. They gave the award to (he and I/him and me).
me	6. The party was for my brother and (I/me).
him	7. I studied with (he/him).
us	8. Tanya and the others arrived after (we/us).
her	9. After the zoo, we stopped at the museum with Bill and (her/she).
him	10. The chips for (he/him) are in the bag on top of the refrigerator.

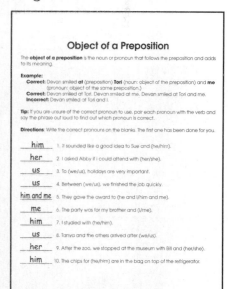

Page 155

Direct Objects

A **direct object** is a noun or pronoun. It answers the question **whom** or **what** after a verb.

Examples:
My mom baked **bread**.
Bread is the direct object. It tells **what** Mom baked.
We saw **Steve**.
Steve is the direct object. It tells **whom** we saw.

Directions: Write a direct object in each sentence.

1. My dog likes _____ WHAT?

2. My favorite drink is _____ WHAT?

3. I saw

Answers will vary.

5. The _____ through the room. WHAT?

6. I packed a _____ for lunch. WHAT?

7. We watched _____ play basketball. WHOM?

8. I finished my _____ WHAT?

9. The artist sketched the _____. WHAT?

10. He greets _____ at the door. WHOM?

11. The team attended the victory _____ WHAT?

12. The beautician cut my _____. WHAT?

13. Tamika will write _____. WHAT?

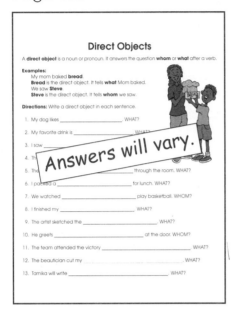

Page 156

Indirect Objects

An **indirect object** is a noun or pronoun which tells **to whom or what** or **for whom or what** the action is performed. An indirect object usually is found between a verb and a direct object.

Example:
I gave **Ellen** my address.
Ellen is the indirect object. It tells **to whom** I gave my address.

Directions: Circle the indirect objects. Underline the direct objects.

1. Joann told (Mary) the <u>secret</u>.

2. Advertisers promise (consumers) the <u>world</u>.

3. The dogs showed (me) their <u>tricks</u>.

4. Aunt Martha gave (Rhonda) a <u>necklace</u> for her birthday.

5. Ramon brought (Mom) a <u>bouquet</u> of fresh flowers.

6. I sent my (niece) a <u>package</u> for Christmas.

7. Mr. Dunbar left his (wife) a <u>note</u> before leaving.

8. Grandma and Grandpa made their (friends) <u>dinner</u>.

9. The baby handed her (mom) a <u>toy</u>.

10. Monica told (Stephanie) the <u>recipe</u> for meatloaf.

11. We sent (Grandma) a <u>card</u>.

12. The waiter served (us) <u>dessert</u>.

13. Mom and Dad sold (us) the <u>farm</u>.

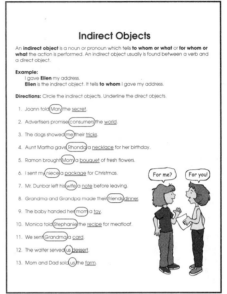

For me?   For you!

Page 159

"Affect" and "Effect"

Affect means to act upon or influence.

Example: Studying will **affect** my test grade.

Effect means to bring about a result or to accomplish something.

Example: The **effect** of his smile was immediate!

Directions: Write **affect** or **effect** in the blanks to complete these sentences correctly. The first one has been done for you.

I HOPE ALL THIS STUDYING AFFECTS MY GRADE!

__affects__ 1. Your behavior (affects/effects) how others feel about you.

__effect__ 2. His (affect/effect) on her was amazing.

__effect__ 3. The (affect/effect) of his jacket was striking.

__affect__ 4. What you say won't (affect/effect) me!

__effect__ 5. There's a relationship between cause and (affect/effect).

__effect__ 6. The (affect/effect) of her behavior was positive.

__affected__ 7. The medicine (affected/effected) my stomach.

__effect__ 8. What was the (affect/effect) of the punishment?

__affect__ 9. Did his behavior (affect/effect) her performance?

__affected__ 10. The cold (affected/effected) her breathing.

__effect__ 11. The (affect/effect) was instantaneous!

__affect__ 12. Your attitude will (affect/effect) your posture.

__effect__ 13. The (affect/effect) on her posture was major.

__effect__ 14. The (affect/effect) of the colored lights was calming.

__affected__ 15. She (affected/effected) his behavior.

Page 160

"Among" and "Between"

Among is a preposition that applies to more than two people or things.

Example: The group divided the cookies **among** themselves.

Between is a preposition that applies to only two people or things.

Example: The cookies were divided **between** Jeremy and Sara.

Directions: Write **between** or **among** in the blanks to complete these sentences correctly. The first one has been done for you.

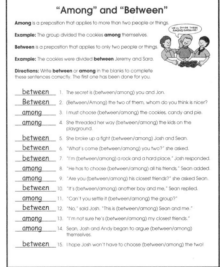

WE'LL DIVIDE THESE AMONG OURSELVES!

__between__ 1. The secret is (between/among) you and Jon.

__Between__ 2. (Between/Among) the two of them, whom do you think is nicer?

__among__ 3. I must choose (between/among) the cookies, candy and pie.

__among__ 4. She threaded her way (between/among) the kids on the playground.

__between__ 5. She broke up a fight (between/among) Josh and Sean.

__between__ 6. "What's come (between/among) you two?" she asked.

__between__ 7. "I'm (between/among) a rock and a hard place," Josh responded.

__among__ 8. "He has to choose (between/among) all his friends," Sean added.

__among__ 9. "Are you (between/among) his closest friends?" she asked Sean.

__between__ 10. "It's (between/among) another boy and me," Sean replied.

__among__ 11. "Can't you settle it (between/among) the group?"

__between__ 12. "No," said Josh. "This is (between/among) Sean and me."

__among__ 13. "I'm not sure he's (between/among) my closest friends."

__among__ 14. Sean, Josh and Andy began to argue (between/among) themselves.

__between__ 15. I hope Josh won't have to choose (between/among) the two!

Page 161

"All Together" and "Altogether"

All together is a phrase meaning everyone or everything in the same place.

Example: We put the eggs **all together** in the bowl.

Altogether is an adverb that means entirely, completely or in all.

Example: The teacher gave **altogether** too much homework.

Directions: Write **altogether** or **all together** in the blanks to complete these sentences correctly. The first one has been done for you.

THE EGGS ARE ALL TOGETHER

__altogether__ 1. "You ate (altogether/all together) too much food."

__all together__ 2. The girls sat (altogether/all together) on the bus.

__All together__ 3. (Altogether/All together) now: one, two, three!

__altogether__ 4. I am (altogether/all together) out of ideas.

__all together__ 5. We are (altogether/all together) on this project.

__altogether__ 6. "You have on (altogether/all together) too much makeup!"

__all together__ 7. They were (altogether/all together) on the same team.

__All together__ 8. (Altogether/All together), we can help stop pollution (altogether/all together).

__altogether__ 9. He was not (altogether/all together) happy with his grades.

__altogether__ 10. The kids were (altogether/all together) too loud.

__All together__ 11. (Altogether/All together), the babies cried gustily.

__altogether__ 12. She was not (altogether/all together) sure what to do.

__all together__ 13. Let's sing the song (altogether/all together).

__altogether__ 14. He was (altogether/all together) too pushy for her taste.

__All together__ 15. (Altogether/All together), the boys yelled the school cheer.

Page 162

"Amount" and "Number"

Amount indicates quantity, bulk or mass.

Example: She carried a large **amount** of money in her purse.

Number indicates units.

Example: What **number** of people volunteered to work?

Directions: Write **amount** or **number** in the blanks to complete these sentences correctly. The first one has been done for you.

- number 1. She did not (amount/number) him among her closest friends.
- amount 2. What (amount/number) of ice cream should we order?
- number 3. The (amount/number) of cookies on her plate was three.
- amount 4. His excuses did not (amount/number) to much.
- amounted 5. Her contribution (amounted/numbered) to half the money raised.
- number 6. The (amount/number) of injured players rose every day.
- amount 7. What a huge (amount/number) of cereal!
- number 8. The (amount/number) of calories in the diet is low.
- number 9. I can't tell you the (amount/number) of friends she has!
- amount 10. The total (amount/number) of money raised was incredible!
- number 11. The (amount/number) of gadgets for sale was amazing.
- number 12. He was startled by the (amount/number) of people present.
- amount 13. He would not do it for any (amount/number) of money.
- number 14. She offered a great (amount/number) of reasons for her actions.
- number 15. Can you guess the (amount/number) of beans in the jar?

Page 163

"Irritate" and "Aggravate"

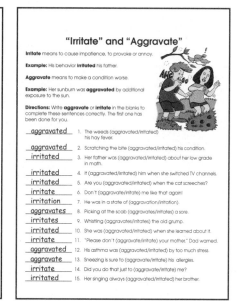

Irritate means to cause impatience, to provoke or annoy.

Example: His behavior **irritated** his father.

Aggravate means to make a condition worse.

Example: Her sunburn was **aggravated** by additional exposure to the sun.

Directions: Write **aggravate** or **irritate** in the blanks to complete these sentences correctly. The first one has been done for you.

- aggravated 1. The weeds (aggravated/irritated) his hay fever.
- aggravated 2. Scratching the bite (aggravated/irritated) his condition.
- irritated 3. Her father was (aggravated/irritated) about her low grade in math.
- irritated 4. It (aggravated/irritated) him when she switched TV channels.
- irritated 5. Are you (aggravated/irritated) when the cat screeches?
- irritate 6. Don't (aggravate/irritate) me like that again!
- irritation 7. He was in a state of (aggravation/irritation).
- aggravates 8. Picking at the scab (aggravates/irritates) a sore.
- irritates 9. Whistling (aggravates/irritates) the old grump.
- irritated 10. She was (aggravated/irritated) when she learned about it.
- irritate 11. "Please don't (aggravate/irritate) your mother," Dad warned.
- aggravated 12. His asthma was (aggravated/irritated) by too much stress.
- aggravate 13. Sneezing is sure to (aggravate/irritate) his allergies.
- irritate 14. Did you do that just to (aggravate/irritate) me?
- irritated 15. Her singing always (aggravated/irritated) her brother.

Page 164

"Principal" and "Principle"

Principal means main, leader or chief, or a sum of money that earns interest.

Examples:
The high school **principal** earned interest on the **principal** in his savings account. The **principal** reason for his savings account was to save for retirement.

Principle means a truth, law or a moral outlook that governs the way someone behaves.

Example:
Einstein discovered some fundamental **principles** of science. Stealing is against her **principles**.

Directions: Write **principle** or **principal** in the blanks to complete these sentences correctly. The first one has been done for you.

- principle 1. A (principle/principal) of biology is "the survival of the fittest."
- principles 2. She was a person of strong (principles/principals).
- principals 3. The (principles/principals) sat together at the district conference.
- principal 4. How much of the total in my savings account is (principle/principal)?
- principal 5. His hay fever was the (principle/principal) reason for his sneezing.
- principles 6. It's not the facts that upset me, it's the (principles/principals) of the case.
- principal 7. The jury heard only the (principle/principal) facts.
- principal 8. Our school (principle/principal) is strict but fair.
- principal 9. Spend the interest, but don't touch the (principle/principal).
- principle 10. Helping others is a guiding (principle/principal) of the homeless shelter.
- principle 11. In (principle/principal), we agree; on the facts, we do not.
- principal 12. The (principle/principal) course at dinner was leg of lamb.
- principles 13. Some mathematical (principles/principals) are difficult to understand.
- principal 14. The baby was the (principle/principal) reason for his happiness.

Page 165

"Good" and "Well"

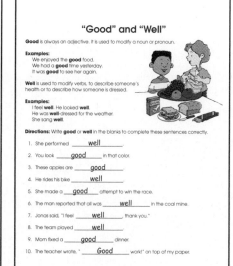

Good is always an adjective. It is used to modify a noun or pronoun.

Examples:
We enjoyed the **good** food.
We had a **good** time yesterday.
It was **good** to see her again.

Well is used to modify verbs, to describe someone's health or to describe how someone is dressed.

Examples:
I feel **well**. He looked **well**.
He was **well**-dressed for the weather.
She sang **well**.

Directions: Write **good** or **well** in the blanks to complete these sentences correctly.

1. She performed ___well___.
2. You look ___good___ in that color.
3. These apples are ___good___.
4. He rides his bike ___well___.
5. She made a ___good___ attempt to win the race.
6. The man reported that all was ___well___ in the coal mine.
7. Jonas said, "I feel ___well___, thank you."
8. The team played ___well___.
9. Mom fixed a ___good___ dinner.
10. The teacher wrote, "___Good___ work!" on top of my paper.

Page 166

"Like" and "As"

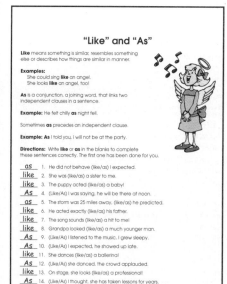

Like means something is similar, resembles something else or describes how things are similar in manner.

Examples:
She could sing **like** an angel.
She looks **like** an angel, too!

As is a conjunction, a joining word, that links two independent clauses in a sentence.

Example: He felt chilly **as** night fell.

Sometimes **as** precedes an independent clause.

Example: As I told you, I will not be at the party.

Directions: Write **like** or **as** in the blanks to complete these sentences correctly. The first one has been done for you.

- as 1. He did not behave (like/as) I expected.
- like 2. She was (like/as) a sister to me.
- like 3. The puppy acted (like/as) a baby!
- As 4. (Like/As) I was saying, he will be there at noon.
- as 5. The storm was 25 miles away, (like/as) he predicted.
- like 6. He acted exactly (like/as) his father.
- like 7. The song sounds (like/as) a hit to me!
- like 8. Grandpa looked (like/as) a much younger man.
- As 9. (Like/As) I listened to the music, I grew sleepy.
- As 10. (Like/As) I expected, he showed up late.
- like 11. She dances (like/as) a ballerina.
- As 12. (Like/As) she danced, the crowd applauded.
- like 13. On stage, she looks (like/as) a professional!
- As 14. (Like/As) I thought, she has taken lessons for years.

Page 168

Capitalization

Capitalize . . .
. . . the first word in a sentence
. . . the first letter of a person's name
. . . proper nouns, like the names of planets, oceans and mountain ranges
. . . titles when used with a person's name, even if abbreviated (Dr., Mr., Lt.)
. . . days of the week and months of the year
. . . cities, states and countries

Directions: Write **C** in the blank if the word or phrase is capitalized correctly. Rewrite the word or phrase if it is incorrect.

1. __C__ President Abraham Lincoln _____
2. __C__ Larry D. Walters _____
3. _____ saturn __Saturn__
4. _____ benjamin franklin __Benjamin Franklin__
5. __C__ August _____
6. __C__ professional _____
7. _____ jupiter __Jupiter__
8. __C__ Pacific Ocean _____
9. _____ white house __White House__
10. __C__ pet _____
11. __C__ Congress _____
12. __C__ Houston _____
13. __C__ federal government _____
14. _____ dr. Samuel White __Dr. Samuel White__
15. _____ milwaukee, Wisconsin __Milwaukee, Wisconsin__
16. _____ Appalachian mountains __Appalachian Mountains__
17. _____ lake michigan __Lake Michigan__
18. __C__ Notre Dame College _____
19. _____ department of the Interior __Department of the Interior__
20. _____ monday and Tuesday __Monday and Tuesday__

Page 169

Capitalization

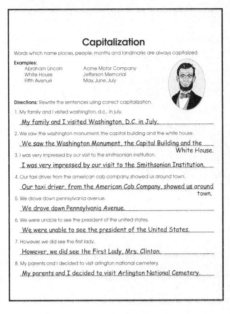

Words which name places, people, months and landmarks are always capitalized.

Examples:
Abraham Lincoln	Acme Motor Company
White House	Jefferson Memorial
Fifth Avenue	May, June, July

Directions: Rewrite the sentences using correct capitalization.

1. My family and I visited washington, d.c. in july.
   My family and I visited Washington, D.C. in July.

2. We saw the washington monument, the capital building and the white house.
   We saw the Washington Monument, the Capital Building and the White House.

3. I was very impressed by our visit to the smithsonian institution.
   I was very impressed by our visit to the Smithsonian Institution.

4. Our taxi driver, from the american cab company, showed us around town.
   Our taxi driver, from the American Cab Company, showed us around town.

5. We drove down pennsylvania avenue.
   We drove down Pennsylvania Avenue.

6. We were unable to see the president of the united states.
   We were unable to see the president of the United States.

7. However, we did see the first lady.
   However, we did see the First Lady, Mrs. Clinton.

8. My parents and I decided to visit arlington national cemetery.
   My parents and I decided to visit Arlington National Cemetery.

Page 170

Commas

Use **commas** . . .
. . . after introductory phrases
. . . to set off nouns of direct address
. . . to set off appositives from the words that go with them
. . . to set off words that interrupt the flow of the sentence
. . . to separate words or groups of words in a series

Examples:
Introductory phrase: Of course, I'd be happy to attend.
Noun of direct address: Ms. Williams, please sit here.
To set off appositives: Lee, the club president, sat beside me.
Words interrupting flow: My cousin, who's 13, will also be there.
Words in a series: I ate popcorn, peanuts, oats and barley.
   or   I ate popcorn, peanuts, oats, and barley.

Note: The final comma is optional when punctuating words in a series.

Directions: Identify how the commas are used in each sentence.
   Write: **I** for introductory phrase
      N for noun of direct address
      A for appositive
      WF for words interrupting flow
      WS for words in a series

__I__ 1. Yes, she is my sister.
__A__ 2. My teacher, Mr. Hopkins, is very fair.
__WS__ 3. Her favorite fruits are oranges, plums and grapes.
__A__ 4. The city mayor, Carla Ellison, is quite young.
__WS__ 5. I will buy bread, milk, fruit and ice cream.
__WF__ 6. Her crying, which was quite loud, soon gave me a headache.
__N__ 7. Stephanie, please answer the question.
__I__ 8. So, do you know her?
__I__ 9. Unfortunately, the item is not returnable.
__WS__ 10. My sister, my cousin and my friend will accompany me on vacation.
__A__ 11. My grandparents, Rose and Bill, are both 57 years old.

Page 171

Commas

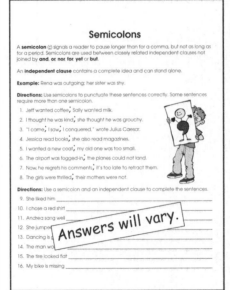

Directions: Use commas to punctuate these sentences correctly.

1. I'll visit her, however, not until I'm ready.
2. She ordered coats, gloves and a hat from the catalog.
3. Eun-Jung, the new girl, looked ill at ease.
4. Certainly, I'll show Eun-Jung around school.
5. Yes, I'll be glad to help her.
6. I paid, nevertheless, I was unhappy with the price.
7. I bought stamps, envelopes and plenty of postcards.
8. No, I told you I was not going.
9. The date, November 12, was not convenient.
10. Her earache, which kept her up all night, stopped at dawn.
11. My nephew, who loves bike riding, will go with us.
12. He'll bring hiking boots, a tent and food.
13. The cat, a Himalayan, was beautiful.
14. The tennis player, a professional in every sense, signed autographs.
15. No, you can't stay out past 10:00 P.M.

Page 172

Semicolons

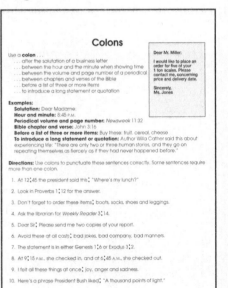

A **semicolon** (;) signals a reader to pause longer than for a comma, but not as long as for a period. Semicolons are used between closely related independent clauses not joined by **and, or, nor, for, yet** or **but**.

An **independent clause** contains a complete idea and can stand alone.

Example: Rena was outgoing; her sister was shy.

Directions: Use semicolons to punctuate these sentences correctly. Some sentences require more than one semicolon.

1. Jeff wanted coffee; Sally wanted milk.
2. I thought he was kind; she thought he was grouchy.
3. "I came; I saw; I conquered," wrote Julius Caesar.
4. Jessica read books; she also read magazines.
5. I wanted a new coat; my old one was too small.
6. The airport was fogged-in; the planes could not land.
7. Now, he regrets his comments; it's too late to retract them.
8. The girls were thrilled; their mothers were not.

Directions: Use a semicolon and an independent clause to complete the sentences.

9. She liked him _____
10. I chose a red shirt _____
11. Andrea sang well _____
12. She jumped _____ *Answers will vary.*
13. Dancing is _____
14. The man wa _____
15. The tire looked flat _____
16. My bike is missing _____

Page 173

Colons

Use a **colon** . . .
. . . after the salutation of a business letter
. . . between the hour and the minute when showing time
. . . between the volume and page number of a periodical
. . . between chapters and verses of the Bible
. . . before a list of three or more items
. . . to introduce a long statement or quotation

Dear Mr. Miller:

I would like to place an order for five of your 1 ton scales. Please contact me, concerning price and delivery date.

Sincerely,
Ms. Jones

Examples:
Salutation: Dear Madame:
Hour and minute: 8:45 P.M.
Periodical volume and page number: Newsweek 11:32
Bible chapter and verse: John 3:16
Before a list of three or more items: Buy these: fruit, cereal, cheese
To introduce a long statement or quotation: Author Willa Cather said this about experiencing life: "There are only two or three human stories, and they go on repeating themselves as fiercely as if they had never happened before."

Directions: Use colons to punctuate these sentences correctly. Some sentences require more than one colon.

1. At 12:45 the president said this: "Where's my lunch?"
2. Look in Proverbs 1:12 for the answer.
3. Don't forget to order these items: boots, socks, shoes and leggings.
4. Ask the librarian for Weekly Reader 3:14.
5. Dear Sir: Please send me two copies of your report.
6. Avoid these at all costs: bad jokes, bad company, bad manners.
7. The statement is in either Genesis 1:6 or Exodus 3:2.
8. At 9:15 P.M. she checked in, and at 6:45 A.M. she checked out.
9. I felt all these things at once: joy, anger and sadness.
10. Here's a phrase President Bush liked: "A thousand points of light."

Page 174

Dashes

Dashes (—) are used to indicate sudden changes of thought.

Examples:
I want milk—no, make that soda—with my lunch.
Wear your old clothes—new ones would get spoiled.

Directions: If the dash is used correctly in the sentence, write **C** in the blank. If the dash is missing or used incorrectly, draw an **X** in the blank. The first one has been done for you.

C 1. No one—not even my dad—knows about the surprise.
X 2. Ask—him—no I will to come to the party.
X 3. I'll tell you the answer oh, the phone just rang!
C 4. Everyone thought—even her brother—that she looked pretty.
C 5. Can you please—oh, forget it!
X 6. Just stop it I really mean it!
C 7. Tell her that I'll—never mind—I'll tell her myself!
X 8. Everyone especially Anna is overwhelmed.
C 9. I wish everyone could—forgive me—I'm sorry!
C 10. The kids—all six of them—piled into the backseat.

Directions: Write two sentences of your own that include dashes.

11. _____

12. Answers will vary.

Page 175

Quotation Marks

Quotation marks are used to enclose a speaker's exact words. Use commas to set off a direct quotation from other words in the sentence.

Examples:
Kira smiled and said, "Quotation marks come in handy."
"Yes," Josh said, "I'll take two."

Directions: If quotation marks and commas are used correctly, write **C** in the blank. If they are used incorrectly, write an **X** in the blank. The first one has been done for you.

C 1. "I suppose," Elizabeth remarked, "that you'll be there on time."
X 2. "Please let me help! insisted Mark.
X 3. I'll be ready in 2 minutes!" her father said.
C 4. "Just breathe slowly," the nurse said, "and calm down."
X 5. "No one understands me" William whined.
C 6. "Would you like more milk?" Jasmine asked politely.
X 7. "No thanks, her grandpa replied, "I have plenty."
C 8. "What a beautiful morning!" Jessica yelled.
X 9. "Yes, it certainly is" her mother agreed.
C 10. "Whose purse is this?" asked Andrea.
X 11. It's mine" said Stephanie. "Thank you."
C 12. "Can you play the piano?" asked Heather.
X 13. "Music is my hobby." Jonathan replied.
X 14. Great!" yelled Harry. Let's play some tunes."
C 15. "I practice a lot," said Jayne proudly.

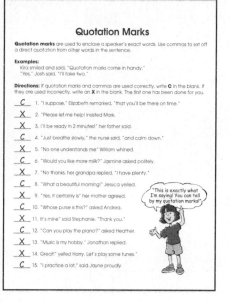

"This is exactly what I'm saying! You can tell by my quotation marks!"

Page 176

Quotation Marks

Directions: Use quotation marks and commas to punctuate these sentences correctly.

1. "No," Ms. Elliot replied, "you may not go.

2. "Watch out!" yelled the coach.

3. "Please bring my coat," called Renee.

4. After thinking for a moment, Paul said, "I don't believe you."

5. Dad said, "Remember to be home by 9:00 P.M."

6. "Finish your projects," said the art instructor.

7. "Go back," instructed Mom, "and comb your hair."

8. "I won't be needing my winter coat anymore," replied Mei-ling.

9. He said, "How did you do that?"

10. I stood and said, "My name is Rosalita."

11. "No," said Misha, "I will not attend."

12. "Don't forget to put your name on your paper," said the teacher.

13. "Pay attention, class," said our history teacher.

14. As I came into the house, Mom called, "Dinner is almost ready!"

15. "Jake, come when I call you," said Mother.

16. "How was your trip to France, Mrs. Shaw?" asked Deborah.

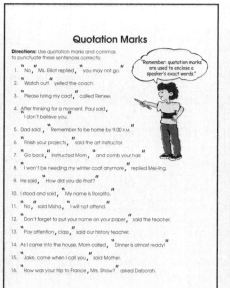

"Remember: quotation marks are used to enclose a speaker's exact words."

Page 177

Apostrophes

Use an **apostrophe** (') in a contraction to show that letters have been left out. A **contraction** is a shortened form of two words, usually a pronoun and a verb.

Add an **apostrophe** and **s** to form the **possessive** of singular nouns. **Plural possessives** are formed two ways. If the noun ends in **s**, simply add an apostrophe at the end of the word. If the noun does not end in **s**, add an apostrophe and **s**.

Examples:
Contraction: He **can't** button his sleeves.
Singular possessive: The **boy's** sleeves are too short.
Plural noun ending in s: The **ladies'** voices were pleasant.
Plural noun not ending in s: The **children's** song was long.

Directions: Use apostrophes to punctuate the sentences correctly. The first one has been done for you.

1. I can't understand that child's game.
2. The farmers' wagons were lined up in a row.
3. She didn't like the chair's covers.
4. Our parents' beliefs are often our own.
5. Sandy's mother's aunt isn't going to visit.
6. Two ladies from work didn't show up.
7. The citizen's group wasn't very happy.
8. The colonists' demands weren't unreasonable.
9. The mothers' babies cried at the same time.
10. Our parents' generation enjoys music.

Directions: Write two sentences of your own that include apostrophes.

11. _____

12. Answers will vary.

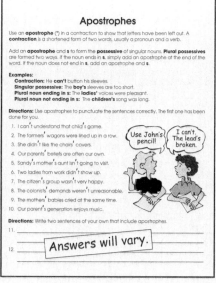

Use John's pencil!

I can't. The lead's broken.

Page 178

Contractions

Examples:
he will = **he'll**
she is = **she's**
they are = **they're**
can not = **can't**

Contraction Chart

Pronoun		Verb		Contraction
I	+	am	=	I'm
we, you, they	+	are	=	we're, you're, they're
he, she, it	+	is	=	he's, she's, it's
I, we, you, they	+	have	=	I've, we've, you've, they've
I, you, we, she, he, they	+	would	=	I'd, you'd, we'd, she'd, he'd, they'd
I, you, we, she, he, they	+	will	=	I'll, you'll, we'll, she'll, he'll, they'll

Directions: Write a sentence using a contraction. The first one has been done for you.

1. I will   I'll see you tomorrow!
2. they are
3. we have
4. she would
5. you a
6. they w   Answers will vary.
7. she is
8. he would
9. they are
10. I am

Page 179

Singular Possessives

Directions: Write the singular possessive form of each word.
Then, add a noun to show possession. The first one has been
done for you.

1. spider __spider's web__
2. clock __clock's__
3. car __car's__
4. book __book's__   (Nouns will vary.)
5. Mom __Mom's__
6. boat __boat's__
7. table __table's__
8. baby __baby's__
9. woman __woman's__
10. writer __writer's__
11. mouse __mouse's__
12. fan __fan's__
13. lamp __lamp's__
14. dog __dog's__
15. boy __boy's__
16. house __house's__

Page 180

Plural Possessives

Directions: Write the plural possessive form of each word. Then add a noun to show
possession. The first one has been done for you.

1. kid __kids' skates__
2. man __men's__   (Nouns will vary.)
3. aunt __aunts'__
4. lion __lions'__
5. giraffe __giraffes'__
6. necklace __necklaces'__
7. mouse __mice's__
8. team __teams'__
9. clown __clowns'__
10. desk __desks'__
11. woman __women's__
12. worker __workers'__

Directions: Write three sentences of your own that include plural possessives.

13. _____

14. ____ *Answers will vary.* ____

15. _____

Page 181

Italics

Use **italics** or **underlining** for titles of books, newspapers, plays, magazines and movies.

Examples:
Book: Have you read *Gone with the Wind*?
Movie: Did you see *The Muppet Movie*?
Newspaper: I like to read *The New York Times*.
Magazine: Some children read *Sports Illustrated*.
Play: *A Doll's House* is a play by Henrik Ibsen.

Since we cannot write in italics, we underline words
that should be in italics.

Directions: Underline the words that should be in italics.
The first one has been done for you.

1. I read about a play titled <u>Cats</u> in <u>The Cleveland Plain Dealer</u>.
2. You can find <u>The New York Times</u> in most libraries.
3. Audrey Wood wrote <u>Elbert's Bad Word</u>.
4. <u>Parents</u> and <u>Newsweek</u> are both popular magazines.
5. The original <u>Miracle on 34th Street</u> was filmed long ago.
6. <u>Cricket</u> and <u>Ranger Rick</u> are magazines for children.
7. <u>Bon Appetit</u> means "good appetite" and is a cooking magazine.
8. <u>Harper's</u>, <u>The New Yorker</u> and <u>Vanity Fair</u> are magazines.
9. <u>David Copperfield</u> was written by Charles Dickens.
10. Harriet Beecher Stowe wrote <u>Uncle Tom's Cabin</u>.
11. Paul Newman was in a movie called <u>The Sting</u>.
12. Have you read <u>Ramona the Pest</u> by Beverly Cleary?
13. The <u>Louisville Courier Journal</u> is a Kentucky newspaper.
14. <u>Teen</u> and <u>Boy's Life</u> are magazines for young readers.
15. Have you seen Jimmy Stewart in <u>It's a Wonderful Life</u>?

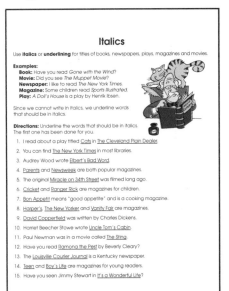

Page 182

Complete Sentences

A **complete sentence** has both a simple subject and a simple predicate. It is a complete
thought. Sentences which are not complete are called **fragments**.

Example:
Complete sentence: The wolf howled at the moon.
Sentence fragment: Howled at the moon.

Directions: Write **C** on the line if the sentence is complete. Write **F** if it is a fragment.

1. _C_ The machine is running.
2. _C_ What will we do today?
3. _F_ Knowing what I do.
4. _C_ That statement is true.
5. _C_ My parents drove to town.
6. _F_ Watching television all afternoon.
7. _C_ The storm devastated the town.
8. _C_ Our friends can go with us.
9. _C_ The palm trees bent in the wind.
10. _F_ Spraying the fire all night.

Directions: Rewrite the sentence fragments from above to make them complete sentences.

Answers will vary.

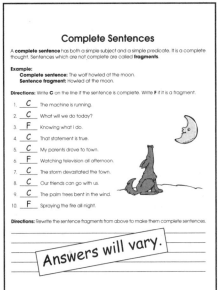

Page 183

Run-On Sentences

A **run-on sentence** occurs when two or more sentences are joined together without
punctuation or a joining word. Run-on sentences should be divided into two or more
separate sentences.

Example:
Run-on sentence: My parents, sister, brother and I went to the park we saw many
animals we had fun.
Correct: My parents, sister, brother and I went to the park. We saw many animals and
had fun.

Directions: Rewrite the run-on sentences correctly.   Sample answers:

1. The dog energetically chased the ball I kept throwing him the ball for a half hour.
   __The dog energetically chased the ball. I kept throwing
   him the ball for a half hour.__

2. The restaurant served scrambled eggs and bacon for breakfast I had some and
   they were delicious.
   __The restaurant served bacon and scrambled eggs for
   breakfast. I had some, and they were delicious.__

3. The lightning struck close to our house it scared my little brother and my grandmother
   called to see if we were safe.
   __The lightning struck close to our
   house. It scared my little
   brother. My grandmother called
   to see if we were safe.__

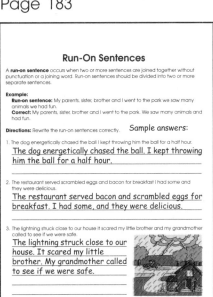

Total Basic Skills Grade 6

Answer Key

Page 184

Finding Spelling Errors

Directions: One word in each sentence below is misspelled. Write the word correctly on the line.

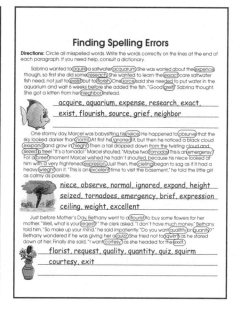

1. Jeff felt discoraged at the comparison between him and his older brother. **discouraged**

2. I got inpatient as my curiosity grew. **impatient**

3. She confided that she had not finished the assignment. **assignment**

4. They made the selection after a brief conference. **conference**

5. Obviusly, it's impolite to sneeze on someone. **Obviously**

6. This skin cream is practicaly invisible. **practically**

7. What would prevent you from taking on additional work? **additional**

8. I can resite the words to that hymn. **recite**

9. In a previous column, the newspaper explained the situation. **column**

10. He decieved me so many times that now I distrust him. **deceived**

11. Please have the curtesy to observe the "No Eating" signs. **courtesy**

12. The advertisement is so small that it's nearly invisible. **invisible**

13. The best way to communicate is in a face-to-face conservation. **conversation**

14. In a cost comparison, salmon is more expensive than tuna. **comparison**

15. Popularity among friends shouldn't depend on your accomplishments. **Popularity**

16. Her campaign was quite an achievement. **achievement**

17. He condemned it as a poor imitation. **condemned**

Page 185

Finding Spelling Errors

Directions: Circle all misspelled words. Write the words correctly on the lines at the end of each paragraph. If you need help, consult a dictionary.

Sabrina wanted to aquire a saltwater aquarum. She was worried about the expence, though, so first she did some reserch. She wanted to learn the exact care saltwater fish need, not just to exsist but to florish. One sorce said she needed to put water in the aquarium and wait 6 weeks before she added the fish. "Good greif," Sabrina thought. She got a kitten from her nieghbor instead.

acquire, aquarium, expense, research, exact, exist, flourish, source, grief, neighbor

One stormy day, Marcel was babysitting his neice. He happened to obsrve that the sky looked darker than norm. At first he ignored it, but then he noticed a black cloud exxpand and grow in hieght. Then a tail dropped down from the twisting cloud and siezed a tree! "It's a tornado!" Marcel shouted. "Maybe two tornados! This is an emergensy!" For a breef moment Marcel wished he hadn't shouted, because his niece looked at him with a very frightened expresion. Just then, the cieling began to sag as if it had a heavy wieght on it. "This is an excelent time to visit the basement," he told the little girl as calmy as possible.

niece, observe, normal, ignored, expand, height seized, tornadoes, emergency, brief, expression ceiling, weight, excellent

Just before Mother's Day, Bethany went to a florist to buy some flowers for her mother. "Well, what is your reqest?" the clerk asked. "I don't have much money," Bethany told him. "So make up your mind," he said impatiently. "Do you want qualitity or quanity?" Bethany wondered if he was giving her a quiz. She tried not to squirm as he stared down at her. Finally he said, "I want cortesy," as she headed for the exit.

florist, request, quality, quantity, quiz, squirm courtesy, exit

Page 186

Writing: Four Types of Sentences

There are four main types of sentences: A **statement** tells something. It ends in a period. A **question** asks something. It ends in a question mark. A **command** tells someone to do something. It ends in a period or an exclamation mark. An **exclamation** shows strong feeling or excitement. It ends in an exclamation mark.

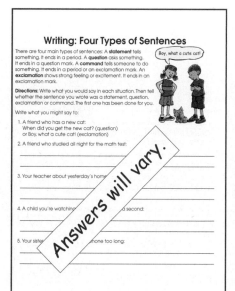

Boy, what a cute cat!

Directions: Write what you would say in each situation. Then tell whether the sentence you wrote was a statement, question, exclamation or command. The first one has been done for you.

Write what you might say to:

1. A friend who has a new cat:
When did you get the new cat? (question)
or Boy, what a cute cat! (exclamation)

2. A friend who studied all night for the math test:

3. Your teacher about yesterday's home...

4. A child you're watching ...a second:

5. Your sister ...phone too long:

Answers will vary.

Page 187

Organizing Paragraphs

A **topic sentence** states the main idea of a paragraph and is usually the first sentence. **Support sentences** follow, providing details about the topic. All sentences in a paragraph should relate to the topic sentence. A paragraph ends with a **conclusion sentence**.

Directions: Rearrange each group of sentences into a paragraph, beginning with the topic sentence. Cross out the sentence in each group that is not related to the topic sentence. Write the new paragraph.

Now, chalk drawings are considered art by themselves. The earliest chalk drawings were found on the walls of caves. Chalk is also used in cement, fertilizer, toothpaste and makeup. Chalk once was used just to make quick sketches. Chalk has been used for drawing for thousands of years. Then the artist would paint pictures from the sketches.

Chalk has been used for drawing for thousands of years. The earliest chalk drawings were found on the walls of caves. Chalk once was used just to make quick sketches. Then the artist would paint pictures from the sketches. Now, chalk drawings are considered art by themselves.

Dams also keep young salmon from swimming downriver to the ocean. Most salmon live in the ocean but return to fresh water to lay their eggs and breed. Dams prevent salmon from swimming upriver to their spawning grounds. Pacific salmon die after they spawn the first time. One kind of fish pass is a series of pools of water that lead the salmon over the dams. Dams are threatening salmon by interfering with their spawning. To help with this problem, some dams have special "fish passes" to allow salmon to swim over the dam.

Dams are threatening salmon by interfering with their spawning. Most salmon live in the ocean but return to fresh water to lay their eggs and breed. Dams prevent salmon from swimming upriver to their spawning grounds. Dams also keep young salmon from swimming downriver to the ocean. To help with this problem, some dams have special "fish passes" to allow salmon to swim over the dam. One kind of fish pass is a series of pools of water that lead the salmon over the dams.

Page 191

Describing People

Often, a writer can show how someone feels by describing how that person looks or what he or she is doing rather than by using emotion words, like angry or happy. This is another way to create word pictures.

Directions: Read the phrases below. Write words to describe how you think that person feels.

1. like a tornado, yelling, raised fists **angry**

2. slumped, walking slowly, head down **depressed, dejected**

3. trembling, breathing quickly, like a cornered animal **frightened**

Directions: Write one or two sentences for each phrase without using emotion words.

4. a runner who has just won a race for his or her school

5. a sixth grader on the first day in a new school

6. a teenager walking down the street ...se on fire

7. a scientist who has just ...for lung cancer

8. a kindergarten child be...ignored by his or her best friend

Answers will vary.

GRADE 6

Page 192

Describing Events in Order

When we write to explain what happened, we need to describe the events in the same order they occurred. Words and phrases such as **at first, then, after that** and **finally** help us relate the order of events.

Directions: Rewrite the paragraph below, putting the topic sentence first and arranging the events in order.

I got dressed, but I didn't really feel like eating breakfast. By the time I got to school, my head felt hot, so I went to the nurse. This day was terrible from the very beginning. Finally, I ended up where I started—back in my own bed. Then she sent me home again! I just had some toast and left for school. When I first woke up in the morning, my stomach hurt.

This day was terrible from the very beginning. When I first woke up in the morning, my stomach hurt. I got dressed, but I didn't really feel like eating breakfast. I just had some toast and left for school. By the time I got to school, my head felt hot, so I went to the nurse. Then she sent me home again! Finally, I ended up where I started—back in my bed!

Directions: Follow these steps to write a paragraph about what happened the last time you tried to cook something or the last time you tried to fix something that was broken.

1. Write your first draft on another sheet of paper. Start with a topic sentence.
2. Add support sentences to explain what happened. Include phrases to keep things in order: **at first, then, after that, finally, in the middle of it, at last.**
3. Read your paragraph out loud to see if it reads smoothly. Make sure the events are in the correct order.
4. Make any needed changes, then write your paragraph below.

Paragraphs will vary.

Page 193

Explaining What Happened

Directions: These pictures tell a story, but they're out of order. Follow these steps to write what happened.

1. On another sheet of paper, write a sentence explaining what is happening in each picture.
2. Put your sentences in order and write a topic sentence.
3. Read the whole paragraph to yourself. Add words to show the order in which things happened.
4. Include adjectives and adverbs and maybe even a simile or metaphor to make your story more interesting.
5. Write your paragraph below. Be sure to give it a title.

Paragraphs will vary.

Page 194

Writing Directions

Directions must be written clearly. They are easiest to follow when they are in numbered steps. Each step should begin with a verb.

How to Peel a Banana:
1. Hold the banana by the stem end.
2. Find a loose edge of peel at the top.
3. Pull the peeling down.
4. Peel the other sections of the banana in the same way.

Directions: Rewrite these directions, number the steps in order and begin with verbs.

How to Feed a Dog

Finally, call the dog to come and eat. Then you carry the filled dish to the place where the dog eats. The can or bag should be opened by you. First, clean the dog's food dish with soap and water. Then get the dog food out of the cupboard. Put the correct amount of food in the dish.

1. Clean the dog's food dish with soap and water.
2. Get the dog food out of the cupboard.
3. Open the can or bag.
4. Put the correct amount of food in the dish.
5. Carry the filled dish to the place where the dog eats.
6. Call the dog to come and eat.

Directions: Follow these steps to write your own directions.

1. On another sheet of paper, draw two symbols, such as a square with a star in one corner or a triangle inside a circle. Don't show your drawing to anyone.
2. On a second sheet of paper, write instructions to make the same drawing. Your directions need to be clear, in order and numbered. Each step needs to begin with a verb.
3. Trade directions (but not pictures) with a partner. See if you can follow each other's directions to make the drawings.
4. Show your partner the drawing you made in step one. Does it look like the one he or she made following your directions? Could you follow your partner's directions? Share what was clear—or not so clear—about each other's instructions.

Page 195

Writing: Stronger Sentences

Sometimes the noun form of a word is not the best way to express an idea. Compare these two sentences:

They made preparations for the party.
They prepared for the party.

The second sentence, using **prepared** as a verb, is shorter and stronger.

Directions: Write one word to replace a whole phrase. Cross out the words you don't need. The first one has been done for you.

1. She ~~made a suggestion~~ that we go on Monday. **suggested**
2. They ~~arranged decorations around~~ the room. **decorated**
3. Let's ~~make a combination of~~ the two ideas. **combine**
4. I ~~have great appreciation for~~ what you did. **appreciate**
5. The buses ~~are acting as transportation for~~ the classes. **transport**
6. The group ~~made an exploration of~~ the Arctic Circle. **explored**
7. Please ~~make a selection of~~ one quickly. **select**
8. The lake ~~is making a reflection of~~ the trees. **reflects**
9. The family ~~had a celebration of~~ the holiday. **celebrated**
10. Would you please ~~provide a solution for~~ this problem? **solve**
11. Don ~~made an imitation of~~ his cat. **imitated**
12. Please ~~give a definition of~~ that word. **define**
13. I ~~made an examination of~~ the broken bike. **examined**
14. Dexter ~~made an invitation for~~ us to join him. **invited**

Write one word to replace a whole phrase.

Page 196

Writing: Descriptive Sentences

Descriptive sentences make writing more interesting to the reader. This is done by using adjectives, adverbs, prepositional phrases, similes and metaphors.

Example:
The dog ran down the hill.
The black and white beagle bounded down the steep embankment as though being chased by an invisible dragon.

Directions: Rewrite these sentences so they are more descriptive.

1. Bill likes collecting stamps.

2. Martina drove into town.

3. I enjoy working on the computer.

4. Riverside won the game.

5. Dinner was great.

6. My mom collects

7. The tea

8. My brother r   a scholarship for college.

Sentences will vary.

Page 197

Writing: Different Points of View

A **fact** is a statement that can be proved. An **opinion** is what someone thinks or believes.

Directions: Write F if the statement is a fact or O if it is an opinion.

1. **F** The amusement park near our town just opened last summer.
2. **O** It's the best one in our state.
3. **F** It has a roller coaster that's 300 feet high.
4. **O** You're a chicken if you don't go on it.

Directions: Think about the last movie or TV show you saw. Write one fact and one opinion about

Fact:

Opinion:

Answers will vary.

In a story, a **point of view** is how one character feels about an event and reacts to it. Different points of view show how characters feel about the same situation.

What if you were at the mall with a friend and saw a CD you really wanted on sale? You didn't bring enough money, so you borrowed five dollars from your friend to buy the CD. Then you lost the money in the store!

Directions: Write a sentence describing what happened from the point of view of each person named below. Explain how each person felt.

Yourself

Your friend

The store clerk who   for the money

The person who found the money

Answers will vary.

Total Basic Skills Grade 6
334
Answer Key

Page 198

Reading Skills: It's Your Opinion

Your opinion is how you feel or think about something. Although other people may have the same opinion, their reasons could not be exactly the same because of their individuality.

When writing an opinion paragraph, it is important to first state your opinion. Then, in at least three sentences, support your opinion. Finally, end your paragraph by restating your opinion in different words.

Example:
I believe dogs are excellent pets. For thousands of years, dogs have guarded and protected their owners. Dogs are faithful and have been known to save the lives of those they love. Dogs offer unconditional love as well as company for the quiet times in our lives. For these reasons, I feel that dogs make wonderful pets.

Directions: Write an opinion paragraph on whether you would or would not like to have lived in Colonial America. Be sure to support your opinion with at least three reasons.

Answers will vary.

Writing Checklist
Reread your paragraph carefully.
- [ ] My paragraph makes sense.
- [ ] There are no jumps in ideas.
- [ ] I used correct punctuation.
- [ ] I have a good opening and ending.
- [ ] I used correct spelling.
- [ ] My paragraph is well-organized.
- [ ] My paragraph is interesting.

Page 199

Persuasive Writing

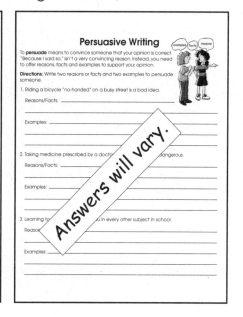

To **persuade** means to convince someone that your opinion is correct. "Because I said so." isn't a very convincing reason. Instead, you need to offer reasons, facts and examples to support your opinion.

Directions: Write two reasons or facts and two examples to persuade someone.

1. Riding a bicycle "no-handed" on a busy street is a bad idea.
   Reasons/Facts: _____
   Examples: _____

2. Taking medicine prescribed by a doctor ___ dangerous.
   Reasons/Facts: _____
   Examples: _____

3. Learning to ___ you in every other subject in school.
   Reason: _____
   Examples: _____

Answers will vary.

Page 200

Describing Characters

When you write a story, your characters must seem like real people. You need to let your reader know not only how they look but how they act, what they look like and how they feel. You could just tell the reader that a character is friendly, scared or angry, but your story will be more interesting if you show these feelings by the characters' actions.

Example:
Character: A frightened child
Adjectives and adverbs: red-haired, freckled, scared, lost, worried
Simile: as frightened as a mouse cornered by a cat
Action: He peeked between his fingers, but his mother was nowhere in sight.

Directions: Write adjectives, adverbs, similes and/or metaphors that tell how each character feels. Then write a sentence that shows how the character feels.

1. an angry woman
   Adjectives and adverbs: _____
   Metaphor or simile: _____
   Sentence: _____

2. a disappointed man
   Adjectives and adverbs: _____
   Metaphor or simile: _____
   Sentence: _____

3. a hungry child
   Adjectives and adverbs: _____
   Metaphor or simile: _____
   Sentence: _____

4. a tired boy
   Adjectives an _____
   Metaphor or simile: _____
   Sentence: _____

Answers will vary.

Page 201

Setting the Scene

Where and when a story takes place is called the **setting**. As with characters, you can tell about a setting—or you can show what the setting is like. Compare these two pairs of sentences:

The sun was shining.
The glaring sun made my eyes burn.

The bus was crowded.
Paige shouldered her way down the aisle, searching for an empty seat on the crowded bus.

If you give your readers a clear picture of your story's setting, they'll feel as if they're standing beside your characters. Include words that describe the sights, sounds, smells, feel and even taste if appropriate.

Directions: Write at least two sentences for each setting, clearly describing it for your readers.

1. an empty kitchen early in the morning _____

2. a locker room after a basketball game _____

3. a dark living room during a scary TV _____

4. a classroom on the fir _____

5. a quiet place i _____

Answers will vary.

Page 202

Creating a Plot

When you're writing a story, the **plot** is the problem your characters face and how they solve it. It's helpful to write a plot outline or summary before beginning a story.

In the beginning of a story, introduce the characters, setting and problem.

Example: Scott and Cindy have never met their mother who lives in another state. They decide they would like very much to meet her. They live with their grandmother and father. On the way home from school, they talk about how they can find and contact her.

In the middle, characters try different ways to solve the problem, usually failing at first.

Example: Scott and Cindy hurry home to ask their grandmother if she can help them find their mother. Their grandmother seems nervous and tells Scott and Cindy to discuss the matter with their father when he gets home from work. When Scott and Cindy's father comes home, they tell him about their plan. Their father is very quiet for several minutes. He says he needs some time to think about it and asks if he can let them know tomorrow. Scott and Cindy can hardly sleep that night. Getting through school the next day is tough as well. After school, Scott and Cindy wait by the window for their father's car to pull in the driveway.

In the end, the characters find a way to solve the problem. Not all stories have happy endings. Sometimes, the characters decide they can live with the situation the way it is.

Example: When their father pulls into the driveway, Scott and Cindy rush out to meet him. Their father hands them airplane tickets. Scott and Cindy hug each other. Then they hug their father.

Directions: How do you think this story ends? Write a summary for the ending of this story.

Answers will vary.

Page 204

Writing Dialogue

When it was Megan's turn to present her book report to the class, she dropped all her notecards! Her face turned red, and she wished she was invisible, but all she could do was stand there and say what she could remember without her cards. It was awful!

Directions: Rewrite each paragraph below. Explain the same scenes and feelings using dialogue.

After class, Megan told her friend Sara she had never been so embarrassed in her life. She saw everyone staring at her, and the teacher looked impatient, but there wasn't anything she could do. Sara assured Megan that no one disliked her because of what had happened.

When Megan got home, she told her mother _____. By then, she felt like crying. Her mother said not to get discouraged ___ days, she would be able to laugh about dropping the cards.

When Megan's older _____ he, he asked her what was wrong. She briefly told him _____ k to school. He started laughing. Megan got mad because she _____ ing at her. Then Jed explained that he had done almost the same _____ sixth grade. He was really embarrassed, too, but not for long.

Answers will vary.

Page 205

Writing: Paraphrasing

Paraphrasing means to restate something in your own words.

Directions: Write the following sentences in your own words. The first one has been done for you.

1. He sat alone and watched movies throughout the cold, rainy night.

   All through the damp, chilly evening, the boy watched television by himself.

2. Many animals such as elephants, zebras and tigers live in the grasslands.

3. In art class, Sarah worked diligently on a clay pitcher, molding and shaping it on the pottery wheel.

Answers will vary.

4. The scientists frantically searched for a cure for the new disease that threatened the entire world population.

5. Quietly, the detective crept around the abandoned building, hoping to find the missing man.

6. The windmill turned lazily in the afternoon breeze.

Page 206

Writing: Paraphrasing

Directions: Using synonyms and different word order, paraphrase the following paragraphs. The first one has been done for you.

Some of the Earth's resources, such as oil and coal, can be used only once. We should always, therefore, be careful how we use them. Some materials that are made from natural resources, including metal, glass and paper, can be reused. This is called recycling.

including Many natural resources, including coal and oil, can be used only one time. For this reason, it is necessary to use them wisely. There are other materials made from resources of the Earth that can be recycled, or used again. Materials that can be recycled include metal, glass and paper.

Recycling helps to conserve the limited resources of our land. For example, there are only small amounts of gold and silver ores in the earth. If we can recycle these metals, less of the ores need to be mined. While there is much more aluminum ore in the earth, recycling is still important. It takes less fuel energy to recycle aluminum than it does to make the metal from ore. Therefore, recycling aluminum helps to conserve fuel.

Answers will vary.

It is impossible to get minerals and fossil fuels from the earth without causing damage to its surface. In the past, people did not think much about making these kinds of changes to the Earth. They did not think about how these actions might affect the future. As a result, much of the land around mines was left useless and ugly. This is not necessary, because such land can be restored to its former beauty.

Page 207

Writing: Summarizing

A **summary** is a brief retelling of the main ideas of a reading selection. To summarize, write the author's most important points in your own words.

Directions: Write a two-sentence summary for each paragraph.

The boll weevil is a small beetle that is native to Mexico. It feeds inside the seed pods, or bolls, of cotton plants. The boll weevil crossed into Texas in the late 1800s. It has since spread into most of the cotton-growing areas of the United States. The boll weevil causes hundreds of millions of dollars worth of damage to cotton crops each year.

Summary:

Each spring, fe ___ with their snouts. T ___ into wormlike grub ___ ___ fall from the plant. ___ eir way from one bud to another. Several generations of boll weevils may be produced in a single season.

Answers will vary.

Summary:

The coming of the boll weevil to the United States caused tremendous damage to cotton crops. Yet, there were some good results, too. Farmers were forced to plant other crops. In areas where a variety of crops were raised, the land is in better condition than it would hav been if only cotton had been grown.

Summary:

Page 208

Writing: Outlining

An **outline** is a skeletal description of the main ideas and important details of a reading selection. Making an outline is a good study aid. It is particularly useful when you must write a paper.

Directions: Read the paragraphs, and then complete the outline below.

Weather has a lot to do with where animals live. Cold-blooded animals' have body temperatures that change with the temperature of the environment. Cold-blooded animals include snakes, frogs and lizards. They cannot live anywhere the temperatures stay below freezing for long periods of time. The body temperatures of warm-blooded animals do not depend on the environment. Any animal with hair or fur—including dogs, elephants and whales—is warm-blooded. Warm-blooded animals can live anywhere in the world where there is enough food to sustain them.

Some warm-blooded animals live where snow covers the ground all winter. These animals have different ways to survive the cold weather. Certain animals store up food to last throughout the snowy season. For example, the tree squirrel may gather nuts to hide in his home. Other animals hibernate in the winter. The ground squirrel, for example, stays in its burrow all winter long, living off the fat reserves in its body.

Sample answers:

Title: Animal Habitats

Main Topic: I. Weather has a lot to do with where animals live.

   Subtopic: A. Cold-blooded animals' temperatures change with environment.

      Detail: 1. They cannot live anywhere it stays below freezing very long.

   Subtopic: B. Warm-blooded animals' temperatures do not depend on the environment.

      Detail: 1. They can live anywhere there is food.

Main Topic: II. Some warm-blooded animals can live in the snow all winter.

   Subtopic: A. Animals have different ways to survive the cold.

      Details: 1. Some animals store food for the winter.

         2. Some animals hibernate in the winter.

Page 209

Using the Right Resources

Directions: Decide where you would look to find information on the following topics. After each question, write one or more of the following references:

- **almanac** — contains tables and charts of statistics and information
- **atlas** — collection of maps
- **card/computer catalog** — library resource showing available books by topic, title or author
- **dictionary** — contains alphabetical listing of words with their meanings, pronunciations and origins
- **encyclopedia** — set of books or CD-ROM with general information on many subjects
- **Readers' Guide to Periodical Literature** — an index of articles in magazines and newspapers
- **thesaurus** — contains synonyms and antonyms of words

1. What is the capital of The Netherlands? **atlas, encyclopedia**

2. What form of government is practiced there? **almanac, encyclopedia**

3. What languages are spoken there? **almanac, encyclopedia**

4. What is the meaning of the word **indigenous**? **dictionary, thesaurus**

5. Where would you find information on conservation? **card/computer catalog, encyclopedia, Readers' Guide to Periodical Literature**

6. What is a synonym for **catastrophe**? **thesaurus**

7. Where would you find a review of the play *Cats*? **Readers' Guide to Periodical Literature**

8. Where would you find statistics on the annual rainfall in the Sahara Desert? **almanac**

9. What is the origin of the word **plentiful**? **dictionary**

10. What are antonyms for the word **plentiful**? **thesaurus**

11. Where would you find statistics for the number of automobiles manufactured in the United States last year? **almanac**

Page 210

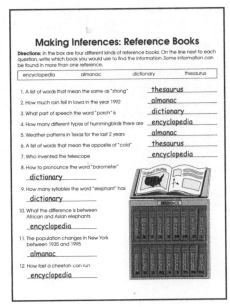

Making Inferences: Reference Books

Directions: In the box are four different kinds of reference books. On the line next to each question, write which book you would use to find the information. Some information can be found in more than one reference.

| encyclopedia | almanac | dictionary | thesaurus |

1. A list of words that mean the same as "strong" — thesaurus
2. How much rain fell in Iowa in the year 1992 — almanac
3. What part of speech the word "porch" is — dictionary
4. How many different types of hummingbirds there are — encyclopedia
5. Weather patterns in Texas for the last 2 years — almanac
6. A list of words that mean the opposite of "cold" — thesaurus
7. Who invented the telescope — encyclopedia
8. How to pronounce the word "barometer" — dictionary
9. How many syllables the word "elephant" has — dictionary
10. What the difference is between African and Asian elephants — encyclopedia
11. The population changes in New York between 1935 and 1995 — almanac
12. How fast a cheetah can run — encyclopedia

Page 211

Table of Contents

The **table of contents**, located in the front of books or magazines, tells a lot about what is inside.

A table of contents in books lists the headings and page numbers for each chapter. **Chapters** are the parts into which books are divided. Also listed are chapter numbers and the sections and subsections, if any. Look at the sample table of contents below:

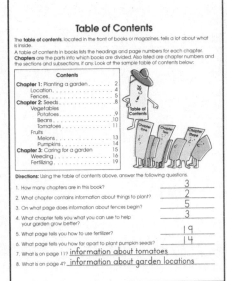

Contents

Chapter 1: Planting a garden 2
  Location 4
  Fences. 5
Chapter 2: Seeds 8
  Vegetables
    Potatoes 9
    Beans 10
    Tomatoes 11
  Fruits
    Melons 13
    Pumpkins 14
Chapter 3: Caring for a garden 15
  Weeding 16
  Fertilizing 19

Directions: Using the table of contents above, answer the following questions.

1. How many chapters are in this book? — 3
2. What chapter contains information about things to plant? — 2
3. On what page does information about fences begin? — 5
4. What chapter tells you what you can use to help your garden grow better? — 3
5. What page tells you how to use fertilizer? — 19
6. What page tells you how far apart to plant pumpkin seeds? — 14
7. What is on page 11? — information about tomatoes
8. What is on page 4? — information about garden locations

Page 212

Indexes

An **index** is an alphabetical listing of names, topics and important words and is found in the back of a book. An index lists every page on which these items appear. For example, in a book about music, dulcimer might be listed like this: Dulcimer 2, 13, 26, 38. Page numbers may also be listed like this: Guitars 18–21. That means that information about guitars begins on page 18 and continues through page 21. **Subject** is the name of the item in an index. **Sub-entry** is a smaller division of the subject. For example, "apples" would be listed under fruit.

Index

		See also planet names.
N		Pleiades 32
Neptune 27		Pluto 12, 27
NGC 5128 (galaxy) . . . 39		Polaris 35, 36
Novas 32		Pole star. See Polaris.
		Project Ozma 41
O		
Observatories. See El Caracol		R
Orbits of planets . . . 10		Rings. See Planet rings.
Orion rocket 43		
		S
P		Sagittarius 37
Planetoids. See Asteroids.		Satellites
Planet rings		Jupiter 24
Jupiter 23		Neptune 27
Saturn 9, 25		Pluto 27
Uranus 26		Saturn 25
Planets		Uranus 26
discovered by Greeks . . 7		See also Galilean satellites.
outside the solar system . . 40		
visible with the naked eye . . 9		Saturn 25

Directions: Answer the questions about the index from this book about the solar system.

1. On what pages is there information about Pluto? — pages 12 and 27
2. On what pages is information about Saturn's first ring found? — page 9 or 25
3. What is on page 41? — information about Project Ozma
4. Where is there information about the pole star? — pages 35 and 36
5. What is on page 43? — information about the Orion rocket
6. On what page would you find information about planets that are visible to the eye? — page 9
7. On what page would you find information about Jupiter's satellites? — page 24

Page 213

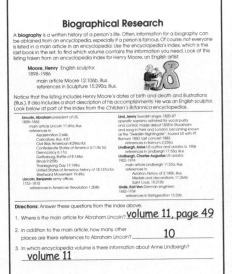

Biographical Research

A **biography** is a written history of a person's life. Often, information for a biography can be obtained from an encyclopedia, especially if a person is famous. Of course, not everyone is listed in a main article in an encyclopedia. Use the encyclopedia's index, which is the last book in the set, to find which volume contains the information you need. Look at this listing taken from an encyclopedia index for Henry Moore, an English artist.

Moore, Henry English sculptor.
1898–1986
main article Moore 12:106b. illus.
references in Sculpture 15:290a. illus.

Notice that the listing includes Henry Moore's dates of birth and death and illustrations (illus.). It also includes a short description of his accomplishments: He was an English sculptor. Look below at part of the index from the *Children's Britannica* encyclopedia.

Lincoln, Abraham president of US,
1809–1865
  main article Lincoln 11:49a. illus.
  references in
    Assassination 2:64b
    Caricature, illus. 4:87
    Civil War, American 4:296a fol.
    Confederate States of America 5:113b fol.
    Democracy 6:17a
    Gettysburg, Battle of 8:144a
    Illinois 9:259b
    Thanksgiving Day 17:199a
    United States of America, history of 18:137a fol.
    Westward Movement 19:49a
Lincoln, Benjamin army officer.
1733–1810
  references in American Revolution 1:204b

Lind, Jenny Swedish singer, 1820–87
operatic soprano admired for vocal purity and song in Paris and London, becoming known as the "Swedish Nightingale"; toured US with P.T. Barnum 1850; last concert 1883.
  references in Barnum 2:235a
Lindbergh, Anne US author and aviator, b. 1906
  references in Lindbergh 11:53a, illus.
Lindbergh, Charles Augustus US aviator,
1902–1974
  main article Lindbergh 11:53a, illus.
  references in
    Aviation, history of 2:140b, illus.
    Medals and decorations, 11:266b
    Saint Louis, 15:215b
Linde, Karl Von German engineer,
1842–1934
  references in Refrigeration 15:32b.

Directions: Answer these questions from the index above.

1. Where is the main article for Abraham Lincoln? — volume 11, page 49
2. In addition to the main article, how many other places are there references to Abraham Lincoln? — 10
3. In which encyclopedia volume is there information about Anne Lindbergh? — volume 11

Page 214

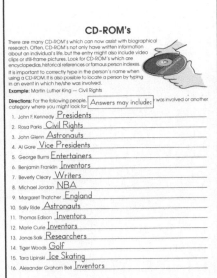

CD-ROM's

There are many CD-ROM's which can now assist with biographical research. Often, CD-ROM's not only have written information about an individual's life, but the entry might also include video clips or still-frame pictures. Look for CD-ROM's which are encyclopedias, historical references or famous person indexes.

It is important to correctly type in the person's name when using a CD-ROM. It is also possible to locate a person by typing in an event in which he/she was involved.

Example: Martin Luther King — Civil Rights

Directions: For the following people, [Answers may include:] was involved or another category where you might look for

1. John F. Kennedy — Presidents
2. Rosa Parks — Civil Rights
3. John Glenn — Astronauts
4. Al Gore — Vice Presidents
5. George Burns — Entertainers
6. Benjamin Franklin — Inventors
7. Beverly Cleary — Writers
8. Michael Jordan — NBA
9. Margaret Thatcher — England
10. Sally Ride — Astronauts
11. Thomas Edison — Inventors
12. Marie Curie — Inventors
13. Jonas Salk — Researchers
14. Tiger Woods — Golf
15. Tara Lipinski — Ice Skating
16. Alexander Graham Bell — Inventors

Page 215

Friendly Letters

Directions: Study the format for writing a letter to a friend. Then answer the questions.

your return address	123 Waverly Road
	Cincinnati, Ohio 45241
date	June 23, 1999
greeting	Dear Josh,
body	How is your summer going? I am enjoying mine so far. I have been swimming twice already this week, and it's only Wednesday! I am glad there is a pool near our house.
	My parents said that you can stay overnight when your family comes for the 4th of July picnic. Do you want to? We can pitch a tent in the back yard and camp out. It will be a lot of fun!
	Please write back to let me know if you can stay over on the 4th. I will see you then!
closing signature	Your friend,
	Michael

Michael Delaney
your return address — 123 Waverly Road
Cincinnati, Ohio 45241

main address — Josh Sommers
2250 West First Ave.
Columbus, OH 43212

1. What words are in the greeting? — Dear Josh
2. What words are in the closing? — Your friend
3. On what street does the writer live? — Waverly Road

Page 218

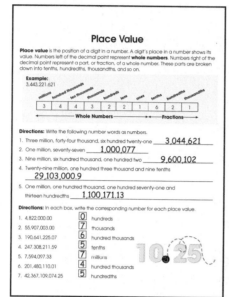

Place Value

Place value is the position of a digit in a number. A digit's place in a number shows its value. Numbers left of the decimal point represent whole numbers. Numbers right of the decimal point represent a part, or fraction, of a whole number. These parts are broken down into tenths, hundredths, thousandths, and so on.

Example:
3,443,221.621

millions	hundred thousands	ten thousands	thousands	hundreds	tens	ones	tenths	hundredths	thousandths
3	4	4	3	2	2	1	6	2	1

Whole Numbers — Fractions

Directions: Write the following number words as numbers.
1. Three million, forty-four thousand, six hundred twenty-one   3,044,621
2. One million, seventy-seven   1,000,077
3. Nine million, six hundred thousand, one hundred two   9,600,102
4. Twenty-nine million, one hundred three thousand and nine tenths
   29,103,000.9
5. One million, one hundred thousand, one hundred seventy-one and thirteen hundredths   1,100,171.13

Directions: In each box, write the corresponding number for each place value.
1. 4,822,000.00   **0** hundreds
2. 55,907,003.00   **7** thousands
3. 190,641,225.07   **6** hundred thousands
4. 247,308,211.59   **5** tenths
5. 7,594,077.33   **7** millions
6. 201,480,110.01   **4** hundred thousands
7. 42,367,109,074.25   **5** hundredths

Page 219

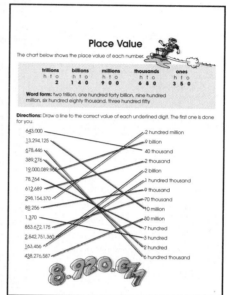

Place Value

The chart below shows the place value of each number.

trillions h t o	billions h t o	millions h t o	thousands h t o	ones h t o
2	1 4 0	9 0 0	6 8 0	3 5 0

Word form: two trillion, one hundred forty billion, nine hundred million, six hundred eighty thousand, three hundred fifty

Directions: Draw a line to the correct value of each underlined digit. The first one is done for you.

643,000
13,294,125
678,446
389,276
19,000,089,966
78,764
612,689
298,154,370
89,256
1,370
853,672,175
2,842,751,360
163,456
438,276,587

2 hundred million
9 billion
40 thousand
2 thousand
2 billion
1 hundred thousand
9 thousand
70 thousand
10 million
80 million
7 hundred
3 hundred
2 hundred
6 hundred thousand

Page 220

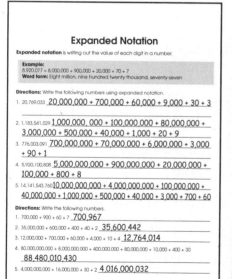

Expanded Notation

Expanded notation is writing out the value of each digit in a number.

Example:
8,920,077 = 8,000,000 + 900,000 + 20,000 + 70 + 7
Word form: Eight million, nine hundred twenty thousand, seventy-seven

Directions: Write the following numbers using expanded notation.
1. 20,769,033   20,000,000 + 700,000 + 60,000 + 9,000 + 30 + 3

2. 1,183,541,029   1,000,000,000 + 100,000,000 + 80,000,000 + 3,000,000 + 500,000 + 40,000 + 1,000 + 20 + 9
3. 776,003,091   700,000,000 + 70,000,000 + 6,000,000 + 3,000 + 90 + 1
4. 5,920,100,808   5,000,000,000 + 900,000,000 + 20,000,000 + 100,000 + 800 + 8
5. 14,141,543,760   10,000,000,000 + 4,000,000,000 + 100,000,000 + 40,000,000 + 1,000,000 + 500,000 + 40,000 + 3,000 + 700 + 60

Directions: Write the following numbers.
1. 700,000 + 900 + 60 + 7   700,967
2. 35,000,000 + 600,000 + 400 + 40 + 2   35,600,442
3. 12,000,000 + 700,000 + 60,000 + 4,000 + 10 + 4   12,764,014
4. 80,000,000,000 + 8,000,000,000 + 400,000,000 + 80,000,000 + 10,000 + 400 + 30
   88,480,010,430
5. 4,000,000,000 + 16,000,000 + 30 + 2   4,016,000,032

Page 221

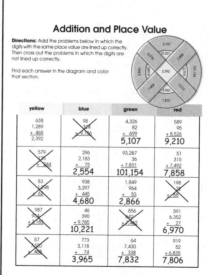

Addition and Place Value

Directions: Add the problems below in which the digits with the same place value are lined up correctly. Then cross out the problems in which the digits are not lined up correctly.

Find each answer in the diagram and color that section.

yellow	blue	green	red
638 1,289 + 465 = 2,392	~~98~~	4,326 82 + 699 = 5,107	589 95 + 8,526 = 9,210
579 ~~125 + 844~~	296 2,183 + 75 = 2,554	93,287 36 + 7,831 = 101,154	51 315 + 7,492 = 7,858
83 ~~298 + 62~~	938 3,297 + 445 = 4,680	1,849 964 + 53 = 2,866	~~198 + 68~~
987 ~~934 + 3,165~~	46 390 + 9,785 = 10,221	856 ~~+ 7,062~~	591 6,352 + 27 = 6,970
57 ~~408~~	773 3,118 + 74 = 3,965	64 7,430 + 338 = 7,832	919 52 + 6,835 = 7,806

Page 222

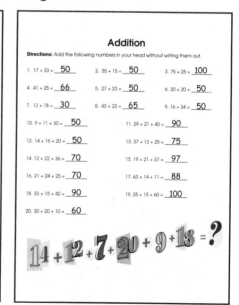

Addition

Directions: Add the following numbers in your head without writing them out.

1. 17 + 33 = 50
2. 35 + 15 = 50
3. 75 + 25 = 100
4. 41 + 25 = 66
5. 27 + 23 = 50
6. 30 + 20 = 50
7. 12 + 18 = 30
8. 43 + 22 = 65
9. 16 + 34 = 50
10. 9 + 11 + 30 = 50
11. 29 + 21 + 40 = 90
12. 14 + 16 + 20 = 50
13. 37 + 13 + 25 = 75
14. 12 + 22 + 36 = 70
15. 19 + 21 + 57 = 97
16. 21 + 24 + 25 = 70
17. 63 + 14 + 11 = 88
18. 33 + 15 + 42 = 90
19. 25 + 15 + 60 = 100
20. 30 + 20 + 10 = 60

14 + 12 + 7 + 20 + 9 + 18 = ?

Page 223

Addition Word Problems

Directions: Solve the following addition word problems.

1. 100 students participated in a sports card show in the school gym. Brad brought his entire collection of 2,000 cards to show his friends. He had 700 football cards and 400 basketball cards. If the rest of his cards were baseball cards, how many baseball cards did he bring with him?

900 baseball cards

2. Refreshments were set up in one area of the gym. Hot dogs were a dollar, soda was 50 cents, chips were 35 cents and cookies were a quarter. If you purchased two of each item, how much money would you need?

$4.20

3. It took each student 30 minutes to set up for the card show and twice as long to put everything away. The show was open for 3 hours. How much time did each student spend on this event?

4 1/2 hours

4. 450 people attended the card show. 55 were mothers of students, 67 were fathers, 23 were grandparents, 8 were aunts and uncles and the rest were kids. How many kids attended?

297 kids

5. Of the 100 students who set up displays, most of them sold or traded some of their cards. Bruce sold 75 cards, traded 15 cards and collected $225. Kevin only sold 15 cards, traded 81 cards and collected $100. Missi traded 200 cards, sold 10 and earned $35. Of those listed, how many cards were sold, how many were traded and how much money was earned?

sold **100**   traded **296**   earned $ **360**

Page 224

Subtraction

Directions: Subtract the following numbers. When subtracting, begin on the right, especially if you need to regroup and borrow.

549 − 162 = **387**	823 − 417 = **406**	370 − 244 = **126**	648 − 79 = **569**
700 − 343 = **357**	475 − 299 = **176**	603 − 425 = **178**	354 − 265 = **89**
1,841 − 952 = **889**	2,597 − 608 = **1,989**	6,832 − 1,774 = **5,058**	9,005 − 3,458 = **5,547**
23,342 − 9,093 = **14,249**	53,790 − 40,813 = **12,977**	29,644 − 19,780 = **9,864**	35,726 − 16,959 = **18,767**
109,432 − 79,145 = **30,287**	350,907 − 14,185 = **336,722**	217,523 − 44,197 = **173,326**	537,411 − 406,514 = **130,897**

Page 225

Subtraction Word Problems

Directions: Solve the following subtraction word problems.

1. Last year, 28,945 people lived in Mike's town. This year there are 31,889. How many people have moved in? **2,944 people**

2. Brad earned $227 mowing lawns. He spent $168 on tapes by his favorite rock group. How much money does he have left? **$59**

3. The school year is 180 days. Carrie has gone to 32 school days so far. How many more days does she have left? **148 days**

4. Craig wants a skateboard that costs $128. He has saved $47. How much more does he need? **$81**

5. To get to school, Jennifer walks 1,275 steps and Carolyn walks 2,618 steps. How many more steps does Carolyn walk than Jennifer? **1,343 steps**

6. Amy has placed 91 of the 389 pieces in a new puzzle she purchased. How many more does she have left to finish? **298 pieces**

7. From New York, it's 2,823 miles to Los Angeles and 1,327 miles to Miami. How much farther away is Los Angeles? **1,496 miles**

8. Shella read that a piece of carrot cake has 236 calories, but a piece of apple pie has 427 calories. How many calories will she save by eating the cake instead of the pie? **191 calories**

9. Tim's summer camp costs $223, while Sam's costs $149. How much more does Tim's camp cost? **$74**

10. Last year, the nation's budget was $45,000,000,000, but the nation spent $52,569,342,000. How much more than its budget did the nation spend? **$ 7,569,342,000**

Page 226

Multiplication

Directions: Multiply the following numbers. Be sure to keep the numbers aligned, and place a 0 in the ones place when multiplying by the tens digit.

Example:

Correct	Incorrect
55 x 15 / 275 / 550 / 825	55 x 15 / 275 / 55 / 330

1. 12 x 6 = **72**
2. 44 x 9 = **396**
3. 27 x 7 = **189**
4. 92 x 6 = **552**
5. 85 x 9 = **765**

6. 78 x 24 = **1,872**
7. 32 x 17 = **544**
8. 19 x 46 = **874**
9. 63 x 12 = **756**
10. 38 x 77 = **2,926**

11. 125 x 6 = **750**
12. 641 x 25 = **16,025**
13. 713 x 47 = **33,511**
14. 586 x 45 = **26,370**
15. 294 x 79 = **23,226**

16. 20 x 4 x 7 = **560**
17. 9 x 5 x 11 = **495**
18. 16 x 2 x 2 = **64**
19. 7 x 6 x 3 = **126**
20. 33 x 11 x 3 = **1,089**
21. 2 x 8 x 10 = **160**

Page 227

Multiplying With Zeros

Directions: Multiply the following numbers. If a number ends with zero, you can eliminate it while calculating the rest of the answer. Then count how many zeros you took off and add them to your answer.

Example:

550 x 50 = 27,500	Take off 2 zeros / Add on 2 zeros	500 x 5 = 2,500	Take off 2 zeros / Add on 2 zeros

1. 300 x 6 = **1,800**
2. 400 x 7 = **2,800**
3. 620 x 5 = **3,100**
4. 290 x 7 = **2,030**

5. 142 x 20 = **2,840**
6. 505 x 50 = **25,250**
7. 340 x 70 = **23,800**
8. 600 x 60 = **36,000**

9. 550 x 380 = **209,000**
10. 290 x 150 = **43,500**
11. 2,040 x 360 = **734,400**
12. 8,800 x 200 = **1,760,000**

13. Bruce traveled 600 miles each day of a 10-day trip. How far did he go during the entire trip? **6,000 miles**

14. 30 children each sold 20 items for the school fund-raiser. Each child earned $100 for the school. How much money did the school collect? **$2,000**

15. 10 x 40 x 2 = **800**
16. 30 x 30 x 10 = **9,000**
17. 100 x 60 x 10 = **60,000**
18. 500 x 11 x 2 = **11,000**
19. 9 x 10 x 10 = **900**
20. 7,000 x 20 x 10 = **1,400,000**

GRADE
6

Page 228

Division

In a division problem, the **dividend** is the number to be divided, the **divisor** is the number used to divide and the **quotient** is the answer. To check your work, multiply your answer times the divisor and you should get the dividend.

```
Example:      130 ← quotient    Check:   130 ← quotient
      divisor→ 4)520 ← dividend          x  4 ← divisor
               4                         520 ← dividend
               12
               12
               00
```

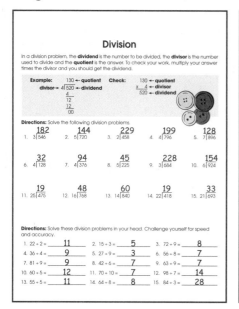

Directions: Solve the following division problems.

1. 3)546 **182**	2. 5)720 **144**	3. 2)458 **229**	4. 4)796 **199**	5. 7)896 **128**
6. 4)128 **32**	7. 4)376 **94**	8. 5)225 **45**	9. 3)684 **228**	10. 6)924 **154**
11. 25)475 **19**	12. 16)768 **48**	13. 14)840 **60**	14. 22)418 **19**	15. 21)693 **33**

Directions: Solve these division problems in your head. Challenge yourself for speed and accuracy.

1. 22 ÷ 2 = **11**   2. 15 ÷ 3 = **5**   3. 72 ÷ 9 = **8**
4. 36 ÷ 4 = **9**   5. 27 ÷ 9 = **3**   6. 56 ÷ 8 = **7**
7. 81 ÷ 9 = **9**   8. 42 ÷ 6 = **7**   9. 63 ÷ 9 = **7**
10. 60 ÷ 5 = **12**   11. 70 ÷ 10 = **7**   12. 98 ÷ 7 = **14**
13. 55 ÷ 5 = **11**   14. 64 ÷ 8 = **8**   15. 84 ÷ 3 = **28**

Page 229

Division Word Problems

In the example below, 368 is being divided by 4. 4 won't divide into 3, so move over one position and divide 4 into 36. 4 goes into 36 nine times. Then multiply 4 x 9 to get 36. Subtract 36 from 36. The answer is 0, less than the divisor, so 9 is the right number. Now bring down the 8, divide 4 into it and repeat the process.

```
Example:     9        92
          4)368     4)368
            36        36
             0        08
                       8
                       0
```

To check your division, multiply 4 x 92 = 368.

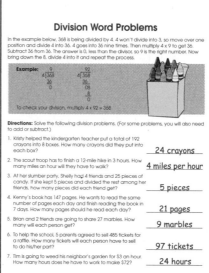

Directions: Solve the following division problems. (For some problems, you will also need to add or subtract.)

1. Kristy helped the kindergarten teacher put a total of 192 crayons in 8 boxes. How many crayons did they put into each box?   **24 crayons**

2. The scout troop has to finish a 12-mile hike in 3 hours. How many miles an hour will they have to walk?   **4 miles per hour**

3. At her slumber party, Shelly had 4 friends and 25 pieces of candy. If she kept 5 pieces and divided the rest among her friends, how many pieces did each friend get?   **5 pieces**

4. Kenny's book has 147 pages. He wants to read the same number of pages each day and finish reading the book in 7 days. How many pages should he read each day?   **21 pages**

5. Brian and 2 friends are going to share 27 marbles. How many will each person get?   **9 marbles**

6. To help the school, 5 parents agreed to sell 485 tickets for a raffle. How many tickets will each person have to sell to do his/her part?   **97 tickets**

7. Tim is going to weed his neighbor's garden for $3 an hour. How many hours does he have to work to make $72?   **24 hours**

Page 230

Equations

In an **equation**, the value on the left of the equal sign must equal the value on the right. Remember the order of operations: solve from left to right, multiply or divide numbers before adding or subtracting and do the operation inside parentheses first.

```
Example:  6 + 4 - 2 = 4 x 2
           10 - 2  →  8
              8  =  8
```

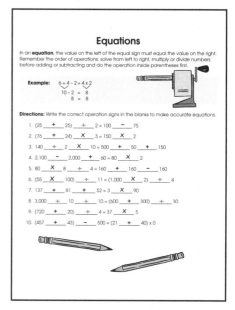

Directions: Write the correct operation signs in the blanks to make accurate equations.

1. (25 **+** 25) **÷** 2 = 100 **−** 75
2. (76 **+** 24) **X** 3 = 150 **X** 2
3. 140 **÷** 2 **X** 10 = 500 **+** 50 **+** 150
4. 2,100 **−** 2,000 **+** 60 = 80 **X** 2
5. 80 **X** 8 **÷** 4 = 160 **+** 160 **−** 160
6. (55 **X** 100) **÷** 11 = (1,000 **X** 2) **+** 4
7. 137 **+** 81 **+** 52 = 3 **X** 90
8. 3,000 **÷** 10 **÷** 10 = (600 **−** 300) **÷** 30
9. (720 **+** 280) **÷** 4 = 37 **X** 5
10. (457 **+** 43) **−** 500 = (21 **+** 40) x 0

Page 231

Equations

Directions: Write the correct operation signs in the blanks to make accurate equations.

1. 5 **+** 5 **+** 5 = 3 **X** 5 **+** 0
2. (50 **+** 0) **X** 2 = 25 **X** 2 **X** 2
3. 2 **X** 2 **X** 2 = 2 **+** 2 **X** 2 **X** 4
4. (4 **X** 5) **+** 5 **+** 5 = 2 **X** 3 **X** 5
5. (25 **+** 5) **X** 2 **X** 3 = 3 **X** 6 **X** 2 **X** 5
6. (125 **X** 7) **+** 3 = 100 **X** 2 **+** 4 **+** 70 **+** 10
7. (100 **X** 10) **÷** 5 **+** 10 = 10 **X** 5 **X** 100 **÷** 10
8. 35 **+** 35 **+** 5 **X** 2 = 5 **X** 3 **X** 2 **X** 5
9. (60 **÷** 2) **X** 3 = 3 **X** 3 **X** 3 **X** 0 **+** 15 **+** (5 **X** 15)
10. (120 **X** 4) **+** 7 = (7 **X** 7) **X** (2 **X** 5)
11. (91 **+** 3 **+** 6) **X** 3 = 2 **X** 1 **X** 3 **X** (2 **X** 5)
12. (16 **X** 4) **−** 8 = 5 **+** 5 **X** (3 **X** 3) **+** 6
13. 0 **X** 5 **+** 15 **−** 4 = 3 **−** 3 **+** 3 **+** 8
14. 16 **X** 3 **+** 12 = (2 **X** 20) = (2 **X** 2) **X** 6 **+** 10 **−** (2 **X** 7)
15. 21 **+** (3 **X** 3) **−** 3 − 1 = 3 **+** 1 **X** 2 **+** 20

Page 232

Rounding and Estimating

Rounding is expressing a number to the nearest whole number, ten, thousand or other value. **Estimating** is using an approximate number instead of an exact one. When rounding a number, we say a country has 98,000,000 citizens instead of 98,347,425. We can round off numbers to the nearest whole number, the nearest hundred or the nearest million— whatever is appropriate.

Here are the steps: 1) Decide where you want to round off the number. 2) If the digit to the right is less than 5, leave the digit at the rounding place unchanged. 3) If the digit to the right is 5 or more, increase the digit at the rounding place by 1.

Examples: 587 rounded to the nearest hundred is 600.
535 rounded to the nearest hundred is 500.
21,897 rounded to the nearest thousand is 22,000.
21,356 rounded to the nearest thousand is 21,000.

When we estimate numbers, we use rounded, approximate numbers instead of exact ones.

Example: A hamburger that costs $1.49 and a drink that costs $0.79 total about $2.30 ($1.50 plus $0.80).

Directions: Use rounding and estimating to find the answers to these questions. You may have to add, subtract, multiply or divide.

1. Debbi is having a party and wants to fill 11 cups from a 67-ounce bottle of pop. About how many ounces should she pour into each cup?   **6 ounces**

2. Tracy studied 28 minutes every day for 4 days. About how long did she study in all?   **120 minutes**

3. About how much does this lunch cost? $1.19 $0.39 $0.49   **$2.00**

4. The numbers below show how long Frank spent studying last week. Estimate how many minutes he studied for the whole week.
Monday: 23 minutes Tuesday: 37 minutes Wednesday: 38 minutes Thursday: 12 minutes   **110 minutes**

5. One elephant at the zoo weighs 1,417 pounds and another one weighs 1,789 pounds. About how much heavier is the second elephant?   **400 lbs.**

6. If Tim studied a total of 122 minutes over 4 days, about how long did he study each day?   **30 minutes**

7. It's 549 miles to Dover and 345 miles to Albany. About how much closer is Albany?   **200 miles**

Page 233

Rounding

Directions: Round off each number, then estimate the answer. You can use a calculator to find the exact answer.

	Estimate	Actual Answer
Round to the nearest ten.		
1. 86 ÷ 9 =	**9**	9.56
2. 237 + 488 =	**730**	725
3. 49 x 11 =	**500**	539
4. 309 + 412 =	**720**	721
5. 625 − 218 =	**410**	407
Round to the nearest hundred.		
6. 790 − 70 =	**700**	720
7. 690 ÷ 70 =	**7**	9.86
8. 2,177 − 955 =	**1,200**	1,222
9. 4,792 + 3,305 =	**8,100**	8,097
10. 5,210 x 90 =	**520,00**	468,900
Round to the nearest thousand.		
11. 4,078 + 2,093 =	**6,000**	6,171
12. 5,525 − 3,065 =	**3,000**	2,460
13. 6,047 + 2,991 =	**2**	2,02
14. 1,913 x 4,216 =	**8,000,000**	8,065,208
15. 7,227 + 8,449 =	**15,000**	15,676

Page 234

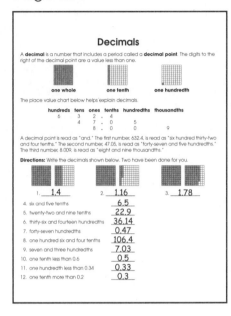

Decimals

A **decimal** is a number that includes a period called a **decimal point**. The digits to the right of the decimal point are a value less than one.

one whole   one tenth   one hundredth

The place value chart below helps explain decimals.

hundreds tens ones tenths hundredths thousandths
6   3   2 . 4
4   7 . 0   5
8   . 0   0   9

A decimal point is read as "and." The first number, 632.4, is read as "six hundred thirty-two and four tenths." The second number, 47.05, is read as "forty-seven and five hundredths." The third number, 8.009, is read as "eight and nine thousandths."

Directions: Write the decimals shown below. Two have been done for you.

1. __1.4__   2. __1.16__   3. __1.78__

4. six and five tenths __6.5__
5. twenty-two and nine tenths __22.9__
6. thirty-six and fourteen hundredths __36.14__
7. forty-seven hundredths __0.47__
8. one hundred six and four tenths __106.4__
9. seven and three hundredths __7.03__
10. one tenth less than 0.6 __0.5__
11. one hundredth less than 0.34 __0.33__
12. one tenth more than 0.2 __0.3__

Page 235

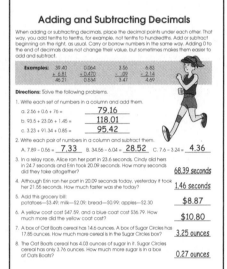

Adding and Subtracting Decimals

When adding or subtracting decimals, place the decimal points under each other. That way, you add tenths to tenths, for example, not tenths to hundredths. Add or subtract beginning on the right, as usual. Carry or borrow numbers in the same way. Adding 0 to the end of decimals does not change their value, but sometimes makes them easier to add and subtract.

Examples:
39.40   0.064   3.56   6.83
+ 6.81   + 0.470   - .09   - 2.14
46.21   0.534   3.47   4.69

Directions: Solve the following problems.

1. Write each set of numbers in a column and add them.
   a. 2.56 + 0.6 + 76 = __79.16__
   b. 93.5 + 23.06 + 1.45 = __118.01__
   c. 3.23 + 91.34 + 0.85 = __95.42__

2. Write each pair of numbers in a column and subtract them.
   A. 7.89 − 0.56 = __7.33__   B. 34.56 − 6.04 = __28.52__   C. 7.6 − 3.24 = __4.36__

3. In a relay race, Alice ran her part in 23.6 seconds, Cindy did hers in 24.7 seconds and Erin took 20.09 seconds. How many seconds did they take altogether? __68.39 seconds__

4. Although Erin ran her part in 20.09 seconds today, yesterday it took her 21.55 seconds. How much faster was she today? __1.46 seconds__

5. Add this grocery bill: potatoes—$3.49; milk—$2.09; bread—$0.99; apples—$2.30 __$8.87__

6. A yellow coat cost $47.59, and a blue coat cost $36.79. How much more did the yellow coat cost? __$10.80__

7. A box of Oat Boats cereal has 14.6 ounces. A box of Sugar Circles has 17.85 ounces. How much more cereal is in the Sugar Circles box? __3.25 ounces__

8. The Oat Boats cereal has 4.03 ounces of sugar in it. Sugar Circles cereal has only 3.76 ounces. How much more sugar is in a box of Oats Boats? __0.27 ounces__

Page 236

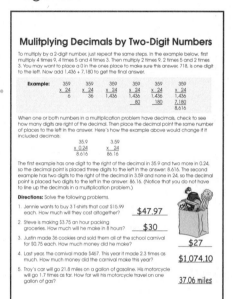

Mulitplying Decimals by Two-Digit Numbers

To multiply by a 2-digit number, just repeat the same steps. In the example below, first multiply 4 times 9, 4 times 5 and 4 times 3. Then multiply 2 times 9, 2 times 5 and 2 times 3. You may want to place a 0 in the ones place to make sure this answer, 718, is one digit to the left. Now add 1,436 + 7,180 to get the final answer.

Example:
359   359   359   359   359   359
x 24   x 24   x 24   x 24   x 24   x 24
6   36   1,436 1,436 1,436 1,436
                           80   180   7,180
                                       8,616

When one or both numbers in a multiplication problem have decimals, check to see how many digits are right of the decimal. Then place the decimal point the same number of places to the left in the answer. Here's how the example above would change if it included decimals.

35.9   3.59
x 0.24   x .24
8.616   86.16

The first example has one digit to the right of the decimal in 35.9 and two more in 0.24, so the decimal point is placed three digits to the left in the answer: 8.616. The second example has two digits to the right of the decimal in 3.59 and none in 24, so the decimal point is placed two digits to the left in the answer: 86.16. (Notice that you do not have to line up the decimals in a multiplication problem.)

Directions: Solve the following problems.

1. Jennie wants to buy 3 T-shirts that cost $15.99 each. How much will they cost altogether? __$47.97__

2. Steve is making $3.75 an hour packing groceries. How much will he make in 8 hours? __$30__

3. Justin made 36 cookies and sold them all at the school carnival for $0.75 each. How much money did he make? __$27__

4. Last year, the carnival made $467. This year it made 2.3 times as much. How much money did the carnival make this year? __$1,074.10__

5. Troy's car will go 21.8 miles on a gallon of gasoline. His motorcycle will go 1.7 times as far. How far will his motorcycle travel on one gallon of gas? __37.06 miles__

Page 237

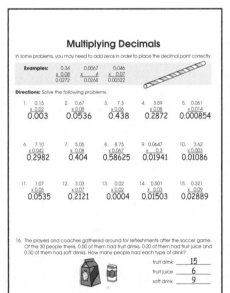

Multiplying Decimals

In some problems, you may need to add zeros in order to place the decimal point correctly.

Examples:
0.34   0.0067   0.046
x 0.08   x   4   x 0.07
0.0272   0.0268   0.00322

Directions: Solve the following problems.

1. 0.15   2. 0.67   3. 7.3   4. 3.59   5. 0.061
   x 0.02   x 0.08   x 0.06   x 0.08   x 0.014
   0.003   0.0536   0.438   0.2872   0.000854

6. 7.10   7. 5.05   8. 8.75   9. 0.0647   10. 3.62
   x 0.042   x 0.08   x 0.067   x 0.3   x 0.003
   0.2982   0.404   0.58625   0.01941   0.01086

11. 1.07   12. 3.03   13. 0.02   14. 0.501   15. 0.321
    x 0.05   x 0.07   x 0.02   x 0.03   x 0.09
    0.0535   0.2121   0.0004   0.01503   0.02889

16. The players and coaches gathered around for refreshments after the soccer game. Of the 30 people there, 0.50 of them had fruit drinks, 0.20 of them had fruit juice and 0.30 of them had soft drinks. How many people had each type of drink?

fruit drink __15__
fruit juice __6__
soft drink __9__

Page 238

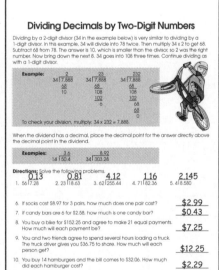

Dividing Decimals by Two-Digit Numbers

Dividing by a 2-digit divisor (34 in the example below) is very similar to dividing by a 1-digit divisor. In this example, 34 will divide into 78 twice. Then multiply 34 x 2 to get 68. Subtract 68 from 78. The answer is 10, which is smaller than the divisor, so 2 was the right number. Now bring down the next 8. 34 goes into 108 three times. Continue dividing as with a 1-digit divisor.

Example:
       2   23   232
34)7.888   34)7.888   34)7.888
   68   68   68
   10   108   108
              102   102
                6   68
                           68
                            6

To check your division, multiply: 34 x 232 = 7,888.

When the dividend has a decimal, place the decimal point for the answer directly above the decimal point in the dividend.

Examples:
      3.6   8.92
14)50.4   34)303.28

Directions: Solve the following problems.
1. 56)7.28 __0.13__   2. 23)18.63 __0.81__   3. 62)255.44 __4.12__   4. 71)82.36 __1.16__   5. 41)8.580 __2.145__

6. If socks cost $8.97 for 3 pairs, how much does one pair cost? __$2.99__
7. If candy bars are 6 for $2.58, how much is one candy bar? __$0.43__
8. You buy a bike for $152.25 and agree to make 21 equal payments. How much will each payment be? __$7.25__
9. You and two friends agree to spend several hours loading a truck. The truck driver gives you $36.75 to share. How much will each person get? __$12.25__
10. You buy 14 hamburgers and the bill comes to $32.06. How much did each hamburger cost? __$2.29__

Page 239

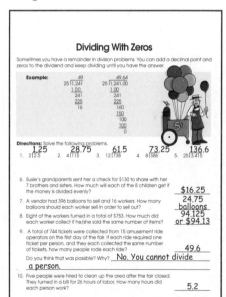

Dividing With Zeros

Sometimes you have a remainder in division problems. You can add a decimal point and zeros to the dividend and keep dividing until you have the answer.

Example:
       49   49.64
25)1.241   25)1,241.00
   1.00   1.00
   241   241
   225   225
    16   160
                 150
                 100
                 100
                   0

Directions: Solve the following problems.
1. 2)25 __1.25__   2. 4)115 __28.75__   3. 12)738 __61.5__   4. 8)586 __73.25__   5. 25)3,415 __136.6__

6. Susie's grandparents sent her a check for $130 to share with her 7 brothers and sisters. How much will each of the 8 children get if the money is divided evenly? __$16.25__

7. A vendor had 396 balloons to sell and 16 workers. How many balloons should each worker sell in order to sell out? __24.75 balloons__

8. Eight of the workers turned in a total of $753. How much did each worker collect if he/she sold the same number of items? __94.125 or $94.13__

9. A total of 744 tickets were collected from 15 amusement ride operators on the first day of the fair. If each ride required each ticket per person, and they each collected the same number of tickets, how many people rode each ride? __49.6__
Do you think that was possible? Why? __No. You cannot divide a person.__

10. Five people were hired to clean up the area after the fair closed. They turned in a bill for 26 hours of labor. How many hours did each person work? __5.2__

Answer Key   341   Total Basic Skills Grade 6

Page 240

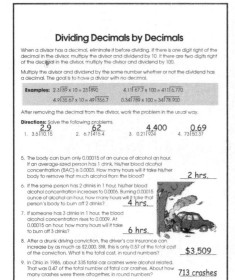

Dividing Decimals by Decimals

When a divisor has a decimal, eliminate it before dividing. If there is one digit right of the decimal in the divisor, multiply the divisor and dividend by 10. If there are two digits right of the decimal in the divisor, multiply the divisor and dividend by 100.

Multiply the divisor and dividend by the same number whether or not the dividend has a decimal. The goal is to have a divisor with no decimal.

Examples: 2.3⟌89 × 10 = 23⟌890   4.11⟌67.7 × 100 = 411⟌6,770
4.9⟌35.67 × 10 = 49⟌356.7   0.34⟌789 × 100 = 34⟌78,900

After removing the decimal from the divisor, work the problem in the usual way.

Directions: Solve the following problems.

1. 3.5⟌10.15 **2.9**
2. 6.7⟌415.4 **62**
3. 0.21⟌924 **4,400**
4. 73⟌50.37 **0.69**

5. The body can burn only 0.00015 of an ounce of alcohol an hour. If an average-sized person has 1 drink, his/her blood alcohol concentration (BAC) is 0.0003. How many hours will it take his/her body to remove that much alcohol from the blood? **2 hrs.**

6. If the same person has 2 drinks in 1 hour, his/her blood alcohol concentration increases to 0.0006. Burning 0.00015 ounce of alcohol an hour, how many hours will it take that person's body to burn off 2 drinks? **4 hrs.**

7. If someone has 3 drinks in 1 hour, the blood alcohol concentration rises to 0.0009. At 0.00015 an hour, how many hours will it take to burn off 3 drinks? **6 hrs.**

8. After a drunk driving conviction, the driver's car insurance can increase by as much as $2,000. Still, this is only 0.57 of the total cost of the conviction. What is the total cost, in round numbers? **$3,509**

9. In Ohio in 1986, about 335 fatal car crashes were alcohol related. That was 0.47 of the total number of fatal car crashes. About how many crashes were there altogether, in round numbers? **713 crashes**

Page 241

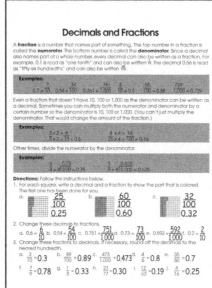

Decimals and Fractions

A **fraction** is a number that names part of something. The top number in a fraction is called the **numerator**. The bottom number is called the **denominator**. Since a decimal also names part of a whole number, every decimal can also be written as a fraction. For example, 0.1 is read as "one tenth" and can also be written 1/10. The decimal 0.56 is read as "fifty-six hundredths" and can also be written 56/100.

Examples: 7/10 = 0.7 34/100 = 0.34 761/1,000 = 0.761 5/10 = 0.5 56/100 = 0.56 729/1,000 = 0.729

Even a fraction that doesn't have 10, 100 or 1,000 as the denominator can be written as a decimal. Sometimes you can multiply both the numerator and denominator by a certain number so the denominator is 10, 100 or 1,000. (You can't just multiply the denominator. That would change the amount of the fraction.)

Examples: 3 × 2 = 6 / 5 × 2 = 10 = 0.6   4 × 4 = 16 / 25 × 4 = 100 = 0.16

Other times, divide the numerator by the denominator.

Examples: 3/4 = 4⟌3.00 = 0.75   5/8 = 8⟌5.000 = 0.625

Directions: Follow the instructions below.
1. For each square, write a decimal and a fraction to show the part that is colored. The first one has been done for you.

a. **25/100 0.25**   b. **60/100 0.60**   c. **32/100 0.32**

2. Change these decimals to fractions.
a. 0.6 = **6/10** b. 0.54 = **54/100** c. 0.751 = **751/1,000** d. 0.73 = **73/100** e. 0.592 = **592/1,000** f. 0.2 = **2/10**

3. Change these fractions to decimals. If necessary, round off the decimals to the nearest hundredth.
a. 3/10 = **0.3** b. 89/100 = **0.89** c. 473/1,000 = **0.473** d. 4/5 = **0.8** e. 35/50 = **0.7**
f. 7/9 = **0.78** g. 1/3 = **0.33** h. 23/77 = **0.30** i. 12/63 = **0.19** j. 4/16 = **0.25**

Page 242

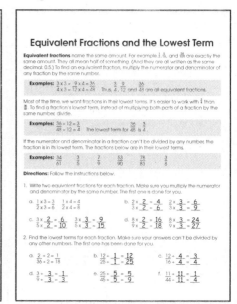

Equivalent Fractions and the Lowest Term

Equivalent fractions name the same amount. For example 1/2, 3/6, and 6/12 are exactly the same amount. They all mean half of something. (And they are all written as the same decimal: 0.5.) To find an equivalent fraction, multiply the numerator and denominator of any fraction by the same number.

Examples: 3 × 3 = 9 / 4 × 3 = 12 × 4 = 36. Thus, 3/4, 9/12 and 36/48 are all equivalent fractions.

Most of the time, we want fractions in their lowest terms. It's easier to work with 1/2 than 3/6. To find a fraction's lowest term, instead of multiplying both parts of a fraction by the same number, divide.

Examples: 36 ÷ 12 = 3 / 48 ÷ 12 = 4   The lowest term for 36/48 is 3/4.

If the numerator and denominator in a fraction can't be divided by any number, the fraction is in its lowest term. The fractions below are in their lowest terms.

Examples: 34/61 3/5 7/9 53/90 76/83 3/8

Directions: Follow the instructions below.

1. Write two equivalent fractions for each fraction. Make sure you multiply the numerator and denominator by the same number. The first one is done for you.

a. 1 × 3 = 3 / 2 × 3 = 6   1 × 4 = 4 / 2 × 4 = 8   b. 2 × 2 = 4 / 3 × 2 = 6   2 × 3 = 6 / 3 × 3 = 9

c. 3 × 2 = 6 / 5 × 2 = 10   3 × 3 = 9 / 5 × 3 = 15   d. 8 × 2 = 16 / 9 × 2 = 18   8 × 3 = 24 / 9 × 3 = 27

2. Find the lowest terms for each fraction. Make sure your answers can't be divided by any other numbers. The first one has been done for you.

a. 2 ÷ 2 = 1 / 36 ÷ 2 = 18   b. 12 ÷ 1 = 12 / 25 ÷ 1 = 25   c. 12 ÷ 4 = 3 / 16 ÷ 4 = 4

d. 3 ÷ 3 = 1 / 9 ÷ 3 = 3   e. 25 ÷ 5 = 5 / 45 ÷ 5 = 9   f. 11 ÷ 11 = 1 / 44 ÷ 11 = 4

Page 243

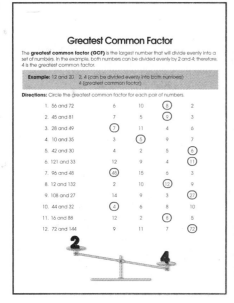

Greatest Common Factor

The **greatest common factor (GCF)** is the largest number that will divide evenly into a set of numbers. In the example, both numbers can be divided evenly by 2 and 4; therefore, 4 is the greatest common factor.

Example: 12 and 20.   2, 4 (can be divided evenly into both numbers)
4 (greatest common factor)

Directions: Circle the greatest common factor for each pair of numbers.

1. 56 and 72   6   10   **8**   2
2. 45 and 81   7   5   **9**   3
3. 28 and 49   **7**   11   4   6
4. 10 and 35   3   **5**   9   7
5. 42 and 30   4   2   5   **6**
6. 121 and 33   12   9   4   **11**
7. 96 and 48   **48**   15   6   3
8. 12 and 132   2   10   **12**   9
9. 108 and 27   14   9   3   **27**
10. 44 and 32   **4**   6   8   10
11. 16 and 88   12   4   **8**   5
12. 72 and 144   9   11   7   **72**

Page 244

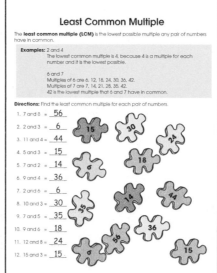

Least Common Multiple

The **least common multiple (LCM)** is the lowest possible multiple any pair of numbers have in common.

Examples: 2 and 4
The lowest common multiple is 4, because 4 is a multiple for each number and it is the lowest possible.

6 and 7
Multiples of 6 are 6, 12, 18, 24, 30, 36, 42.
Multiples of 7 are 7, 14, 21, 28, 35, 42.
42 is the lowest multiple that 6 and 7 have in common.

Directions: Find the least common multiple for each pair of numbers.

1. 7 and 8 = **56**
2. 2 and 3 = **6**
3. 11 and 4 = **44**
4. 5 and 3 = **15**
5. 7 and 2 = **14**
6. 9 and 4 = **36**
7. 2 and 6 = **6**
8. 10 and 3 = **30**
9. 7 and 5 = **35**
10. 9 and 6 = **18**
11. 12 and 8 = **24**
12. 15 and 3 = **15**

Page 245

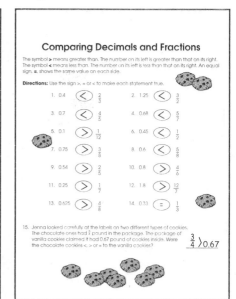

Comparing Decimals and Fractions

The symbol > means greater than. The number on its left is greater than that on its right. The symbol < means less than. The number on the left is less than that on its right. An equal sign, =, shows the same value on each side.

Directions: Use the sign >, = or < to make each statement true.

1. 0.4 **<** 2/3   2. 1.25 **<** 3/2
3. 0.7 **<** 4/5   4. 0.68 **<** 5/7
5. 0.1 **>** 1/12   6. 0.45 **<** 4/5
7. 0.75 **>** 3/8   8. 0.6 **<** 5/8
9. 0.54 **>** 2/5   10. 0.8 **>** 3/4
11. 0.25 **>** 1/7   12. 1.8 **>** 12/7
13. 0.625 **>** 4/8   14. 0.33 **=** 1/3

15. Jenna looked carefully at the labels on two different types of cookies. The chocolate ones had 3/4 pound in the package. The package of vanilla cookies claimed it had 0.67 pound of cookies inside. Were the chocolate cookies <, > or = to the vanilla cookies? **3/4 > 0.67**

Page 246

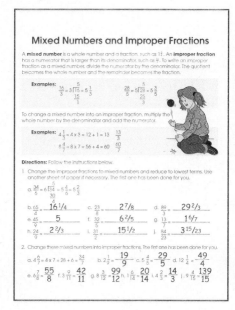

Mixed Numbers and Improper Fractions

A **mixed number** is a whole number and a fraction, such as $1\frac{2}{3}$. An **improper fraction** has a numerator that is larger than its denominator, such as $\frac{9}{7}$. To write an improper fraction as a mixed number, divide the numerator by the denominator. The quotient becomes the whole number and the remainder becomes the fraction.

Examples:
$$\frac{16}{3} = 3\overline{)16} = 5\frac{1}{3} \qquad \frac{28}{5} = 5\overline{)28} = 5\frac{3}{5}$$

To change a mixed number into an improper fraction, multiply the whole number by the denominator and add the numerator.

Examples:
$$4\frac{1}{3} = 4 \times 3 = 12 + 1 = 13 \qquad \frac{13}{3}$$
$$8\frac{4}{7} = 8 \times 7 = 56 + 4 = 60 \qquad \frac{60}{7}$$

Directions: Follow the instructions below.

1. Change the improper fractions to mixed numbers and reduce to lowest terms. Use another sheet of paper if necessary. The first one has been done for you.

a. $\frac{34}{6} = 6\overline{)34} = 5\frac{4}{6} = 5\frac{2}{3}$

b. $\frac{65}{4}$ **16 1/4**   c. $\frac{23}{8}$ **2 7/8**   d. $\frac{89}{3}$ **29 2/3**

e. $\frac{45}{9}$ **5**   f. $\frac{32}{5}$ **6 2/5**   g. $\frac{89}{?}$ **1 6/7**

h. $\frac{24}{9}$ **2 2/3**   i. $\frac{31}{2}$ **15 1/2**   j. $\frac{84}{23}$ **3 15/23**

2. Change these mixed numbers into improper fractions. The first one has been done for you.

a. $4\frac{6}{7} = 4 \times 7 = 28 + 6 = \frac{34}{7}$ b. $2\frac{1}{9}$ **19/9** c. $5\frac{4}{5}$ **29/5** d. $12\frac{1}{4}$ **49/4**

e. $6\frac{7}{8}$ **55/8** f. $3\frac{9}{11}$ **42/11** g. $8\frac{3}{12}$ **99/12** h. $1\frac{6}{14}$ **20/14** i. $4\frac{2}{3}$ **14/3** j. $9\frac{4}{15}$ **139/15**

Page 247

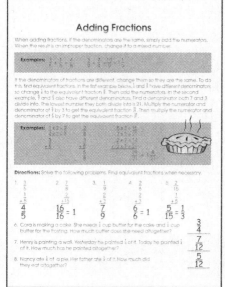

Adding Fractions

When adding fractions, if the denominators are the same, simply add the numerators. When the result is an improper fraction, change it to a mixed number.

Examples: ...

If the denominators of fractions are different, change them so they are the same. ...

Directions: Solve the following problems. Find equivalent fractions when necessary.

1. $\frac{3}{5} + \frac{1}{5} = \frac{4}{5}$

2. $\frac{7}{8} + \frac{9}{8} = \frac{16}{16} = 1$

3. $\frac{1}{9} + \frac{?}{?} = \frac{7}{9}$

4. $\frac{2}{6} + \frac{?}{6} = \frac{5}{6} = 1$

5. $\frac{?}{15} + \frac{?}{15} = 1\frac{1}{15}$

6. Cora is making a cake. She needs $\frac{1}{2}$ cup butter for the cake and $\frac{1}{4}$ cup butter for the frosting. How much butter does she need altogether? **3/4**

7. Henry is painting a wall. Yesterday he painted $\frac{1}{3}$ of it. Today he painted $\frac{1}{4}$ of it. How much has he painted altogether? **7/12**

8. Nancy ate $\frac{1}{12}$ of a pie. Her father ate $\frac{4}{12}$ of it. How much did they eat altogether? **5/12**

Page 248

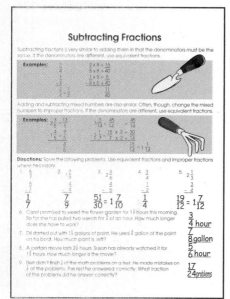

Subtracting Fractions

Subtracting fractions is very similar to adding them in that the denominators must be the same. If the denominators are different, use equivalent fractions.

Examples: ...

Adding and subtracting mixed numbers are also similar. Often, though, change the mixed numbers to improper fractions. If the denominators are different, use equivalent fractions.

Examples: ...

Directions: Solve the following problems. Use equivalent fractions and improper fractions where necessary.

1. $\frac{6}{7} - \frac{?}{7} = \frac{1}{7}$

2. $\frac{7}{9} - \frac{?}{9} = \frac{7}{9}$

3. $2\frac{3}{4} - \frac{?}{?} = \frac{51}{10} = 1\frac{7}{10}$

4. $\frac{3}{4} - \frac{?}{4} = \frac{1}{4}$

5. $2\frac{1}{3} - \frac{?}{?} = \frac{19}{12} = 1\frac{7}{12}$

6. Carol promised to weed the flower garden for $1\frac{1}{4}$ hours this morning. So far she has pulled two weeds for $\frac{1}{2}$ of an hour. How much longer does she have to work? **3/4 hour**

7. Bill started out with $4\frac{3}{8}$ gallons of paint. He used $\frac{1}{2}$ gallon of the paint on his boat. How much paint is left? **7/8 gallon**

8. A certain movie lasts $2\frac{1}{3}$ hours. Susan has already watched it for $1\frac{1}{2}$ hours. How much longer is the movie? **5/6 hour**

9. Bert didn't finish $\frac{1}{4}$ of the math problems on a test. He made mistakes on $\frac{1}{3}$ of the problems. The rest he answered correctly. What fraction of the problems did he answer correctly? **17/24 problems**

Page 249

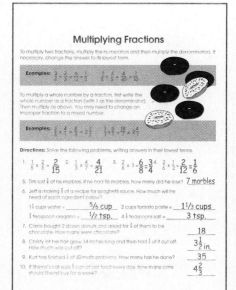

Multiplying Fractions

To multiply two fractions, multiply the numerators and then multiply the denominators. If necessary, change the answer to its lowest term.

Examples: ...

To multiply a whole number by a fraction, first write the whole number as a fraction (with 1 as the denominator). Then multiply as above. You may need to change an improper fraction to a mixed number.

Examples: ...

Directions: Solve the following problems, writing answers in their lowest terms.

1. $\frac{1}{5} \times \frac{2}{3} = \frac{2}{15}$ 2. $\frac{1}{3} \times \frac{4}{7} = \frac{4}{21}$ 3. $\frac{2}{3} \times 3 = \frac{6}{3} = 2$ 4. $\frac{3}{4}$ ... $= \frac{2}{12} = \frac{1}{6}$

5. Tim lost $\frac{1}{8}$ of his marbles. If he had 56 marbles, how many did he lose? **7 marbles**

6. Jeff is making $\frac{2}{3}$ of a recipe for spaghetti sauce. How much will he need of each ingredient below?

$1\frac{1}{4}$ cups water = **5/6 cup**   2 cups tomato paste = **1 1/3 cups**

$\frac{3}{4}$ teaspoon oregano = **1/2 tsp.** $4\frac{1}{2}$ teaspoons salt = **3 tsp.**

7. Carrie bought 2 dozen donuts and asked for $\frac{3}{4}$ of them to be chocolate. How many were chocolate? **18**

8. Christy let her hair grow 14 inches long and then had $\frac{1}{4}$ of it cut off. How much was cut off? **3 1/2 in.**

9. Kurt has finished $\frac{7}{8}$ of 40 math problems. How many has he done? **35**

10. If Sherry's cat eats $\frac{2}{3}$ can of cat food every day, how many cans should Sherry buy for a week? **4 2/3**

Page 250

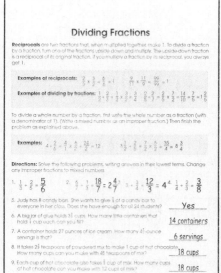

Dividing Fractions

Reciprocals are two fractions that, when multiplied together, make 1. To divide a fraction by a fraction, turn one of the fractions upside down and multiply. The upside-down fraction is a reciprocal of its original fraction. If you multiply a fraction by its reciprocal, you always get 1.

Examples of reciprocals: ...

Examples of dividing by fractions: ...

To divide a whole number by a fraction, first write the whole number as a fraction (with a denominator of 1). (Write a mixed number as an improper fraction.) Then finish the problem as explained above.

Examples: ...

Directions: Solve the following problems, writing answers in lowest terms. Change any improper fractions to mixed numbers.

1. $\frac{1}{3} \div \frac{2}{5} = \frac{5}{6}$ 2. $\frac{6}{7} \div \frac{1}{3} = \frac{18}{7} = 2\frac{4}{7}$ 3. $\frac{?}{?} \div \frac{12}{?} = 4\frac{1}{4}$ 4. $\frac{2}{3} = \frac{3}{8}$

5. Judy has 8 candy bars. She wants to give $\frac{1}{3}$ of a candy bar to everyone in her class. Does she have enough for all 24 students? **Yes**

6. A big jar of glue holds $3\frac{1}{2}$ cups. How many little containers that hold $\frac{1}{4}$ cup each can you fill? **14 containers**

7. A container holds 27 ounces of ice cream. How many $4\frac{1}{2}$-ounce servings is that? **6 servings**

8. It takes $2\frac{1}{2}$ teaspoons of powdered mix to make 1 cup of hot chocolate. How many cups can you make with 45 teaspoons of mix? **18 cups**

9. Each cup of hot chocolate also takes $\frac{2}{3}$ cup of milk. How many cups of hot chocolate can you make with 12 cups of milk? **18 cups**

Page 251

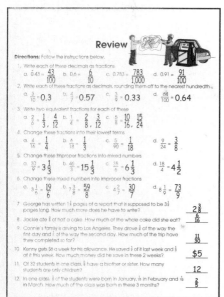

Review

Directions: Follow the instructions below.

1. Write each of these decimals as fractions.

a. $0.43 = \frac{43}{100}$ b. $\frac{6}{10}$ c. $0.783 = \frac{783}{1,000}$ d. $\frac{91}{100}$

2. Write each of these fractions as decimals, rounding them off to the nearest hundredth.

a. $\frac{3}{10} = 0.3$ b. $\frac{4}{7} = 0.57$ c. $\frac{3}{9} = 0.33$ d. $\frac{64}{100} = 0.64$

3. Write two equivalent fractions for each of these.

a. $\frac{2}{6} = \frac{1}{3}, \frac{4}{12}$ b. $\frac{1}{4} = \frac{2}{8}, \frac{3}{12}$ c. $\frac{5}{8} = \frac{10}{16}, \frac{15}{24}$

4. Change these fractions into their lowest terms.

a. $\frac{4}{16} = \frac{1}{4}$ b. $\frac{5}{90} = \frac{1}{18}$ c. $\frac{9}{24} = \frac{3}{8}$

5. Change these improper fractions into mixed numbers.

a. $\frac{30}{9} = 3\frac{3}{9}$ b. $\frac{46}{3} = 15\frac{1}{3}$ c. $\frac{55}{9} = 6\frac{1}{9}$ d. $\frac{18}{4} = 4\frac{1}{2}$

6. Change these mixed numbers into improper fractions.

a. $3\frac{1}{6} = \frac{19}{6}$ b. $7\frac{3}{8} = \frac{59}{8}$ c. $4\frac{2}{7} = \frac{30}{7}$ d. $8\frac{1}{9} = \frac{73}{9}$

7. George has written $1\frac{1}{8}$ pages of a report that is supposed to be $3\frac{1}{2}$ pages long. How much more does he have to write? **2 3/8**

8. Jackie ate $\frac{3}{8}$ of half a cake. How much of the whole cake did she eat? **6/16**

9. Connie's family is driving to Los Angeles. They drove $\frac{4}{9}$ of the way the first day and $\frac{1}{5}$ of the way the second day. How much of the trip have they completed so far? **11/30**

10. Kenny gets $6 a week for his allowance. He saved $\frac{1}{2}$ of it last week and $\frac{1}{3}$ of it this week. How much money did he save in these 2 weeks? **$5**

11. Of 32 students in one class, $\frac{3}{8}$ have a brother or sister. How many students are only children? **12**

12. In one class, $\frac{2}{9}$ of the students were born in January, $\frac{1}{9}$ in February and $\frac{1}{9}$ in March. How much of the class was born in these 3 months? **2/5**

Page 252

Review

Directions: Follow the instructions below.

Add.

1. $\frac{4}{16} + \frac{5}{8} = \frac{14}{16} = \frac{7}{8}$ 2. $\frac{1}{6} + \frac{1}{3} = \frac{3}{6} = \frac{1}{2}$ 3. $\frac{2}{10} + \frac{4}{10} = \frac{10}{10} = 1$ 4. $\frac{3}{5} + \frac{9}{10} = \frac{15}{10} = 1\frac{1}{2}$

Subtract.

1. $\frac{15}{9} - \frac{2}{9} = \frac{9}{9} = 1$ 2. $\frac{3}{8} - \frac{1}{8} = \frac{3}{8}$ 3. $\frac{4}{7} - \frac{2}{14} = \frac{6}{14} = \frac{3}{7}$ 4. $\frac{3}{5} - \frac{1}{10} = \frac{5}{10} = \frac{1}{2}$

Multiply.

1. $\frac{1}{2} \times \frac{4}{16} = \frac{4}{32} = \frac{1}{8}$ 2. $\frac{1}{3} \times \frac{4}{9} = \frac{4}{27}$ 3. $\frac{5}{12} \times \frac{1}{4} = \frac{5}{48}$ 4. $\frac{3}{16} \times \frac{3}{4} = \frac{9}{64}$

Divide.

1. $\frac{1}{3} \div \frac{1}{3} = \frac{9}{5} = 1\frac{4}{5}$ 2. $4 \div \frac{1}{2} = \frac{8}{1} = 8$ 3. $\frac{1}{4} \div \frac{1}{3} = \frac{3}{4}$ 4. $3\frac{3}{4} \div \frac{1}{3} = \frac{45}{4} = 11\frac{1}{4}$

Write >, < or = to make the statements true.

1. 0.5 $<$ $\frac{5}{8}$ 2. 0.8 $=$ $\frac{4}{5}$ 3. 0.35 $<$ $\frac{2}{5}$ 4. 1.3 $>$ $\frac{7}{8}$

Page 253

Trial and Error

Often, the quickest way to solve a problem is to make a logical guess and test it to see if it works. The first guess, or trial, will probably not be the correct answer—but it should help figure out a better, more reasonable guess.

Directions: Use trial and error to find the solutions to these problems.

1. Mr. McFerrson is between 30 and 50 years old. The sum of the digits in his age is 11. His age is an even number. How old is Mr. McFerrson?

He is 38 years old.

2. The key for number 5 does not work on Rusty's calculator. How can he use his broken calculator to subtract 108 from 351?

Sample answer: Add 10 to each number and subtract 118 from 361, equalling 243.

3. Tasha likes to swim a certain number of miles each day for 3 days straight. Then, she increases her mileage by 1 for the next 3 days, and so on. Over a nine day period, Tasha swims a total of 27 miles. She swims equal mileage Monday, Tuesday and Wednesday. She swims another amount on Thursday, Friday and Saturday. She swims yet a third amount on Sunday, Monday and Tuesday. How many miles does Tasha swim each day?

2 Monday	2 Tuesday	2 Wednesday
3 Thursday	3 Friday	3 Saturday
4 Sunday	4 Monday	4 Tuesday

Page 254

Trial and Error

Directions: Use trial and error to complete each diagram so all the equations work.

Example: 6, 7 + → 13, × → 42

7, 4 + → 11, × → 28   4, 8 + → 12, × → 32

4, 4 + → 8, × → 16   7, 0 + → 7, × → 0

8, 7 + → 15, × → 56   8, 9 + → 17, × → 72

6, 9 + → 15, × → 54   15, 16 + → 31, × → 240

10, 1 + → 11, × → 10   100, 1 + → 101, × → 100

Page 255

Choosing a Method

This table explains different methods of computation that can be used to solve a problem.

Method		
Mental Math	– Calculating in your head.	– Use with small numbers, memorized facts and multiples of tens, hundreds, thousands, and so on.
Objects/Diagram	– Drawing or using an object to represent the problem.	– Use to model the situation.
Pencil and Paper	– Calculating the answer on paper.	– Use when a calculator is not available and the problem is too difficult to solve mentally.
Calculator	– Using a calculator or computer to find the solution.	– Use with large numbers or for a quick answer.
Trial and Error	– Making a guess at the answer and trying to see if it works.	– Use when unsure what to do or if none of the methods above work.

Directions: Circle the method of computation that seems best for solving each problem. Then solve the problem.

1. The School Days Fun Fair has 38 booths and 23 games. How many booths and games total are in the fair?
   - **Paper and Pencil**
   - Objects/Diagram

   Answer: 61

2. The lemonade stand was stocked with 230 cups. On the first day, 147 drinks were sold. How many cups were left?
   - Objects/Diagram
   - **Paper and Pencil**

   Answer: 83

3. There are 3 cars in the tram to transport people from the parking lot to the fair. Each car can seat 9 people. How many people can ride the tram at one time?
   - **Objects/Diagram**
   - Trial and Error

   Answer: 27

Page 256

Choosing a Method

Directions: Write what method you will use for each problem. Then find the answer.

1. Jenna receives an allowance of $3.50 a week. This week, her mother pays her in nickels, dimes and quarters. She received more di[...] coin did her mom use to pay her?

   Answers may include:

   Method: Trial and Error

   Answer: 8 quarters, 13 dimes, 4 nickels

2. You are buying your lunch at school. There are 4 people in front of you and 7 people behind you. How many people are standing in line? (Hint: it's not 11 people.)

   Method: mental math

   Answer: 12 people

3. A runner can run 1 mile in 12 minutes. He ran for 30 minutes today. How far did he run?

   Method: calculator

   Answer: 2.5 miles

4. A family of four goes out to dinner. They decide to order a 16-cut pizza. Each person likes something different on his/her pizza, but each will eat equal amounts. Maria likes pepperoni and sausage. Tony likes ham and pineapple. Mom likes cheese only and Dad likes mushrooms. Maria is allergic to mushrooms, so her slices can't be next to Dad's. Mom detests pineapple, so her slices can't be next to Tony's. How will the restaurant arrange their pizza?

   Method: objects/diagram

   Answer: starting at top of pizza: Dad's, Mom's, Maria's, Tony's

5. The Petting Zoo has 72 animals in aquariums, 32 animals in cages and 57 animals fenced in. How many animals does the Petting Zoo have?

   Method: pencil and paper

   Answer: 161

Page 257

Multi-Step Problems

Some problems take more than one step to solve. First, plan each step needed to find the solution. Then solve each part to find the answer.

Example: Tickets for a bargain matinee cost $4 for adults and $3 for children. How much would tickets cost for a family of 2 adults and 3 children?

Step 1: Find the cost of the adults' tickets.

Step 2: Find the cost of the children's tickets.

Step 3: Add to find the sum of the tickets.

2 adults	x	$4 each ticket	=	$8 total
3 children	x	$3 each ticket	=	$9 total
$8 adults		+ $9 children	=	$17 total

The tickets cost $17 total.

Directions: Write the operations you will use to solve each problem. Then find the answer.

Operations: 1. Add the miles they've gone; 2. Subtract from total miles.

Answer: 29

Operations: 1. Devise a formula: number of mi. ÷ mph = time; 2. Add the time totals; 3. Convert to hours.

Answer: 3 hrs. and 5 min.

Operations: 1. Find total cost of raspberries; 2. Add to the cost of blueberries and strawberries.

Answer: $5.89

Page 258

Hidden Questions

When solving a story problem, you may find that some information you want is not stated in the problem. You must ask yourself what information you need and decide how you can use the data in the problem to find this information. The problem contains a hidden question to find before you can solve it.

Example: Chris and his mother are building a birdhouse. He buys 4 pieces of wood for $2.20 each. How much change should he get back from $10?

Step 1: Find the hidden question:
What is the total cost of the wood? $2.20 x 4 = $8.80

Step 2: Use your answer to the hidden
question to solve the problem. $10.00 - $8.80 = $1.20

Directions: Write the hidden questions. Then solve the problems.

1. Chris used 3 nails to attach each board to the frame. After nailing 6 boards, he had 1 nail left. How many nails did Chris have before he started?
Hidden Question: How many nails had he used?
Answer: 19 nails

2. Chris sawed a 72-inch post into 3 pieces. Two of the pieces were each 20 inches long. How long was the third piece?
Hidden Question: How long where the 2 pieces total?
Answer: 32 inches long

3. It took Chris and his mom 15 hours to make a birdhouse. They thought it would take 3 days. How many hours early did they complete the job?
Hidden Question: How many hours are in 3 days?
Answer: 57 hours early

4. It takes Chris 15 hours to make a birdhouse and 9 hours to make a birdfeeder. He worked for 42 hours and made 1 birdhouse and some birdfeeders. How many birdfeeders did Chris make?
Hidden Question: How much time total did he spend on birdfeeders?
Answer: 3 birdfeeders

Page 259

Logic Problems

Directions: Use the clues below to figure out this logic problem.

Three friends all enjoy sports. Each of their favorite sports involves a ball. Two of these sports are played on courts, and one is played on a field.

- Rachel likes to run, and doesn't have to be a good catcher.
- Melinda is a good jumper.
- Betsy is also a good jumper, but she is a good ball handler.

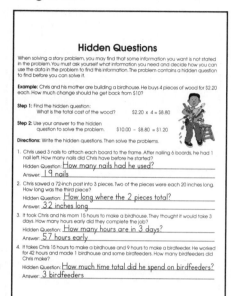

Which sport does each girl play?

Melinda   Volleyball

Betsy   Basketball

Rachel   Soccer

Page 260

A Cool Logic Problem

A family with five children went to the ice-cream shop. The children all ordered different flavors.

Directions: Use the clues and the chart to help you write which child ate which flavor of ice cream. Write a dot in the chart for the correct answer. Cross out all the other boxes in that row and column.

- No person had ice cream with the same first initial as his/her name.
- Neither of the twins, Corey and Cody, like peanut butter. Corey thinks vanilla is boring.
- The children are the twins, Vicki, the brother who got chocolate and the sister who ate peanut butter.

	Rocky Road	Chocolate Chip	Vanilla	Chocolate	Peanut Butter
Corey	•	X	X	X	X
Cody	X	X	•	X	X
Randa	X	X	X	X	•
Vicki	X	•	X	X	X
Paul	X	X	X	•	X

Who ate which flavor?

Corey   Rocky Road

Cody   Vanilla

Randa   Peanut Butter

Vicki   Chocolate Chip

Paul   Chocolate

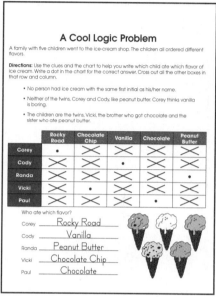

Page 261

Perimeter

The **perimeter** is the distance around a shape formed by straight lines, such as a square or triangle. To find the perimeter of a shape, add the lengths of its sides.

Examples:

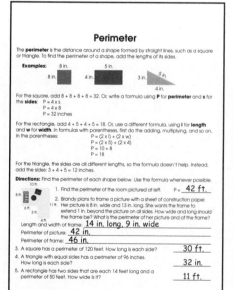

For the square, add 8 + 8 + 8 + 8 = 32. Or, write a formula using **P** for **perimeter** and **s** for the sides:
$P = 4 \times s$
$P = 4 \times 8$
$P = 32$ inches

For the rectangle, add 4 + 5 + 4 + 5 = 18. Or, use a different formula, using **l** for **length** and **w** for **width**. In formulas with parentheses, first do the adding, multiplying, and so on, in the parentheses:
$P = (2 \times l) + (2 \times w)$
$P = (2 \times 5) + (2 \times 4)$
$P = 10 + 8$
$P = 18$

For the triangle, the sides are all different lengths, so the formula doesn't help. Instead, add the sides: 3 + 4 + 5 = 12 inches.

Directions: Find the perimeter of each shape below. Use the formula whenever possible.

1. Find the perimeter of the room pictured at left.   P = 42 ft.

2. Brandy plans to frame a picture with a sheet of construction paper. Her picture is 8 in. wide and 13 in. long. She wants the frame to extend 1 in. beyond the picture on all sides. How wide and long should the frame be? What is the perimeter of her picture and of the frame?
Length and width of frame: 14 in. long, 9 in. wide
Perimeter of picture: 42 in.
Perimeter of frame: 46 in.

3. A square has a perimeter of 120 feet. How long is each side?   30 ft.

4. A triangle with equal sides has a perimeter of 96 inches. How long is each side?   32 in.

5. A rectangle has two sides that are each 14 feet long and a perimeter of 50 feet. How wide is it?   11 ft.

Page 262

Perimeter

Directions: Find the perimeter of each shape below.

1.   P = 12
2.   P = 32
3.   P = 128
4.   P = 18
5.   P = 16
6.   P = 14
7.   P = 25
8.   P = 21

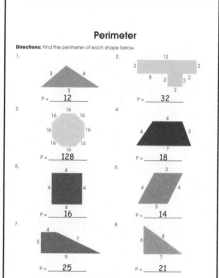

Page 263

Area: Squares and Rectangles

The **area** is the number of square units that covers a certain space. To find the area, multiply the length by the width. The answer is in square units, shown by adding a superscript 2 (²) to the number.

Examples:

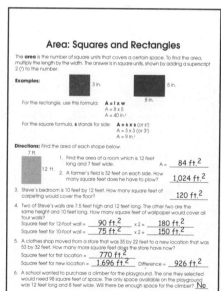

For the rectangle, use this formula: $A = l \times w$
$A = 8 \times 5$
$A = 40$ in.²

For the square formula, **s** stands for side: $A = s \times s$ (or s^2)
$A = 3 \times 3$ (or 3^2)
$A = 9$ in.²

Directions: Find the area of each shape below.

1. Find the area of a room which is 12 feet long and 7 feet wide.   A = 84 ft.²

2. A farmer's field is 32 feet on each side. How many square feet does he have to plow?   1,024 ft.²

3. Steve's bedroom is 10 feet by 12 feet. How many square feet of carpeting would cover the floor?   120 ft.²

4. Two of Steve's walls are 7.5 feet high and 12 feet long. The other two are the same height and 10 feet long. How many square feet of wallpaper would cover all four walls?
Square feet for 12-foot wall = 90 ft.²   x 2 = 180 ft.²
Square feet for 10-foot wall = 75 ft.²   x 2 = 150 ft.²

5. A clothes shop moved from a store that was 35 by 22 feet to a new location that was 53 by 32 feet. How many more square feet does the store have now?
Square feet for first location = 770 ft.²
Square feet for new location = 1,696 ft.²   Difference = 926 ft.²

6. A school wanted to purchase a climber for the playground. The one they selected would need 98 square feet of space. The only space available for the playground was 12 feet long and 8 feet wide. Will there be enough space for the climber? No

Page 264

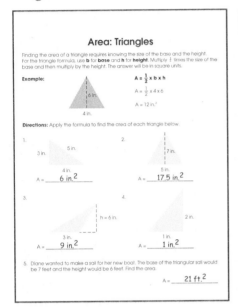

Area: Triangles

Finding the area of a triangle requires knowing the size of the base and the height. For the triangle formula, use **b** for **base** and **h** for **height**. Multiply ½ times the size of the base and then multiply by the height. The answer will be in square units.

Example:

$A = \frac{1}{2} \times b \times h$

$A = \frac{1}{2} \times 4 \times 6$

$A = 12$ in.²

Directions: Apply the formula to find the area of each triangle below.

1. A = __6 in.²__
2. A = __17.5 in.²__
3. A = __9 in.²__
4. A = __1 in.²__

5. Diane wanted to make a sail for her new boat. The base of the triangular sail would be 7 feet and the height would be 6 feet. Find the area.

A = __21 ft.²__

Page 265

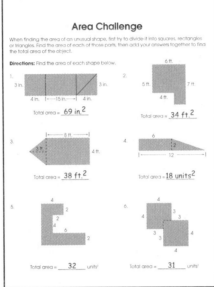

Area Challenge

When finding the area of an unusual shape, first try to divide it into squares, rectangles or triangles. Find the area of each of those parts, then add your answers together to find the total area of the object.

Directions: Find the area of each shape below.

1. Total area = __69 in.²__
2. Total area = __34 ft.²__
3. Total area = __38 ft.²__
4. Total area = __18 units²__
5. Total area = __32__ units²
6. Total area = __31__ units²

Page 266

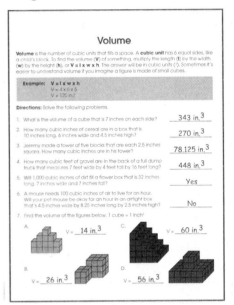

Volume

Volume is the number of cubic units that fills a space. A **cubic unit** has 6 equal sides, like a child's block. To find the volume (**V**) of something, multiply the length (**l**) by the width (**w**) by the height (**h**), or **V = l x w x h**. The answer will be in cubic units (³). Sometimes it's easier to understand volume if you imagine a figure is made of small cubes.

Example: V = l x w x h
V = 4 x 6 x 5
V = 120 in.³

Directions: Solve the following problems.

1. What is the volume of a cube that is 7 inches on each side? __343 in.³__

2. How many cubic inches of cereal are in a box that is 10 inches long, 6 inches wide and 4.5 inches high? __270 in.³__

3. Jeremy made a tower of five blocks that are each 2.5 inches square. How many cubic inches are in his tower? __78.125 in.³__

4. How many cubic feet of gravel are in the back of a full dump truck that measures 7 feet wide by 4 feet tall by 16 feet long? __448 in.³__

5. Will 1,000 cubic inches of dirt fill a flower box that is 32 inches long, 7 inches wide and 7 inches tall? __Yes__

6. A mouse needs 100 cubic inches of air to live for an hour. Will your pet mouse be okay for an hour in an airtight box that's 4.5 inches wide by 8.25 inches long by 2.5 inches high? __No__

7. Find the volume of the figures below. 1 cube = 1 inch³

A. V = __14 in.³__
B. V = __26 in.³__
C. V = __60 in.³__
D. V = __56 in.³__

Page 267

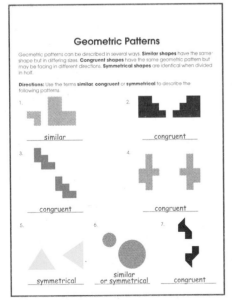

Geometric Patterns

Geometric patterns can be described in several ways. **Similar shapes** have the same shape but in differing sizes. **Congruent shapes** have the same geometric pattern but may be facing in different directions. **Symmetrical shapes** are identical when divided in half.

Directions: Use the terms **similar**, **congruent** or **symmetrical** to describe the following patterns.

1. __similar__
2. __congruent__
3. __congruent__
4. __congruent__
5. __symmetrical__
6. __similar or symmetrical__
7. __congruent__

Page 268

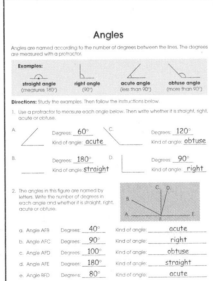

Angles

Angles are named according to the number of degrees between the lines. The degrees are measured with a protractor.

Examples:

straight angle (measures 180°)
right angle (90°)
acute angle (less than 90°)
obtuse angle (more than 90°)

Directions: Study the examples. Then follow the instructions below.

1. Use a protractor to measure each angle below. Then write whether it is straight, right, acute or obtuse.

A. Degrees: __60°__ Kind of angle: __acute__
B. Degrees: __180°__ Kind of angle: __straight__
C. Degrees: __120°__ Kind of angle: __obtuse__
D. Degrees: __90°__ Kind of angle: __right__

2. The angles in this figure are named by letters. Write the number of degrees in each angle and whether it is straight, right, acute or obtuse.

a. Angle AFB   Degrees: __40°__   Kind of angle: __acute__
b. Angle AFC   Degrees: __90°__   Kind of angle: __right__
c. Angle AFD   Degrees: __100°__   Kind of angle: __obtuse__
d. Angle AFE   Degrees: __180°__   Kind of angle: __straight__
e. Angle BFD   Degrees: __80°__   Kind of angle: __acute__

Page 269

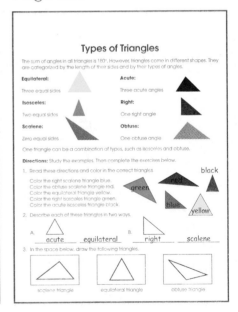

Types of Triangles

The sum of angles in all triangles is 180°. However, triangles come in different shapes. They are categorized by the length of their sides and by their types of angles.

Equilateral: Three equal sides
Acute: Three acute angles
Isosceles: Two equal sides
Right: One right angle
Scalene: Zero equal sides
Obtuse: One obtuse angle

One triangle can be a combination of types, such as isosceles and obtuse.

Directions: Study the examples. Then complete the exercises below.

1. Read these directions and color in the correct triangles.
   Color the right scalene triangle blue.
   Color the obtuse scalene triangle red.
   Color the equilateral triangle yellow.
   Color the right isosceles triangle green.
   Color the acute isosceles triangle black.

black, green, red, blue, yellow

2. Describe each of these triangles in two ways.
A. __acute__ __equilateral__
B. __right__ __scalene__

3. In the space below, draw the following triangles.
scalene triangle   equilateral triangle   obtuse triangle

Page 270

Finding Angles

All triangles have three angles. The sum of these angles is 180°. Therefore, if we know the number of degrees in two of the angles, we can add them together, then subtract from 180 to find the size of the third angle.

Directions: Follow the instructions below.

1. Circle the number that shows the third angle of triangles A through F. Then describe each triangle two ways. The first one has been done for you.

A. 60°, 60°   45° 50° (60°)   equilateral, acute
B. 35°, 55°   27° (90°) 132°   scalene, right
C. 30°, 120°   (30°) 74° 112°   isosceles, obtuse
D. 15°, 78°   65° (87°) 98°   scalene, acute
E. 28°, 93°   61° (59°) 70°   scalene, obtuse
F. 12°, 114°   60° 50° (54°)   scalene, obtuse

2. Find the number of degrees in the third angle of each triangle below.

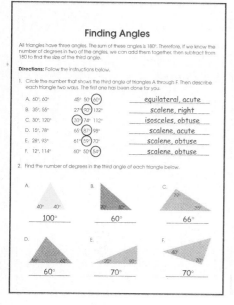

A. 100°   B. 60°   C. 66°
D. 60°   E. 70°   F. 70°

Page 271

Types of Quadrilaterals

A **quadrilateral** is a shape with four sides and four angles. The sum of angles in all quadrilaterals is 360°. Like triangles, quadrilaterals come in different shapes and are categorized by their sides and their angles.

A **square** has four parallel sides of equal length and four 90° angles.

A **rectangle** has four parallel sides, but only its opposite sides are equal length; it has four 90° angles.

A **parallelogram** has four parallel sides, with the opposite sides of equal length.

A **trapezoid** has two opposite sides that are parallel; its sides may or may not be equal length; its angles may include none, one or two that are 90°.

Directions: Study the examples. Then complete the exercises below.

1. Color in the correct quadrilateral.

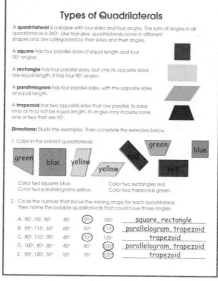

Color two squares blue.
Color two parallelograms yellow.
Color two rectangles red.
Color two trapezoids green.

2. Circle the number that shows the missing angle for each quadrilateral. Then name the possible quadrilaterals that could have those angles.

A. 90°, 90°, 90°   45° (90°) 180°   square, rectangle
B. 65°, 115°, 65°   65° 90° (115°)   parallelogram, trapezoid
C. 90°, 110°, 90°   45° (70°) 90°   trapezoid
D. 100°, 80°, 80°   40° 80° (100°)   parallelogram, trapezoid
E. 90°, 120°, 50°   50° 75° (100°)   trapezoid

Page 272

Length in Customary Units

The **customary system** of measurement is the most widely used in the United States. It measures length in inches, feet, yards and miles.

Examples:
12 inches (in.) = 1 foot (ft.)
3 ft. (36 in.) = 1 yard (yd.)
5,280 ft. (1,760 yds.) = 1 mile (mi.)

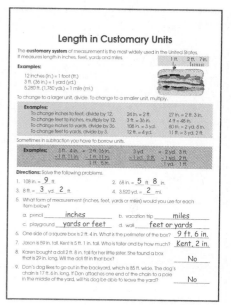

To change to a larger unit, divide. To change to a smaller unit, multiply.

Examples:
To change inches to feet, divide by 12.   24 in. = 2 ft.   27 in. = 2 ft. 3 in.
To change feet to inches, multiply by 12.   3 ft. = 36 in.   4 ft = 48 in.
To change inches to yards, divide by 36.   108 in. = 3 yd.   80 in. = 2 yd. 8 in.
To change feet to yards, divide by 3.   12 ft. = 4 yd.   11 ft. = 3 yd. 2 ft.

Sometimes in subtraction you have to borrow units.

Examples: 3 ft. 4 in. = 2 ft. 15 in.   3 yd. = 2 yd. 3 ft.
   -1 ft. 11 in. = -1 ft. 11 in.   -1 yd. 2 ft. = -1 yd. 2 ft.
   1 ft. 5 in.   -1 yd. 1 ft.

Directions: Solve the following problems.

1. 108 in. = __9__ ft.   2. 68 in. = __5__ ft. __8__ in.
3. 8 ft. = __3__ yd. __2__ ft.   4. 3,520 yds. = __2__ mi.

5. What form of measurement (inches, feet, yards or miles) would you use for each item below?
   a. pencil __inches__   b. vacation trip __miles__
   c. playground __yards or feet__   d. wall __feet or yards__

6. One side of a square box is 2 ft. 4 in. What is the perimeter of the box? __9 ft. 6 in.__
7. Jason is 59 in. tall. Kent is 5 ft. 1 in. tall. Who is taller and by how much? __Kent, 2 in.__
8. Karen bought a doll 2 ft. 8 in. tall for her little sister. She found a box that is 29 in. long. Will the doll fit in that box? __No__
9. Don's dog likes to go out in the backyard, which is 85 ft. wide. The dog's chain is 17 ft. 6 in. long. If Don attaches one end of the chain to a pole in the middle of the yard, will his dog be able to leave the yard? __No__

Page 273

Length in Metric Units

The **metric system** measures length in meters, centimeters, millimeters, and kilometers.

Examples:
A **meter (m)** is about 40 inches or 3.3 feet.
A **centimeter (cm)** is ¹⁄₁₀₀ of a meter or 0.4 inches.
A **millimeter (mm)** is ¹⁄₁₀₀₀ of a meter or 0.04 inches.
A **kilometer (km)** is 1,000 meters or 0.6 miles.

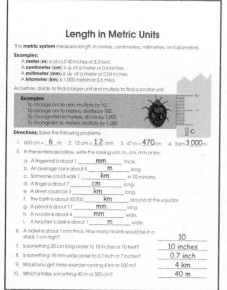

As before, divide to find a larger unit and multiply to find a smaller unit.

Examples:
To change cm to mm, multiply by 10.
To change cm to meters, divide by 100.
To change mm to meters, divide by 1,000.
To change km to meters, multiply by 1,000.

Directions: Solve the following problems.

1. 600 cm = __6__ m   2. 12 cm = __1.2__ mm   3. 47 m = __470__ cm   4. 3 km = __3,000__ m

5. In the sentences below, write the missing unit: m, cm, mm or km.
   a. A fingernail is about 1 __mm__ thick.
   b. An average car is about 5 __m__ long.
   c. Someone could walk 1 __km__ in 10 minutes.
   d. A finger is about 7 __cm__ long.
   e. A street could be 3 __km__ long.
   f. The Earth is about 40,000 __km__ around at the equator.
   g. A pencil is about 17 __mm__ long.
   h. A noodle is about 4 __mm__ wide.
   i. A teacher's desk is about 1 __m__ high.

6. A nickel is about 1 mm thick. How many nickels would be in a stack 1 cm high? __10__
7. Is something 25 cm long closer to 10 inches or 10 feet? __10 inches__
8. Is something 18 mm wide closer to 0.7 inch or 7 inches? __0.7 inch__
9. Would you get more exercise running 4 km or 500 m? __4 km__
10. Which is taller, something 40 m or 350 cm? __40 m__

Page 274

Weight in Customary Units

Here are the main ways to measure weight in customary units:
16 ounces (oz.) = 1 pound (lb.)
2,000 lb. = 1 ton (tn.)
To change ounces to pounds, divide by 16.
To change pounds to ounces, multiply by 16.

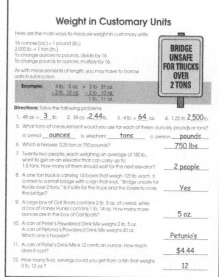

BRIDGE UNSAFE FOR TRUCKS OVER 2 TONS

As with measurements of length, you may have to borrow units in subtraction.

Example: 4 lb. 5 oz. = 3 lb. 21 oz.
   -2 lb. 10 oz. = -2 lb. 10 oz.
   1 lb. 11 oz.

Directions: Solve the following problems.

1. 48 oz. = __3__ lb.   2. 39 oz. = __2.44__ lb.   3. 4 lb. = __64__ oz.   4. 1.25 tn. = __2,500__ lb.

5. What form of measurement would you use for each of these: ounces, pounds or tons?
   a. pencil __ounces__   b. elephant __tons__   c. person __pounds__
6. Which is heavier, 0.25 ton or 750 pounds? __750 lbs.__
7. Twenty-two people, each weighing an average of 150 lb., want to get on an elevator that can carry up to 1.5 tons. How many of them should wait for the next elevator? __2 people__
8. A one ton truck is carrying 14 boxes that weigh 125 lb. each. It comes to a small bridge with a sign that says, "Bridge unsafe for trucks over 2 tons." Is it safe for the truck and the boxes to cross the bridge? __Yes__
9. A large box of Oat Boats contains 2 lb. 3 oz. of cereal, while a box of Honey Hunks contains 1 lb. 14 oz. How many more ounces are in the box of Oat Boats? __5 oz.__
10. A can of Peter's Powdered Drink Mix weighs 2 lb. 5 oz. A can of Petunia's Powdered Drink Mix weighs 40 oz. Which one is heavier? __Petunia's__
11. A can of Peter's Drink Mix is 12 cents an ounce. How much does it cost? __$4.44__
12. How many 5-oz. servings could you get from a fish that weighs 3 lb. 12 oz.? __12__

Page 275

Weight in Metric Units

A **gram (g)** is about 0.035 oz.
A **milligram (mg)** is ¹⁄₁₀₀₀ g or about 0.000035 oz.
A **kilogram (kg)** is 1,000 g or about 2.2 lb.
A **metric ton (t)** is 1,000 kg or about 1.1 tn.

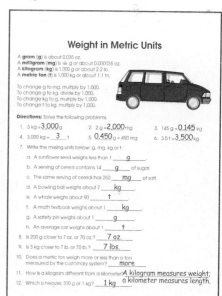

To change g to mg, multiply by 1,000.
To change g to kg, divide by 1,000.
To change kg to g, multiply by 1,000.
To change t to kg, multiply by 1,000.

Directions: Solve the following problems.

1. 3 kg = __3,000__ g   2. 2 g = __2,000__ mg   3. 145 g = __0.145__ kg
4. 3,000 kg = __3__ t   5. __0.450__ g = 450 mg   6. 3.5 t = __3,500__ kg

7. Write the missing units below: g, mg, kg or t.
   a. A sunflower seed weighs less than 1 __g__.
   b. A serving of cereal contains 14 __g__ of sugar.
   c. The same serving of cereal has 250 __mg__ of salt.
   d. A bowling ball weighs about 7 __kg__.
   e. A whale weighs about 90 __t__.
   f. A math textbook weighs about 1 __kg__.
   g. A safety pin weighs about 1 __g__.
   h. An average car weighs about 1 __t__.

8. Is 200 g closer to 7 oz. or 70 oz.? __7 oz.__
9. Is 3 kg closer to 7 lb. or 70 lb.? __7 lbs.__
10. Does a metric ton weigh more or less than a ton measured by the customary system? __more__
11. How is a kilogram different from a kilometer? __A kilogram measures weight; a kilometer measures length.__
12. Which is heavier, 300 g or 1 kg? __1 kg__

GRADE 6

Page 276

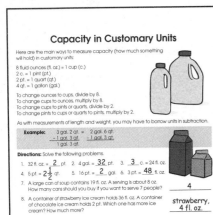

Capacity in Customary Units

Here are the main ways to measure capacity (how much something will hold) in customary units:

8 fluid ounces (fl. oz.) = 1 cup (c.)
2 c. = 1 pint (pt.)
2 pt. = 1 quart (qt.)
4 qt. = 1 gallon (gal.)

To change ounces to cups, divide by 8.
To change cups to ounces, multiply by 8.
To change cups to pints or quarts, divide by 2.
To change pints to cups or quarts to pints, multiply by 2.

As with measurements of length and weight, you may have to borrow units in subtraction.

Example: 3 gal. 2 qt. =   2 gal. 6 qt.
              – 1 gal. 3 qt.   – 1 gal. 3 qt.
                               1 gal. 3 qt.

Directions: Solve the following problems.

1. 32 fl. oz. = __2__ pt.   2. 4 gal. = __32__ fl. oz.   3. __3__ c. = 24 fl. oz.
4. 5 pt. = 2½ qt.   5. 16 pt. = __2__ qt.   6. 3 pt. = __48__ fl. oz.
7. A large can of soup contains 19 fl. oz. A serving is about 8 oz. How many cans should you buy if you want to serve 7 people? — __4__
8. A container of strawberry ice cream holds 36 fl. oz. A container of chocolate ice cream holds 2 pt. Which one has more ice cream? How much more? — __strawberry, 4 fl. oz.__
9. A day-care worker wants to give 15 children each 6 fl. oz. of milk. How many quarts of milk does she need? — __3 qt.__
10. This morning, the day-care supervisor bought 3 gal. of milk. The kids drank 2 gal. 3 c. How much milk is left for tomorrow? — __13 cups__
11. Harriet bought 3 gal. 2 qt. of paint for her living room. She used 2 gal. 3 qt. How much paint is left over? — __3 qt.__
12. Jason's favorite punch takes a pint of raspberry sherbet. If he wants to make 1½ times the recipe, how many fl. oz. of sherbet does he need? — __24 fl. oz.__

Page 277

Capacity in Metric Units

A **liter (L)** is a little over 1 quart.
A **milliliter (mL)** is ¹⁄₁₀₀₀ of a liter or about 0.03 oz.
A **kiloliter (kL)** is 1,000 liters or about 250 gallons.

Directions: Solve the following problems.

1. 5,000 mL = __5__ L
2. 2,000 L = __2__ kL
3. 3 L = __3,000__ mL
4. Write the missing unit: L, mL or kL.
   a. A swimming pool holds about 100 __kL__ of water.
   b. An eyedropper is marked for 1 and 2 __mL__.
   c. A pitcher could hold 1 or 2 __L__ of juice.
   d. A teaspoon holds about 5 __mL__ of medicine.
   e. A birdbath might hold 5 __L__ of water.
   f. A tablespoon holds about 15 __mL__ of salt.
   g. A bowl holds about 250 __mL__ of soup.
   h. We drank about 4 __L__ of punch at the party.
5. Which is more, 3 L or a gallon? — __gallon__
6. Which is more, 400 mL or 40 oz.? — __40 oz.__
7. Which is more, 1 kL or 500 L? — __1 kL__
8. Is 4 L closer to a quart or a gallon? — __gallon__
9. Is 480 mL closer to 2 cups or 2 pints? — __2 cups__
10. Is a mL closer to 4 drops or 4 teaspoonful? — __4 drops__
11. How many glasses of juice containing 250 mL each could you pour from a 1-L jug? — __4 glasses__
12. How much water would you need to water an average-sized lawn, 1 kL or 1 L? — __1 kL__

Page 278

Temperature in Customary and Metric Units

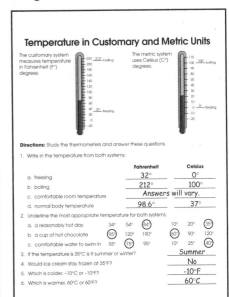

The customary system measures temperature in Fahrenheit (F°) degrees.

The metric system uses Celsius (C°) degrees.

Directions: Study the thermometers and answer these questions.

1. Write in the temperature from both systems.

	Fahrenheit	Celsius
a. freezing	32°	0°
b. boiling	212°	100°
c. comfortable room temperature	Answers will vary.	
d. normal body temperature	98.6°	37°

2. Underline the most appropriate temperature for both systems.
   a. a reasonably hot day   34°   54°   (84°)   10°   20°   (35°)
   b. a cup of hot chocolate   (95°)   120°   190°   (60°)   90°   120°
   c. comfortable water to swim in   55°   (75°)   95°   10°   25°   (40°)
3. If the temperature is 35°C is it summer or winter? — __Summer__
4. Would ice cream stay frozen at 35°C? — __No__
5. Which is colder, –10°C or –10°F? — __–10°F__
6. Which is warmer, 60°C or 60°F? — __60°C__

Page 279

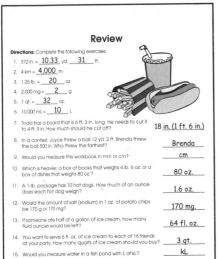

Review

Directions: Complete the following exercises.

1. 372 in. = __10.33__ yd. __31__ ft.
2. 4 km = __4,000__ m
3. 1.25 kl = __20__ L
4. 2,000 mg = __2__ g
5. 1 qt. = __32__ oz.
6. 10,000 mL = __10__ L
7. Todd has a board that is 6 ft. 3 in. long. He needs to cut it to 4 ft. 9 in. How much should he cut off? — __18 in. (1 ft. 6 in.)__
8. In a contest, Joyce threw a ball 12 yd. 2 ft. Brenda threw the ball 500 in. Who threw the farthest? — __Brenda__
9. Would you measure this workbook in mm or cm? — __cm__
10. Which is heavier, a box of books that weighs 4 lb. 6 oz. or a box of dishes that weighs 80 oz.? — __80 oz.__
11. A 1-lb. package has 10 hot dogs. How much of an ounce does each hot dog weigh? — __1.6 oz.__
12. Would the amount of salt (sodium) in 1 oz. of potato chips be 170 mg or 170 mg? — __170 mg.__
13. If someone ate half of a gallon of ice cream, how many fluid ounces would be left? — __64 fl. oz.__
14. You want to serve 6 fl. oz. of ice cream to each of 16 friends at your party. How many quarts of ice cream should you buy? — __3 qt.__
15. Would you measure water in a fish pond with L or kL? — __kL__
16. Would popsicles melt at 5°C? — __Yes__
17. Would soup be steaming hot at 100°F? — __Yes__

Page 280

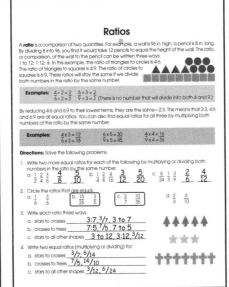

Ratios

A **ratio** is a comparison of two quantities. For example, a wall is 96 in. high; a pencil is 8 in. long. By dividing 8 into 96, you find it would take 12 pencils to equal the height of the wall. The ratio, or comparison, of the wall to the pencil can be written three ways:
1 to 12; 1:12; ¹⁄₁₂. In this example, the ratio of triangles to circles is 4:6.
The ratio of triangles to squares is 4:9. The ratio of circles to squares is 6:9. These ratios will stay the same if we divide both numbers in the ratio by the same number.

Examples: 4 ÷ 2 = 2   2 = 2   (There is no number that will divide into both 4 and 9.)
              6 ÷ 2 = 3   9 ÷ 3 = 3

By reducing 4:6 and 6:9 to their lowest terms, they are the same—2:3. This means that 2:3, 4:6 and 6:9 are all equal ratios. You can also find equal ratios for all three by multiplying both numbers of the ratio by the same number.

Examples: 4 × 3 = 12   6 × 5 = 30   4 × 4 = 16
              6 × 3 = 18   9 × 5 = 45   9 × 4 = 36

Directions: Solve the following problems.

1. Write two more equal ratios for each of the following by multiplying or dividing both numbers in the ratio by the same number.
   a. 1/2 __3/6__ __5/10__   b. 2/4 __5/12__ __3/20__   c. 8/24 __2/6__ __4/12__
2. Circle the ratios that are equal.
   a. 1/3   b. (15/25   3/5)   c. (2/7   10/35)   d. 2/5   6/10
3. Write each ratio three ways.
   a. stars to crosses — 3:7, 3/7, 3 to 7
   b. crosses to trees — 7:5, 7/5, 7 to 5
   c. stars to all other shapes — 3 to 12, 3:12, 3/12
4. Write two equal ratios (multiplying or dividing) for:
   a. stars to crosses — 3/7, 6/14
   b. crosses to trees — 7/5, 14/10
   c. stars to all other shapes — 3/12, 6/24

Page 281

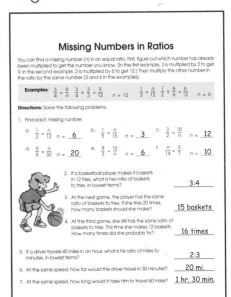

Missing Numbers in Ratios

You can find a missing number (n) in an equal ratio. First, figure out which number has already been multiplied to get the number you know. (In the first example, 3 is multiplied by 3 to get 9; in the second example, 2 is multiplied by 6 to get 12.) Then multiply the other number in the ratio by the same number (3 and 6 in the examples).

Examples: 3/4 = 9/12   3/4 × 3/3 = 9/12   n = 12   1/2 = 6/12   1/2 × 6/6 = 6/12   n = 6

Directions: Solve the following problems.

1. Find each missing number.
   a. 1/2 = n/12   n = __6__   b. 1/5 = n/15   n = __3__   c. 3/2 = 18/n   n = __12__
   d. 5/8 = n/32   n = __20__   e. 8/3 = 16/n   n = __6__   f. 4/14 = 5/7   n = __10__

2. If a basketball player makes 9 baskets in 12 tries, what is her ratio of baskets to tries, in lowest terms? — __3:4__
3. At the next game, the player has the same ratio of baskets to tries. If she tries 20 times, how many baskets should she make? — __15 baskets__
4. At the third game, she still has the same ratio of baskets to tries. This time she makes 12 baskets. How many times did she probably try? — __16 times__
5. If a driver travels 40 miles in an hour, what is his ratio of miles to minutes, in lowest terms? — __2:3__
6. At the same speed, how far would the driver travel in 30 minutes? — __20 mi.__
7. At the same speed, how long would it take him to travel 60 miles? — __1 hr. 30 min.__

Total Basic Skills Grade 6

348

Answer Key

GRADE 6

Page 282

Proportions

A **proportion** is a statement that two ratios are equal. To make sure ratios are equal, called a proportion, we multiply the cross products.

Examples of proportions: $\frac{1}{5} = \frac{2}{10} \quad \frac{1}{2} \times \frac{10}{5} = \frac{10}{10} \quad \frac{3}{7} = \frac{15}{35} \quad \frac{3}{7} \times \frac{35}{15} = \frac{105}{105}$

These two ratios are not a proportion: $\frac{4}{3} = \frac{5}{4} \quad \frac{4}{3} \times \frac{6}{5} = \frac{24}{15}$

To find a missing number (n) in a proportion, multiply the cross products and divide.

Examples: $\frac{n}{30} = \frac{1}{6} \quad n \times 6 = 1 \times 30 \quad n \times 6 = 30$
$n = \frac{30}{6}$
$n = 5$

Directions: Solve the following problems.

1. Write = between the ratios if they are a proportion. Write ≠ if they are not a proportion. The first one has been done for you.

   a. $\frac{1}{2}$ (=) $\frac{6}{12}$ b. $\frac{13}{18}$ (≠) $\frac{20}{22}$ c. $\frac{2}{6}$ (=) $\frac{5}{15}$ d. $\frac{5}{6}$ (=) $\frac{20}{24}$

2. Find the missing numbers in these proportions.

   a. $\frac{2}{5} = \frac{n}{15}$ n = __6__   b. $\frac{3}{7} = \frac{9}{n}$ n = __24__   c. $\frac{n}{18} = \frac{4}{12}$ n = __6__

3. One issue of a magazine costs $2.99, but if you buy a subscription, 12 issues cost $35.88. Is the price at the same proportion? __Yes__

4. A cookie recipe calls for 3 cups of flour to make 36 cookies. How much flour is needed for 48 cookies? __4__

5. The same recipe requires 4 teaspoons of cinnamon for 36 cookies. How many teaspoons is needed to make 48 cookies? (Answer will include a fraction.) __$5\frac{1}{3}$__

6. The recipe also calls for 2 cups of sugar for 36 cookies. How much sugar should you use for 48 cookies? (Answer will include a fraction.) __$2\frac{2}{3}$__

7. If 2 kids can eat 12 cookies, how many can 8 kids eat? __48__

Page 283

Percents

Percent means "per 100." A percent is a ratio that compares a number with 100. The same number can be written as a decimal and a percent. To change a decimal to a percent, move the decimal point two places to the right and add the % sign. To change a percent to a decimal, drop the % sign and place a decimal point two places to the left.

Examples: 0.25 = 25%   0.1 = 10%   1.456 = 145.6%
32% = 0.32   99% = 0.99   203% = 2.03

A percent or decimal can also be written as a ratio or fraction.

Example: $0.25 = 25\% = \frac{25}{100} = \frac{1}{4} = 1:4$

To change a fraction or ratio to a percent, first change it to a decimal. Divide the numerator by the denominator.

Examples: $\frac{1}{3} = 3\overline{\smash{\big)}1.00}^{0.33\frac{1}{3} = 33\frac{1}{3}\%}$ $\frac{2}{5} = 5\overline{\smash{\big)}2.0}^{0.4 = 40\%}$

Directions: Solve the following problems.

1. Change the percents to decimals.

   a. 3% = __0.03__   b. 75% = __0.75__   c. 14% = __0.14__   d. 115% = __1.15__

2. Change the decimals and fractions to percents.

   a. 0.56 = __56__ %   b. 0.03 = __3__ %   c. $\frac{3}{4}$ = __75__ %   d. $\frac{1}{5}$ = __20__ %

3. Change the percents to ratios in their lowest terms. The first one has been done for you.

   a. 75% = $\frac{75}{100} = 3/4 = 3:4$ b. 40% = $\frac{40}{100} = 2/5 = 2:5$

   c. 35% = $\frac{35}{100} = 7/20 = 7:20$ d. 70% = $\frac{70}{100} = 7/10 = 7:10$

4. The class was 45% girls. What percent was boys? __55%__

5. Half the shoes in one store were on sale. What percent of the shoes were their ordinary price? __50%__

6. Kim read 84 pages of a 100-page book. What percent of the book did she read? __84%__

Page 284

Percents

To find the percent of a number, change the percent to a decimal and multiply.

Examples: 45% of $20 = 0.45 × $20 = $9.00
125% of 30 = 1.25 × 30 = 37.50

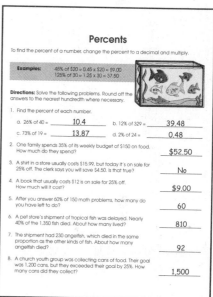

Directions: Solve the following problems. Round off the answers to the nearest hundredth where necessary.

1. Find the percent of each number.

   a. 26% of 40 = __10.4__   b. 12% of 329 = __39.48__
   c. 73% of 19 = __13.87__   d. 2% of 24 = __0.48__

2. One family spends 35% of its weekly budget of $150 on food. How much do they spend? __$52.50__

3. A shirt in a store usually costs $15.99, but today it's on sale for 25% off. The clerk says you will save $4.50. Is that true? __No__

4. A book that usually costs $12 is on sale for 25% off. How much will it cost? __$9.00__

5. After you answer 60% of 150 math problems, how many do you have left to do? __60__

6. A pet store's shipment of tropical fish was delayed. Nearly 40% of the 1,350 fish died. About how many lived? __810__

7. The shipment had 230 angelfish, which died in the same proportion as the other kinds of fish. About how many angelfish died? __92__

8. A church youth group was collecting cans of food. Their goal was 1,200 cans, but they exceeded their goal by 25%. How many cans did they collect? __1,500__

Page 285

Probability

Probability is the ratio of favorable outcomes to possible outcomes in an experiment. You can use probability (P) to figure out how likely something is to happen. For example, six picture cards are turned facedown—3 cards have stars, 2 have triangles and 1 has a circle. What is the probability of picking the circle? Using the formula below, you have a 1 in 6 probability of picking the circle, a 2 in 6 probability of picking a triangle and a 3 in 6 probability of picking a star.

Example: P = $\frac{\text{number of favorable outcomes}}{\text{number of trials}}$ P = $\frac{1}{6}$ = 1:6

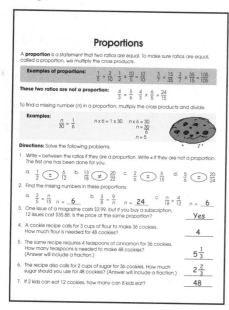

Directions: Solve the following problems.

1. A class has 14 girls and 15 boys. If all of their names are put on separate slips in a hat, what is the probability of each person's name being chosen? __1:29__

2. In the same class, what is the probability that a girl's name will be chosen? __14:29__

3. In this class, 3 boys are named Mike. What is the probability that a slip with "Mike" written on it will be chosen? __3:29__

4. A spinner on a board game has the numbers 1–8. What is the probability of spinning and getting a 4? __1:8__

5. A paper bag holds these colors of wooden beads: 4 blue, 5 red and 6 yellow. If you select a bead without looking, do you have an equal probability of getting each color? __No__

6. Using the same bag of beads, what is the probability of reaching in and drawing out a red bead (in lowest terms)? __1:3__

7. In the same bag, what is the probability of not getting a blue bead? __2:1__

8. In a carnival game, plastic ducks have spots. The probability of picking a duck with a yellow spot is 2:15. There is twice as much probability of picking a duck with a red spot. What is the probability of picking a duck with a red spot? __4:15__

9. In this game, all the other ducks have green spots. What is the probability of picking a duck with a green spot (in lowest terms)? __3:5__

Page 286

Possible Combinations

Today the cafeteria is offering 4 kinds of sandwiches, 3 kinds of drinks and 2 kinds of cookies. How many possible combinations could you make? To find out, multiply the number of choices together.

Example: 4 x 3 x 2 = 24 possible combinations

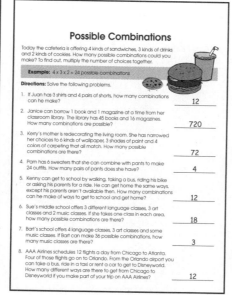

Directions: Solve the following problems.

1. If Juan has 3 shirts and 4 pairs of shorts, how many combinations can he make? __12__

2. Janice can borrow 1 book and 1 magazine at a time from her classroom library. The library has 45 books and 16 magazines. How many combinations are possible? __720__

3. Kerry's mother is redecorating the living room. She has narrowed her choices to 6 kinds of wallpaper, 3 shades of paint and 4 colors of carpeting that all match. How many possible combinations are there? __72__

4. Pam has 6 sweaters that she can combine with pants to make 24 outfits. How many pairs of pants does she have? __4__

5. Kenny can get to school by walking, taking a bus, riding his bike or asking his parents for a ride. He can get home the same ways, except his parents aren't available then. How many combinations can he make of ways to get to school and get home? __12__

6. Sue's middle school offers 3 different language classes, 3 art classes and 2 music classes. If she takes one class in each area, how many possible combinations are there? __18__

7. Bart's school offers 4 language classes, 3 art classes and some music classes. If Bart can make 36 possible combinations, how many music classes are there? __3__

8. AAA Airlines schedules 12 flights a day from Chicago to Atlanta. Four of those flights go on to Orlando. From the Orlando airport you can take a bus, ride in a taxi or rent a car to get to Disneyworld. How many different ways are there to get from Chicago to Disneyworld if you make part of your trip on AAA Airlines? __12__

Page 287

Review

Directions: Solve the following problems. Round answers to the nearest hundredth where necessary.

1. Write an equal ratio for each of these:

   a. $\frac{1}{7} = \frac{2}{14}$ b. $\frac{5}{8} = \frac{15}{24}$ c. $\frac{15}{3} = \frac{30}{6}$ d. $\frac{6}{24} = \frac{12}{48}$

2. State the ratios below in lowest terms.

   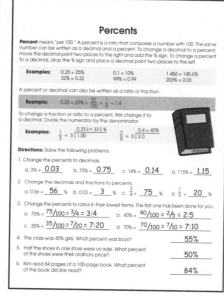

   a. cats to bugs = __4:6 = 2:3__
   b. cats to dogs = __4:5__
   c. dogs to all other objects = __5:10 = 1:5__

3. If Shawn drives 45 miles an hour, how far could he go in 40 minutes? __30 miles__

4. At the same speed, how many minutes would it take Shawn to drive 120 miles? __2 hrs. 40 min.__

5. Mr. Herman is building a doghouse in proportion to his family's house. The family's house is 30 ft. high and the doghouse is 5 ft. high. If the family house is 42 ft. wide, how wide should the doghouse be? __7 ft.__

6. The family house is 24 ft. from front to back. How big should Mr. Herman make the doghouse? __4 ft.__

7. Change these numbers to percents.

   a. 0.56 = __56%__   b. $\frac{4}{5}$ = __80%__   c. 0.04 = __4%__   d. $\frac{3}{8}$ = __37.5%__

8. Which is a better deal, a blue bike for $125 at 25% off or a red bike for $130 at 30% off? __red bike__

9. If sales tax is 6%, what would be the total price of the blue bike? __$99.38__

10. Richard bought 6 raffle tickets for a free bike. If 462 tickets were sold, what is Richard's probability of winning? __6:462 = 1:77__

11. Lori bought 48 tickets in the same raffle. What are her chances of winning? __48:462 = 8:77__

GRADE
6

Page 288

Comparing Data

Data (**datum**—singular) are gathered information. The **range** is the difference between the highest and lowest number in a group of numbers. The **median** is the number in the middle when numbers are listed in order. The **mean** is the average of the numbers. We can compare numbers or data by finding the range, median and mean.

Example: 16, 43, 34, 78, 8, 91, 26

To compare these numbers, we first need to put them in order: 8 16 26 34 43 78 91. By subtracting the lowest number (8) from the highest one (91), we find the range: 83. By finding the number that falls in the middle, we have the median: 34 (If no number fell exactly in the middle, we would average the two middle numbers.) By adding them and dividing by the number of numbers (7), we get the mean: 42.29 (rounded to the nearest hundredth).

Directions: Solve the following problems. Round answers to the nearest hundredth where necessary.

1. Find the range, median and mean of these numbers: 19, 5, 84, 27, 106, 38, 75.

   Range: 101 Median: 38 Mean: 50.57

2. Find the range, median and mean finishing times for 6 runners in a race. Here are their times in seconds: 14.2, 12.9, 13.5, 10.3, 14.8, 14.7.

   Range: 4.5 Median: 13.85 Mean: 13.4

3. If the runner who won the race in 10.3 seconds had run even faster and finished in 7 seconds, would the mean time be higher or lower? Lower

4. If that runner had finished in 7 seconds, what would be the median time? 13.85 (same)

5. Here are the high temperatures in one city for a week: 65, 72, 68, 74, 81, 68, 85. Find the range, median and mean temperatures.

   Range: 20 Median: 72 Mean: 73.29

6. Find the range, median and mean test scores for this group of students: 41, 32, 45, 36, 48, 38, 37, 42, 39, 36.

   Range: 16 Median: 38.5 Mean: 39.4

Page 289

Tables

Organizing data into tables makes it easier to compare numbers. As evident in the example, putting many numbers in a paragraph is confusing. When the same numbers are organized in a table, you can compare numbers in a glance. Tables can be arranged several ways and still be easy to read and understand.

Example: Money spent on groceries:
Family A: week 1 — $68.50; week 2 — $72.25; week 3 — $67.00; week 4 — $74.50.
Family B: week 1 — $42.25; week 2 — $47.50; week 3 — $50.25; week 4 — $53.50.

	Week 1	Week 2	Week 3	Week 4
Family A	$68.50	$72.25	$67.00	$74.50
Family B	$42.25	$47.50	$50.25	$53.50

Directions: Complete the following exercises.

1. Finish the table below, then answer the questions.
   Data: Steve weighs 230 lb. and is 6 ft. 2 in. tall. George weighs 218 lb. and is 6 ft. 3 in. tall. Chuck weighs 225 lb. and is 6 ft. 1 in. tall. Henry weighs 205 lb. and is 6 ft. tall.

	Henry	George	Chuck	Steve
Weight	205 lbs.	218 lbs.	225 lbs.	230 lbs.
Height	6 ft.	6 ft. 3 in.	6 ft. 1 in.	6 ft. 2 in.

   a. Who is tallest? George b. Who weighs the least? Henry

2. On another sheet of paper, prepare 2 tables comparing the amount of money made by 3 booths at the school carnival this year and last year. In the first table, write the names of the games in the left-hand column (like **Family A** and **Family B** in the example). In the second table (using the same data), write the years in the left-hand column. Here is the data: fish pond—this year $15.60, last year $13.50; bean-bag toss—this year $13.45, last year $10.25; ring toss—this year $23.80, last year $18.80. After you complete both tables, answer the following questions.

   a. Which booth made the most money this year? ring toss
   b. Which booth made the biggest improvement from last year to this year? ring toss

Page 290

Bar Graphs

Another way to organize information is a **bar graph**. The bar graph in the example compares the number of students in 4 elementary schools. Each bar stands for 1 school. You can easily see that School A has the most students and School C has the least. The numbers along the left show how many students attend each school.

Example:

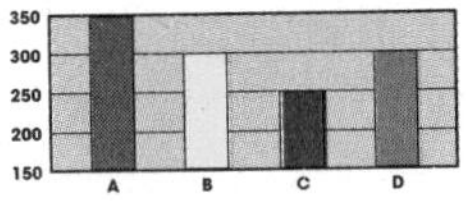
350
300
250
200
150
A
B
C
D

Directions: Complete the following exercises.

1. This bar graph will show how many calories are in 1 serving of 4 kinds of cereal. Draw the bars the correct height and label each with the name of the cereal. After completing the bar graph, answer the questions. Data: Korn Kernals—150 calories; Oat Floats—160 calories; Rite Rice—110 calories; Sugar Shapes—200 calories.

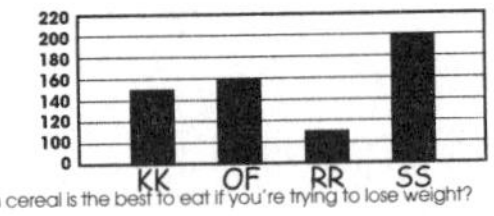
220
200
180
160
140
120
100
0
KK
OF
RR
SS

   A. Which cereal is the best to eat if you're trying to lose weight? Rite Rice
   B. Which cereal has nearly the same number of calories as Oat Floats? Korn Kernals

2. On another sheet of paper, draw your own graph, showing the number of TV commercials in 1 week for each of the 4 cereals in the graph above. After completing the graph, answer the questions. Data: Oat Boats—27 commercials; Rite Rice—15; Sugar Shapes—35; Korn Kernals—28.

   A. Which cereal is most heavily advertised? Sugar Shapes
   B. What similarities do you notice between the graph of calories and the graph of Sugar Shapes is highest in sugar and advertisements

Page 291

Picture Graphs

Newspapers and textbooks often use pictures in graphs instead of bars. Each picture stands for a certain number of objects. Half a picture means half the number. The picture graph in the example indicates the number of games each team won. The Astros won 7 games, so they have $3\frac{1}{2}$ balls.

Example:

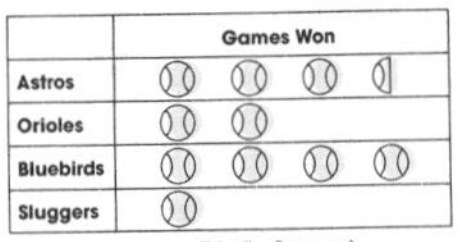
Games Won
Astros
Orioles
Bluebirds
Sluggers

(1 ball = 2 games)

Directions: Complete the following exercises.

Finish this picture graph, showing the number of students who have dogs in 4 sixth-grade classes. Draw simple dogs in the graph, letting each drawing stand for 2 dogs. Data: Class 1—12 dogs; Class 2—16 dogs; Class 3—22 dogs; Class 4—12 dogs. After completing the graph, answer the questions.

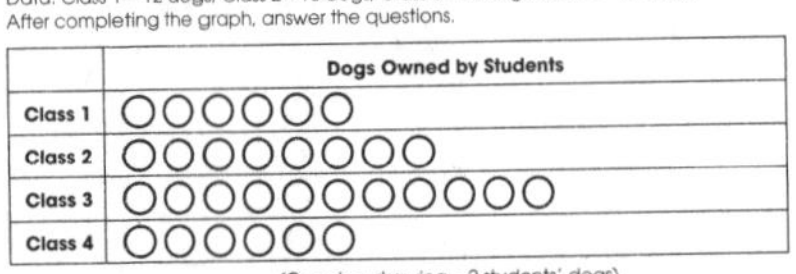
Dogs Owned by Students
Class 1
Class 2
Class 3
Class 4

(One dog drawing = 2 students' dogs)

1. Why do you think newspapers use picture graphs? Answers will vary. It simplifies information and is easier to read.
2. Would picture graphs be appropriate to show exact number of dogs living in America? Why or why not? There are too many!

Page 292

Line Graphs

Still another way to display information is a line graph. The same data can often be shown in both a bar graph and a line graph. Nevertheless, line graphs are especially useful in showing changes over a period of time.

The line graph in the example shows changes in the number of students enrolled in a school over a 5-year period. Enrollment was highest in 1988 and has decreased gradually each year since then. Notice how labeling the years and enrollment numbers make the graph easy to understand.

Example:

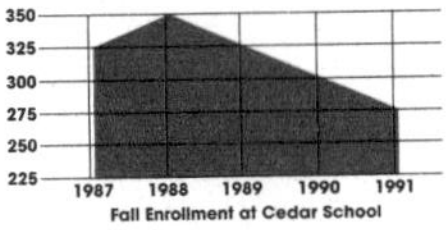
350
325
300
275
250
225
1987
1988
1989
1990
1991

Fall Enrollment at Cedar School

Directions: Complete the following exercises.

1. On another sheet of paper, draw a line graph that displays the growth of a corn plant over a 6-week period. Mark the correct points, using the data below, and connect them with a line. After completing the graph, answer the questions. Data: week 1—3.5 in.; week 2—4.5 in.; week 3—5 in.; week 4—5.5 in.; week 5—5.75 in.; week 6—6 in.

   a. Between which weeks was the growth fastest? 1 and 2
   b. Between which weeks was the growth slowest? 4 and 5; 5 and 6

2. On another sheet of paper draw a line graph to show how the high temperature varied during one week. Then answer the questions. Data: Sunday—high of 53 degrees; Monday—51; Tuesday—56; Wednesday—60; Thursday—58; Friday—67; Saturday—73. Don't forget to label the numbers.

   a. In general, did the days get warmer or cooler? warmer
   b. Do you think this data would have been as clear in a bar graph? No
   Explain your answer. Line graphs show a trend up and down across the graph.

Page 293

Circle Graphs

Circle graphs are useful in showing how something is divided into parts. The circle graph in the example shows how Carly spent her $10 allowance. Each section is a fraction of her whole allowance. For example, the movie tickets section is $\frac{1}{2}$ of the circle, showing that she spent $\frac{1}{2}$ of her allowance, $5, on movie tickets.

MOVIE TICKETS
FOOD
STAMPS

Directions: Complete the following exercises.

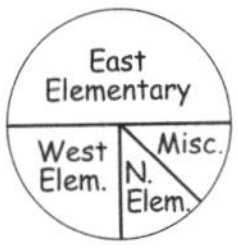
East Elementary
West Elem.
Misc.
N. Elem.

1. When the middle school opened last fall, $\frac{1}{2}$ of the students came from East Elementary, $\frac{1}{4}$ came from West Elementary, $\frac{1}{8}$ came from North Elementary and the remaining students moved into the town from other cities. Make a circle graph showing these proportions. Label each section. Then answer the questions.

   a. What fraction of students at the new school moved into the area from other cities? $\frac{1}{8}$
   b. If the new middle school has 450 students enrolled, how many used to go to East Elementary? 225

2. This circle graph will show the hair color of 24 students in one class. Divide the circle into 4 sections to show this data: black hair—8 students; brown hair—10 students; blonde hair—4 students; red hair—2 students. (Hint: 8 students are $\frac{8}{24}$ or $\frac{1}{3}$ of the class.) Be sure to label each section by hair color. Then answer the questions.

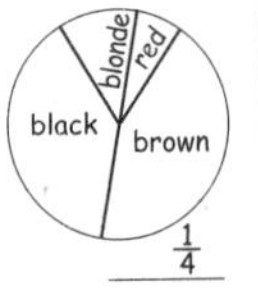
blonde
red
black
brown

   a. Looking at your graph, what fraction of the class is the combined group of blonde- and red-haired students? $\frac{1}{4}$
   b. Which two fractions of hair color combine to total half the class? red/brown

Page 294

Comparing Presentation Methods

Tables and different kinds of graphs have different purposes. Some are more helpful for certain kinds of information. The table and three graphs below all show basically the same information—the amount of money Mike and Margaret made in their lawn-mowing business over a 4-month period.

Directions: Study the graphs and table. Then circle the one that answers each question below.

1. Which one shows the fraction of the total income that Mike and Margaret made in August?

   table   line graph   bar graph   (circle graph)

2. Which one compares Mike's earnings with Margaret's?

   (table)   line graph   bar graph   circle graph

3. Which one has the most exact numbers?

   (table)   line graph   bar graph   circle graph

4. Which one has no numbers?

   table   line graph   bar graph   (circle graph)

5. Which two best show how Mike and Margaret's income changed from month to month?

   table   (line graph)   (bar graph)   circle graph

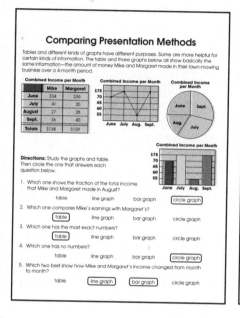

Page 295

Graphing Data

Directions: Complete the following exercises.

1. Use the following information to create a bar graph.

Cities	Population (in 1,000's)
Dover	20
Newton Falls	12
Springdale	25
Hampton	17
Riverside	5

2. Study the data and create a line graph showing the number of baskets Jonah scored during the season.

   Game 1 — 10
   Game 2 — 7
   Game 3 — 11
   Game 4 — 10
   Game 5 — 9
   Game 6 — 5
   Game 7 — 9

   Fill in the blanks.
   a. High game: __3__
   b. Low game: __6__
   c. Average baskets per game: __8.7__

3. Study the graph, then answer the questions.

   a. Which flavor is the most popular? __chocolate__

   b. Which flavor sold the least? __Blue Moon__

   c. What decimal represents the two highest sellers? __0.75__

   d. Which flavor had ⅒ of the sales? __vanilla__

   Ice-Cream Sales

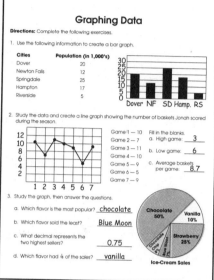

Page 296

Integers

An **integer** is a whole number above or below 0: -2, -1, 0, +1, +2, and so on. **Opposite integers** are two integers the same distance from 0, but in different directions, such as -2 and +2.

Think of the water level in the picture as 0. The part of the iceberg sticking out of the water is positive. The iceberg has +3 feet above water. The part of the iceberg below the water is negative. The iceberg extends - 9 feet under water.

Numbers greater than 0 are **positive** numbers. Numbers less than 0 are **negative** numbers. Pairs of positive and negative numbers are called **opposite integers**.

Examples of opposite integers:
-5 and +5
losing 3 pounds and gaining 3 pounds
earning $12 and spending $12

Directions: Complete the following exercises.

1. Write each of these as an integer. The first one is done for you.
   a. positive 6 = __+6__   b. losing $5 = __-$5__
   c. 5 degrees below 0 = __-5__   d. receiving $12 = __+$12__

2. Write the **opposite** integer of each of these. The first one is done for you.
   a. negative 4 = __+4__   b. positive 10 = __-10__
   c. 2 floors below ground level = __+2__   d. winning a card game by 6 points = __-6__

3. Write integers to show each idea.
   a. A train that arrives 2 hours after it was scheduled: __-2__
   b. A package that has 3 fewer cups than it should: __-3__
   c. A board that's 3 inches too short: __-3__   d. A golf score 5 over par: __+5__
   e. A paycheck that doesn't cover $35 of a family's expenses: __-$35__
   f. 30 seconds before a missile launch: __-30__
   g. A team that won 6 games and lost 2: __+4__

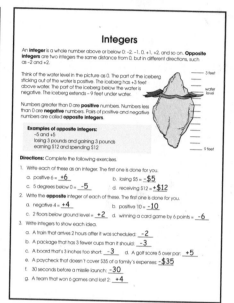

Page 297

Comparing Integers

Comparing two integers can be confusing unless you think of them as being on a number line, as shown below. Remember that the integer farther to the right is greater. Thus, +2 is greater than -3, 0 is greater than -4 and -2 is greater than -5.

Directions: Study the number line. Then complete the following exercises.

1. Write in integers to number the number line.

2. Write < for "less than" or > for "greater than" to compare the integers. The first one is done for you.

   a. -5 __<__ +5   b. +3 __>__ -3   c. +2 __>__ -4
   d. -4 __<__ -3   e. -1 __<__ +3   f. -1 __>__ -5

3. Write **T** for true or **F** for false. (All degrees are in Fahrenheit.)

   a. +7 degrees is colder than -3 degrees. __F__
   b. -14 degrees is colder than -7 degrees. __T__
   c. +23 degrees is colder than -44 degrees. __F__
   d. -5 degrees is colder than +4 degrees. __T__

4. Draw an **X** by the series of integers that are in order from least to greatest.

   ___ +2, +3, -4
   _X_ -3, 0, +1
   _X_ -7, -4, -1
   ___ -3, -4, -5

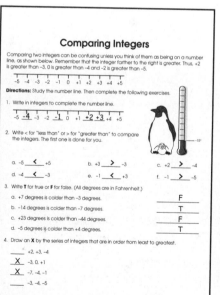

Page 298

Adding Integers

The sum of two positive integers is a positive integer.
Thus, +4 + 1 = +5.
The sum of two negative integers is a negative integer.
Thus, -5 + -2 = -7.
The sum of a positive and a negative integer has the sign of the integer that is farther from 0.
Thus, -6 + +3 = -3.
The sum of opposite integers is 0.
Thus, +2 + -2 = 0

Directions: Complete the following exercises.

1. Add these integers.
   a. +2 + +7 = __+9__   b. -4 + -2 = __-6__   c. +5 + -3 = __+2__   d. +4 + -4 = __0__
   e. -10 + -2 = __-12__   f. +6 + -1 = __+5__   g. +45 + -30 = __+15__   h. -39 + +26 = __-13__

2. Write the problems as integers. The first one has been done for you.

   a. One cold morning, the temperature was -14 degrees. The afternoon high was 20 degrees warmer. What was the high temperature that day?
   __-14 + +20 = +6__

   b. Another day, the high temperature was 26 degrees, but the temperature dropped 35 degrees during the night. What was the low that night?
   __+26 + -35 = -9__

   c. Sherri's allowance was $7. She paid $4 for a movie ticket. How much money did she have left?
   __+$7 + -$4 = +$3__

   d. The temperature in a meat freezer was -10 degrees, but the power went off and the temperature rose 6 degrees. How cold was the freezer then?
   __-10 + +6 = -4__

   e. The school carnival took in $235, but it had expenses of $185. How much money did the carnival make after paying its expenses?
   __+$235 + -$185 = +$50__

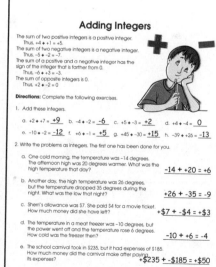

Page 299

Subtracting Integers

To subtract an integer, change its sign to the opposite and add it. If you are subtracting a negative integer, make it positive and add it: +4 - -6 = +4 + +6 = +10. If you are subtracting a positive integer, make it negative and add it: +8 - +2 = +8 + -2 = +6.

More examples: -5 - -8 = -5 + +8 = +3
+3 - +7 = +3 + -7 = -4

Directions: Complete the following exercises.

1. Before subtracting these integers, rewrite each problem. The first one has been done for you.

   -6 - -8 = __-6 + +8 = +2__   +3 - -4 = __+3 + +4 = +7__
   +9 - -3 = __+9 + -3 = +6__   -1 - -7 = __-1 + +7 = +6__
   +7 - -5 = __+7 + +5 = +12__   -4 - +3 = __-4 + -3 = -7__

2. Write these problems as integers. The first one is done for you.

   a. The high temperature in the Arctic Circle one day was -42 degrees. The low was -67 degrees. What was the difference between the two?
   __-42 - -67 = -42 + +67 = +25__

   b. At the equator one day, the high temperature was +106 degrees. The low was +85 degrees. What was the difference between the two?
   __+106 - +85 = +106 + -85 = +21__

   c. At George's house one morning, the thermometer showed it was +7 degrees. The radio announcer said it was -2 degrees. What is the difference between the two temperatures?
   __+7 - -2 = +7 + +2 = +9__

   d. What is the difference between a temperature of +11 degrees and a wind-chill factor of -15 degrees?
   __+11 - -15 = +11 + +15 = +26__

   e. During a dry spell, the level of a river dropped from 3 feet above normal to 13 feet below normal. How many feet did it drop?
   __+3 - -13 = +3 + +13 = +16__

   f. Here are the average temperatures in a meat freezer for four days: -12, -11, -14 and -9 degrees. What is the difference between the highest and lowest temperature?
   __-14 - -9 = -14 + +9 = -5__

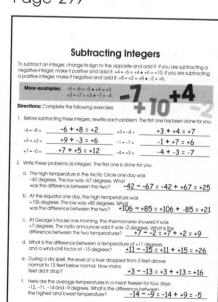

Answer Key

351

Total Basic Skills Grade 6

Page 300

Plotting Graphs

A graph with horizontal and vertical number lines can show the location of certain points. The horizontal number line is called the **x axis**, and the vertical number line is called the **y axis**. Two numbers, called the **x coordinate** and the **y coordinate**, show where a point is on the graph.

The first coordinate, x, tells how many units to the right or left of 0 the point is located. On the example graph, point A is +2, two units to the right of 0.

The second coordinate, y, tells how many units above or below 0 the point is located. On the example, point A is −3, three units below 0.

Thus, the coordinates of A are +2, −3. The coordinates of B are −3, +2. (Notice the order of the coordinates.) The coordinates of C are +3, +1; and D, −2, −2.

Directions: Study the example. Then answer these questions about the graph below.

1. What towns are at these coordinates?

+1, +3	Patterson
+1, −3	Harlow
−4, +1	Stewart
−2, −3	Clinton
−3, −2	Weston
−3, +3	Hillsville

2. What are the coordinates of these towns?

Hampton	−2, +1
Wooster	+3, +2
Beachwood	+2, −4
Middletown	+1, −1
Kirby	−4, −1
Arbor	+3, −2

Page 301

Ordered Pairs

Ordered pairs is another term used to describe pairs of integers used to locate points on a graph.

Directions: Complete the following exercises.

1. Place the following points on the graph, using the ordered pairs as data.

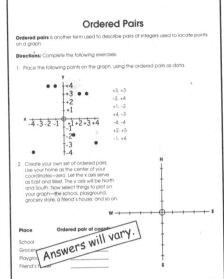

+3, +3	
−2, +4	
+1, −2	
+4, −3	
−4, −4	
+2, +4	
−1, +4	

2. Create your own set of ordered pairs. Use your home as the center of your coordinates—zero. Let the x axis serve as East and West. The y axis will be North and South. Now select things to plot on your graph—the school, playground, grocery store, a friend's house, and so on.

Place	Ordered pair of coordinates
School	
Grocery	
Playground	
Friend's house	

Answers will vary.

Page 302

Review

Directions: Complete the following exercises.

1. Write the **opposite** integers of the following:

a. 14 degrees above 0 __−14__

b. Spending $21 __+$21__

2. Write integers to show these ideas.

a. 4 seconds after the launch of the space shuttle __+4__

b. A lake 3 feet below its usual level __−3__

c. 2 days before your birthday __−2__

3. Write < for "less than" or > for "greater than" to compare these integers.

−2 _>_ −4   +2 _>_ −3   −1 _<_ +1

4. Add the integers.

−14 + −11 = __−25__   −6 + +5 = __−1__   −7 + +7 = __0__

5. Subtract the integers.

−4 − −5 = __+1__   +3 − −6 = __+9__   +7 − +2 = __+5__

6. Write **T** for true or **F** for false.

a. The x coordinate is on the horizontal number line. __T__

b. Add the x and y coordinates to find the location of a point. __F__

c. Always state the x coordinate first. __T__

d. A y coordinate of +2 would be above the horizontal number line. __T__

e. An x coordinate of +2 would be to the right of the vertical number line. __T__

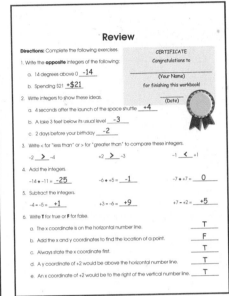

CERTIFICATE
Congratulations to
_____
(Your Name)
for finishing this workbook!
_____
(Date)

Ready Reference
The Metric System

Linear Measure					
1 millimeter	=		=	0.03937 inch
1 centimeter	=	10 millimeters	=	0.3937 inch
1 decimeter	=	10 centimeters	=	3.937 inches
1 meter	=	10 decimeters	=	39.37 inches
1 meter	=	10 decimeters	=	3.2808 feet
1 decameter	=	10 meters	=	393.7 inches
1 hectometer	=	10 decameters	=	328.08 feet
1 kilometer	=	10 hectometers	=	0.621 mile
1 kilometer	=	10 hectometers	=	3,280.8 feet

Square Measure				
1 square millimeter	=		=	0.00155 square inch
1 square centimeter	=	100 square millimeters	=	0.15499 square inch
1 square decimeter	=	100 square centimeters	=	15.499 square inches
1 square meter	=	100 square decimeters	=	1,549.9 square inches
1 square meter	=	100 square decimeters	=	1.196 square yards
1 square decameter	=	100 square meters	=	119.6 square yards
1 square hectometer	=	100 square decameters	=	2.471 acres
1 square kilometer	=	100 square hectometers	=	0.386 square mile
1 square kilometer	=	100 square hectometers	=	247.1 acres

Land Measure				
1 centiare	=	1 square meter	=	1,549.9 square inches
1 are	=	100 centiares	=	119.6 square yards
1 hectare	=	100 ares	=	2.471 acres
1 square kilometer	=	100 hectares	=	0.386 square mile
1 square kilometer	=	100 hectares	=	247.1 acres

Volume Measure				
1 cubic centimeter	=	1,000 cubic millimeters	=	0.06102 cubic inch
1 cubic decimeter	=	1,000 cubic centimeters	=	61.023 cubic inches
1 cubic decimeter	=	1,000 cubic centimeters	=	0.0353 cubic foot
1 cubic meter	=	1,000 cubic decimeters	=	35.314 cubic feet
1 cubic meter	=	1,000 cubic decimeters	=	1.308 cubic yards

Capacity Measure				
1 centiliter	=	10 milliliters	=	0.338 fluid ounce
1 deciliter	=	10 centiliters	=	3.38 fluid ounces
1 deciliter	=	10 centiliters	=	0.1057 liquid quart
1 liter	=	10 deciliters	=	1.0567 liquid quarts
1 liter	=	10 deciliters	=	0.9081 dry quart
1 decaliter	=	10 liters	=	2.64 gallons
1 decaliter	=	10 liters	=	0.284 bushel
1 hectoliter	=	10 decaliters	=	26.418 gallons
1 hectoliter	=	10 decaliters	=	2.838 bushels
1 kiloliter	=	10 hectoliters	=	264.18 gallons
1 kiloliter	=	10 hectoliters	=	35.315 cubic feet

Weights				
1 centigram	=	10 milligrams	=	0.1543 grain
1 centigram	=	10 milligrams	=	0.000353 ounce
1 decigram	=	10 centigrams	=	1.5432 grains
1 gram	=	10 decigrams	=	15.432 grains
1 gram	=	10 decigrams	=	0.035274 ounce
1 decagram	=	10 grams	=	0.3527 ounce
1 hectogram	=	10 decagrams	=	3.5274 ounces
1 kilogram	=	10 hectograms	=	2.2046 pounds
1 myriagram	=	10 kilograms	=	22.046 pounds
1 quintal	=	10 myriagrams	=	220.46 pounds
1 metric ton	=	10 quintals	=	2,204.6 pounds

GRADE 6

Ready Reference Conversion Chart

Linear Measure

To convert:	Multiply by:	To convert:	Multiply by:
inches to millimeters	25.4	millimeters to inches	0.039
inches to centimeters	2.54	centimeters to inches	0.394
feet to meters	0.305	meters to feet	3.281
yards to meters	0.914	meter to yards	1.094
miles to kilometers	1.609	kilometers to miles	0.621

Square Measure

To convert:	Multiply by:	To convert:	Multiply by:
sq. inches to sq. centimeters	6.452	sq. centimeters to sq. inches	0.155
sq. feet to sq. meters	0.093	sq. meters to sq. feet	10.764
sq. yards to sq. meters	0.836	sq. meters to sq. yards	1.196
acres to hectares	0.405	hectares to acres	2.471

Cubic Measure

To convert:	Multiply by:	To convert:	Multiply by:
cu. inches to cu. centimeters	16.387	cu. centimeters to cu. inches	0.061
cu. feet to cu. meters	0.028	cu. meters to cu. feet	35.315
cu. yards to cu. meters	0.765	cu. meters to cu. yards	1.308

Liquid Measure

To convert:	Multiply by:	To convert:	Multiply by:
fluid ounces to liters	0.03	liters to fluid ounces	33.814
quarts to liters	0.946	liters to quarts	1.057
gallons to liters	3.785	liters to gallons	0.264
imperial gallons to liters	4.546	liters to imperial gallons	0.220

Weights

To convert:	Multiply by:	To convert:	Multiply by:
ounces avoirdupois to grams	28.35	grams to ounces avoirdupois	0.035
pounds avoirdupois to kilograms	0.454	kilograms to pounds avoirdupois	2.205
tons to metric tons	0.907	metric tons to tons	1.102

Temperature

	Fahrenheit	Celsius
Freezing point of water	32° F	0° C
Boiling point of water	212° F	100° C
Body temperature	98.6° F	37° C

- To find degrees Celsius, subtract 32 from degrees Fahrenheit and divide by 1.8
  Example: 68° F = (68 – 32)/1.8 = 20° C

- To find degrees Fahrenheit, multiply degrees Celsius by 1.8 and add 32
  Example: 35° C = (35 x 1.8) + 32 = 95° F